Examining Writing

Research and practice in assessing second language writing

Examining Writing

Research and practice in assessing second language writing

Stuart D Shaw
Validation Officer
University of Cambridge ESOL Examinations

and

Cyril J Weir
Powdrill Professor in English Language Acquisition
University of Bedfordshire

CAMBRIDGE
UNIVERSITY PRESS

CAMBRIDGE UNIVERSITY PRESS
Cambridge, New York, Melbourne, Madrid, Cape Town, Singapore, São Paulo

Cambridge University Press
The Edinburgh Building, Cambridge CB2 8RU, UK

www.cambridge.org
Information on this title: www.cambridge.org/9780521692939

First published 2007

Printed in the United Kingdom at the University Press, Cambridge

A catalogue record for this publication is available from the British Library

Library of Congress Cataloging in Publication Data
Shaw, Stuart D., 1962-
Examining writing : research and practice in assessing second language
writing / Stuart D. Shaw, Cyril J. Weir.
          p.   cm. – (Studies in language testing ; 26)
Includes bibliographical references and index.
ISBN 978-0-521-69293-9
1. Language and languages – Ability testing. 2. Rhetoric – Ability testing.
I. Weir, Cyril J. II. Title. III. Series.
P53.27.S53 2007
418′.0076 – dc22   2007016909

ISBN 978-0-521-69293-9

Contents

Abbreviations

AE	Assistant Examiner
ALTE	Association of Language Testers in Europe
ANOVA	Analysis of variance
ANCOVA	Analysis of covariance
APE	Assistant Principal Examiner
AWL	Academic Word List
BEC	Business English Certificates
BMF	Batch Monitoring Form
BNC	British National Corpus
BULATS	Business Language Testing Service
CAE	Certificate in Advanced English
CB	Computer-based
CB IELTS	Computer-based International English Language Testing System
CB PET	Computer-based Preliminary English Test
CBT	Computer-based testing
CCSE	Certificates in Communicative Skills in English
CEFR	Common European Framework of Reference
CELS	Certificates in English Language Skills
CET	College English Test
CIS	Candidate Information Sheet
CLC	Cambridge Learner Corpus
CM	Clerical Marker
CMS	Clerical Marking Supervisor
Co-Ex	Co-ordinating Examiner
CPE	Certificate of Proficiency in English
CRELLA	Centre for Research in English Language Learning and Assessment
CSW	Common Scale for Writing
CUEFL	Communicative Use of English as a Foreign Language
DIF	Differential Item Functioning
EAP	English for Academic Purposes
EAQUALS	The European Association for Quality Language Services
EFL	English as a Foreign Language
ELT	English Language Teaching

EM	Examinations Manager
EPS	Examinations Processing System
ERM	Electronic Return of Marks
ESL	English as a Second Language
ESLPE	English as a Second Language Placement Examination
ESM	Electronic Script Management
ESOL	English for Speakers of Other Languages
ESP	English for Specific Purposes
ETS	Educational Testing Service
FCE	First Certificate in English
FSI	Foreign Service Institute
FUEL	File Uploads from External Locations
GMAT	Graduate Management Admission Test
GMS	General Mark Scheme
IATM	Instrument for the Analysis of Textbook Materials
IEA	Intelligent Essay Assessor
IELTS	International English Language Testing System
IIS	IELTS Impact Study
ILEC	International Legal English Certificate
ILSSIEA	Instructions to Local Secretaries, Supervisors and Invigilators for Examination Administration
IRT	Item Response Theory
KET	Key English Test
LIBS	Local Item Banking System
LSA	Latent Semantic Analysis
LTRC	Language Testing Research Colloquium
MFI	Mark from Image
MFO	Mark from Object
MFR	Multi-faceted Rasch
MFRM	Multi-faceted Rasch Measurement
MFS	Mark from Script
MS	Main Suite
NLP	Natural Language Processing
NNS	Non-native speaker
NS	Native speaker
OMR	Optical Mark Reader
PA	Paper Administrator
PE	Principal Examiner
PEG	Project Essay Grader
PET	Preliminary English Test
QPP	Question Paper Production
QPT	Quick Placement Test
RCEAL	Research Centre for English and Applied Linguistics

Abbreviations

RITCME	Recruitment, Induction, Training, Co-ordination, Monitoring, Evaluation
RNIB	Royal National Institute for the Blind
RTL	Regional Team Leader
SEM	Standard Error of Measurement
SO	Subject Officer
TCT	Text Categorisation Techniques
TEEP	Test in English for Educational Purposes
TKT	Teaching Knowledge Test
TL	Team Leader
TOEFL	Test of English as a Foreign Language
TSMS	Task Specific Mark Scheme
TWE	Test of Written English
UCLES	University of Cambridge Local Examinations Syndicate
VRIP	Validity, Reliability, Impact, Practicality
YLE	Young Learners English Tests

Series Editors' note

Cambridge ESOL has long experience of the direct assessment of second language writing ability going back to the introduction of the Cambridge Proficiency in English (CPE) examination almost a century ago. In 1913 CPE required test takers to complete a two-hour English Essay, a Writing task modelled on the traditional UK school/university-based assessments of the time. By 1938 the CPE Writing component had been renamed English Composition; it included a new summary Writing task alongside the established essay and the time allocation had increased to two and a half hours. When the Lower Certificate in English (later First Certificate – FCE) was introduced in 1939 it incorporated an English Composition and Language paper lasting two hours; candidates were provided with a choice of subjects for a free composition, such as a letter or an essay on a given subject.

Since then a direct test of second language writing (and of speaking) ability has been added to subsequent examinations developed by Cambridge as and when this has been appropriate. The examination board's commitment over many decades to direct performance assessment reflects a strong view (or construct) of proficiency as being about the *ability to use* language rather than simply *possess knowledge about* language. Individual examinations adopt an approach to assessing writing ability that is appropriate to the proficiency level, test purpose, context of use, and test-taking candidature for which they are designed; the approach shapes features such as choice of test format, task design, assessment criteria and rating descriptors. Today the Writing components in Cambridge ESOL examinations continue to be considered as useful measures of learners' ability to communicate in written English.

The credibility of any language examination is determined by the faithfulness with which it represents a coherent understanding and articulation of the underlying abilities or construct(s) that it seeks to measure. For example, if the construct of second language writing ability is not well defined and operationalised, then it will be difficult for examination developers to support claims they wish to make about the usefulness of their writing tests. This includes claims that the tests do not suffer from factors such as *construct under-representation* (i.e. the test is too narrow in focus and fails to include important elements of the construct of interest) or *construct irrelevant variance* (i.e. the test score is prone to systematic measurement error perhaps due to factors other than the construct of interest, such as background/cultural knowledge or unreliable scoring). Construct under-representation and construct irrelevant variance are widely regarded as the two most important threats to construct validity.

The need for clear construct definition becomes especially important when an examination developer offers writing tests at different proficiency levels (e.g. beginner, intermediate, advanced) since it presupposes a clear understanding of how the nature of second language writing ability changes across the proficiency continuum and how this can be operationalised in terms of differentiated task demands for writing tests targeted at different levels (e.g. KET, FCE, CPE).

This volume sets out to explicate the theoretical basis on which Cambridge ESOL currently tests different levels of second language writing ability across its range of test products, particularly those within its traditional Main Suite of general English examinations (KET–CPE) which span Levels A2–C2 of the Common European Framework of Reference. It does so by presenting an explicit validation framework for the testing of Writing. Building on Weir (2005), Shaw and Weir present a socio-cognitive framework which views language testing and validation within a contemporary evidence-based paradigm. They use this framework to conduct a comprehensive description and evaluation of Cambridge ESOL's current approach to examining the skill of second language writing according to a number of dimensions or parameters.

A comprehensive model of second language proficiency remains elusive in theoretical terms; nevertheless, international language proficiency test developers such as Cambridge ESOL need to have recourse to a well-informed and coherent language proficiency model in order to operationalise it for practical assessment purposes. Such a model needs to deal satisfactorily with the twin dimensions of: (1) aspects of cognition, i.e. the language user's or test taker's cognitive abilities; and (2) features of the language use context, i.e. task and situation, in the testing event and beyond the test. These two dimensions constitute two of the core components within the Cambridge ESOL view of construct definition. In the specific context of practical language testing/assessment, which is where the theoretical construct must be operationalised, there exists an important third dimension: (3) the process of marking/rating/scoring itself. In other words, at the heart of any language testing activity there is a triangular relationship between three critical components:

- the test-taker's cognitive abilities
- the context in which the task is performed, and
- the scoring process.

These three 'internal' dimensions of any language test – referred to in this volume as *cognitive validity, context validity* and *scoring validity* – constitute an innovative conceptualisation of construct validity, which has sound theoretical and direct practical relevance for language testers. By maintaining a strong focus on these three components and by undertaking a careful analysis of tests in relation to these three dimensions, it becomes possible to provide theoretical, logical and empirical evidence to support validity claims and arguments about the quality and usefulness of writing tests. Having a clear and well articulated position on the underlying construct(s) can also help guide writing test revision projects and inform any future modifications.

The symbiotic relationship between the contextual parameters laid out in the task and the cognitive processing involved in task performance is stressed throughout this volume. Language testers need to give both the socio and the cognitive elements an appropriate place and emphasis within the whole, and avoid privileging one over another. The framework reminds us that language use – and also language assessment – is both a socially situated and a cognitively processed phenomenon. The twin 'external' dimensions of a test which are discussed in this volume – *consequential validity* and *criterion-related validity* – also reflect this understanding of the nature of language assessment from a wider perspective. The socio-cognitive framework thus seeks to marry the individual psycholinguistic perspective with the individual and group sociolinguistic perspectives. It could be argued that the socio-cognitive approach helps promote a more 'person-oriented' than 'instrument-oriented' view of the testing/assessment process than earlier models/frameworks; it implies a strong focus on the language learner or test taker, rather than the test or measurement instrument, as being at the centre of the assessment process, and it acknowledges the extent to which that assessment process is itself part of a larger social endeavour. This humanistic tradition has been a fundamental feature of the Cambridge ESOL examinations since the earliest days.

From the Cambridge ESOL perspective, the socio-cognitive framework may be the first framework which allows for serious theoretical consideration of the issues and is at the same time capable of being applied practically – hence its relevance and value to an operational language testing context. Although other frameworks (e.g. Bachman 1990) have been extremely helpful in provoking language test practitioners to think about key issues from a theoretical perspective, they have often proved difficult to operationalise in a manageable and meaningful way in the context of large-scale, international language assessment such as that undertaken by Cambridge ESOL.

In terms of the contribution it makes to research and practice in examining second language writing, the socio-cognitive framework helps to clarify, both theoretically and practically, the various constituent parts of the testing endeavour as far as 'validity' is concerned. The validation process presented in this volume is conceptualised in a temporal frame thereby identifying the various types of validity evidence that need to be collected at each stage in the test development and post implementation cycle. Within each of these, individual criterial parameters that help distinguish between adjacent proficiency levels have been identified and are summarised at the end of each chapter.

The framework gives us all a valuable opportunity to revisit many of our traditional terms and concepts, to redefine them more clearly, and to grow in our understanding. It accommodates and strengthens Cambridge ESOL's existing Validity, Reliability, Impact and Practicality (VRIP) approach (see Saville in Weir and Milanovic 2003); while seeking to establish similar evidence, it also attempts to reconfigure validity to show how its constituent parts interact with one another. The results from developing and operationalising the framework in this volume with regard to testing writing ability in the Main Suite examinations are encouraging, and evidence to date suggests that where it has been applied to other Cambridge examinations/tests it has proved useful in generating validity evidence in those cases too, e.g. in the International Legal English Certificate, The Teaching Knowledge Test, and BEC and BULATS (see O'Sullivan 2006). As well as showing where current examinations are performing satisfactorily in respect of a particular validity parameter, areas for possible improvement are highlighted, constituting a future research agenda in Writing not only for Cambridge ESOL but potentially for the wider research community.

It would be illuminating for other examination boards offering English language tests at a variety of proficiency levels to compare their own exams in terms of the validity parameters mapped out in this volume. In this way the nature of language proficiency across 'natural' levels in terms of how it is operationalised through examinations/tests may be more firmly grounded in theory and thus better understood.

Michael Milanovic
Cyril Weir
Cambridge
December 2006

Acknowledgements

In bringing this volume to fruition, the authors are deeply indebted to a great many individuals. Their patience, co-operation and expert counsel has undoubtedly contributed to the success of the volume.

The first group of individuals, instrumental in terms of shaping, reading and commenting on the whole manuscript, include Professor Liz Hamp-Lyons (University of Hong Kong); Dr Sara Cushing Weigle (Georgia State University, USA); and Carole Sedgwick (Roehampton University).

The authors are very appreciative of a number of specialists in the field of language testing who provided expert input and reflection on individual chapters: Dr John Field (Reading University) for his work on cognitive validity; Dr Norbert Schmitt (University of Nottingham) and Dr Felicity O'Dell (Cambridge ESOL Testing Consultant) for their contributions to the chapter on context validity; Dr Paul Thompson (University of Reading) for his review of the scoring validity chapter; and Dr Roger Hawkey (Cambridge ESOL Testing Consultant and University of Bedfordshire) for his reviews of both the consequential validity and criterion-related validity chapters.

Sincere thanks are also due to Dr Barry O'Sullivan (Roehampton University) and Sarah Gysen (Katholieke Universiteit, Leuven) who made a number of insightful comments on various drafts of the manuscripts.

This volume could not have been completed without the additional co-operation of numerous Cambridge ESOL personnel, many of whom enabled the authors to represent fully the various voices within the organisation. We would like first to take the opportunity to acknowledge several individuals from the Assessment and Operations Group who reviewed portions of the manuscript for its comprehensibility and accuracy: Roger Johnson (Director); Anne Gutch (Assistant Director); Edward Hackett (KET/PET Subject Manager); Margaret Cooze (KET/FCE Subject Officer); Beth Weighill (formerly FCE Subject Officer); Mick Ashton (PET Subject Officer); Cris Betts (CAE Subject Officer); and Steve Murray (CPE Subject Officer).

We wish to express our special thanks to Angela ffrench in her role as FCE/CAE/CPE Subject Manager in providing an excellent liaison mechanism between the Research and Validation Group and the Assessment and Operations Group. Her insightful and patient guidance was very much appreciated.

Particular thanks goes to the Chairs of the Writing papers for the diligent and attentive reviews of text relating to their respective areas of interest: Laura Matthews; Elaine Boyd; Diana Fried-Booth; and Annette Capel.

We are also very thankful for the thoughtful and invaluable contributions made by members of the Research and Validation Group: Nick Saville (Director) for overseeing the project; Lynda Taylor (Assistant Director) especially in her editorial capacity; and to the Senior Research and Validation Co-ordinators (Neil Jones, Hanan Khalifa Louhichi and Ardeshir Geranpayeh) for their encouragement and judicious reviewing. Additional thanks goes to Anthony Green (Validation Officer), Fiona Barker (Validation Officer) and Louise Maycock (Validation Officer) for their expert guidance in selected reviews of the volume.

We would like to acknowledge the efforts of Paul Seddon (Projects Office, Cambridge ESOL) for his review of the section relating to computer-based testing and to Meredyth Rodgers (Projects Office, Cambridge ESOL) who was kind enough to critically read those portions of the text describing areas of technological assessment (particularly Electronic Script Management).

And finally we should like to recognise the contribution of Mike Milanovic (Chief Executive of Cambridge ESOL Examinations) for his encouragement throughout the entire project, and his willingness to support future research into issues raised by this study.

The publishers are grateful to the copyright holders for permission to use the copyright material reproduced in this book. Cambridge University Press for extracts and Table 5.1 from *Assessing Writing* by Sara Cushing Weigle, 2002. Cambridge University Press for Table 1.1 from *Common European Framework of Languages: Learning, teaching, assessment* by Council of Europe, 2001. Longman Pearson for Table 2H based on *Measuring Second Language Performance* by Tim McNamara, 1996. Palgrave Macmillan for extracts and Figure 1.1 from *Language Testing and Validation* by Cyril J. Weir, 2005.

1 Introduction

Purpose of the volume

Language testing in Europe is faced with increasing demands for accountability in respect of all examinations offered to the public. Examination boards are increasingly being required by their own governments and by European authorities to demonstrate that the language ability constructs they are attempting to measure are well grounded in the examinations they offer. Furthermore, examination boards in Europe are being encouraged to map their examinations on to the Common European Framework of Reference (CEFR) (Council of Europe 2001), although some reservations have been expressed within the testing community as to the comprehensiveness of this instrument for practical test development and comparability purposes.

Weir (2005a) argues that a more comprehensive, coherent and transparent form of the CEFR would better serve language testing. For example, the descriptor scales could take increased account of how variation in terms of contextual parameters (i.e. specific features of the Writing task or context) may affect test performance; differing contextual parameters can lead to the raising or lowering of the level of difficulty involved in carrying out the target writing activity represented by a Can Do statement, e.g. 'can write short, simple formulaic notes'. In addition, a test's cognitive validity, which is a function of the cognitive processing involved in carrying out a writing activity, must also be explicitly addressed by any specification on which a test is based. Without such contextual and cognitive-based validity parameters, i.e. a comprehensive definition of the construct to be tested, current attempts to use the CEFR as the basis for developing comparable test forms within and across languages and levels are weakened, and attempts to link separate assessments particularly through social moderation by expert judges hampered.

Weir feels that the CEFR is best seen as a heuristic device rather than a prescriptive one, which can be refined and developed by language testers to better meet their needs. For this particular constituency its current limitations mean that comparisons based on the illustrative scales alone might prove to be misleading given the insufficient attention paid in these scales to issues of validity. The CEFR as presently constituted is not designed to say with any degree of precision or confidence whether or not tests are comparable, nor does it equip us to develop comparable tests. Instead, a more explicit test validation framework is required which better enables examination providers to furnish comprehensive evidence in support of any claims about the sound theoretical basis of their tests.

Examination boards and other institutions offering high-stakes tests need to demonstrate and share how they are seeking to meet the demands of validity in their tests and, more specifically, how they actually operationalise criterial distinctions between the tests they offer at different levels on the proficiency continuum. This volume represents a first attempt to articulate the Cambridge ESOL approach to assessment in the skill area of writing. The perceived benefits of a clearly articulated theoretical and practical position for assessing writing skills in the context of Cambridge ESOL tests are essentially twofold:

- Within Cambridge ESOL – it will deepen understanding of the current theoretical basis upon which Cambridge ESOL tests different levels of language proficiency across its range of test products, and will inform current and future test development projects in the light of this analysis. It will thereby enhance the development of equivalent test forms and tasks.

- Beyond Cambridge ESOL – it will communicate in the public domain the theoretical basis for the tests and provide a more clearly understood rationale for the way in which Cambridge ESOL operationalises this in its tests. It will provide a framework for others interested in validating their own examinations and thereby offer a more principled basis for comparison of language examinations across the proficiency range than is currently available.

We build on Cambridge ESOL's traditional approach to validating tests, namely the VRIP approach where the concern is with Validity (the conventional sources of validity evidence: construct, content, criterion), Reliability, Impact and Practicality. The work of Bachman (1990) and early work of Bachman and Palmer (1996) underpinned the adoption of the VRIP approach, as set out in Weir and Milanovic (2003), and it can be traced back to about 1993 in various Cambridge ESOL documents on validity.

We explore below how a socio-cognitive validity framework described in Weir's *Language Testing and Validation: An evidence-based approach* (2005b) might contribute to an enhanced validation framework for use with Cambridge ESOL examinations. Weir's approach covers much of the same ground as VRIP but it attempts to reconfigure validity to show how its constituent parts (context, cognitive processing and scoring) interact with each other. The construct is not just the underlying traits of communicative language ability but is the result of the constructed triangle of trait, context and score (including its interpretation). The traditional 'trait-based' approach to assessment had to be reconciled with the traditional 'task-based' approach (the CUEFL/CCSE approach and to some extent traditional Cambridge approach). The approach adopted in this volume is therefore effectively an *interactionalist* position which sees the construct as residing in the interactions between the underlying cognitive ability and the context of use – hence the socio-cognitive model.

In addition it conceptualises the validation process in a *temporal frame* thereby identifying the various types of validity evidence that need to be collected at each stage in the test development, monitoring and evaluation cycle. A further difference of the socio-cognitive approach as against traditional approaches is that the construct is now defined more specifically. Within each constituent part of the validation framework, criterial individual parameters for distinguishing between adjacent proficiency levels are also identified.

The conceptualisation of test performance suggested by Weir (2005b) is represented graphically in Figure 1.1.

The framework is socio-cognitive in that the abilities to be tested are demonstrated by the mental processing of the candidate (the cognitive dimension); equally, the use of language in performing tasks is viewed as a social rather than a purely linguistic phenomenon. The framework represents a unified approach to establishing the overall validity of a test. The pictorial representation is intended to depict how the various validity components (the different types of validity evidence) fit together both temporally and conceptually. 'The arrows indicate the principal direction(s) of any hypothesised relationships: what has an effect on what, and the timeline runs from top to bottom: before the test is finalised, then administered and finally what happens after the test event' (2005b:43). Conceptualising validity in terms of temporal sequencing is of value as it offers a plan of what should be happening in relation to validation and when it should be happening.

The framework represented in Figure 1.1 comprises both *a priori* (before-the-test event) validation components of context and cognitive validity and *a posteriori* (after-the-test event) components of scoring validity, consequential validity and criterion-related validity. Weir notes:

> The more comprehensive the approach to validation, the more evidence
> collected on each of the components of this framework, the more secure
> we can be in our claims for the validity of a test. The higher the stakes of
> the test the stricter the demands we might make in respect of all of these
> (Weir 2005b:47).

A number of critical questions will be addressed in applying this socio-cognitive validation framework to Cambridge ESOL examinations across the proficiency spectrum:

Figure 1.1 A framework for conceptualising writing test performance (adapted from Weir 2005b:47)

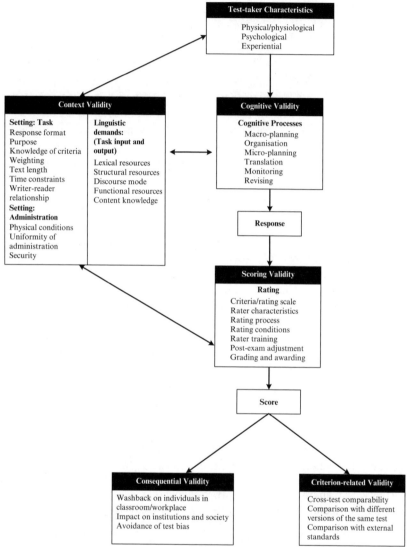

- How are the physical/physiological, psychological and experiential characteristics of candidates catered for by this test? (focus on the test taker)
- Are the cognitive processes required to complete the test tasks appropriate? (focus on cognitive validity)

- Are the characteristics of the test tasks and their administration appropriate and fair to the candidates who are taking them? (focus on context validity)
- How far can we depend on the scores which result from the test? (focus on scoring validity)
- What effects do the test and test scores have on various stakeholders? (focus on consequential validity)
- What external evidence is there outside of the test scores themselves that the test is fair? (focus on criterion-related validity)

These are precisely the sorts of critical questions that anyone intending to take a particular test or to use scores from that test would be advised to ask of the test developers in order to be confident that the nature and quality of the test matches up to their requirements. The *test-taker characteristics* box in Figure 1.1 connects directly to the *cognitive* and *context validity* boxes because:

> these individual characteristics will directly impact on the way the individuals process the test task set up by the context validity box. Obviously, the tasks themselves will also be constructed with the overall test population and the target use situation clearly in mind as well as with concern for their [cognitive] validity (Weir 2005b:51).

Individual test-taker characteristics can be sub-divided into three main categories:

- physical/physiological characteristics – e.g. individuals may have special needs that must be accommodated, such as partial sightedness or dyslexia
- psychological characteristics – e.g. a test-taker's interest or motivation may affect the way a task is managed, or other factors such as preferred learning styles or personality type may have an influence on performance
- experiential characteristics – e.g. the degree of a test-taker's familiarity with a particular test may affect the way the task is managed.

All three types of characteristics have the potential to affect test performance.

The term content validity was traditionally used to refer to the content coverage of the task. *Context validity* is preferred here as the more inclusive superordinate which signals the need to consider not just linguistic content parameters, but also the social and cultural contexts in which the task is performed. Context validity for a Writing task thus addresses the particular performance conditions, the setting under which it is to be performed (such as purpose of the task, time available, length, specified addressee, known marking criteria as well as the linguistic demands inherent in the successful performance of the task) together with the actual examination conditions resulting from the administrative setting (Weir 2005b:19).

Cognitive validity involves collecting both *a priori* evidence on the cognitive processing activated by the test task through piloting and trialling before the test event (e.g. through verbal reports from test takers), and also *a posteriori* evidence on constructs measured involving statistical analysis of scores following test administration. Weir stresses the importance of both:

> There is a need for validation at the *a priori* stage of test development. The more fully we are able to describe the construct we are attempting to measure at the *a priori* stage the more meaningful might be the statistical procedures contributing to construct validation that can subsequently be applied to the results of the test (Weir 2005b:18).

Language test constructors need to be aware of the established theory relating to the cognitive processing that underpins equivalent operations in real-life language use.

Scoring validity is linked directly to both context and cognitive validity and is employed as a superordinate term for all aspects of reliability (see Weir 2005b: chapter 9). Scoring validity accounts for the extent to which test scores are based on appropriate criteria, exhibit consensual agreement in their marking, are as free as possible from measurement error, stable over time, consistent in terms of their content sampling and engender confidence as reliable decision-making indicators.

Criterion-related validity is a predominantly quantitative and *a posteriori* concept, concerned with the extent to which test scores correlate with a suitable external criterion of performance with established properties (see Anastasi 1988:145; Messick 1989:16). A test is said to have criterion-related validity if a relationship can be demonstrated between test scores and some external criterion which is believed to be a measure of the same ability. Criterion-related validity sub-divides into two forms: concurrent and predictive. Concurrent validity seeks an external indicator that has a proven track record of measuring the ability being tested (Bachman 1990:248). It involves the comparison of the test scores with this other measure for the same candidates taken at roughly the same time as the test. This other measure may consist of scores from some other tests, or ratings of the candidate by teachers, subject specialists, or other informants (Alderson, Clapham and Wall 1995). Predictive validity entails the comparison of test scores with some other measure for the same candidates taken some time after the test has been given (Alderson et al 1995).

Messick (1989) argued the case for also considering *consequential validity* in judging the validity of a test. From this point of view it is necessary in validity studies to ascertain whether the social consequences of test interpretation support the intended testing purpose(s) and are consistent with other social values. There is also a concern here with the washback of the test on the learning and teaching that precedes it as well as with its impact on institutions and society more broadly. The further issue of test bias takes us back to the *test-taker characteristics* box. The evidence we collect on the test taker should be used to check that no unfair bias has occurred for individuals as a result of decisions taken earlier with regard to contextual features of the test.

Validity as a unitary concept

Although for descriptive purposes the various elements of the model in Figure 1.1 are presented as being independent of each other, there is undoubtedly a 'symbiotic' relationship that exists between context, cognitive and scoring validity, which together constitute what is frequently referred to as *construct validity*. Decisions taken with regard to parameters in terms of task context will impact on the processing that takes place in task completion. Likewise scoring criteria where made known to candidates in advance will similarly affect executive processing in task planning, and monitoring and revision. The scoring criteria in writing are an important part of the construct in addition to context and processing since they describe the level of performance that is required. Particularly at the upper levels of writing ability, it is the quality of the performance that enables distinctions to be made between levels (Hawkey and Barker 2004). The interactions between, and especially within, these different aspects of validity may well eventually offer further insights into a closer definition of different levels of task difficulty. For the purposes of the present volume, however, the separability of the various aspects of validity will be maintained since they offer the reader a helpful descriptive route through the socio-cognitive validation framework and, more importantly, a clear and systematic perspective on the literature which informs it.

Audience for the volume

This volume is aimed primarily at those working professionally in the field of language testing such as key personnel in examination agencies and those with an academic interest in language testing/examining. It is intended as a high level academic statement of the theoretical construct on which Cambridge examinations are based. As such it is hoped that it will offer other institutions a useful framework for reviewing their own examinations.

However, some parts of the volume may also be of interest and relevance to anyone who is directly involved in practical writing assessment activity and/or Cambridge ESOL examinations in some way, e.g. writing curriculum and materials developers, teachers preparing candidates for the Cambridge Writing tests, etc.

Voices in the volume

As the reader progresses through the volume, it will become apparent that there are several 'voices' in the book, along with various styles of expression.

First, there is the voice of the wider academic community in Applied Linguistics and Language Testing which provides the theoretical base for the framework we have adopted and the guiding principles on which we feel good practice should be based. In discussing each section of the above framework an account is first given of contemporary thinking on the parameter under discussion.

Then there is the voice of the language testing practitioners within Cambridge ESOL who are responsible for developing, administering and validating versions of the tests. Alongside this may be detected the voice of the large community of external professionals who are actively associated with the production and delivery of Cambridge ESOL tests (e.g. test item writers, Writing examiners, centre administrators, etc.).

These latter voices are referred to after we have addressed the current thinking on a particular element of the framework. Sometimes they take the form of case studies to exemplify particular issues, at others they exist in quotations from, or references to, external and internal documentation such as examination handbooks, item writer guidelines, examination and centre reports.

It will become clear that, in compiling the volume, we have drawn together important material from a variety of sources within the organisation relating to the operationalisation of Cambridge ESOL's exams in relation to the theoretical framework; some of this information is extracted from previously internal and confidential documentation and is appearing in the public domain for the first time. It reflects Cambridge ESOL's ongoing commitment to increasing transparency and accountability.

The presence of multiple voices, together with the assembly of information from a wide variety of different documentary sources, inevitably means that differing styles of expression can be detected in certain parts of the volume. Apparent shifts in voice or style simply testify to the complex network of stakeholders which exists in relation to any large-scale testing practice and the fact that any large-scale testing enterprise constitutes a complex, and sometimes sensitive, ecosystem (see Weir and Milanovic 2003 for further discussion of this).

Focus of the volume

Research into the assessment of second language writing normally concerns itself with the direct testing of language performance. By a 'direct test' we mean one which tests writing through involving candidates in the actual construction of text in contrast to 'indirect' or 'objective' tests of writing which principally focus on knowledge of microlinguistic elements of writing, e.g. through multiple choice, cloze, gap filling or error recognition response formats (Hyland 2002:8–9). In these indirect tests writing is divided into more specific 'discrete' elements, e.g. of grammar, vocabulary, spelling, punctuation and orthography, and attempts are made to test these formal features of text by the use of objective test formats. These tests are indirect in that they are only measuring parts of what we understand to be the construct of writing ability. What they test may be related to proficient writing as statistical studies have indicated (De Mauro 1992), but they cannot represent what proficient writers can do (Hamp-Lyons 1990). It would be difficult to generalise from these types of test to how candidates might perform on more productive tasks which required construction of a complete text. It would be difficult from these discrete item tests to make direct statements about how good a writer is or what he or she can do in writing.

As a general principle, it is here argued that language tests should, as far as is practicable, place the same requirements on test takers as are involved in writers' responses to communicative settings in non-test 'real-life' situations. This approach requires attention to both cognitive and social dimensions of communication. According to Hyland, the purpose for writing in this new paradigm is communication rather than accuracy. He argues that tasks within this paradigm are concerned with the psychological reality rather than statistical reliability (Hyland 2002:8, 230). Jacobs, Zinkgraf, Wormuth, Hartfiel and Hughey (1981:3) draw attention to the additional communicative dimension of writing as a social interaction with its emphasis on communicative purpose and the importance of the effect on the reader in the process. Hamp-Lyons and Kroll (1997:8) similarly emphasise that writing is a social and cultural act as well as a cognitive activity with *context, purpose* and *audience* as key parameters.

These views on direct Writing tasks (see Grabe and Kaplan 1996 and Hyland 2002 for excellent overviews of writing) reflect a concern with *authenticity* which has been a dominant theme in recent years for adherents of the *communicative testing* approach as they attempt to develop tests that approximate to the 'reality' of non-test language use (real-life performance) (see Hawkey 2004b, Morrow 1979, Weigle 2002, Weir 1983, 1993 and 2005b).The 'Real-Life' (RL) approach (Bachman 1990:41), though initially the subject of much criticism in the USA, has proved useful as a means of guiding practical test development. It is particularly useful in situations in which the domain of language use is relatively homogeneous and identifiable (see O'Sullivan 2006 on the development of Cambridge Business English examinations).

With regard to Cambridge ESOL examinations, authenticity is considered to have two characteristics. First, *interactional authenticity*, which is a feature of the cognitive activities of the test taker in performing the test task (see Chapter 3 on cognitive validity), and second, *situational authenticity* which attempts to take into account the contextual requirements of the tasks (see Chapter 4 on context validity). Cambridge ESOL adopts an approach which recognises the importance of both situational and interactional authenticity (see Bachman and Palmer 1996 for discussion of these concepts).

The concern with situational authenticity requires writers to respond to contexts which simulate 'real life' in terms of criterial parameters without necessarily replicating it exactly. As far as possible, attempts are made to use situations and tasks which are likely to be familiar and relevant to the intended test taker. In providing contexts, the purpose for carrying out a particular Writing task is made clear, as well as the intended audience, and the criterion for success in completing the task.

Saville (2003:67) positions Cambridge ESOL examinations as follows:

> The authenticity of the tasks and materials in the Cambridge EFL examinations is often referred to as a major strength of the approach . . . The examination content must be designed to provide sufficient evidence of the underlying abilities (i.e. construct) through the way the test taker responds to this input. The authenticity of test content and the authenticity of the candidate's interaction with that content are important considerations for the examination developer in achieving high validity.

There is a strong argument for making tests as direct as possible. The more features of real-life use of language, in this case of writing, that can be built into test tasks the greater the potential for positive washback on the learning that precedes the test-taking experience and the easier it will be from the test to make statements about what students can or cannot do as regards writing. If we want an estimate of a candidate's writing ability, it seems a waste of time to be training students in ways of improving their scores on indirect tests of writing, such as multiple-choice tests of written expression as has happened in the past in some tests of writing. If the purpose is to measure writing ability, examination boards should be employing Writing tasks that encourage teachers to equip candidates with the writing abilities they will need for performing in a real-world context.

Hamp-Lyons (1991a:5–6) suggested that a direct test of writing should minimally feature the following characteristics:

- The sample of written performance produced by the test taker in response to the test must comprise at least 100 words of continuous text. Such a sample, Hamp-Lyons contends, is a length generally accepted as a minimum.
- The writer is afforded substantial scope within which to fashion a response to the task prompt despite the prompt offering the test taker both specific instructions and other input stimulus material.
- Every written response is read by at least one, and more often two, human raters (with a third in case of extreme disagreement), who have undertaken preparatory training to equip them with the necessary writing evaluation skills.
- Judgements arrived at by raters should conform to, or be associated with, a common 'standard' which may comprise a set of exemplar performances or a clear depiction of expected performance at specific proficiency levels.
- The raters' judgements are explicitly stated in numerical terms, instead of or supplemental to, written or verbal articulations. A permanent record of test scores is created and made available for subsequent retrieval for review purposes by a higher authority as and when required.

In this volume, we will be principally concerned with direct tests of writing. Furthermore, almost all the Cambridge ESOL examinations include a direct writing test designed to assess a candidate's skill in writing above the sentence level and the quality of the output produced by a candidate in response to a task is assessed by one or more examiners according to specified criteria.

Although some writers have suggested that second language performance assessment dates from the mid-1950s (Lowe 1988; McNamara 1996), it is worth noting that Cambridge ESOL examinations have included performance assessment components for much longer; for example, a face-to-face interview and an essay-Writing task were both included in the Certificate of Proficiency in English (CPE) from 1913, and the Lower Certificate of English, introduced in 1939 (and later renamed the First Certificate in English) incorporated both a written composition paper and an oral interview (see Weir 2003). As new tests have been added to the Cambridge suite over the past 30 years, direct Writing tasks and a face-to-face Speaking test have continued to be integral components of the Cambridge ESOL examinations.

The Main Suite (MS) examinations offer a picture of how writing ability is measured by Cambridge ESOL across a broad language proficiency continuum and they will form a major source of reference in this volume for illustrating how the writing construct differs from level to level in Cambridge ESOL examinations. In addition we will make reference to other Writing papers from examinations in the Cambridge ESOL family such as the International English Language Testing System (IELTS) examination and Business English Certificates (BEC). This is intended to provide further clarification of how various performance parameters help establish distinctions between different levels of proficiency in writing. It will also demonstrate how research, though specifically conducted in relation to these examinations, has had wider effects throughout the range of examinations offered, for example in helping improve scoring validity. It is worth noting that non-MS examinations are well documented in their own right in other volumes in the Studies in Language Testing series (see Davies forthcoming for IELTS, Hawkey 2004b for Certificates in English Language Skills and O'Sullivan 2006 for BEC) and the reader is referred to these for comprehensive coverage of their history, operationalisation and validity.

In its Main Suite examinations, Cambridge ESOL offers Writing tests at five levels corresponding to equivalent levels of the Common European Framework of Reference (CEFR) (Council of Europe 2001). These five levels are often thought to correspond to the natural levels of language ability familiar to English language teachers around the world, i.e. beginner, pre-intermediate, intermediate, upper intermediate and advanced. The relationship claimed between Cambridge ESOL levels and the CEFR is discussed in detail in Chapter 7.

An overview of the Writing tasks in the Cambridge ESOL 5-level Main Suite examinations is presented in Tables 1.1 and 1.2, starting with descriptors used in the CEFR.

Reference is also made in this volume to the Business English Certificate (BEC) examinations and the International English Language Testing System (IELTS) and overviews of the written elements of these examinations are shown in Tables 1.3 and 1.4. BEC examinations are taken by those wishing to gain a qualification in business English as a result of the growing internationalisation of business and the need for employees to interact in more than just a single language (see O'Sullivan 2006 for full details of this test). IELTS is an English for Academic Purposes (EAP) test principally used for admissions purposes into tertiary level institutions throughout the world (see Davies forthcoming, for a detailed history of the developments in EAP testing leading up to the introduction of IELTS).

The relationships between the Writing tests in terms of level of proficiency is reviewed in Chapter 7 where research is reported on comparability studies

Table 1.1 Common European Framework of Reference level descriptors for second language writing (based on Council of Europe 2001:61, 83)

Level – What language users at these levels are actually able to do in writing. Each level subsumes command of the level below

KET	PET	FCE	CAE	CPE
CEFR A2 Waystage	CEFR B1 Threshold	CEFR B2 Vantage	CEFR C1 Effective Mastery Operational	CEFR C2 Proficiency
Overall Written Production*	*Overall Written Production*	*Overall Written Production*	*Overall Written Production*	*Overall Written Production*
Can write a series of simple phrases and sentences linked with simple connectors like 'and', 'but' and 'because'.	Can write straightforward connected texts on a range of familiar subjects within their field of interest, by linking a series of shorter discrete elements into a linear sequence.	Can write clear, detailed texts on a variety of subjects related to their field of interest, synthesising and evaluating information and arguments from a number of sources.	Can write clear, well-structured texts of complex subjects, underlining the relevant salient issues, expanding and supporting points of view at some length with subsidiary points, reasons and relevant examples, and rounding off with an appropriate conclusion.	Can write clear, smoothly flowing, complex texts in an appropriate and effective style and a logical structure which helps the reader to find significant points.
Overall Written Interaction**	*Overall Written Interaction*	*Overall Written Interaction*	*Overall Written Interaction*	*Overall Written Interaction*
Can write short, simple formulaic notes relating to matters in areas of immediate need.	Can convey information and ideas on broad and everyday topics, check information and ask about or explain problems with reasonable precision. Can write personal letters and notes asking for or conveying simple information of immediate relevance, getting across the point he/she feels to be important.	Can express news and views effectively in writing, and relate to those of others.	Can express him/ herself with clarity and precision, relating to the addressee flexibly and effectively.	In CEFR same as C1.

* *'In written production (writing) activities the language user as writer produces a written text which is received by a readership of one or more readers' (Council of Europe 2001:61).*
** *'Interaction through the medium of written language includes such activities as: passing and exchanging notes, memos, etc. when spoken interaction is impossible and inappropriate; correspondence by letter, fax, e-mail, etc.; negotiating the text of agreements, contracts, communiqués, etc. by reformulating and exchanging drafts, amendments, proof corrections, etc.; participating in on-line or off-line computer conferences' (Council of Europe 2001:82).*

Table 1.2 Descriptions from the examination handbooks of the Writing tasks used in the Cambridge ESOL 5-level Main Suite examinations

KET (A2)	PET (B1)	FCE (B2)	CAE (C1)	CPE (C2)
KET candidates are expected to be able to produce items of vocabulary from a short definition, select appropriate lexis to complete one-word gaps in a simple text, and to transfer information from a text to a form (Parts 6–8). They also need to show their ability to complete a short everyday Writing task appropriately, coherently and showing reasonable control of structure, and vocabulary, (Part 9).	PET candidates are expected to be able to give information, report events and describe people, objects and places as well as convey reactions to situations, express hopes, regrets, pleasure, etc. They should also be able to use the words they know appropriately and accurately in different written contexts and be capable of producing variations on simple sentences (Part 3).	FCE candidates are expected to be able to write non-specialised text types such as letters, articles, reports and compositions given purpose and target reader, covering a range of topics. One of the optional tasks in Part 2 is based on the reading of one of five set books.	CAE candidates are expected to be able to use the structures of a language with ease and fluency. They are aware of the relationship between the language and the culture it exists in, and of the significance of register. The Writing paper is designed to test a candidate's ability to write continuous English appropriate to a given task. CAE candidates are expected to complete Writing tasks in response to the stimuli provided (input text and task instructions). The candidate's situation, purpose of writing and target readership are clearly stated.	CPE candidates are expected to be able to write clear, fluent text in an appropriate style. They should be able to write complex letters, reports, essays, reviews or articles using an effective logical structure which helps the reader notice and remember significant points. A candidate at CPE level should also be able to write reviews of professional or literary works.

Table 1.3 BEC Writing examinations

	BEC Preliminary	BEC Vantage	BEC Higher
Level Description	This is an examination for candidates at a level similar to Cambridge MS PET level [CEF B1]	This is an examination for candidates at a level similar to Cambridge MS FCE level [CEF B2]	This is an examination for candidates at a level similar to Cambridge MS CAE level [CEF C1]
Language Use	Learners at this level can: • read and understand a variety of business-related texts • interpret charts and diagrams • produce a variety of written texts in order to convey specific information or feeling.	Learners at this level can: • read and understand general business letters, reports, articles and leaflets • produce letters, memos and simple reports.	Learners at this level can: • understand most correspondence, articles and reports where information is overtly stated • write reports and draft instructions.

Table 1.4   IELTS Academic Writing task

Module format
IELTS Academic Writing consists of two tasks (Writing task 1 and Writing task 2) and candidates must answer BOTH tasks.

Task 1
For Writing task 1 candidates are given some visual information which may be presented in the form of one or more related diagrams, charts, graphs or tables. Candidates are asked to describe the information or data.

Task 2
For Writing task 2, candidates are presented with an opinion, problem or issue which they must discuss. They may be asked to present the solution to a problem, present and justify an opinion, compare and contrast evidence or opinions, or evaluate and challenge an argument or idea.

of how the same candidates have performed on the different tests at particular proficiency levels.

Structure of the volume

The outline shape for the volume closely follows the organisation of the framework described above in Figure 1.1 with its six component parts: test taker; cognitive validity; context validity; scoring validity; consequential validity; and criterion-related validity.

Chapter 2, on test-taker characteristics, reviews the research literature in this area paying particular attention to research undertaken into Cambridge ESOL tests. The ways in which ESOL tests take account of test-taker characteristics are then considered. This includes special considerations and special circumstances as well as the nature of the general candidature and how this is reflected in the tests at different levels. This twin focus on research and practice is followed throughout the book.

In Chapter 3, on cognitive validity, the available research literature on the processing involved in writing is reviewed and then the cognitive processing involved in Cambridge Writing examinations is examined in detail. Given the relative paucity of L2 research in this area, findings from L1 studies are also taken into account.

The purpose of Chapter 4, on context validity, is to review the again limited research literature on the impact of contextual variables on performance. The available research in this area relating to Cambridge ESOL Writing products is also explored. The chapter then examines the ways in which Cambridge ESOL Writing tests operationalise various contextual variables. Of particular interest here is the variation of parameters across tasks intended for test takers at different levels of ability.

Chapter 5, on scoring validity, looks at issues relating to the scoring of Writing tests. The available research literature is reviewed and extensive research by Cambridge ESOL in this area is highlighted. The procedures developed by Cambridge ESOL in each of the elements of this part of the framework are exemplified.

In Chapters 6 and 7, the value of the test score in terms of criterion-related and consequential validity is discussed. Again Cambridge ESOL Writing tests and research are the basis for the examples.

In the final chapter, we summarise our findings from applying this validity framework to Cambridge Writing examinations. We suggest where the current tests embody and operationalise current knowledge and understanding about the writing ability construct as well as where, in due course, improvements might be made in terms of various parameters from the validity components. Suggestions are also made for further research which might be of value to Cambridge ESOL as well as the wider testing community.

Postscript

In this introductory chapter we have highlighted the need for test developers to provide a clear explication of the ability constructs which underpin the tests they offer in the public domain; such an explication is increasingly necessary if claims about the validity of test score interpretation and use are to be supported both logically and with empirical evidence.

We have proposed a comprehensive test validation framework which adopts a socio-cognitive perspective in terms of its underlying theory and which conceptualises validity as a unitary concept; at the same time the framework embraces six core components which reflect the practical nature and quality of an actual testing event. We have suggested that an understanding and analysis of the framework and its components in relation to specific tests can assist test developers to more effectively operationalise their tests, especially in relation to criterial distinctions across test levels. We have also explained how this volume proposes to apply the validation framework and its components to a set of actual tests produced by Cambridge, taking as its focus the construct of writing ability. Finally, in this chapter we have highlighted the extent to which this volume is informed from multiple professional perspectives and has drawn on a wide variety of documentary and other sources in its attempt to communicate effectively to its intended audience.

In Chapter 2 we will address in greater detail the first of the six components of our validation framework – the test taker – in order to examine the specific parameters which test developers need to take account of in developing their tests.

2 Test-taker characteristics

An examination is normally developed with both test takers and the target situation context in mind. As we discussed in Chapter 1, real-life perform-ance is increasingly seen as the criterion of choice against which test tasks are judged and we deal at length with authenticity of task in Chapters 3 and 4. It is important to remember however, that it is the test taker, rather than the test task, which is at the heart of the assessment event. While it is clear that success in language learning and performance assessment depends primarily on an individual's ability in the intended construct, there are of course many other variables which are likely to impact on performance and which relate to personal characteristics of the individual test taker; these include factors such as age, interests, experience, knowledge and motivation. The range and complexity of these variables has been increasingly acknowledged by testing specialists over recent years leading to a growth in theoretical and empirical studies (see for example Bachman 1990, 2004, Bachman and Palmer 1996, Kunnan 1995, O'Sullivan 2000, Purpura 1999). Test developers would, in as far as it is possible to do so, normally wish to take these into account in test development to ensure they are 'testing for best'.

Despite the central importance of the test taker in any assessment activity, it is often difficult for an exam provider to cater for individual variation across test takers and at the same time adhere to the requirement for test fair-ness. This becomes a critical issue when dealing with a large and/or highly heterogeneous test population, e.g. an international test candidature or a population of test takers with a potential age range from 17 to 70. For example, in an international English language examination taken on all con-tinents it is clearly impossible to take full account of the many linguistic vari-eties of English which are now recognised around the world. Instead, examination boards tend to adopt a largely pragmatic approach, selecting those varieties of English which have the greatest exposure or appealing to some general notion of international English as the standard (for a fuller dis-cussion of this particular issue see Taylor 2006).

Catering for each of the varied cultural backgrounds of a multi-ethnic candidature is again impossible in large-scale examinations (although it may be possible to achieve at the local and regional level). At best, steps must be taken at the test development stage to ensure that no candidate is disadvan-taged in relation to other candidates by the socio-cultural content of the test.

Tasks and topics should normally be neutral with regard to candidates, and materials should be trialled in advance to confirm this and to filter out any material which may be culturally inaccessible or inappropriate. Feedback from candidates on the accessibility of topics and tasks should be elicited in such trialling and used in modifying materials where necessary. In Chapter 4 on context validity we discuss steps that are taken with regard to content to try and avoid biasing the test against people of particular backgrounds, i.e. in terms of their age, topical knowledge or probable life experience. In Chapter 6 on consequential validity we detail ways in which exam boards can check that bias has been avoided in the tests they offer.

In relation to writing assessment, differences may also occur in the ways L2 writers exhibit L1 cultural preferences when drawing on the resources available to them. Hyland (2002:37) with reference to Grabe and Kaplan (1996:239) draws attention to possible cultural influences from L1 writing where rhetorical features are transferred from the writer's L1 into their L2 writing. Grabe and Kaplan describe how studies in contrastive rhetoric indicate that different communities can have different cultural preferences for organising writing, structuring arguments, using secondary material, catering for the reader, and using cohesion and overt linguistic features which may be inappropriate for native English-speaking settings. Consideration needs to be given as to how such L1 cultural preferences will be handled in the marking scheme (see Chapter 5 on scoring validity). Current practice tends to assume that, with an international candidature, test takers will conform to the norms of the target discourse community.

In the main we limit ourselves in this chapter to consideration of those test-taker characteristics that can reasonably be addressed by examining boards, e.g. special accommodations for candidates with some form of physical/physiological disability. Our intention is not to downgrade the importance of other characteristics which are undoubtedly relevant to theories of writing and writing assessment; while acknowledging these, we recognise that it is more difficult for test developers to take account of them and at the same time maintain the requirement for test fairness. The touchstone of any decisions taken in respect of background variables is that no candidate should be discriminated against except in terms of their ability in the intended construct.

We begin with an overview of research findings on selected test-taker characteristics and move on to describe and discuss aspects of Cambridge ESOL practice in this area.

Test taker

Bachman (1990) details how personal attributes or '*test-taker characteristics*' are either *systematic*, in that they will consistently affect an individual's test performance, or *unsystematic* or random and therefore largely beyond the control of test developers/administrators (Bachman 2004a:156). Test developers need to be concerned primarily about the former and to consider how these can be addressed. The latter are more difficult to cater for precisely because they are more difficult to predict. The systematic attributes referred to by Bachman (1990:164) include both individual characteristics, e.g. cognitive style and content knowledge, and group characteristics such as gender or L1. These characteristics may be systematic in the sense of having a continued effect on performance, though the precise nature of the effect may vary over differing task contexts. As we will see later in this chapter, Cambridge ESOL takes these systematic attributes into account at each stage: in guidelines for item writers, in the pre-editing of test material and also in the review of centre and candidate feedback following trialling.

The assessment of writing entails a series of complex interactions between individual test takers, raters and task (see Milanovic and Saville 1996, Ruth and Murphy 1984). In a forthcoming companion volume on Speaking, O'Sullivan and Green cite Edgeworth (1888:615) on the 'elements of uncertainty' which may contribute to measurement error in examinations, and note his identification of factors 'too subtle for the Calculus and Probabilities to handle: such as the variation of the candidate's spirits'. Since that time the potential effect on test performance of a range of factors associated with the test taker has received relatively little attention (see O'Sullivan 2000 for a summary of this rather disparate literature). However, current concerns with test fairness highlight the need to avoid bias against certain candidates in those cases where personal facets can be accounted for.

A number of Test of English as a Foreign Language (TOEFL) research studies have identified variables associated with test takers that were potential sources of construct irrelevant variance – 'a type of systematic measurement error where there is some variance in the test scores that is due to factors other than the construct in question' (Davies et al 1999:32). Item performance on TOEFL across native language groups was looked at by a number of researchers (Alderman and Holland 1981, Angoff and Sharon 1974, Oltman et al 1988, Swinton and Powers 1980) who all found significant variation among the groups examined. In investigating gender of the test taker (Blanchard and Reedy 1970, O'Sullivan 2000, Wilson 1982) only Wilson found significant differences. Kunnan (1990, 1994) and Ryan and Bachman (1992), Brown and Iwashita (1998), and Hill (1998) looked at differential item functioning (DIF) in terms of a number of background variables. Tittle (1990) discussed the contexts in which test bias can happen and details various methodologies for establishing whether it has occurred or not.

O'Sullivan (2000) suggests that the variables associated with the individual candidate that might influence performance on tests can be presented as in Table 2.1.

The framework in Table 2.1 will be used to describe some aspects of Cambridge ESOL practice with particular regard to the assessment of writing.

Table 2.1 Characteristics of the test taker (based on O'Sullivan 2000)

Physical/Physiological	Psychological	Experiential
Short term ailments (*toothache, cold etc.*)	Personality	Education
	Memory	Examination preparedness
Longer term disabilities (*speaking, hearing, vision*)	Cognitive style	Examination experience
	Affective schemata	Communication experience
	Concentration	Target language –
Age	Motivation	Country residence
Sex	Emotional state	

Test taker: Cambridge practice

The physical characteristics of the test taker have a visible impact on the test development process. Most serious tests address the special arrangements, or accommodations, necessary to ensure that all test takers are given an equal opportunity to demonstrate their language skills to the best of their ability.

Physical/physiological characteristics

Cambridge ESOL makes appropriate special provisions once decisions have been made on the acceptability of a request for an accommodation in respect of one or more of these characteristics. *Special Arrangements*, made before the candidate sits the examination, are provisions for candidates who have a permanent or long-term disability (such as a visual difficulty or dyslexia) or a temporary difficulty (such as a broken arm). Special Arrangements enable candidates to understand questions and tasks, to express their answers and to demonstrate their English to the best of their ability. The purpose of these arrangements is to permit such candidates' level of attainment to be fairly and objectively assessed.

Provisions are generally intended:

- to remove, as far as practicably possible, the effects of the disability on the candidate's ability to demonstrate their true level of attainment in relation to the assessment objectives
- to ensure that the Special Arrangements do not provide disabled candidates with an unfair advantage over their counterparts
- to avoid misleading the user of the certificate about the candidate's attainment.

The type of provision offered by Cambridge ESOL depends on the nature and context of the disability. Details of all provisions which can be offered are publicly available and any request made by a test taker for Special Arrangements is normally supported by appropriate documentation, e.g. a medical certificate or doctor's letter.

Table 2.2 shows the range and volume of provision made for candidates taking Main Suite Writing papers over a six-year period (2000–2005). Major categories of Special Arrangements across the Cambridge ESOL range of tests include additional time and/or supervised breaks and modified question papers. The nature of these and other arrangements offered are explained in more detail below.

Table 2.2 Number of provisions made for candidates taking Main Suite Writing papers 2000–2005

	2000	2001	2002	2003	2004	2005*
Braille papers	20	27	31	21	20	11
Enlarged print papers	59	43	52	50	39	48
Dyslexic candidates	356	542	889	1,594	767	437
Separate marking***	82	171	390	950	254*	N/A
Extra time			281**	953	793	530
Use of amanuensis			19**	66	54	23
Use of word processor/ typewriter			14**	31	35	21
Supervised breaks			13**	27	42	7
Use of copier			16**	24	26	11

* March/June only
** December only
*** Not provided from December 2004 onwards.

In certain situations, candidates require *additional time* either to read their paper or write their responses. Examples of difficulties which may warrant extra time would include dyslexia, visual difficulties or difficulties with writing due to, for example, cerebral palsy. Additional time up to 25% of the prescribed duration of an examination session invariably meets the requirements of most candidates although greater time allowance may be recommended according to the respective needs of candidates. Blind candidates often need 100% extra time.

For some candidates, *supervised breaks* may be appropriate instead of, or in addition to, the extra time allowance. An example would be a candidate who had difficulty concentrating for long periods of time, or one who had repetitive strain injury in the writing hand.

Candidates may require *modified question papers* if they have severe visual or hearing difficulties. Modifications – which are made in accordance with recommendations of nationally recognised organisations such as the Royal

National Institute for the Blind (RNIB) – can be made to most Writing question papers and include:

- *Braille* versions of question papers in either contracted or uncontracted form. Braille papers are usually modified, particularly where there is any visual element, and may be shortened.
- *Enlarged print question papers*, which are also available for use by visually impaired candidates for most Cambridge ESOL examinations.

Candidates with special needs sometimes require *assistance in recording their answers*. Examples of how candidates with particular difficulties can record their Writing responses include blind candidates who can either dictate their answers to an amanuensis, or use a Braille machine alone or with assistance, or use a typewriter or word processor. Visually impaired candidates or candidates with specific writing problems can also dictate their answers to an amanuensis or use a typewriter or word processor.

Provision for the *use of a computer/word processor* is restricted to candidates with a disability which prevents them from writing by hand in the usual way. The object of Special Arrangements is to enable candidates with disabilities to demonstrate their true levels of attainment in relation to the assessment objectives of a syllabus. This principle applies to the use of computers just as it does to other types of Special Arrangement. Use of the computer must not create a misleading impression of attainment or confer an unfair advantage over and above other candidates so it is important before provision is granted to evaluate what effect, if any, the use of the computer will have on the ability to assess the candidate fairly. Use of a computer requires that the candidate possesses a degree of computer proficiency together with familiarity with any associated program. Some candidates may additionally request the use of *computer assistive software* such as Zoomtext for the visually impaired, or voice to text software.

Provision for the *use of an amanuensis* is restricted to candidates with a disability which prevents them from writing at all; in other words they are unable to write by hand or to use a Braille writer, a typewriter or a word processor. As with the use of a computer, use of an amanuensis must not engender wrong impressions of candidate attainment or offer any advantage over other candidates.

Sometimes the presentation of a candidate's answers may cause difficulty for an examiner, for example where a disability or an injury to the hand results in poor quality handwriting and largely illegible text; in such cases, provision for the *production of a transcript* exists. The purpose of the transcript – which is produced immediately after the Writing examination and usually in the presence of the candidate – is to aid the examiner in the marking of a candidate's answers.

Provision for candidates with specific learning difficulties, such as dyslexia, includes *additional time* (normally 25% or if required up to 50%) as well as permission to use a typewriter or word processor; in addition, test takers do not have to transfer answers to OMR (Optical Mark Reader) sheets and separate invigilation is also sometimes offered. Until recently provision for FCE, CAE and CPE candidates with dyslexia also included 'separate marking', i.e. the option to have their answers separately marked, with mistakes in spelling being disregarded by examiners. This provision was discontinued from December 2004, however, following internal studies into its validity, reliability and practicality (see Case Study A below).

As can be seen from the description and discussion so far, Cambridge ESOL's Special Arrangements policy and practice seeks to reflect current knowledge and professional expertise on assessing learners with various types of disability. Policy and practice in this area are kept under regular review by the examination board and, as far as possible, are informed by internal validation and research studies to confirm the suitability of particular provision and to identify where and how improvements might be made. A set of studies undertaken prior to the recent policy change on 'separate marking' provision for test takers with dyslexia demonstrates this approach in action; for this reason the studies are summarised and presented below in the form of a case study – the first of several such case studies in this volume. The case studies have been included to illustrate the type of investigations which examination boards may need to engage in as part of their ongoing commitment to quality and fairness.

Case Study A: Investigating provision for candidates with dyslexia

Background

In 2002 Cambridge ESOL undertook a review of its Special Arrangements provision to identify any issues needing attention. One particular area of concern highlighted was the appropriateness or otherwise of the separate marking Special Arrangement for candidates with dyslexia taking FCE, CAE or CPE. This Special Arrangement involved disregarding the quality of the candidate's spelling (only) in their Writing test performance. Provision of this Special Arrangement triggered an endorsement on the candidate's certificate with a note on the reverse side declaring '*The candidate was exempt from satisfying the full range of assessment objectives in the examination*'. Attention was drawn to the note by means of a small symbol on the front of the certificate.

Concerns focused on the continuing justification for the separate marking arrangement in terms of its *theoretical validity, equity and practicality*. Although demand for this provision appeared to be growing rapidly year on year, there was concern that the overwhelming majority of requests (95%) originated from a single European country, with most of the remaining 5% coming from a second country in Europe.

Dyslexia is an area which is receiving increasing attention within education (both in the UK and internationally) and about which there is growing awareness and understanding; it was acknowledged that recent theoretical and empirical work in this field should directly feed into decisions about Cambridge ESOL policy and practice.

The nature of the investigation

A series of small-scale investigative studies set out to explore four key areas:

- current theory and practice within the 'expert' community on L2 learners and dyslexia, and possible implications for Cambridge ESOL policy/practice
- the nature of the writing performance produced in Cambridge ESOL examinations by candidates with dyslexia who requested separate marking, and a comparison with the performance of candidates who did not request it
- the actual process of separate marking from the perspective of the Writing examiner, and its impact on final task score
- possible educational and social reasons for the growing take-up of the separate marking Special Arrangement, especially in certain European countries.

The approach adopted to investigate these four key areas is described briefly below together with a summary of the findings (Taylor 2004).

Study 1

To gain greater insights into the issues of L2 learners with dyslexia and the potential implications for assessment, a dyslexia specialist at the University of Edinburgh was commissioned to write a report for Cambridge ESOL and to give a presentation of his findings to relevant ESOL personnel (Reid 2003).

General background questions addressed by the report included:

- How is dyslexia defined? Do definitions vary from country to country?
- What sorts of tests are used to diagnose dyslexia?
- Do approaches to diagnosis/intervention vary from country to country?
- Are there any specific nationalities/language groups where the incidence of dyslexia appears to be significantly high?

Questions relating specifically to L2 learners with dyslexia included:

- What difficulties do L2 learners with dyslexia face in their learning?
- Do these vary across different age groups – children, teenagers, adults?

- What is the general impact on different skill areas – reading, writing, listening, speaking?
- What is the specific impact in the area of writing performance (both micro and extended writing)?
- What difficulties might L2 learners with dyslexia face in terms of language assessment?
- What implications might this have for test design and format, administrative procedures, score reporting, etc?
- What research has been done to date in any of these areas?

The report confirmed that learners with dyslexia have particular problems with various aspects of language: not only with spelling but also with grammar and organisation; also that dyslexia can manifest itself in different 'bundles' of difficulties from individual to individual. Extra time is generally considered the most appropriate provision in formal assessment contexts but it is also common practice to disregard form-focused features of writing performance in content-based tests such as history or mathematics (i.e. where the assessment focus is content rather than language).

Study 2

A small quantitative/qualitative study of FCE and CAE writing performance was set up in December 2002 to compare the writing performance of L2 candidates with dyslexia who requested separate marking, and L2 candidates who did not request separate marking (and who might therefore be assumed not to suffer from dyslexia). All candidates shared the same first language to avoid L1 or nationality as a confounding variable.

Specific research questions included:

- How does the writing performance of L2 learners with dyslexia compare with that of other L2 learners who share the same L1?
- Does it contain more spelling and other errors likely to be influenced by the L1?
- Does it contain more spelling and other errors less easily attributable to L1 influence?

Data for analysis comprised eight CAE Paper 2 scripts (two tasks) and 16 FCE Paper 2 scripts (two tasks); 'non-dyslexic' scripts were taken from the Cambridge Learner Corpus (CLC); 'dyslexic' scripts were taken from the separate marking scripts allocation and included both scripts where examiners judged that separate marking apparently made a difference to the final score assigned and others where it appeared to make no difference (see Study 3 below).

Qualitative and quantitative methodologies were employed to analyse the data and involved:

- a reflective exercise by one of the analysts (UK based) on likely features of performance by learners in the country of interest, followed by
- a close qualitative/quantitative analysis of each script and a summary of observations; this was used to compare features across all scripts.

One of the analysts involved shared the L1 of the test takers, and both analysts had recent experience of teaching EFL in the country of interest.

Analysis revealed that the frequency of typical learner spelling errors and the frequency of 'unusual' (and therefore possibly dyslexia-related) spelling errors was higher overall across the 'dyslexic' script sample for both CAE and FCE; but no clear pattern emerged when looking at the individual scripts in the set.

Study 3

One of the responsibilities of the Principal Examiner for any Cambridge ESOL Writing test was to deal with scripts where the separate marking Special Arrangement applies. Over a period of about 18 months, Principal Examiners were asked to monitor during their marking whether – in their view – their disregard of spelling quality actually made a difference to the final task score assigned to that candidate. Remembering that this Special Arrangement requires that the quality of the candidate's spelling only should be disregarded, they reported that:

- in December 2001 it appeared to make a difference in 46% of cases
- in December 2002 it appeared to make a difference in 63% of cases.

This would imply that in December 2001, more than half of the candidates (54%) receiving this Special Arrangement provision may have received, in respect of their writing performance, an unnecessary endorsement on their final certificate. Endorsements are added to certificates where some of the objectives of the relevant examination have not been assessed on account of a particular disability of the candidate and where the candidate's performance in the examination was assessed on the basis of modified criteria to take account of particular learning disabilities, such as dyslexia. Whilst the figure was lower in December 2002 it was still nearly 40%.

Study 4

In order to investigate the disproportionately large number of separate marking requests emanating from one particular European country, referred to here as Country X, Cambridge ESOL commissioned an ESOL special needs consultant to conduct interviews with two EFL teachers for whom the national language of Country X was their first language. One was resident and working in the country whilst the other was living in the UK (Gutteridge 2003).

The following key questions were addressed in the course of this investigation:

- Why are such large numbers of dyslexic candidates from Country X opting for separate marking?
- Apart from the use of a 'Candidate with Dyslexia' form, what other reasons might there be for candidates opting for separate marking?
- What national attitudes to the area of Specific Learning Difficulties might be relevant?
- What relevant conclusions can be drawn from analysing scripts from dyslexic candidates?
- Are dyslexic ESOL candidates aware of the limitations of separate marking?
- Are dyslexic candidates aware that separate marking makes no difference in many cases?
- Are there any relevant issues regarding the certification of dyslexic ESOL candidates?

Responses to the questions above suggested that a number of specific social and educational factors provided a rationale for why so many candidates were requesting this Special Arrangement.

Conclusions

The results of investigation into the four areas described above led to extensive internal discussion within Cambridge ESOL and ultimately to the conclusion that 'separate marking' of writing is not an appropriate Special Arrangement in language-focused assessment (even though it is common practice in content-focused assessment). For this reason, from December 2004, the provision of separate marking for candidates with dyslexia was no longer offered. The change in policy is consistent with expert advice in the field and with the policy/practice of other assessment providers. The additional time provision is generally acknowledged to be the most appropriate provision for candidates with dyslexia.

Psychological characteristics

As previously mentioned, a test taker's interest or motivation may influence the way a task is dealt with (Berry 2004). Given a desire to elicit the best sample of a student's performance, Cambridge ESOL attempts to make test events as positive as possible in the full knowledge that some stress is probably unavoidable and may even be desirable if it enhances performance. A range of Writing tasks is offered, and sometimes a degree of choice in the anticipation that test takers will respond to or select tasks which align, to at least some degree, with their personal interests and motivation. Some tasks will appeal to candidates who want to write about personal experience;

others are designed to permit a more objective treatment, for example, a report on a holiday resort.

Although factors such as preferred learning styles or personality type could affect test performance (Berry 2004), it is difficult to see how the former might be catered for in the testing (as opposed to the teaching/learning) context. Cambridge ESOL takes the view that a candidate's psychological characteristics will affect their real-life performance just as it may affect their test performance, but that their psychological make-up need not necessarily prevent them from performing well. It is important to note that offering a multiplicity of tasks in an attempt to take account of individual learning styles or personality types raises issues of test sampling and comparability and could lead to real problems in scoring validity. It seems unlikely that much can be done to cater for individual differences in these respects except to put the candidates at their ease as far as is possible in ways described next under experiential characteristics. It is interesting to speculate whether computer-based assessment, including computer-adaptive assessment, might offer a better and more flexible solution in the future to help take account of individual test-taker differences.

Experiential characteristics

Candidates need to be familiar with examination format and other environmental features before sitting a test as familiarity with the demands of a particular test may affect the way they deal with the tasks. Provision of specimen past papers and clear test specifications help to ensure that test takers are fully aware of the test's demands. Examination handbooks for candidates and teachers contain sample Writing tasks along with examples of candidates' written responses and mark schemes, and these are readily available in both electronic (www.CambridgeESOL.org/support/handbooks) and hard copy.

Experiential characteristics comprise those influences external to the test taker, and include their past learning experiences especially where directly connected with the examination in question; they may have prepared for an examination through a course of study, for example, or taken the same examination on a previous occasion. Familiarity with the mode of test delivery is increasingly important. For example, the computer literacy of test takers needs to be established in the light of the impetus towards computer-delivered tests (Eignor et al 1998, Kirsch et al 1998, Taylor et al 1998). Weir et al (2005) report on the development of a Computer Familiarity and Anxiety questionnaire in their study into the effect on performance in IELTS of writing using pencil-and-paper and computer modes. Findings from this study suggested that for the majority of candidates mode had no significant effect on their test scores.

An investigation into the effects of computer familiarity and attitudes towards CB IELTS on candidate performance was undertaken by Maycock (2004). The study concluded that attitudes towards CB IELTS are generally positive. Candidate characteristics (L1 = Chinese and age range) were also found to have significant but minimal effects on the difference in scores. However, computer experience and ability were not found to have any significant effects, indicating that CB IELTS is not biased towards candidates with advanced computer skills over those with basic skills.

Candidates who took part in the CB PET comparability trial in February 2005 (Maycock and Green 2005) were asked to complete a questionnaire regarding their attitudes towards the test and their levels of computer familiarity. The aim of the study was to address issues such as whether candidates preferred taking PET on paper or computer and how user-friendly they found the navigation of the test, and to discover any aspects which might cause problems for candidates on the launch of CB PET. Results again indicated a very positive response to the computer-based test and no evidence of bias due to lack of computer familiarity.

The issue of computer familiarity in these studies is further discussed in detail in Chapter 5.

Main Suite candidature

Test-taker information is collected about Cambridge ESOL's Main Suite candidature at each examination session, when candidates fill in *Candidate Information Sheets* (CIS) – included as Appendix B. These sheets gather essential information, which is needed, for example, to analyse whether certain types of question cause difficulties for candidates in particular age ranges or from particular language backgrounds (see Chapter 6 for discussion of the issue of test bias). They also allow ongoing monitoring of the demographic make-up of the candidature of a given examination and enable any changes in the test taking population to be observed so that these can inform later review and revision of the test in question. The information provided by candidates is treated as confidential and is covered by the Data Protection Act of the United Kingdom. The answers that candidates give to the questions on the CIS do not affect their result in any way. Typical CIS data for candidates across the five proficiency levels is summarised below in Table 2.3 and it reveals some interesting trends in the test-taker populations across the proficiency levels:

- the average age of test takers and the range of their ages increases steadily across the levels from KET to CPE
- the proportion of female to male test takers also increases steadily up the proficiency continuum, from around 50:50 to 65:35

Table 2.3 Typical breakdown of KET–CPE test takers based on CIS data for 2005

	Nationality	Age	Gender	Employment	Exam preparation	Reasons for taking
KET	More than 60 countries, mainly Europe, South America, and Asia-Pacific region.	About 90% are 18 or under. 6% are in the 19–30 age group.	Approximately 54% are female.	Most are studying full-time.	Approximately 80% attend preparation classes.	About 14% for personal interest, 21% for employment reasons, about 30% interested in further study.
PET	Taken in over 80 countries, mainly in Europe and South America.	About 70% are age 20 or under. 20% are in the 21–30 age group.	Approximately 56% are female.	Most are studying full-time.	About 89% attend preparation classes. On average, they study for about 4.5 years in total prior to entry.	About 14% for personal reasons, while nearly 31% to improve their future employment prospects. Nearly 20% are interested in further study of English.
FCE	About 100 countries although more than 150 nationalities are represented. Mainly European (many in the UK) and South American.	About 83% are under 25, with an average age being about 20. In some countries the average age is lower (e.g. Greece is about 16).	About 59% are female.	Most are students, although there are considerable differences in the proportion of students in different countries.	About 86% undertake a preparatory course. Most of these courses last between 8 and 24 weeks.	Reasons are roughly distributed as: 31% to gain employment, 20% for further study, 10% out of personal interest.

	Countries	Age	Gender	Education	Preparatory course		Reasons
CAE	Taken in about 67 countries although more than 175 nationalities are represented.	Nearly 73% are under 25, with the average age being about 22. In some countries the average age is lower (e.g. Greece is about 19).	About 62% are female.	Most are students, although there are considerable differences in the proportion of students in different countries.	About 83% undertake a preparatory course.		Reasons are roughly distributed as: 22% for study, 31% for work.
CPE	Taken in about 90 countries. The majority (80%) are European – but South America also provides considerable numbers of candidates.	Most in late teens or early 20s. Almost 78% are 25 and under. Only around 5% are 31 or over. Some countries have a narrow age range. Greece and Portugal – a younger population – almost 44% (GR) / 53% (PT) are 16–20.	About 64% are female.	Most have studied English for at least 6 years. 32% are educated to secondary level up to 19 and another 68% have completed further education to degree level or equivalent.	Around 74% undertake a preparatory course.	Many have taken other Cambridge exams before. The most popular is FCE followed by CAE and PET.	Most frequent reason is to help career. Other reasons include further study of English and other subjects.

- at all levels candidates taking the Main Suite tests are for the most part still in education (rather than in employment)
- the proportion of test takers taking preparation courses prior to the test decreases somewhat from PET onwards
- a significant number of test takers at all levels are motivated to take the test in order to improve their study or employment prospects.

Postscript

Wherever feasible, appropriate and equitable, knowledge of the test takers – both as individuals and as a group – should be reflected in test format, test task design, topics, test administration and assessment.

Careful consideration needs to be given at the test development stage to ensuring that in respect of all the contextual features of the task to be discussed in Chapter 4 no bias is introduced into the test. Post test statistical analysis should be used to check on this utilising demographic data available from the CIS located at Appendix B (see also Chapter 6 for discussion of these procedures). Such bias can easily arise through ignorance or oversight of those test-taker characteristics that it is possible for examining boards catering for a multi-ethnic population to do something about. It is crucial that test developers know their test population and that they routinely gather and analyse appropriate data in order to achieve this; the design of the CIS needs to be periodically revisited in the light of emerging research to ensure that characteristics which might unfairly impact on performance can be properly monitored.

Accommodations should be available where a strong case can be made for such by the candidate. Whenever such accommodations are made, however, examination boards need evidence of their impact in terms of the test construct. The guiding principle must remain that the validity of the test should not be compromised by any accommodations that are made, and ongoing research needs to investigate that no unfair advantages or disadvantages result from the accommodations made or from the physical challenges faced. As the American Psychological Association Standards (1999) point out, professional judgement clearly plays a key role in decisions about the nature and extent of accommodations in test development and delivery. While professional judgement can be informed by findings from empirical studies, such studies are often few in number due to the practical constraints of research in this field, e.g. small sample size, non-random selection of test takers with disabilities, etc. In the light of this the various investigations undertaken by Cambridge ESOL assume increased significance.

Cambridge ESOL addresses directly and proactively many of the physical and physiological features that we have identified in our framework but for the present, given the heterogeneous nature of the candidature and the general nature of many of its examinations, it is limited to avoiding bias arising from these features against individuals rather than catering specifically for psychological and experiential preferences or background.

The literature on the test taker is now growing as fairness in examining receives the recognition it deserves. Cognitive validity, on the other hand, to which we turn next in Chapter 3, is still very much an under-researched area of validity in L2 language studies. Here the interest is in what happens cognitively at the test-taker level when an individual processes a test task/item.

3 Cognitive validity

Overview

The cognitive validity of a Writing task is a measure of how closely it represents the cognitive processing involved in writing contexts beyond the test itself, i.e. in performing the task in real life. Drawing extensively on the work of the authors cited in this chapter, we propose a framework of processing levels or cognitive validity parameters as shown in Figure 3.1. We believe that such a framework can be operationalised on a regular basis by examination boards to assist them in establishing the cognitive validity of their Writing tests.

It is worth noting here that demonstrating the cognitive validity of any testing instrument is rarely an easy matter. Where exams appear in multiple forms and on numerous occasions, practical constraints on exam developers mean that they will have to rely mainly on expert judgement and student introspection at the piloting stage to generate evidence concerning the nature of the cognitive processing involved in performing a task. Further evidence is available from the scripts produced by the candidates, which reveal their achievement in terms of rhetorical and content parameters and also provide some further insights into the levels of processing attainable across a skilled–unskilled writer continuum (see pages 43–44). The cognitive processes shown in Figure 3.1 are all amenable to such investigation as we shall discuss below, and their importance is testified to by their close relationship with the accepted criteria for assessing Writing in Cambridge ESOL examinations (see Chapter 5). We have not included the processes of storage, programming

Figure 3.1 Cognitive validity parameters in writing

Cognitive validity
Cognitive processes   • Macro-planning   • Organisation   • Micro-planning   • Translation   • Monitoring   • Revising

and execution (see Field 2004, 2005) as these are not susceptible to direct investigation and it is difficult to see how they can form part of any validity argument for a test.

A cognitive processing framework for L2 writing

The cognitive processing activities involved in writing (particularly L1 writing) are described in varying degrees of detail by Emig (1971), Hayes and Flower (1980), Hayes (1996), Bereiter and Scardamalia (1987), Grabe and Kaplan (1996), Kellogg (1994, 1996), Field (2004) and Eysenck and Keane (2005). Though all these authors are concerned with the nature of writing, they do not all identify the levels of processing and operations which take place at each level. Additionally, the models differ in the goals they set themselves and in the theoretical background upon which they draw.

The cognitive psychology literature that is cited here draws mainly on L1 research, but is nevertheless of interest to us, since an L1 model of writing proficiency is commonly used as the metric in examining L2 writing. The literature on processing in L2 writing is in any case comparatively scarce. We have thus sought to identify the various components and phases of the L1 writing process and to adopt as a pre-theoretical assumption the view that they constitute the goal towards which good L2 teachers and successful L2 learners strive.

The original Hayes and Flower model (1980) identified three phases of the L1 writing process, which the authors termed 'planning', 'translating' and 'reviewing'. However, they were at pains to stress that writing is not a linear process but an extended problem-solving exercise, subject at any time to multiple constraints. The phases are not necessarily sequential and the model allows for multiple recursions. The latest version of the model (Hayes 1996) omits the concept of writing as a staged activity altogether and instead focuses upon the essential components of the writing process: the social environment, the physical environment, motivation/affect, working memory, long-term memory and the cognitive processes that link these components.

No claims are made as to precisely how the various components interact, other than at a very general level, and none about the order in which they are applied. Although the work of Hayes and Flower provides some useful insights for our purposes, including their description of the nature of content knowledge, their model has been criticised in that it does not fully reflect the way in which writing varies according to task and does not distinguish skilled from unskilled writing (see section on Scardamalia and Bereiter (1987) on page 43).

Grabe and Kaplan (1996) adapt a general model of L2 language processing to specifically represent the processing demands of L2 writing. Their work is part of a limited literature available on cognitive processing in L2 writing. It is not a sequential model, though it attempts to show how a number of the components of processing interact. Although Grabe and Kaplan claim that the original model has a sound basis in cognitive psychology, some of the terms and concepts employed do not seem to accord with current theory. In particular, the model fails to distinguish adequately the resources stored in long-term memory (e.g. language competence or world knowledge) from the operations of short-term memory.

Our view is that the Grabe and Kaplan model begs a number of questions, and they themselves admit that it has certain limitations. But the taxonomy proposed for the planning of writing (or 'goal setting') is useful for the type of framework that is discussed in this chapter.

'Goal setting' in the Grabe and Kaplan model refers to setting goals and purposes based on the contextual situation (see Chapter 4 below and Grabe and Kaplan 1996:226–27). Grabe and Kaplan argue (230) that goal setting involves:

- an assessment of the context
- a preliminary representation of the writing product
- an evaluation of possible problems in task execution
- an initial consideration of the genre required
- an organisational plan.

We would wish to emphasise in our framework (see Chapter 4 for details) that context should specifically include consideration of the reader and of the purpose for writing. In addition, it is perhaps useful to make a distinction between a stage at which the components are gathered together and the task defined, and a later stage at which the components are organised (note the separate characterisation of macro-planning, micro-planning and organisation in Figure 3.1 above).

For Grabe and Kaplan, goal setting in turn activates three components in what they refer to as the 'verbal processing unit': language competence, a world knowledge component, and metacognitive processing as necessary for assembling world and language knowledge. They point out that the effect of context on verbal working memory is always mediated by internal goal setting and that metacognitive awareness and monitoring have an important role to play in this process.

Grabe and Kaplan consider that metacognitive awareness covers conscious directed attentional activity as against the largely automaticised and procedural verbal processing involved in the 'online processing assembly'. It involves monitoring, evaluating and revising output, both text development and content development, in accordance with internal goal setting. They point out that metacognitive awareness and control abilities may operate throughout working memory space except that space used for online processing (1996:229).

Field (2004:329–31) provides an account of information processing which aims to represent the operations a writer performs when engaged in the writing process. Field's model attempts to extrapolate a widely accepted framework from the work of others based upon information-processing principles. Much of the model draws upon the phases of processing proposed by Kellogg (1994, 1996) and employs some of Kellogg's terminology. Kellogg's account to some extent draws upon that of Hayes and Flower and on an earlier proposal by Brown, McDonald, Brown and Carr (1988). It is also strongly influenced by Levelt's (1989) sequential model of the speaking process.

What is important to note here is that the Field/Kellogg model is more closely based upon psycholinguistic theory and evidence than that of Grabe and Kaplan. Another advantage is that it aims to provide a detailed account of the stages (and within them the operations) through which a writer proceeds, though the stages are represented as interactive, with multiple possibilities of looping back. Because the Field/Kellogg model identifies levels of processing and the operations which take place at those levels, it provides a more accessible, detailed and structured framework than the other models currently available to us; as such it is the most useful for the surface analysis of Cambridge ESOL examinations at different levels of ability described later in this chapter.

Field diverges from the models proposed by Kellogg and Levelt in one important way. Levelt proposes a stage of 'conceptualisation' where the speaker selects a topic and draws upon world knowledge. This operation is in an abstract pre-linguistic form. Kellogg follows Levelt, identifying a similar stage which he terms 'planning' and which includes generating ideas, organising the ideas and setting goals. Field's account, however, recognises that writing differs from speaking (in most circumstances) in that:

1. It is not time-constrained in most real-life situations other than exams and there is a much greater element of conscious planning.
2. Planning embraces decisions at text level (including long-distance decisions about readership, goals, genre etc.) as well as decisions at what one might term utterance level (Field: personal communication, 2005).

Field therefore divides what Levelt terms *conceptualisation* and Kellogg terms *planning* into three stages: macro-planning, organisation and micro-planning. In this, Field follows the early Hayes and Flower (1980) model, which recognised, within 'planning', three different operations characterised as 'generating', 'organising' and 'goal setting'. The remainder of Field's model follows Kellogg quite closely.

Because of the centrality of the Field/Kellogg model to our evaluation of the cognitive validity of Cambridge ESOL examinations later in this chapter, we describe the components relevant for our purposes in detail below.

Macro-planning: *Gathering of ideas and identification of major constraints (genre, readership, goals).*

Field describes how writers generate ideas in response to a task by drawing upon content knowledge. They determine what is necessary for successful task completion, including consideration of the target readership, of the *genre* of the text and of the level of formality required.

This aspect of processing can be addressed by a number of criteria in a mark scheme for a Writing task including: the relevance and adequacy of content to the task set, the appropriateness of the language used for the topic and the readership, and at higher levels the effect of the writing on the reader. This is a critical activity and all efforts need to be made both in prior training, through proactive task rubrics and task structure, through appropriate rating criteria and in time allocated to ensure that it takes place.

Organisation: *Ordering the ideas; identifying relationships between them; determining which are central to the goals of the text and which are of secondary importance.*

Field argues that there is provisional organisation of ideas in abstract form both in relation to the overall text and to each other. The writer evaluates the relative importance of the ideas, and decides on their relative prominence in the text. This activity might result in a set of rough notes. This was included as part of goal setting by Grabe and Kaplan but for our purposes it is useful to have it as a separate category (see the section on cognitive processing and Cambridge practice on pages 53–57) as it is closely related to the organisational aspect of the marking criteria which features strongly in FCE, CAE and CPE examinations.

Hyland (2002:26) presents a summary of the findings of research by Silva (1993) and Krapels (1990) into L1 and L2 process writing research. In general, the composing process patterns in both L1 and L2 appear somewhat similar. Skilled writers, it would seem, both compose differently from their unskilled counterparts and tend to use more effective planning and revising strategies. Moreover, it is not clear whether L1 strategies are transferred to L2 contexts. L2 writers are thought to plan and organise less than L1 writers and unskilled L2 writers are unlikely to engage in organisation. One reason may be that unskilled L2 writers experience a heavy cognitive load in simply encoding their thoughts in linguistic form so that the resources available for building cohesion and coherence may be severely limited.

This shortfall in attentional capacity in unskilled writers is reflected in KET and PET examinations where at KET level the organisational structure of the writing is made clear to the candidate and a content schema is provided for candidates at both KET and PET Part 2 tasks. This is also the case in the first task at FCE. In Part 2 of FCE, and the tasks in CAE and CPE there is less scaffolding of tasks as appropriate at these levels and any deficits in content or rhetorical space occasioned by lack of planning and/or organisation are catered for in the mark scheme (see pages 53–57 for details of reports on performance in these areas in Cambridge examinations, Chapter 4 for further discussion of these parameters in the known criteria section and Chapter 5 for scoring criteria).

Micro-planning: *Focusing on the part of the text that is about to be produced. Here, the planning takes place on at least two levels: the goal of the paragraph, itself aligned with the overall goal of the writing activity; within the paragraph, the immediate need to structure an upcoming sentence in terms of information.*

Field (2004:329) provides a useful reminder that organisation and planning may also take place at the sentence and paragraph level, with constant reference back both to overall parameters established earlier (goals, organisational plan) and to the actual text as it develops (immediately preceding sentence or paragraph(s)). In addition, consideration is given by the writer to whether knowledge is shared by the reader either through access to previous world knowledge or through information supplied earlier in the text itself. The evolving textual output thus becomes part of the context itself. A weakness of Grabe and Kaplan's model is that it does not take adequate account of the 'text so far' and the way in which the text can both drive further planning and be subject to revision.

The output of micro-planning is stored in the mind in the form of abstract goals at paragraph and sentence level – the latter are ultimately translated into linguistic form. It is these micro-plans, not macro-plans which get turned into linguistic output, but nevertheless Field (2005) recognises a kind of trickle-down effect. Thus, decisions made at macro-level about readership, genre and goals will heavily constrain choices made in micro-planning and in translation. They will also form the yardstick against which drafts are measured at the monitoring stage.

Translation: *Propositional content previously held in abstract form is converted to linguistic form.*

Field (2005) notes that it is at this critical point that the writer moves from an internal 'private' representation, which is abstract and only understood by him or her, to its expression in the 'public' shared code of language. Up to this point, the writer's ideas are not specific to any language (though they are most probably based on experience in an L1 context and even associated with L1 lexis). Kellogg (1994:64) makes an important distinction between the personal symbols used in planning and the linguistic consensual symbols which are employed when communicating with the reader. The unencoded ideas of the writer have to be converted into a shared form that can be comprehended by others. By contrast with processes that might be transferred from L1, a number of the decisions now made by L2 writers are closely dependent upon the writer's knowledge of the target language. They have to be shaped specifically to take account of the nature of L2.

It is at this point that L2 writers face particular problems related to the translation of ideas for which they may not possess the necessary language resources. Part of the additional cognitive demand upon the writer consists of the need to apply communication strategies where their knowledge of lexis or grammar may not be adequate to represent the ideas selected during macro-planning.

Field (2004:66–67) describes the use of 'avoidance' behaviour on the part of writers in order to circumvent a topic, grammatical structure or lexical item. A second behaviour identified by Field is 'achievement' behaviour which involves attempting to reach a linguistic goal by less direct methods than in L1, perhaps by employing a more general term, paraphrasing or employing simpler syntactic structures. Such L2 behaviours are assessed by examiners through the criteria employed in the mark scheme where for example, lexical range, different levels of appropriateness and sophistication in language use can be identified.

It is at the translation stage that decisions made at the macro-level must be given concrete form: choices must be made about discourse features – the linguistic elements of style – such as rhetorical and functional language. Many of the decisions made at a higher level (about genre, reader, goal) will continue to constrain the choices that are made. Thus the writer has to find appropriate language not simply to represent ideas identified during macro-planning but also to ensure that rhetorical demands are met. The language required needs to be not just lexically and syntactically appropriate, but functionally appropriate as well. Greater demands in terms of fulfilling rhetorical goals are likely to be a characteristic of the higher examinations.

Issues also arise in relation to text-level considerations, some of which are dependent upon socio-cultural understanding. Here, the writer is reliant upon awareness of role in relation to the task, target reader and appropriate stylistic level, as well as upon an understanding of the discourse and genre requirements of the L2 context. In relation to the proposed framework, it is assumed that an ability to write effectively in a range of genres and in particular an understanding of argument structure will be the mark of those taking the higher exams in the suite (CAE and CPE).

Field (personal communication, 2005) hypothesises that certain features of a text are intentionally put in by a skilled writer in order to assist the reader in building an appropriate meaning representation. These features of coherence and cohesion might include topic foregrounding, inferential connections and features such as reference and anaphora which support the integration of current text into 'text so far'. The presence or absence of such features of textual content may be described in the task specific mark scheme for a task.

Monitoring: *At a basic level monitoring involves checking the mechanical accuracy of spelling, punctuation and syntax. At a more advanced level, it can involve examining the text to determine whether it reflects the writer's intentions and fits the developing argument structure of the text.*

Grabe and Kaplan have little to say on monitoring *per se* which is a critical if often neglected aspect in L2 writing performance. Field (2004:330) describes how self-monitoring in the writing process is a complex operation which may occur at different stages of the process (after writing a word, a sentence, a paragraph or a complete text) and may relate to different levels of analysis.

It appears that L2 writers do less monitoring than L1 (Eysenck and Keane 2005). Their monitoring tends to become fixated at a linguistic level especially for unskilled L2 writers (Field 2005). At the lowest level, the concern is normally with the accuracy of spelling, punctuation and syntax. At a higher level, monitoring should involve consideration of the extent to which the text produced accords with the writer's goals, its relevance to and adequacy for the task set and the development of the discourse structure of the text. There might also be consideration of the possible impact of the text upon the intended reader or readers and its appropriateness for the intended discourse community. Finally, attention might be paid to features of cohesion and coherence such as topic foregrounding and reference. The cognitive demands of monitoring and revision are considerable, especially if they occur while the writer is still engaged in the process of producing text. Field (2004:330) therefore suggests that writers are likely to focus on one level of representation at a time. Writers are likely to monitor at the level of the sentence, the paragraph, the 'text so far' and the completed first draft. In the actual process of text construction, attention might be given to lower-level features, with higher-level features reserved for a post production revision stage. The matching of linguistic form against predetermined goals is especially important at the translation stage.

Field (2005) points out that so far as the possible transfer of skills from L1 is concerned we need to be aware that the cognitive demands of using unfamiliar and incomplete vocabulary and syntax might impede access to such skills. The attentional resources of a writer are finite and, at least in the early stages of L2 development, one might expect a large part of those resources to be diverted away from planning and monitoring towards more low-level considerations concerning the linguistic code. The effort of translation makes considerable cognitive demands on the less skilled L2 writer and as a result is likely to become the principal focus of attention for many.

The demand for attentional resources has ramifications for Writing tests set at different levels. It means that tasks requiring planning and organisation may be less suitable below a B2 level in the CEFR, (FCE in Cambridge Main Suite examinations). Various Association of Language Testers in Europe (ALTE) members have commented on the problems encountered in attempts to include such processing activities below this level. The presence of such 'cognitive demands' also provides a convincing rationale for the view that there should be a heavier emphasis upon planning and monitoring in the more advanced exams of the Cambridge Main Suite examinations.

It may well be that examination boards might wish to encourage monitoring even more proactively in more advanced Writing tests. Weir (1983) included an editing task in the Test in English for Educational Purposes (TEEP) in an attempt to encourage positive washback in the teaching for the test (see Weir 1993 for an example of this task). It was felt that requiring students to monitor and revise inaccurate or inappropriate written text could only be beneficial for their future studies.

Revising: *As a result of monitoring activities a writer will return to those aspects of the text considered unsatisfactory and make corrections or adjustments perhaps after each sentence, each paragraph or when the whole text has been written.*

Field (2004:330) argues that monitoring and revising may interface with any of the previous stages, and may result in alterations to the original macroplan, to rewording of translated text or in correcting an error.

Hayes and Flower (1986) indicate that skilled writers spend more time revising when writing than do unskilled writers and pay more attention to higher-level aspects of the composing process such as coherence and argumentation. Eysenck and Keane (2005:417) cite evidence that skilled writers are much more concerned with revision that involves changes to meaning than are unskilled writers and that they are also better at identifying problems in a text (418).

To the extent that a test does not result in appropriate cognitive processing as laid out above it might be considered deficient and raise concern about any attempt to generalise from the test task to the real-life language use. For example, using a multiple-choice test of structure and written expression as an indirect indicator of writing ability might be deemed seriously inadequate in terms of cognitive validity (one reason why Cambridge ESOL does not employ such tests). However, direct tests of writing that do not activate planning, monitoring and revision levels of processing are open to criticism for failing to include these important processing abilities.

From a cognitive perspective, a valid Writing test would involve candidates engaging in all the processing components described above as appropriate to the level of proficiency being assessed. The issue of interest for language testers is how these components of processing relate to different levels of language proficiency. This leads us back to another of the central concerns of this volume: the identification of different levels of proficiency in L2 writing.

What is 'skilled' L2 writing?

So far the discussion has focused upon attempts within cognitive psychology to model the various components and stages which constitute the writing process. A parallel strand of research and thinking attempts to specify what it is that characterises the processing undertaken by a skilled writer and that distinguishes it from the processing of a novice or less able writer.

Eysenck and Keane (2005:418) argue that it is the planning process that is most likely to help differentiate writers of contrasting expertise. Similarly, Scardamalia and Bereiter (1987) argue that different processing models exist at different developmental stages of writing and describe two major strategies, *knowledge telling* and *knowledge transforming*, which occur principally during the planning stage and which exemplify the differences between skilled and less skilled writers. In knowledge telling, novice writers plan very little, and focus on generating content from within remembered existing resources in line with the task, topic, or genre. Knowledge transforming by the skilled writer entails a heightened awareness of problems as and when they arise – whether in the areas of ideas, planning and organisation (content), or in those of goals and readership (rhetoric) – with movement of information in both directions. Writers establish problem spaces relating to content and to rhetoric within which they resolve the demands of the writing process by reference to the constraints they have laid down for the current task.

Hyland notes (2002:28) that, in knowledge transforming, skilled writers consider the complexities of a task, and analyse and solve problems of task achievement in terms of content, audience, register, and set goals. All the while there is an ongoing interaction between their developing knowledge and the text. This continuous reflection and development of plans means that ideas as well as text may be changed by the experience.

Turning specifically to the processes adopted by novice second language writers, Hyland (2002:26) notes that although the composing patterns seem to be similar between L1 and L2 writers, the latter tend to plan less than L1 writers and encounter more difficulty in setting goals and generating text. Their inter-language may be less developed along a number of dimensions and the increased cognitive load occasioned by this in the writing process will affect their performances in a number of ways, for example in the amount of attention they can devote to planning, monitoring and reflection on what they have written. According to Hyland's review of the research, L2 writers are less fluent than L1 writers and the texts they write are less accurate and effective. The criteria for assessing the product of their processing will need to address this as appropriate to the tasks set at each level of examination (see the section on criteria/rating scale on pages 146–53 in Chapter 5).

Field (2004:331–2) points out that skilled writers pay a lot more attention to planning and monitoring their productions than do unskilled writers. They take pains when considering goals, assessing rhetorical impact and locating possible areas for revision. The skilled writer considers task and text demands, and monitors and improves the text both during and after writing. Field suggests a number of questions the skilled writer seeks to answer during monitoring. The questions relate to the linguistic accuracy of the text, its cohesion and coherence, its relation to goals set, its impact on the reader, the knowledge state of the reader in relation to the developing text content and its logic.

Field (2005) notes that writing in a second language imposes additional cognitive demands in the form of the need to allocate attention at several different levels (spelling, syntax, lexical retrieval). This then has implications both for fluency of writing and for the extent to which a pre-writing plan can be sustained during the process of putting words on the page.

One limitation of the work of Scardamalia and Bereiter (1987) is that while they present a very useful account of the skilled versus unskilled writer they do not make clear what are the stages of development from being a 'knowledge telling' writer to being a 'knowledge transforming' one; little help is available to understand how people progress from one to the other. However, their conceptualisation of a skilled knowledge transforming writer versus an unskilled knowledge telling writer is helpful in characterising the shift in the level of writing expected between KET and PET, and the higher levels of FCE, CAE and CPE Cambridge ESOL examinations (see the five-level summary chart at the end of this chapter). It clearly marks a contrast between a linear writing process, presenting ideas as they occur, and one which entails organising ideas in terms of their relationship to each other and to the goals of the text. This characterisation can be associated more transparently with the types of writing which are required at different ESOL levels: narrative or instructional texts at the lower levels clearly demanding knowledge telling skills rather than knowledge transforming ones. Conversely, texts involving argument at the higher levels require knowledge transforming skills.

Cognitive processing: Cambridge practice

Having reviewed the academic literature relating to cognitive processes in writing we now turn to a descriptive analysis of the cognitive processes that underlie the efforts of candidates tackling Writing tasks at the different proficiency levels in the Cambridge Main Suite. We will focus on the processing underlying these tasks using those parameters discussed in the previous section which are amenable to investigation through expert judgement:

- macro-planning
- organisation
- translation
- monitoring and revising.

The descriptive analysis which follows draws on a number of sources, including the practical experience of test design and development for the Cambridge ESOL Main Suite tests and the extensive documentation which now exists to support these activities, e.g. test handbooks, item writer guidelines, examiner training materials, etc. In one sense, the analysis on the following pages represents the *voice* of the language testing practitioners within the Cambridge ESOL organisation who are responsible in their day-to-day work for developing, administering and validating versions of the tests. Where appropriate, comments are also supplied from routine Examination Reports (March 2004 KET (Part 9) and PET (Parts 2 and 3) and FCE, CAE and CPE December 2003 – FCE 0100, CAE 0150, CPE 0300) to illustrate the points being made in relation to candidates' actual performances. This represents another *voice* – that of the large community of external professionals who are actively associated with the production and delivery of Cambridge ESOL tests (e.g. test item writers, Writing examiners, centre administrators, etc.). The actual Writing tasks, as presented to the test takers in the above sessions and discussed below, are given in Appendix A.

We are of course aware of the limitations of this subjective approach and would encourage future empirical research in the area where a diversity of methodological procedures might better ground the discussion below. However, at an operational level exam boards may have to restrict themselves to this type of surface-level exploration where exams appear in multiple forms and on numerous occasions per annum. Despite its limitations, such a surface-level exploration nevertheless permits a more explicit analysis of the ways in which cognitive processing demands of Writing tasks change across the different proficiency levels; such an analysis is likely to enhance our understanding of the developmental progression involved in L2 writing ability as well as provide cognitive validity evidence for our tests.

Macro-planning: goal setting and task representation

As we noted above this kind of planning is likely to be employed by most candidates in writing in their L1 but the literature suggests that it does not happen as much in L2 especially at lower levels. This is probably because of the greater cognitive demands entailed in writing at lower levels in L2. Accordingly at the lowest levels in the exams described below (KET, PET) limited planning is required by the task as the content focuses are clearly indicated to the candidate (see Appendix A for copies of these tasks).

In the subsequent discussion, quotations from Examination Reports for each of the Main Suite exams are cited by year and page number only but appear in the References under the heading 'University of Cambridge'.

KET Syllabus 0085/1 (March 2004 session)

Part 9, Question 56: Continuous writing

Description of task

The task input on which the test takers must base their note in this March 2004 KET task is made up of prompts or cues in the form of three questions and supported by the input text. All the essential content or topic points that the test taker is expected to address are explicitly presented in the input material.

In this task, candidates were required to cover three points:

- 'Where shall we eat?'
- 'What time can you come?'
- 'Where can I park my car?'

There is minimal need on the part of the candidate to generate further knowledge in order to answer this question. Part of the task expectation is to add a piece of information (giving details of meeting for dinner), suggestion (places to eat) and advice (where to park the car) in order to expand their demonstration of range. The KET candidate attempts to look for things to write about regarding the words 'meeting for dinner', generating ideas about what people might expect to do when organising a dinner. The writer also has to respond in the form of a note as this is the genre being called for. Nearly all of what is retrieved will be inextricably linked to the topic, the bullet points providing a coherence to the response.

Examination Report

The note genre, its organisational conventions and format is assumed familiar to the writer so success is largely predicted in this aspect of processing. However, the relevant KET Examination Report suggests that such familiarity was not always manifest for this particular task: 'Candidates must remember to cover all three pieces of information. If they are asked to write a note, they should remember to begin appropriately (e.g. "Dear Sara") and to sign it, as they would in real life' (2004:7).

Process

Macro-planning for KET candidates might entail:

- an assessment of the context (the need for a note to a friend in order to arrange dinner; appreciation and understanding of the three questions raised in the input text (place to eat, time of arrival, car parking location); points for inclusion in response and what they constitute in terms of functions)
- a preliminary representation of the writing outcome (a 25–35 word note)
- an evaluation of the potential problems in undertaking the task (understanding input text, coverage of content bullet points, appropriate note)
- an initial activation of certain aspects of the genre
- perhaps also strategic considerations – avoiding what they cannot say.

The primary objective of KET candidates is to *tell* what they have retrieved. This is a linear writing process, presenting ideas as they occur. The *knowledge telling* process enables less-skilled writers to produce enough on-topic material whilst working within manageable cognitive complexity constraints (Grabe and Kaplan 1996:124).

PET Syllabus 0090/1 (March 2004 session)

Part 2, Question 6: Short communicative message

Description of task

In Part 2 candidates were shown a picture postcard bought at an art gallery and had to imagine they were sending this postcard to a friend in Australia. In common with all Part 2 tasks, there were three content points to include: candidates had to say something about the art gallery, give an explanation as to why they chose this postcard, and ask the friend a question about the weather in Australia.

Examination Report

Performance in relation to relevance and adequacy of answers for this task is described in the PET Examination Report: ' "Most candidates handled the task well." Candidates who wrote unduly long answers tended to lose marks because the clarity of their writing suffered and some irrelevant material was introduced' (2004:10).

Part 3, Question 7 or 8: Continuous writing

Description of task

In Part 3: Question 7, the letter, asked candidates to write to a friend about birthday presents for teenage boys.

Question 8, the story, had the title 'A very unusual evening'.

PET candidates, like their KET counterparts, are largely restricted to *knowledge telling*. They look for things to write about by looking at the questions; seeing the words *What do teenage boys like getting as presents?* (Question 7) will prompt them to think about what they like. Alternately, reading the words *A very unusual evening* (Question 8) will set them thinking about what they did during a personal and very unusual evening. Further content will be generated by considering what people deem to be either an unusual evening or what most teenage boys like as a present.

Examination Report

As regards topic familiarity in Part 3 (Questions 7 and 8): 'Both tasks appear to have been accessible in terms of topic, but more candidates chose Question 7, possibly because they were familiar with the "traditional" PET letter format' (2004:7). For the letter (Part 3), there is some need to activate additional world knowledge resources. The topic and information in the task together with the macro-planning generates world knowledge appropriate to describing the central theme i.e. advising on the suitability of a gift for a male teenager.

The story, whilst familiar to candidates in terms of conventions requires the generation of substantially more invented material (i.e. recounting/ inventing a suitable narrative). Yet, despite this, overall candidate performance revealed: 'Question 8 gave rise to some imaginative stories, written in either the first or the third person' (2004:10).

Process

In terms of PET questions (Parts 2 and 3), macro-planning might involve:

- an assessment of the context: the need for a postcard to a friend relating information about an art gallery and rationale for choice of card, a story written for a teacher to read about a very unusual evening, a letter to a penfriend giving advice on presents; points for inclusion in response and what they constitute in terms of functions

- an initial activation of certain aspects of the genre
- a preliminary representation of the writing outcome (Part 2 – 35–45 word postcard; Part 3 – 100 word story or letter)
- an evaluation of the potential problems in undertaking the task (understanding input text, accurate response to main/relevant features/content points in input text).

The processing, retrieval and evaluation demands placed upon the PET candidate are generally relatively simple and largely involve knowledge telling.

While at KET and PET levels the primary objective is for candidates to engage in knowledge telling writing activity, at FCE Writing tasks begin to involve knowledge transformation, albeit at a basic level. Much is still 'given' as most of the ideas are presented in the rubric. But where FCE seems to represent a step up is in demanding: rhetorical decisions related to the purpose of the text and to the reader; that in order to provide coherence, the writer integrates information as new paragraphs are written; that the writer needs to distinguish 'given' and 'new' information.

FCE Syllabus 0100/2 (December 2003)

Compulsory Part 1: Transactional letter

Description of task

The task input on which the test takers must base their letter is made up of prompts or cues in the form of very brief notes and supported by the letter. All the essential content or topic points that are expected to be addressed by the test taker are explicitly presented in the input material. The letter genre, its organisational conventions and format, is assumed familiar to the writer so success in this aspect of processing is largely predicted. Information about the target reader and the reason for writing is given in the question to help the test taker. For example, candidates might be required to write a letter to a penfriend about a forthcoming visit, confirming arrangements, making suggestions and requesting information.

The functional goal for test takers is to write a transactional letter. There will be little need to generate much additional world knowledge resources; just some invention of appropriate contextual supporting information. The test taker will engage internal macro-planning and establish a physical objective of one piece of extended writing in the form of an informal letter of between 120–180 words.

Examination Report

The transactional letter genre is familiar to the writer (through preparation courses and handbook documentation) so some degree of success is anticipated: 'The general scenario was clear to candidates and they found the task relatively straightforward' (December 2003 (0100): 9). The task is to produce a short informal letter addressing all five content points given in the task input material. The five content points are presented as the candidate's own notes down the sides of the input letter and the rubric states that the candidates must use all their notes: 'Candidates are expected to include all 5 points and nearly all did' (2003:8).

Process

Macro-planning for FCE candidates in Part 1 might entail:

- an assessment of the purpose (letter to penfriend; informal friendly tone; appreciation of all content points for inclusion in response and what they constitute in terms of functions; text length)
- an initial activation of certain aspects of the genre: in this example a familiar informal letter
- a preliminary representation of the writing outcome (one page letter draft)
- an evaluation of the potential problems in undertaking the task (including all content points and weaving them into a coherent whole – set of appropriately linking paragraphs.

Writing tasks at the more advanced levels demand ever more complex language processing, and planning is increasingly required at the CAE and CPE levels.

CAE Syllabus 0150/2 (December 2003)

Compulsory Part 1: Report writing

Description of task

CAE test takers are expected to read the opening paragraphs and instructions in the task to make sure they know what their role as a writer is and whom they are writing to. Decisions have to be taken as regards goal and readership. For instance, candidates in this example were required to write a report to their fellow members of an English language club, comparing two types of accommodation for the club's forthcoming trip and recommending one hotel for the trip. The task involved processing the information given on the members' requirements and the two hotels, extracting and collating the relevant information and using the language of explanation, opinion and suggestion. Factors that have to be borne in mind at this level include: relevance, relative importance, formal schemata, and rhetoric: 'make recommendations'.

Candidates are given considerable freedom in terms of their reactions to the input, their perceived relationship with the target audience and the decision they make about how to organise their writing. The functional goal for test takers is to process the task input, summarise the salient features, find the main points, report them and make recommendations. There should be very little need to generate additional world knowledge resources because the test taker will be familiar with the concepts in the input reading texts. The topic – accommodation – (reinforced by the reading of the text) as well as the macro-planning will generate world knowledge that is appropriate. Students are made aware of the need to adopt an appropriate style, layout and register for the format (or text type) of the Writing task and so sociocultural knowledge will also play a part here.

Examination Report

'Weaker candidates . . . often tried to include every piece of information' (2003:9). Clearly, less successful candidates attempt to include all the information in the input, rather than judiciously selecting what is appropriate for their answer.

Process

Macro-planning for CAE candidates might entail:

- an assessment of the context (the need for a report for fellow students on accommodation in the area; appreciation of main features of student accommodation requirements/ expectations and available facilities, points for inclusion in response and what they constitute in terms of functions)

- a preliminary representation of the writing outcome (a 250-word report)

- an evaluation of the potential problems in undertaking the task (understanding input text, accurate identification and extraction of main/relevant features in input text)

- an initial activation of certain aspects of the genre: appropriate report presentation and format.

CPE Syllabus 0300/2 (December 2003)

Compulsory Part 1: Essay writing

Description of task

CPE test takers are expected to read the questions very carefully, decide exactly what information is being asked of them, identify the target reader, their role as writer and their purpose in writing, check what text type they are being asked to write and organise their ideas before they begin to write. For example this December 2003 Part 1 question requires candidates to write an essay for their tutor evaluating the advantages of major international sports competitions, based on quoted comments made during a class discussion and their own views and opinions on the subject.

When the points to address are given as an extract of text, the candidate must identify the required points. Once the points have been identified, the test taker's own views on the points should also be noted. The object is not merely to restate the points, but to develop them and use them as the basis for a piece of discursive writing of the appropriate task type.

Examination Report

The Examination Report states that candidates must be careful when reading the question, in order to identify what is expected in their response:

> Very careful reading of the question will show what information needs to be included. The question will also indicate the appropriate register for the piece of writing. It is also very important that students learn to distinguish between the various task types required by the questions. If these factors, together with an understanding of the purpose in writing, are not fully grasped, there is little chance that the piece of writing will be effective (2003:11).

In terms of topic:

> The topic was familiar to all candidates and the question attracted a wide range of responses . . . The issues around sports events are almost certainly topic areas that students will have discussed in their preparation courses and are therefore familiar with, but examiners are looking for evidence that candidates can use the input plus their own knowledge and ideas to produce a reasoned discussion which approaches the subject in the way outlined in the question (2003:9).

Process

Macro-planning for CPE candidates entails:

- an assessment of the context (the need to evaluate the advantages of major international sports competitions; semi-formal tone, appreciation of all the comments made during the class discussion including the three comments highlighted, justification of international sports competitions, recognising points for inclusion in response and what they constitute in terms of functions expressed)
- an initial activation of certain aspects of the genre: presentation and format
- a preliminary representation of the writing outcome (a 300–350 word proposal)
- an evaluation of the potential problems in undertaking the task (understanding input text, good grasp and appreciation of issues associated with each of the three comments supplied, giving sound, reasoned and balanced arguments for each of the three options).

The demands made by the task on the language competence of CPE test takers are great.

CPE writers must be able to access and activate knowledge resources whilst processing input information more or less simultaneously. The knowledge transforming process at the highest level requires the candidate to reflect carefully on the complexity of the CPE task, and leads them to arrive at the most appropriate method for addressing the complexities. Candidates who are likely to be most successful at this level are those who have practised the types of Writing tasks which develop knowledge transforming skills. Less skilled writers rarely encounter such tasks.

Organisation

Skilled writers' provisional organisation of ideas in abstract form both in relation to the overall text and to each other normally takes place in the initial stages of the writing process. The writer evaluates their relative importance, and decides on their relative prominence in the text. As we noted above unskilled L2 writers are unlikely to engage in organisation. One reason may be that unskilled L2 writers experience a heavy enough cognitive load in simply encoding their thoughts in linguistic form so that the resources available for meaning building may be severely limited.

KET

Process

There is no requirement on the part of the test taker to note main ideas in order to generate a stronger organisational plan as the points in the task constitute the structure for the note to the pen friend. General performance on this task suggests that the organisation of the message followed the order of presentation of the points as presented in the task.

At PET level no organisation is required on the part of the writer in Part 2, but it is in Part 3.

PET

Process

In Part 2 the organisation for the writing is provided. Candidates are presented with a task through the rubric, where the content required is laid out as three bulleted points. This is not the case, however, in Part 3 where the candidate is responsible for organising the text.

Examination Report

'In relation to the letter/story, better candidates organised their writing effectively' (2004:10). The text type (narrative) is familiar to candidates at this level and is normally concerned with knowledge telling only. Although preparation practice is advocated, candidates are advised not to spend time making a full rough copy for Writing Part 3. The time available to test takers is insufficient for this and it is not a requirement of the task.

FCE

Process: Part 1

There is no requirement on the part of the test taker to note main ideas in order to generate a stronger organisational plan as the points in the task constitute the structure for the Part 1 letter. So this is a good example of knowledge telling without any attempt to organise the knowledge.

Examination Report: Part 1

General performance on this task suggests that the organisation of the letter followed the order of presentation of the points as presented in the task:

> Most candidates followed order of the points as given in Maria's letter/their notes, and this worked well because the sequence of ideas was logical (2003:8).

However, departure from task order did engender difficulties:

> ... some candidates changed the order, which did not work so well, and candidates are advised to think carefully about whether this is appropriate (2003:8).

Process: Part 2

In Part 2 no structure is provided for use in answering the various options. There seems to be a requirement to recognise paragraph structure at the micro-planning stage: topic sentence plus exemplification.

Examination Report: Part 2

The Examination Report recommended the need to point out to students:

> how a content point can be developed, perhaps by the use of obviously contrasting sample answers, where one is only minimally expanded and the other includes good development ... Where candidates develop the point, they generally score higher marks (2003:11).

Students are advised through a variety of mechanisms to make a plan for their answer, noting what to include in each paragraph:

> Working with past papers in pairs or groups, where students spend time identifying the reader, the text type, and the important content points, is all useful in planning what to write (2003:10).

There was some evidence, from the general performance on this task that test takers would indeed benefit from constructing a plan prior to writing:

> Students should be encouraged to make a plan before they start writing, and should then think carefully about what they can say on each point (2003:11).

Comments in the Examination Report made about the need to write a plan suggest a lack of brainstorming on the part of the test taker.

Overall, candidate performance prompted the following recommendation to expend more time and effort on organisation:

> Spending time on organisation, encouraging sensible use of paragraphing and a variety of linkers. This is another reason for developing a plan prior to writing (2003:11).

FCE writers are provided with some autonomy and responsibility for shaping and planning the structure and outcome of the discourse in Part 2 only. In Part 1 such organisation is provided for the candidate through the input. This seems anomalous when one looks at what is required in PET Part 3.

CAE

Process

Part of the task is to prioritise and plan the presentation of information. No organising principles are offered to CAE candidates in the task.

Examination Report

The CAE Examination Report made reference to good organisation and textual structuring by the more able candidates:

> This question was answered fairly well with a majority of candidates achieving a satisfactory mark or above and gaining a higher score than in Part 2. Strong candidates organised and structured their report well, paying attention to linking devices . . . Weaker candidates failed to plan their answers and often tried to include every piece of information (2003:9).

Students are advised to make a plan for their answer, but are informed that they do not necessarily have to use all the input information, only that which addresses the content points of the task. Weaker students 'tried to include every piece of information' in their response when this is not necessary.

At CPE level, like CAE level, tasks normally lack any direct reference to how candidates should organise their responses. An awareness of the relative importance of topics and the ability to foreground would also seem to play a progressively more important part at the organisational level. Coherence between ideas and developing a clear overall argument structure are also expected at the upper two Main Suite levels.

CPE

Process

Relevance is again an important criterion with the need for candidates to be selective.

Examination Report

Lack of planning/organisation accounted for under and/or over length scripts and the inclusion of rambling and 'off-topic' content:

> Students should get into the habit of planning their answers carefully before they begin to write. This will help them to produce the appropriate number of words. It should also prevent the inclusion of irrelevant digression and avoid the possibility of running out of time before the answer has been completed . . .CPE candidates are permitted to use blank pages in the answer booklet for notes in order to aid their writing. In practice few candidates use them for this purpose although quite a number of candidates do use them to complete their answers if they run out of lined pages in the booklet (2003:11).

Translation

At this stage the writer moves from an internal 'private' representation which is abstract and only understood by him/her to its expression in the 'public' shared code of language; the propositional content previously held in abstract form is converted to linguistic form. This process is largely automaticised and the process is therefore not susceptible to direct investigation. However, examiner reports on student scripts provide an insight into the product of such processing.

At KET level, candidates need to have appropriate language for the preestablished genre.

KET

Examination Report

The task emphasis:

> should be on the successful communication of a message, though it is also important to avoid errors of structure, vocabulary, spelling and punctuation (2004:9).

At PET level candidates are encouraged to be ambitious in their use of language.

PET

Examination Report

Candidates are advised to be ambitious and use a range of language in Part 3 (2004:12). General performance on Questions 7 and 8 prompted the following statements: First, in relation to strong and weak performance on Question 7 (letter):

> . . . better candidates showed good use and range of language, but weaker candidates did not develop their answers beyond merely listing their ideas of presents to buy (2004:10).

And second, with regard to strong and weak performance on Question 8 (story):

> Better candidates showed an excellent range of language and organised their writing effectively. Weaker candidates often got into difficulties when attempting to use a range of past tenses and the lack of accuracy of irregular past tense forms was a recurrent problem (2004:10).

Candidates:

> ... should be discouraged from using any phrases that appear on the question paper, since this may not be the most natural way of communicating a given function in informal language and will not show their true language ability (2004:11).

> ... should regularly be encouraged to be more ambitious, for example, using a variety of adjectives instead of 'playing safe' with one or two, and varying how they start their sentences. Work on simple linking devices may also be required (2004:11).

At FCE level lexical variety is rewarded. Register, style and rhetoric have to be balanced against the considerable cognitive demands of assembling the language.

FCE

Examination Report

> Candidates who use a variety of adjectives rather than repeating the word 'beautiful' six times will usually score a higher mark ... Better candidates were able to demonstrate their range of vocabulary and expression, and found ample opportunity to expand on points 2, 3 and 5 (2003:9).

Average candidates were able to express the main points and functions adequately, but often used an inappropriate tone (audience-related), and lacked the ability to expand appropriately.

Weaker candidates seemed unaware of the notion of register and the need to translate ideas into appropriate and consistent language in a suitable tone:

> Where students have to write an informal letter to a person they know, as here ... in this type of task especially, they need to consider the 'bigger picture' of why they are writing and be sensitive to the type of scenario described ... they need to be trained to produce ... informal language in a suitable tone (2003:11).

At CAE level, despite the significant amount of input text, better candidates are able to process information well translating their thoughts into complex and well connected text using correct sentence structures.

CAE

Examination Report

> In general these [strong] candidates processed the given information appropriately. Strong candidates successfully reworded or paraphrased language from the input and used complex sentences suitable to the functions required . . . Whereas weaker candidates were unable to express their ideas into appropriate, cohesive and coherent text relying on language copied verbatim from the input material . . . Weaker candidates . . . used simple sentences and lifted language directly from the question. In some cases this lifted language was spelt incorrectly (2003:9).

CPE

Examination Report

The candidate is expected to develop ideas by paying attention to a number of linguistic aspects. Higher-level translation skills required would appear to include an ability to employ lexical variety and syntactic complexity to express subtle differences of meaning and attitude. The length of text produced by candidates at this level has ramifications for the various processing levels and particularly for organisation and translation.

As candidates move upwards through each of the levels mastery of the demands of all the levels below are assumed.

Monitoring and revising

At a basic level, monitoring involves checking the mechanical accuracy of spelling, punctuation and syntax. At a more advanced level, it can involve examining the text to determine whether it reflects the writer's intentions and fits the developing argument structure of the text. As a result of monitoring activities a writer will return to those aspects of the text considered unsatisfactory and make corrections or adjustments perhaps after each sentence, each paragraph or when the whole text has been written.

KET

Examination Report

In the view of examiners revision is focused at the level of spelling – lexis – morphology – basic syntactic structure.

At PET level revision of basic organisation as well as accuracy of language is required. Candidates are also expected to use a greater range of language.

PET

Examination Report

Overall candidate performance would suggest that regular practice in writing short communicative messages would benefit Part 2 particularly in the context of the writer reviewing his/her own work (2004:11).

Providing students with regular opportunities to write extended answers of around 100 words to Part 3 would enable candidates to evaluate, revise and review their work more effectively (2004:11).

At FCE level some evaluation of content is required.

FCE

Examination Report

Performance on this task merited the following comments regarding the production of draft versions to improve the quality of writing:

It is often very instructive for students to work on a second draft of a home-work answer. In this way, the teacher, or fellow students, can make useful suggestions regarding organisation, language, and content omissions . . . The second draft can then be compared to the first, which is not only instructive regarding weaknesses, but also builds confidence. Students should be encouraged to experiment with a wider range of language in the second draft, for example replacing any repeated words with near synonyms (2003:10).

The fact that most test takers included all five points given in the notes in order to achieve a mark in Band 3 or above attests to the fact that some evaluation of content development took place (monitoring text to ensure inclusion of all content points). Cohesion and coherence are addressed in the mark scheme so monitoring for this is also required in FCE, CAE and CPE examinations.

At CAE and CPE multiple monitoring is called for at different levels.

CAE and CPE

Examination Report

Evidence from examiners' reports on performance on these tasks would suggest that better candidates were able to review the appropriateness of the contents and their order, the correctness of sentences, and the appropriateness of words while writing. There is an expectation that takers will operate in the problem spaces relating to both rhetoric and content and will do so both while writing and post writing.

Based on the description of cognitive processing in the last section we summarise in Figure 3.2 our analysis of the cognitive processing that appears to be taking place at the various levels in the Cambridge Main Suite examinations.

Figure 3.2 Summary table of cognitive processing across Main Suite examinations

	KET (A2)	PET (B1)	FCE (B2)	CAE (C1)	CPE (C2)
Cognitive processing	knowledge telling	knowledge telling	knowledge telling (knowledge transforming)	knowledge transforming: rhetorical and organisational	knowledge transforming: rhetorical and organisational
		analysis and evaluation	analysis and evaluation	analysis and evaluation	analysis and evaluation
	limited planning encouraged; lower level monitoring and revision of vocabulary, grammar and spelling	limited planning encouraged; monitoring and revision of vocabulary, grammar and basic organisation	planning, monitoring and revision of style and content required	planning, monitoring and revision of style and content required	planning, monitoring and revision of style and content required
	organisational structure provided	organisational structure provided in Part 2 but not in Part 3	organisational structure provided in Part 1 but not in Part 2	organisation required	organisation required

Summary of cognitive processing across Cambridge ESOL levels

In all Writing tasks at all levels careful task specification (e.g. in terms of purpose, readership, length, known assessment criteria) promotes the stages of macro-planning, organisation, micro-planning, translation, monitoring, and revision.

From PET Part 3 writers are provided with some autonomy and responsibility for shaping and planning the structure and outcome of their discourse. Planning, monitoring and revising written work for content and organisation is increasingly necessary in FCE, CAE and CPE particularly at CAE and CPE levels. From FCE upwards there is a need to engage in knowledge transforming rather than knowledge telling though this is not always required at FCE.

The relationship between cognitive validity and contextual validity

Approaches to writing in the recent past have followed a number of different conceptualisations (e.g. genre and process developments) which space and focus preclude from treating here. Hamp-Lyons (2002) and Hyland (2002) provide excellent accounts of these and the interested reader is referred to them.

However, one approach is very much germane to the discussion of our validation argument. In some quarters writing has been decontextualised and regarded as product oriented where the various elements are coherently and accurately put together according to a rule governed system (Hyland 2002:6). The text was seen as an autonomous object and writing was considered independent of particular writers or readers (Hyland 2002:6). Written products were viewed as ideal forms capable of being analysed independently of any real-life uses.

In contrast to this position, we feel that as well as identifying the nature of the cognitive processing activated by a task, we need to account for any interaction of these cognitive parameters with the context within which the task is located. The model adopted for Writing tasks by Cambridge ESOL follows a socio-cognitive model of *writing as communicative language use*, which takes into account both internal processing and contextual factors in writing (see Hyland 2002:30–3). It looks beyond the surface structure manifested by the text and regards the text as an attempt to engage the reader communicatively. The text is viewed as *discourse*, which Hyland (2002:11) characterises as referring to 'language as use' and to the purposes and functions linguistic forms serve in texts. In his view the linguistic patterns employed in a piece of writing are influenced by contexts beyond the page which bring with them a variety of social constraints and choices. The writers' goals, relationship with readers and the content knowledge they want to impart are accomplished by the forms of a text appropriate to that social context.

In Chapter 4 we detail how decisions taken on task setting and the linguistic and content demands of the task affect the processing and resources required to successfully complete a test task.

4 Context validity

Cognitive processing in a Writing test never occurs in a vacuum but is activated in response to the contextual parameters set out in the wording of the task. Context validity relates to the linguistic and content demands that must be met for successful task realisation and to features of the task setting that serve to describe the performance required. In developing test tasks attention needs to be paid to both context and cognitive validity.

Test-task performance needs to be generalisable to the wider domain of real-world Writing tasks that candidates may be exposed to and it is, therefore, important to be able to describe target writing activities in terms of their criterial parameters (context and cognitive) and to operationalise as many of these parameters as possible in the test task(s).

Given that performance tests attempt to reflect specific authentic communicative tasks, they inevitably encounter problems of generalisability to other performances (Hawkey 2004b). Weir (1993:11) perceives rigour in the specification of direct performance tasks as one possible way to increase generalisability. The sample of communicative language ability selected for a test should be 'as representative as possible' and the test tasks should be selected in accordance with 'the general descriptive parameters of the intended target situation particularly with regard to the skills necessary for successful participation in that situation'.

Tests should approximate to 'the performance conditions' of the authentic real-life context. According to Weir the important role of context as a determinant of communicative language ability is paramount. The context must be acceptable to the candidates as a suitable milieu for assessing particular language abilities. The conditions under which tasks are normally performed should obtain as far as is possible in a test of these abilities. A conscious effort should be made to build into tests as many real life conditions as are feasible and considered criterial by the test writers and their peers.

> If the test tasks reflect real-life tasks in terms of important identified conditions and operations it is easier to state what a student can do through the medium of English . . . unless steps are taken to identify and incorporate such features it would seem imprudent to make statements about a candidate's ability to function in normal conditions in his/her future target situation (Weir 1993:28).

In its tests Cambridge ESOL aims to approximate to such situational authenticity (see Bachman and Palmer 1996, Douglas 2000, O'Sullivan 2006). Full authenticity of setting is not attainable but the contextual parameters operationalised in a test should mirror as many of the criterial features of the target situation as possible.

Having established the criterial parameters that characterise task performance, test developers need to establish how such parameters vary across tests set at different levels of language proficiency. In this chapter we will examine closely how these parameters vary from level to level in Cambridge Main Suite examinations.

In Figure 4.1 below, we draw on the contextual parameters suggested by Weir (2005a, b) as being most likely to have an impact on test performance.

Figure 4.1 Aspects of context validity for writing (adapted from Weir 2005b:47)

Context validity	
Setting: task	**Linguistic demands:**
• Response format	**Task input and output**
• Purpose	• Lexical resources
• Knowledge of	• Structural resources
criteria	• Discourse mode
• Weighting	• Functional resources
• Text length	• Content knowledge
• Time constraints	
• Writer–reader relationship	
Setting: administration	
• Physical conditions	
• Uniformity of administration	
• Security	

Using this framework as our informing source, the rest of this chapter explores the parameters of context validity in terms of *Setting: (task* and *administration)* and *Linguistic demands (task input and output)*.

Mirroring our treatment of cognitive validity in the previous chapter, we first provide a review of the academic research we have discovered on each parameter. We will then exemplify each parameter in relation to Cambridge ESOL examinations at different levels by reference to the voices of the language testing practitioners within the Cambridge ESOL organisation who are responsible in their day-to-day work for developing, administering and validating versions of the tests and to the large community of external professionals who are actively associated with the production and delivery of Cambridge ESOL tests.

At the end of the discussion on each parameter we summarise how different levels of Cambridge ESOL examinations vary and attempt to establish where the critical differences are.

Task setting and linguistic demands are conveyed through the wording of the task supplied to the candidates. In the case of a direct test of writing it is generally accepted (Bachman 1990, Bachman and Palmer 1996, Weigle 2002) that the information provided in the task input (the material contained in a given test task) and in the task rubric (incorporating aspects of the task which relate to the provision of task structure and guidance on successful task completion (Bachman and Palmer 1996:50)) is presented to the test taker in an explicit manner: test takers should be clear of any production demands placed upon them.

Test rubrics specify how the test taker is expected to undertake the test. Bachman (1990:118) suggests three characteristics of task rubrics:

- test organisation
- time allocation and
- instructions.

The wording of the task comprises certain characteristics that specify exactly how the test taker is expected to successfully accomplish the test. Given the requirement to make certain inferences on the basis of test-taker performance, it is crucial that instructions to test takers are both transparent and accessible. Instructions specify the task the test taker is expected to complete, and test-taker performance is enhanced when there is a greater appreciation of the task or of what is required of the test taker.

For Bachman and Palmer (1996:181) well-written instructions make it clear to the candidate exactly what is being asked of them by the test procedure and task, the nature of their expected response and in some cases how this will be rated. According to Bachman (1990:124) the necessity for clarity of instructions concerning the expectations placed on the candidate by the test task increases in importance commensurate with the complexity of the task and its familiarity to the test taker.

One source of test-taker anxiety, according to Madsen (1982), is unclear or ambiguously phrased instructions. Offering the candidate clear instructions is a crucially important aspect in the overall design and implementation of a valid test. Bachman and Palmer (1996:121) offer three essential guidelines for instructions. They should be:

1. Simple enough for test takers to understand.
2. Short enough so as not to take up too much of the test administration time.

3. Sufficiently detailed for test takers to know exactly what is expected of them.

Instructions in relation to expected/anticipated length of the test-taker response tend to adopt one of several types: a suggested word count (offered to the test taker as either a range or single figure), a structural unit (such as a sentence or paragraph) or, as has been suggested by Carson (2000), page units defined in terms of a page(s), e.g. half a page, one or more pages.

In Cambridge ESOL examinations the rubric specifies the appropriate task setting parameters and linguistic demands required for the candidate to deal with the task effectively and efficiently. Additional information and exemplification is provided in the handbooks that accompany each examination.

Setting: task

Response format

Alderson et al (2004:10) note that there is nothing in the CEFR about response format even though the CEFR claims to be a reference point for assessment. Weir (2005b: Chapter 8) points out that the techniques selected will have clear implications for the context and cognitive validity of the assessment. In writing, choice of format will determine whether knowledge telling or knowledge transformation occurs in task completion; two very different processing experiences.

There is some evidence that the *response format* can affect the test taker's performance and score (for example, Alderson et al 1995, Berry 1997). Alderson et al (1995) have suggested that a test should include a range of response formats in order to ensure that all candidates will have an opportunity to perform at their best and to reduce the possibility of construct irrelevant variance being introduced by the use of a single format.

Accordingly a wide variety of tasks is employed in KET and PET examinations and at the higher levels candidates are offered a choice of tasks in Part 2 of the test.

Response format: Cambridge practice

Examples of the tasks used in each of the Main Suite examinations can be found in Appendix A. An idea of the whole task can be gained from these. Readers may find it useful to refer to these in following the discussion below which focuses on only one specific contextual parameter at a time.

KET has three papers, covering the four skills. The Reading and Writing component consists of nine parts with Parts 6–9 concentrating on testing basic writing skills. The Writing parts of KET embrace a wide variety of formats (Parts 6–8 are suitable techniques for testing 'productive writing ability' only in a very guided sense) and these are summarised in the box below.

	Response format
Part 6	*Word completion* (*5 items*) In Part 6, candidates have to produce five items of vocabulary and to spell them correctly. The five items of vocabulary all belong to the same lexical field, for example jobs, food, household objects, etc. For each word, candidates are given a 'definition' of the type found in a learner's dictionary, followed by the first letter of the required word and a set of dashes to represent the number of the remaining letters. Each of the five definitions contains no more than 16 words. A completed example from the lexical set is given at the beginning.
Part 7	*Open cloze* (*Gap-filling*) (*10 items*) In Part 7, candidates have to complete a gapped text of 80–100 words (including gaps, addresses and salutations). Deletions in the text focus on grammatical structure and vocabulary.
Part 8	*Information transfer* (*Form-filling*) (*5 items*) In Part 8, candidates complete a simple information transfer task. They must use the information in two short texts totalling about 90 words to complete someone's notes. Candidates have to understand the text(s) in order to complete the task, and the focus is on both writing and reading ability. The required written production is at word and phrase level, not sentence level.
Part 9	*Continuous writing* (*1 task*) In Part 9, candidates have to show that they can communicate a written message of an authentic type. This task constitutes a very general, open-ended writing exercise. The input text requires minimal reading on the part of the candidate (maximum 65 words, which includes the entire rubric). The instructions indicate the type of message required, whom it is for and what kind of information should be included. Candidates have to respond to all three points. Alternatively, the candidates may be asked to read and respond appropriately to three elements contained within a short note from a friend.

PET Reading and Writing, like KET, are combined in one question paper. The Reading and Writing component consists of eight parts: Reading (Parts 1–5) and Writing (Parts 1–3). The Writing parts of PET are summarised in the box below.

	Response format
Part 1	*Sentence transformation (5 items)* Part 1 focuses on grammatical precision and requires candidates to complete five sentences, all sharing a common theme or topic. For each question, candidates are given a complete sentence, together with a 'gapped' sentence below it. The first and second sentence contain no more than 12 words, including the gapped words. Candidates have to write between one and three words to fill this gap. The second sentence, when complete, must mean the same as the first sentence. A completed example is given.
Part 2	*Short communicative message (1 task)* The wording of this task does not exceed 60 words, including the rubric. Candidates are told whom they are writing to and why, and must include three content points, which are laid out as bullet points in the question.
Part 3	*A longer piece of continuous writing (1 from 2)* Part 3 offers candidates a choice of task: either an informal letter or a story. For the informal letter, candidates are given an extract of a letter from a friend, which provides cues on the topic they must write about. For the story, candidates are given either a short title or the first sentence. The total reading load for the *informal letter* task does not exceed 60 words and for the *story* task does not exceed 40 words, including the entire rubric.

For FCE, Writing is a separate paper and candidates are required to carry out two tasks (summarised in the table below); a compulsory one in Part 1 and one from a choice of four in Part 2. FCE candidates will require greater language knowledge than their KET/PET counterparts in order to process the longer input text.

	Response format
Part 1 Q 1	*Transactional letter (1 task)* Part 1 – a compulsory task – requires candidates to write a trans-actional letter which may be formal or informal, in response to a request for action or to initiate action. The usual conventions of

	letter writing, specifically opening salutation, paragraphing and closing phrasing are required but it is not necessary to include postal addresses.
	The input on which the candidates must base their letter is made up of varied combinations of text and notes, sometimes supported by illustrations. Candidates have to deal with textual material of up to 250 words. These texts are commonly annotated with notes which may be presented on a separate piece of realia, such as a notepad.
Part 2 Q 2–4 Q 5 (a or b)	*Optional question (1 task from 4 options)* Candidates must choose one from four questions, one of which offers two set-text options. The input for these five tasks is considerably less than in Part 1 but a context, a purpose for writing and a target reader are indicated. Attention to every element in the rubric is essential for effective task achievement. Question 5 consists of a choice of two tasks based on a set of five reading texts, as specified in the Examination Regulations every year. Candidates who base their answer on another book not on the list receive Band 0. The two questions are general enough to be applicable to any of the five set texts. In order to encourage adequate reference to the text which the candidate has read, the target reader is often defined as someone who may not have read the book. A plot summary is not, however, a substitute for the task.

Like FCE, CAE Writing is also a single paper and candidates are required to carry out two tasks (summarised in the table below); a compulsory one in Part 1 and one from a choice of four in Part 2.

	Response format
Part 1 Q 1	*Compulsory question (1 task)* Part 1 is a compulsory contextualised Writing task giving candidates guidance to the content required through instructions and one or more texts and/or visual prompts. The task requires candidates to process up to about 400 words of input material. Candidates are required to transform the input in some way and not lift large chunks of the input (to expand notes, to summarise, to change the register or tone, for instance). The question may occasionally involve candidates in writing more than one piece, e.g. an article and a short note.

Part 2 Q 2–5	*Optional question (1 task from 4 options)* Candidates have to choose one of four contextualised Writing tasks which are specified in no more than 80 words. Candidates are given all the necessary information about what they have to write, whom they are writing to, and why they are writing. The rubric always specifies what genre is required. It could appear as an advertisement, an extract from a letter or in some other 'authentic' form.

CPE Writing is also a single paper and candidates are required to carry out two tasks (summarised in the table below); a compulsory one in Part 1 and one from a choice of four in Part 2.

	Response format
Part 1 Q 1	*Compulsory question (1 task)* Part 1 is compulsory and candidates are asked to write in response to instructions and a short text or texts, totalling approximately 100 words. These text(s) may come from a variety of sources, for example, extracts from newspapers, magazines, books, letters or advertisements, or could be quotations from speakers in a discussion. Visuals, such as a diagram, simple graph or picture, may be included with the text(s) to support or extend a topic.
	Although stimulus material may have an authentic source, the final input is unlikely to be wholly authentic, as the required number of words restricts the density of the argument. The input text always contains three distinct points which should be addressed by the candidate in their response. Candidates are expected to add their own ideas, so input material is made suitable for them to expand on the discussion points. Examples of appropriate sources are: academic notes, advertisements, book, article, newspaper or magazine extracts, headlines, journals, letters/correspondence notes, opening paragraphs, quotations.
	Line drawings to clarify topic and visual material such as pie charts or block graphs are sometimes included for supporting or extending a topic, but are never the sole focus of the input.
Part 2 Q 2–5	*Optional question (1 task from 4 options)* Candidates have to choose one of four contextualised Writing tasks one of which offers three set-text options. The tasks are specified in no more than 70 words excluding the standard rubric. Candidates are given all the necessary information about what

> they have to write, whom they are writing to, and why they are writing. The rubric always specifies what genre is required.
>
> Question 5 requires illustrated description and discussion within the context of the task as evidence of having read and appreciated a text rather than merely a reproduction of the plot of the book.

Summary of response formats across Cambridge ESOL levels

KET is characterised by controlled tasks at the word level and limited semi-controlled tasks at the text level. PET Part 1 is controlled, Part 2 and the Part 3 tasks are semi-controlled. At FCE, CAE and CPE there is a mixture of semi-controlled tasks where the task is framed by the rubric and/or input texts but candidates are expected to make their own contribution.

Purpose

The rubric must present candidates with clear, precise and unequivocal information regarding the purpose for completing the Writing task. This purpose should provide a reason for completing the task that goes beyond a ritual display of knowledge for assessment. Giving the writer a clear and acceptable communicative purpose is thought to enhance performance (Weir 2005b).

The purpose of a test task is critical to any macro-planning that might take place. Weir (2005b) argues that there is a close relationship between the choices we make in relation to purpose and the processing that results in task completion. Having a clear purpose will facilitate planning and monitoring – two key cognitive strategies in language processing that were discussed above under cognitive validity (see Chapter 3).

Scoring validity (see Chapter 5) is also related to task control. When the task developer designs a clear and unambiguous task, there is a greater likelihood that the task will result in a performance that can be measured with a greater degree of consistency. Where the purpose of a task is unclear (in the mind of either the task constructor or the test taker) there is a real risk that macro-planning (as envisaged by the task constructor) will be misinterpreted by the test taker or that task performance will be misjudged by the examiner. The way the prompt is worded has been shown to affect what the candidate sees as the purpose of the task (Moore and Morton 1999). For example, a term like 'discuss' is open to different interpretations unless further specified (see also Dudley-Evans 1988, Hale et al 1996, Horowitz 1986).

Weigle (2002:10) provides a useful model of writing discourse originally laid out by Vahapassi (1982) in which she presents text types 'categorized along two major dimensions: cognitive processing, and dominant intention or purpose' (2002:10). Weigle lists six different dominant intentions or purposes which follow a scheme originally proposed by Jakobson (1960):

- metalingual mathetic (intended to learn)
- referential (intended to inform)
- conative (intended to persuade or convince)
- emotive (intended to convey feelings or emotions)
- poetic (intended to entertain, delight, please)
- phatic (intended to keep in touch).

In addition, Weigle (2002:10) shows how writing for these purposes can be further categorised according to three different levels of cognitive processing: reproduction, organising known information, and generation of new ideas and information. Reproduction involves writing down information that has already been linguistically encoded as in dictation or filling out a form. Organisation involves arranging already known information such as a narrative report, a description or biography. Generation of new ideas as in expository writing or argument places the greatest demands on cognitive processing. These categories are useful in that they help to explain the important distinction between the cognitive processes involved in knowledge telling and knowledge transformation (see Chapter 3 for discussion of the distinction between these).

The importance of giving test takers a clear purpose for each task (albeit often involving a degree of simulation/role play) is recognised by Cambridge ESOL. The tasks discussed below are framed with a clear purpose for the candidate and the rubric makes this as explicit as possible. The categorisation suggested by Weigle is followed in the following analyses of Cambridge ESOL examinations.

Purpose: Cambridge practice

In terms of continuous writing KET candidates in Part 9 need to show their ability to complete one short everyday Writing task. This provides candidates with the opportunity to show that they can communicate a written message of an authentic type, for example, a note, letter or postcard to a friend. The focus of the guided Writing task is on the communicative ability of the candidate. The purposes for writing are referential (and possibly phatic) and may include:

- carrying out certain transactions: making arrangements
- giving and obtaining factual information: personal, non-personal (places, times, etc.)
- establishing and maintaining social contacts: meeting people, extending and receiving invitations, proposing/arranging a course of action, exchanging information, views, feelings and wishes.

PET candidates need to be able to give information, report events, and describe people, objects and places as well as convey reactions to situations, express dreams, hopes, ambitions, pleasure. The focus of the Part 1 sentence transformation task is on the identification and accurate production of the target structure. Part 2 is a guided Writing task with a communicative purpose. Purposes are mainly referential but sometimes emotive and/or phatic. Part 3 comprises a choice of extended Writing tasks. The introduction of choice (from March 2004) has meant that the exam better reflects the range of Writing texts that PET-level students are currently producing in the ESOL classroom. For one of the tasks, candidates are asked to create a story from a title or an initial sentence. This might be considered as a poetic use of language in Vahapassi's taxonomy (see Weigle 2002:9).

At FCE level, tasks are usually referential in orientation, and sometimes conative. Less often is the focus emotive and only occasionally is phatic use of language required. However, as language for conative purposes is often a required dimension of the compulsory task in Part 1, language used for this purpose can be considered as a differentiating feature from the level below. In Part 2, conative use of language is currently required in a number of questions but not all. Conative purpose makes an appearance for the first time in the Main Suite in some of the FCE Writing tasks.

In Part 1 (Q1), candidates are required to write a compulsory transactional letter which may be formal or informal, in response to a request for action or to initiate action. The range of functions of this letter may include: providing information, requesting information, giving opinions, agreeing and disagreeing, making complaints, correcting erroneous information, making suggestions, stating preferences, giving reasons.

In Part 2 (Q2–4) candidates may be asked to write a letter of application, an article, a composition, an informal letter, report or story. Each of these text-types is described more fully below.

letter of application: The letter of application will probably be for a job (of a temporary or part-time nature). Since candidates will probably not have any work experience, the jobs are normally suitable for a school leaver, e.g. temporary holiday jobs. Referential and conative language is often required.

article: The question makes reference to where the article will be published. This information, together with an indication of the magazine's readership defines the style of the article. Often, the question includes an 'authentic' announcement from the magazine itself and the request for articles may take the form of a competition. The main purpose is to inform, but the candidate will also have to interest the reader.

composition: Candidates write a composition in answer to a question, or give their opinion on a statement. Always written for a teacher, the context and reason for writing is usually established through reference to a previous class activity. Compositions are generally intended to inform.

informal letter: This letter is non-transactional and might involve sharing an experience or explaining feelings or personal opinions, providing information, giving a choice or making suggestions.

report: The focus of the report is factual and impersonal, although candidates are often asked to include their own recommendations or suggestions.

story: A short story is normally written for a magazine or anthology for which the typical reader might be a fellow student. The immediate purpose of the story is to engage the interest of the reader.

In Part 2 (Q5 a and b – the set-text question), questions are of a universal nature and commonly focus on such aspects as action, character and place. The five texts include at least one set of short stories (candidates are asked to write about one of these stories). The tasks require one of the types of writing given above, i.e. article, letter, composition or report, and usually involve both informational and conative use of language.

At CAE level comprehension and processing of the input texts is essential for successful completion of the Part 1 task. Such reading into writing activities are well supported in the current research literature (Grabe and Stoller 2002:14) and are increasingly used in high-stakes Writing tests around the world, for example, in new TOEFL and since the 1980s in TEEP (see Weir 1983).

The objectives of the task, or combination of tasks, that might form the basis of Part 1 are, for example:

- finding differences between one text and another (correcting an inaccurate newspaper report compared with an accurate eye-witness account)
- transferring from one register to another (e.g. writing a formal complaint on the basis of informal notes)
- collating different pieces of information in order to come up with one piece of writing (e.g. writing a report on possible locations)
- transferring from one format to another (for instance, expressing information from a table/questionnaire in an article or a report).

These Part 1 tasks involve mainly referential and conative use of language. Boyd (2005) argues that:

> there is a cline of persuasion in Part 1 CAE tasks ranging from overtly and strongly persuading someone to do something (for the writer or a general body), to a milder form where the writer is merely trying to

persuade the audience to accept his or her point of view or simply that the writer has a case.

Three elements feed into the strength of persuasion: what the writer wants to achieve (e.g. action or agreement); who the persuasion benefits; what form the persuasion takes.

(a) The strongest form of persuasion is where the writer wants action and presents this in the form of a proposal. This is perhaps where the writer is most involved and most concerned about the outcome.

(b) Slightly weaker is persuasion by describing a problem(s) and suggesting a solution or resolution that the audience should consider.

(c) A more subtle form of persuasion is persuading by describing something in an enticing way – but clearly wanting a positive response, e.g. an invitation.

(d) At the opposite end of the scale to (a) is where the writer merely wants the audience to accept his or her view and presents that view in an article. In this case, the writer has no personal involvement with the audience and, as no overt response is required, this could be said to be the mildest form of persuasion.

Boyd thus argues that persuasion is not only a distinctive element in all the nine Part 1 tasks she surveyed but is in fact the focus of the tasks.

Part 2 covers a range of task types, such as articles, reports and leaflets, proposals, character references, text for guidebooks, reviews, etc. and includes a work-oriented task as the last of the four questions. Candidates must be aware of the need to adopt an appropriate style, layout and register for the text type of each Writing task since the overall aim of the task is to have a positive effect on the target reader. These tasks normally involve conative use of language as well as referential use.

The work-oriented task in Question 5 is aimed at candidates with some experience of the workplace rather than candidates with specialist business knowledge. Candidates are unlikely to be able to do the task well if they have just followed a course of business study but not had any significant work experience.

CPE Part 1 is compulsory and candidates are asked to write an article, an essay, a letter or a proposal in response to instructions and a short text or texts which may be supported by a visual. All questions in this part have a discursive focus. For example, candidates may be required to defend or attack a particular argument or opinion, compare or contrast aspects of an argument, explain a problem and suggest a solution, or make recommendations having evaluated an idea.

In Part 2, candidates choose one from four tasks, one of which offers three set-text options. Candidates are able to select the task and topic which best suits their interests or which they think they can perform best on. The focuses are mainly referential but some also involve conative use of language and occasionally emotive use of language is called for. Candidates are expected to be able to produce the following text types for this part of the Writing paper:

article: An article will usually be activated by a central idea which provides a point or purpose to the writing or reading of the article. Referential and conative uses of language are usually involved.

letter: An example would be a letter to a newspaper giving an opinion and making a point. The purpose of the task, simulated by the input given and further developed with the candidate's own ideas, is usually referential but sometimes involves a conative dimension.

report: Candidates are given an appropriate prompt, in response to which they then have to produce a report for a specified audience, which could be a superior, e.g. a line manager at work, or a peer group, e.g. colleagues. A report will involve candidates in giving information, describing, analysing, summarising, hypothesising, etc. and requires candidates to draw upon their ability to persuade the specified audience. Compared to some of the other formats in Part 2 this task invariably involves conative use of language.

proposal: A proposal has a similar format to the report but contains an added element of making recommendations for discussion. The proposal is not used for set texts. An example of a proposal would be a bid for funds for a project defined in the task, and would entail outlining the way the funds would be spent, the benefits which would accrue, and the way progress would be monitored and evaluated if the bid were to be successful. A proposal in Part 2 will not have as a main focus the discursive requirement. It will rely more on the presentation of ideas and recommendations rather than a justification of and argument for a particular point of view, although justification could be involved in terms of persuasion. Thus both conative and referential use of language is often required.

review: A review of a book, film, concert or play should be informative and interesting as well as draw on skills such as evaluating, summarising, describing, comparing/contrasting, drawing conclusions. Emotive as well as referential uses of language may be called for.

set texts: The set-text option in Part 2 consists of three tasks based on the set reading texts, as specified in the Examination Regulations issued every year. This option is intended to encourage extended reading (an intended washback feature) as a basis for the enrichment of language study, and a variety of texts is included in the list of prescribed titles. Questions on set texts may use the following types: article, essay, letter, report, review. This task largely requires referential use of language.

essay: The essay in Part 2 only appears in the set-text question. The essay should be complete in itself and be united by a central concept which provides a purpose to the writing and reading of the essay.

Summary of purpose across Cambridge ESOL levels

There is a transition from KET to CPE in terms of purpose with the possibility of having to deal with conative purpose from the FCE level upwards. Only at CPE, however, is the discursive task compulsory. Within the higher levels (FCE, CAE, CPE) the same broad range of purposes for writing may occur at each of the three levels.

Knowledge of criteria

Weir (2005b) points out that, as well as having a clear idea of what they are expected to do in the task and how to set about this, candidates should also be fully aware which criteria are to be used in the marking. This will have an effect on planning and monitoring in the cognitive processing involved in task completion (see Chapter 3). This information should be available to candidates and their teachers prior to the examination. If, in the unlikely situation that mechanical accuracy (e.g. spelling and punctuation) were not to be assessed in a Writing task, candidates would be wasting their time monitoring their output with regard to this. If organisation is not as important as mechanical accuracy then planning would be less important.

The Standards for Educational and Psychological Testing (AERA 1999:85) state that the higher the consequences of the test for the candidates, the more important it is that they are fully informed about the test process, the uses that will be made of results, the rating criteria, testing policy, and protection of confidentiality consistent with the need to obtain valid responses. These requirements are echoed in the *ETS Standards for Quality and Fairness* (Educational Testing Service 2002:61) in terms of test-taker rights and responsibilities, which declare that candidates have a right to information about the nature and purpose of the test. Cambridge ESOL addresses this standard in its examinations, and regards the provision of such information as an important element of the scoring validity of the test (see Chapter 5 for full discussion of this).

Knowledge of criteria: Cambridge practice

Published information about how the tasks are scored, including criteria for correctness, and procedures used for scoring, are provided in the Cambridge ESOL *Examination Handbooks*.

The handbooks for each examination include details of the General Mark Scheme (GMS) for each level and examples of Task Specific Mark Schemes (TSMS) which relate to specific questions. In combination, these mark schemes address what is expected of candidates at each level. An adequate performance at each level is further explained through the Cambridge ESOL Common Scale for Writing (CSW). The scale attempts to aid the production of a framework of descriptor bands including key criteria for the assessment of writing across exams at levels already specified by the Common European Framework.

The draft common scale derived from the research undertaken by Cambridge ESOL has been adapted to appear in Cambridge ESOL exam handbooks in a way similar to the Common Scale for Speaking. This user-oriented Common Scale for Writing, as it appears in the revised FCE Handbook, for example, is reproduced here together with accompanying explanatory text. Further detail of the Common Scale for Writing Project is provided in Chapter 5.

The Cambridge ESOL Common Scale for Writing has been developed to allow users to:

- interpret levels of performance in the Cambridge tests from beginner to advanced
- identify typical performance qualities at particular levels
- locate performance in one examination against performance in another.

The Common Scale is designed to be useful to test candidates and other test users (e.g. admissions officers or employers). The description at each level of the Common Scale is not intended as a specification for the test content, but rather aims to provide a brief, general description of the nature of written language ability at a particular level in real-world contexts. In this way the wording offers an easily understandable description of performance which can be used, for example, in specifying requirements to language trainers, formulating job descriptions and specifying language requirements for new posts.

Cambridge ESOL Common Scale Levels for Writing

LEVEL MASTERY C2 (CEF)
CERTIFICATE OF PROFICIENCY IN ENGLISH:
Fully operational command of the written language

- Can write on a very wide range of topics.
- Is able to engage the reader by effectively exploiting stylistic devices such as sentence length, variety and appropriacy of vocabulary, word order, idiom and humour.
- Can write with only very rare inaccuracies of grammar or vocabulary.
- Is able to write at length organising ideas effectively.

LEVEL EFFECTIVE OPERATIONAL PROFICIENCY C1 (CEF)
CERTIFICATE IN ADVANCED ENGLISH:
Good operational command of the written language

- Can write on most topics.
- Is able to engage the reader by using stylistic devices such as sentence length, variety and appropriacy of vocabulary, word order, idiom and humour though not always appropriately.
- Can communicate effectively with only occasional inaccuracies of grammar and vocabulary.
- Is able to construct extended stretches of discourse using accurate and mainly appropriate complex language which is organisationally sound.

LEVEL VANTAGE B2 (CEF)
FIRST CERTIFICATE IN ENGLISH:
Generally effective command of the written language

- Can write on familiar topics.
- Shows some ability to use stylistic devices such as variety and appropriacy of vocabulary and idiom though not always appropriately.
- Can communicate clearly using extended stretches of discourse and some complex language despite some inaccuracies of grammar and vocabulary.
- Can organise extended writing which is generally coherent.

LEVEL THRESHOLD B1 (CEF)
PRELIMINARY ENGLISH TEST:
Limited but effective command of the written language

- Can write on most familiar and predictable topics.
- Can communicate clearly using longer stretches of discourse and simple language despite relatively frequent inaccuracies of grammar or vocabulary.
- Can organise writing to a limited extent.

LEVEL WAYSTAGE A2 (CEF)
KEY ENGLISH TEST:
Basic command of the written language

- Can write short basic messages on very familiar or highly predictable topics possibly using rehearsed or fixed expressions.
- May find it difficult to communicate the message because of frequent inaccuracies of grammar or vocabulary.

In addition to the criteria, the front covers of Main Suite examination question papers carry details of marks. The KET Reading and Writing question paper informs candidates that there are nine parts to the combined test (it does not distinguish between Reading and Writing sections) and that Questions 36–55 (in Parts 6, 7, and 8) carry one mark each and Question 56 in Part 9 carries five marks. PET separates information on the reading parts from that on the Writing parts, showing: Questions 1–5 carry one mark each, Part 2 (Question 6) carries five marks and Part 3 (Question 7 or 8) carries fifteen marks. FCE, CAE and CPE question papers inform candidates that each part carries equal marks.

In publicising the criteria, Cambridge ESOL conforms to established standards discussed above in respect of test-taker rights.

Weighting

Weighting occurs when a different number of maximum points are assigned to a test item, task or component in order to change its relative contribution in relation to other parts of a test. Weir (2005b) points out that if different parts of the test are weighted differently then the timing or marks to be awarded should reflect this and any such differential weighting should be made clear to the test takers so that they can allocate their time accordingly, particularly in the macro-planning phase of processing.

It may well be possible to determine differential weighting at the task level, for example, writing an essay is perhaps more important than writing a postcard and places far greater linguistic demands on candidates in terms of the framework above. The weighting of different parts of a Writing test should always be based on a clearly defined rationale and reflect the perceived importance, or lack of importance of that aspect of the test in relation to other tasks.

At the individual task level, if any of the marking criteria to be used in assessing a Writing task are to receive differential weighting, then candidates need to know this and allocate time and attention for monitoring their output accordingly.

Weighting: Cambridge practice

At the lowest level, KET, the direct Writing tasks carry a greater weighting per question, but the greater number of questions overall for the more form-focused elements in the test mean that greater weighting is actually given to these microlinguistic elements. By PET level, the direct tasks are weighted more highly, putting the emphasis in the test overall on productive writing. In FCE, CAE and CPE all tasks are equally weighted as are the criteria of assessment employed to evaluate them, so this parameter (along with input type and nature of information) does not contribute to any differentiation between these higher levels of ability.

Table 4.1 Weighting of tasks in Main Suite examinations

KET	Parts 6–9 are unequally weighted.
	Part 6 consists of 5 questions (Q36–40), Part 7 consists of 10 questions (Q41–50), Part 8 consists of 5 questions (Q51–55) and Part 9 consists of 1 question (Q56).
	Each item carries one mark, except for the Part 9 question which is marked out of 5. This gives a maximum total of 60 marks (Reading and Writing combined), which is weighted to a final mark out of 50, representing 50% of total marks for the whole examination (including Reading).
PET	Parts 1–3 are unequally weighted.
	Part 1 consists of 5 questions (Q1–5), Part 2 consists of 1 question (Q6) and Part 3 consists of 1 question (Q7 or Q8).
	Questions 1–5 carry one mark each. Question 6 is marked out of 5; and Question 7/8 is marked out of 15. This gives a maximum total of 25 which represents 25% of total marks for the whole examination.
FCE	Parts 1 and 2 are equally weighted. Each question in the paper carries equal marks (20 marks spread over five band levels per question).
	The maximum total for both parts is 40 which constitutes 20% of the examination total.
CAE	Parts 1 and 2 are equally weighted. Each question in the paper carries equal marks. The first examiner's total mark for both parts is out of 10 which is double weighted, i.e. a mark out of 20.
	The second examiner's total mark for both parts is out of 10 which is double weighted, i.e. a mark out of 20.
	The maximum total number of marks from both examiners is 40 which constitutes 20% of the examination total.
CPE	Parts 1 and 2 are equally weighted. Each question in the paper carries equal marks. (20 marks spread over five band levels per question).
	The maximum total for both parts is 40 which constitutes 20% of the examination total.

Text length

Alderson et al (2004) point out that length is defined in the CEFR as 'short' or 'long', arguing that it is difficult for individuals to determine for themselves what is 'short' or 'long'. Text length potentially has an important effect in terms of the resources that will be called into play in cognitive processing. In general, the longer the text candidates have to produce, the greater the language, content knowledge, organisational and monitoring metacognitive abilities that might be required in processing. If short texts are not making the demands on these resources that occur in real-life situations cognitive validity is compromised.

Text length: Cambridge practice

In KET and PET candidates are not sufficiently proficient to be able to cope with extended direct Writing tasks, though attempts are made to encourage them in this direction (see section on time constraints on page 83). The minimally sufficient length for production of written text that can be considered a test of direct writing is reached in PET Part 3 but not Parts 1 and 2. In FCE, CAE and CPE candidates are expected to produce text of a sufficient length to ensure that all appropriate generic criteria can be applied. All pieces of written work in these examinations meet the stipulations for a direct Writing task discussed in the introduction to this volume. All require texts of a length that far exceed the minimal requirement for valid assessment as suggested by Jacobs et al (1981) and Hamp-Lyons (1990).

Table 4.2 Text length in Main Suite examinations

	Text length
KET	Part 6
	Candidates are expected to supply five items of vocabulary.
	Part 7
	Candidates are expected to supply one word for each gap.
	Part 8
	Candidates have to write between five and ten words filling in five gaps on a form or set of notes.
	Part 9
	The output text could be a note, postcard, or email of 25 to 35 words.
PET	Part 1
	Candidates are expected to supply no more than three words.
	Part 2
	Candidates are expected to write the task within the word limit stipulated (35 to 45 words).
	Part 3
	Candidates are expected to produce about 100 words.
FCE	In both parts the candidates are expected to produce 120 to 180 words giving an overall word length of 240 to 360 words.
CAE	In both parts the candidates are expected to produce approximately 250 words giving an overall word length of 500 words.
CPE	In both parts the candidates are expected to produce 300 to 350 words giving an overall word length of 600 to 700 words.

Summary of text length across Cambridge ESOL levels

In general there is an increase of about 100 words between each of the first three levels if one takes the minimum amount required as the benchmark.

The upper word limit at FCE is substantially greater than that which is expected of KET and PET candidates. There is also substantial difference between the minimum required at CAE and at FCE. Longer pieces of writing will in themselves add to the cognitive pressures on the writer.

Time constraints

In writing, test constructors are concerned with the time available for task completion: speed at which processing must take place; length of time available to write; whether it is an exam or hand-in assignment; and the number of revisions/drafts allowed (process element). Outside of examination answers, in the real world, Writing tasks would not necessarily be timed as strictly. In some working contexts, e.g. journalism, timing is clearly very important, whereas in other situations there may be more flexibility regarding timing. Where time in the workplace is not of the essence, employees would be allowed maximum opportunity and access to resources. However considerations such as time constraints and reliability issues make longer, process-oriented tests impractical in most situations.

The actual amount of time allowed for an essay has implications. Weigle (2002:101–2) cites a study by Powers and Fowles (1996) in which the researchers observed that:

> students performed somewhat better on writing tasks for the Graduate Management Admissions Test (GMAT) when given 60 minutes than when they were given 40 minutes, but they note in their review of related literature that such effects have not been found uniformly in other research.

The study suggests that 'time limits do not differentially benefit or disadvantage certain groups of students' (2002:101). Weigle also notes that the cultural preferences and practices of test takers constitute yet another dimension relating to the issue of time allocation: 'Purves (1992) notes that the amount of time students will take is largely dependent upon what they are used to' (Weigle 2002:101–2).

Weir (2005b:66) points out that the texts we ask candidates to produce obviously have to be long enough for them to be scored in a reliable manner. If we want to establish whether a student can organise a written product into a coherent whole, length is obviously a key factor. As regards an appropriate time for completion of product-oriented Writing tasks in an actual examination setting, Jacobs et al (1981:19), in their research on the Michigan Composition Test, found that a time allowance of 30 minutes probably gave most students enough time to produce an adequate sample of their writing ability. This, of course, depends on the expectations of the sample produced.

One might reasonably expect that time-restricted test tasks cannot represent what writers are capable of producing in normal written discourse where time constraints may be less limited. Kroll (1990:140–54) reports on research comparing timed classroom essays and essays written at home over a 10–14 day period. Contrary to what one might have expected, the study indicated that in general time does not buy very much for students in either their control over syntax – the distribution of specific language errors being remarkably similar in both – or in their organisational skills. However, as no qualitative data was collected on the process one does not know how much time was actually taken up with the take-home assignment. Weigle (2002:101) also notes that the research undertaken on time allotment does not wholly support the notion that more time is better.

Issues associated with the allocation of time are inevitably related to the number of tasks in a Writing test. This raises the concept of information yield. More tasks, it could be argued, will produce more useful information about the candidate's ability. Weigle (2002:102) argues that there are validity arguments for both enlarging and limiting the number of tasks presented to a candidate in a Writing test. A greater number of tasks offers the candidate more choice and an opportunity to demonstrate their best work. The PET Part 3 story, for example, may well give rise to 'better' output than the letter task, in that candidates have more opportunity to display range. Conversely, many short and easily written tasks may well be less challenging and less representative of the types of writing students encounter in their respective fields of study. Ruth and Murphy (1984) have suggested that higher proficiency candidates engaged in, and more cognisant of, complex writing processes might be frustrated by shorter tasks which would not allow them the freedom to exhibit their language proficiency.

In the final analysis, the number of tasks and the time given over to those tasks will depend on the proficiency of the candidate and the level of the examination. 'To discriminate between higher levels of writing proficiency, therefore, it may make sense to provide fewer long tasks rather than more shorter tasks' (Weigle 2002:102–3).

Henning (1991:288) contends that though in general reliability is improved through providing more time and by sampling across a range of tasks, and increasing the number of raters, any improvement in reliability soon reaches a point of diminishing returns.

These considerations have affected time allocation in Cambridge ESOL examinations and the *sine qua non* is that there should be sufficient time available for candidates to produce a situationally and interactionally authentic written product appropriate to level. These parameters of time and length are always systematically checked at the trialling stage (see Appendix E). In line with the above discussion in regard to other parameters, more than one sample should be taken to address coverage and scoring validity requirements (see Chapter 5).

Time constraints: Cambridge practice

Although the overall time available for the whole test is printed on the front of the question paper, the time which should be spent on each Main Suite task is not specified on the question test paper. Centre invigilators and test administrators are expected to adopt a non-interventionist stance, as time management is seen as the responsibility of the test taker. Despite this, candidates sitting Main Suite examinations do receive ten- and five-minute warnings from the administrators. It should also be noted that test takers are usually well-prepared in advance of the examination; classroom preparation generally aims to make sure they are fully aware of the timings involved and how to make the best use of the time available to them.

From the timings shown in Table 4.3, it is clear that as language proficiency increases, the time available for completion of Main Suite tasks extends. The speed at which any processing takes place and the length of time given over to writing, by necessity, need to increase with improving language ability and with the demands placed upon candidates. Moreover, the texts that candidates are expected to produce need to be long enough for them to be marked in a reliable manner. If we want to establish whether a candidate can organise a written product into a coherent whole, length – and time available – are key factors. FCE, CAE and CPE examinations require that candidates produce between 240 and 700 words in one-and-a-half to two hours; KET and PET examinations require (for the continuous Writing tasks) that candidates produce between 25 and 100 words. In the case of CAE and CPE, additional time is given to candidates to reflect the greater complexity of the tasks set and the longer pieces of writing required as output (readers are referred to the section on direct tests of writing in Chapter 1, see pages 9–12).

Table 4.3 Time constraints in Main Suite examinations

KET	PET	FCE	CAE	CPE
70 minutes (including Reading test)	90 minutes (including Reading test)	90 minutes	120 minutes	120 minutes

Summary of time constraints across Cambridge ESOL levels

At FCE the time available is dedicated time for the Writing tasks alone rather than time being shared with the Reading tasks as in KET and PET. There is a substantial increase in the amount of time available at CAE and CPE. This increase in time allocation matches the increase in length of writing output.

Writer–reader relationship

Hyland (2002:5) suggests three general approaches to the teaching and researching of writing which focus on:

- the products of writing by analysing texts in a variety of ways (e.g. Systemic Functional Linguistics, Discourse and Genre Analysis)
- the writer and the processes employed to generate textual output
- the nature and role that readers and social community play in writing, i.e. writing as social interaction and writing as social construction.

In language teaching and testing, we have moved on from the perspective of those theoretical linguists who restrict their attention to form and treat texts as autonomous objects and ignore completely the dimensions of communication in real-world contexts. For researchers like Hyland (2002:22–48) communicative writing is viewed from a different paradigm and most usefully seen as interactive and socially constructed, as well as cognitive, i.e. concerned with the orientation of both the reader and writer (see also Hamp-Lyons and Kroll 1997). We have discussed the cognitive approach in relation to the individual writer in detail in Chapter 3, so in this chapter we will broaden our perspective to the social context and consider reader-oriented approaches which help explain the influences outside the individual that clarify problems and solutions and shape writing.

The reader-oriented dimension of writing can be thought of in terms of social interaction and social construction:

Writing as social interaction

Writing viewed as interaction between writers and readers adds a communicative dimension. Nystrand (1989:75) sees writing as developing text in accordance with what the reader is likely to know or expect and reading as a process of predicting text in line with what is assumed to be the writer's purpose. Both parties presume an ability on the part of the other to make sense of what is written or read. The reader or audience is, according to Grabe and Kaplan (1996:207), critical to the generation of text and meaning. Ede and Lunsford (1984) describe two models of audience: *audience addressed* and *audience invoked*. Audience addressed refers to the real or intended readership definable by the writer who exists apart from the text. Audience invoked is a fictitious readership invoked by the reader for a rhetorical purpose.

Hyland (2002) notes that for a text to have an appropriate impact on the target audience the writer has to gauge accurately the reader's capacity for interpreting it and probable reaction to it.

Hyland (2002:72) gives the example of a thank-you letter written by a child to his or her friend and argues that this will probably differ from one written to an older relation who is not well known to the writer, in terms of what is disclosed about self, level of formality, amount, if any, of deference and whether topic elaboration is needed to achieve common ground.

It is clear that a notion of audience – the target reader – will have a profound impact on the discourse of the written product. Grabe and Kaplan (1996) list five factors ('parameters of audience influence') they consider to be responsible for constraining decisions taken by the writer and which have implications for textual variation:

1. The numerical size of the readership, that is, the number of persons expected to read the text.
2. The degree to which the readership is either known or unknown.
3. The status of the reader.
4. The extent of shared background knowledge possessed by the readership.
5. The extent of specific topical knowledge both reader and writer share.

Expressivists, cognitivists and interactionists: views of audience

For expressivists, the audience is a construction of the writer (Ede and Lunsford 1984) because, essentially, writing is for its own sake. Clearly, this might be difficult to support in an L2 situation in which writers very often write in real-world contexts for specific audiences and specific purposes (although this said, the audience is often the teacher). The extent to which this mainly L1 approach to teaching writing may be relevant relates to the make-up of the Cambridge ESOL candidature. The candidature is predominantly young in KET and PET (approximately 70 per cent of the test-taking population are under 20). In KET and PET opportunities are provided for candidates to use their own experience and tasks which for the most part involve only knowledge telling, narrative or description.

The issue of audience is complicated for cognitivists and interactionists. Both recognise the importance of anticipating the informational and linguistic needs of the audience. However, English as a Second Language (ESL) reading research literature makes it clear that the relationship between reader and text is extremely complex (Carrell et al 1988) and as a consequence text is often open to multiple interpretation.

Social interactionists see the writer as an 'outsider' to the discourse community with the reader being all powerful. This is particularly appropriate in EAP tests in which the marker can mirror the role of academic tutor. However, in most of the Cambridge ESOL range this is not the case. For these tests, the marker is not the invoked or notional audience indicated by the task rubric even though he or she effectively makes the assessment decision about the writing and is constrained by having to mark to a specific standard for assessment purposes. However, particularly in FCE, CAE and CPE it is considered essential that the candidate is able to address properly the audience specified by the task. The marker is required to assess a candidate's performance for its effectiveness in doing this.

Writing as social construction

Writing as an activity premised on social structures is a view which has become widely accepted and is premised on social structures (Cooper 1986:336). Hyland (2002:69) argues that in an attempt to legitimise their sense of membership and create identity through discourse, writers characteristically locate themselves and their own ideas with respect to other ideas and texts within their communities. He notes that despite reservations in the research literature, the notion of *discourse community*, the location of writing in wider social and discursive practice, has nevertheless become a useful way of making connections between writers, texts and readers on which there is now a fair degree of agreement and one that has proved important to research in the field.

Hyland (2002:69) suggests that all acts of writing are part of wider social and discursive practices which assume certain things about relationships between those involved and how practices are carried out. Whether a personal or a business letter or an email, each has conventional ways of transmitting content and addressing readers, which, Hyland argues, are based on legitimate ways of conducting such relationships.

Hayes (1996:5) similarly emphasises the social dimension of writing noting that it is a social artifact conducted in a social context, constrained by social convention and influenced by our own personal history of production in such social interaction and by our exposure to the writing of others.

In English for Academic Purposes (EAP) and English for Specific Purposes (ESP) examinations in the Cambridge examinations, there is a clear expectation that the norms of the relevant discourse community are observed. Thus in IELTS the relevance and adequacy of content, the organisation of ideas and appropriate register are regarded as important criteria to be met in completing test tasks just as in academic life (see Bridgeman and Carlson 1983, Horowitz 1991, Weir 1983). For its General English examinations, the criteria employed are generic across levels and cover the criteria that examination stakeholders in society at large regard as important. Appropriate criteria have been established for these more general Writing tasks in the Main Suite examinations through extensive discussion with the discourse community of teachers and users of test information (see Weir and Milanovic 2003).

At higher levels, there is a progressive need to address the wider social and discursive practices identified by Hyland, for example in terms of context, purpose, audience and genre. At all levels (with the exception of KET) the effect of the writing on the reader is taken into account in the marking.

Writer–reader relationship: Cambridge practice

Efforts are made to address this important aspect of writing in Cambridge ESOL Writing examinations by providing candidates with an audience and social context in the ways described in Table 4.4.

Table 4.4 The writer–reader relationship

KET	In view of the divergent KET candidature, which comprises students at school and college, and general adult learners, material is accessible to the younger learner (i.e. not too cognitively demanding for a 14-year-old) and reasonably appealing (i.e. not puerile) to an adult.
	Part 9 The writer communicates a written message of an authentic type to an intended target reader (friend).
PET	Again, in view of the divergent PET candidature, material is accessible to the younger learner (i.e. not too cognitively demanding for a 14-year-old) and reasonably appealing (i.e. not puerile) to an adult.
	Part 2 The task involves a defined and named reader.
	Part 3 The target audience (defined in the task) tends to be appropriate to both a school-age focus (14–16) or adult focus (16+).
FCE	In Part 1, the writer must be aware that the overall aim of the task is to achieve a positive effect on the target reader and write in a style (appropriacy of register and format) appropriate to that reader.
	The different task types in Part 2 are intended to provide frameworks for the candidates so that they can put together ideas on a topic with a reader in mind. For example: A composition is always written for a teacher. An article would be written for a magazine for which the reader may be someone with a similar interest to the writer or, as in the case of a college magazine, be in the writer's peer group. A report could be written for a superior (e.g. a teacher) or a peer group (club members, colleagues). A letter of application could be written to an individual or a formal reader such as an employer. An informal letter would always be written for a known reader, e.g. a pen friend. A story would be written for a magazine (or anthology) for which the typical reader might be a fellow student. The target reader in the set text question is defined as someone who may not have read the book in order to encourage adequate reference to the text which the candidate has read.

Table 4.4 (Continued)

CAE	As with FCE, task types in Part 1 vary and may include formal letters, informal letters, reports, articles, notes or any combination of these. Scope is given to the candidate to assess and define their own relationship to the target reader. Like FCE, Part 2 offers a range of different task types: A letter would not be a personal letter to a friend as this would not generate CAE level language. A proposal or a report is predicated on there being a likely reason for the target reader to elicit the candidate's opinion, i.e. who wants the report/proposal and why is both clear and convincing to the candidate. A competition entry would require candidates to persuade the 'judges' who are the target readership. A contribution to a guidebook, etc. should be appropriate for the intended readership of the text. A work-related task might be addressed to a *superior* (requesting some personal development from boss e.g. to work abroad); *management* (making suggestions for the department in which the candidate may work e.g. more equipment); *peers* (reporting back on a particular work experience e.g. attendance at a trade fair).
CPE	Candidates are expected to write within an appropriate context in an appropriate register and to demonstrate sensitivity to their audience. Part 1 task types include: A letter which is addressed to a target reader who would need to understand the writer's point of view, for example, an editor selecting appropriate responses for inclusion in a newspaper; a store manager receiving a letter of complaint. An article which is written for a specified audience which may be an editor of a newspaper, magazine or newsletter. A proposal, which is similar to a report and is written for a specified audience. The proposal/report readership more often than not is a superior (e.g. a boss at work) or a peer group (e.g. one's colleagues). An essay which will be structured to suit a particular audience, for example a tutor. The task types for Part 2 are similar to those of Part 1 and the potential readers for Part 2 would be the same as for Part 1.

Summary of writer–reader relationship across Cambridge ESOL levels

There is a gradual progression through the levels from personally known (e.g. friend or teacher) to specified audiences with whom candidates are not personally acquainted (e.g. an editor or magazine readers). Addressing a broader range of audience is required between PET and FCE as candidates only write to people they know personally in KET and PET. By PET, the candidates also need to take greater account of their audience by considering what the potential reader is likely to know about the subject, the amount of explanation required and what can be left implicit. By CAE, candidates are no longer writing to people they know personally. A slightly wider range of unacquainted audience distinguishes CAE and CPE. At these two levels candidates must decide what sorts of evidence the reader is likely to find persuasive. With the exception of KET, the effect of the writing on the reader is taken into account in the marking.

Linguistic demands: task input and output

Our description of linguistic knowledge is based on a communicative approach to modelling language ability first appearing in Hymes (1972), extended by Canale and Swain (1980), and developed further by Canale (1983), Bachman (1990), and Bachman and Palmer (1996). These linguistic demands need to be as similar as possible to those made by equivalent tasks in real-life language use at the level of performance we are targeting if we are to generalise from test performance to language use in the future domain of interest.

Lexical resources

Cambridge ESOL, in line with other ALTE members, aligns its examinations with the Common European Framework of Reference (CEFR) which has six levels A1 to C2 corresponding to the natural levels of ability familiar to teachers in EFL, namely beginner, elementary, lower intermediate, intermediate, upper intermediate and advanced (Council of Europe 2001). Weir (2005a:292–3) notes, however, that:

> The CEFR provides little assistance in identifying the breadth and depth of productive or receptive lexis that might be needed to operate at the various levels. Some general guidance is given on the learner's lexical resources for productive language use but as Huhta et al (2002:131) point out 'no examples of typical vocabulary or structures are included in the descriptors'. The argument that the CEFR 'is intended to be applicable to a wide range of different languages' (op. cit.) is used as an explanation, but this offers little comfort to the test writer who has to select texts or activities uncertain as to the lexical breadth or knowledge required at a particular level within the CEFR.

Alderson et al (2004:13) make a related point that many of the terms in the CEFR remain undefined. They cite the use of 'simple' in the scales and argue that difficulties arise in interpreting it because the CEFR has no advice on what this might mean for structures, lexis or any other linguistic feature. They suggest that for each language that is tested, the CEFR would need to be supplemented with lists of grammatical structures and lexical items before terms like 'simple' are meaningful for those involved in item writing.

The generic function of the CEFR suggested above may mean that it cannot reasonably be expected to provide test writers with detailed guidelines on how lexical resources operate differentially at the various levels in their particular language; but test writers clearly require this sort of detailed guidance – usually in the form of reference lists – if they are to successfully create tests targeting specific levels of difficulty or covering particular domains.

Supplementary lists such as those suggested above by Alderson et al (2004) have been in existence for many years and have been used extensively in teaching and assessment; some lists (e.g. the Cambridge English Lexicon, Hindmarsh 1980) were developed more intuitively than empirically; others form part of a more functionally-oriented specification (e.g. 1990 Waystage and Threshold levels) and later came to underpin some of the lower reference levels of the CEFR.

More recently, the development of both native speaker (NS) and L2 learner corpora (i.e. computerised collections of written and spoken texts) and the application of corpus linguistic tools to these bodies of evidence, have made it easier to derive more empirically grounded word lists for use in pedagogy and assessment contexts; these can be used to help validate and improve existing word lists, as well as create new word lists sometimes with a specific level/domain focus.

Over the past 10 years examination boards (e.g. Cambridge ESOL, the Educational Testing Service (ETS), Michigan) have been at the forefront of advances in the application of corpus findings not only to practical language test development but also to the development of second language proficiency. (See Granger 2004 for a summary of learner corpora, and Taylor and Barker, forthcoming, for an overview of the use of corpora in assessment.)

Cambridge ESOL, for example, has been building corpora since the early 1990s and using outcomes from corpus studies to inform language test development and validation (see Barker 2004 for an overview) particularly with regard to lexical content. The Cambridge Learner Corpus (CLC), developed jointly with Cambridge University Press, is a learner corpus of over 75,000 candidates' written exam scripts from 20 Cambridge examinations, initially for General English exams (Main Suite) but now also for Business English (BEC) and Academic English (IELTS). The CLC currently contains 23 million words of learner English from over a hundred L1 backgrounds (see the CLC website for more information: www.cambridge.org/elt/corpus/learner_corpus.htm). The scripts in the corpus are a representative first-language based sample and are keyed in to create an anonymised machine-readable form; candidates' errors are also manually coded using a series of error-tags (see Nicholls 2003). Scripts are accompanied by score data and candidate background information such as age, gender, L1, or grade achieved on the Writing paper as well as by error-tags. The CLC can be searched by particular types of error (e.g. missing prepositions or tense errors) or lexically through a concordancer, collocation search or frequency word lists.

Together with NS corpora, the CLC is used by Cambridge ESOL for operational test development and validation purposes as well as by Cambridge University Press for publication of market- or level-specific books. Corpus studies have been used to inform test revision projects (e.g. CPE, see Weir and Milanovic 2003), devise new test formats (Hargreaves 2000), and create or revise test writer and candidate word lists (see Ball 2002, Barker 2004). The error-coded portion of the CLC can also be used to help identify typical errors at a given proficiency level which can inform the focus of test items or tasks for a particular test-taker population as well as test preparation publications (see Cambridge University Press website for corpus-informed examples). Corpora are also increasingly used for longer-term research into skills-focused construct-related areas such as developing a common scale for assessing L2 writing from criterial features of perform-ance at different proficiency levels (Hawkey and Barker 2004, and also Chapter 5 below).

Cambridge ESOL's Local Item Banking System (LIBS) can also be con-sidered as a type of corpus since it contains large quantities of tasks and items from Cambridge test versions delivered over the past 10 years or so (see Marshall 2006). In this way, LIBS functions as a powerful archive whose content is amenable to searching for particular lexical items or topics to check whether a word, phrase or structure has been tested before and in what contexts. The functionality of LIBS continues to be enhanced so that ques-tions relating to features of test input at particular proficiency levels can be explored more closely.

At the time of writing, Cambridge ESOL is exploiting a range of different corpora, including the CLC, to conduct research into both productive and receptive vocabulary across different proficiency levels and for different types of English. A major motivation for this work is to contribute to academic knowledge and understanding in the broader field of L2 vocabulary acquisi-tion, learning and assessment; another, more instrumental, motivation is to develop over time a revised Lexicon for Item Writers for the Cambridge exams at the five levels (i.e. a set of level- and domain-focused reference wordlists).

A current project is using the CLC together with spoken learner data from the Cambridge Speaking tests to investigate vocabulary use at the six proficiency levels (A1–C2) of the CEFR (Council of Europe 2001). Findings will feed into a larger collaborative project to produce a comprehensive refer-ence level description for English (see the section on the English Profile Project in Chapter 8).

The research literature indicates that receptive and productive vocabular-ies are different and that differences between passive and active vocabulary size may increase as proficiency improves (Laufer 1998, Melka 1997). Receptive vocabulary is widely believed to be greater than productive and to encompass it, as well as include words that are only partly known, low frequency words not readily available for use and words that are avoided in active use. Because of these differences in size and nature, productive vocabulary is unlikely to provide a reliable guide to receptive vocabulary knowledge, and analysis of learner corpora alone, e.g. the CLC, would be unsuitable as the basis for compiling a lexicon to guide the compilation of Reading or Listening papers.

Leech, Rayson and Wilson (2001) found that the British National Corpus list of comparative frequencies of occurrence of words in speech and writing seems to reveal significant differences in the positioning of words according to their medium of use (see also Read 2000). Corpus evidence reveals a larger core of written vocabulary than spoken vocabulary; analyses of corpus and other language data have also shown clear differences in the nature of written and spoken language, e.g. lexical density and variety (Carter and McCarthy 2002). Spoken and written corpora therefore need to be compiled separately, and the content of derived wordlists from such corpora may need to reflect this distinction across the two different modes. The literature strongly indicates that any lexicon should reflect depth of vocabulary knowledge as well as breadth of vocabulary knowledge though this feature is considerably more difficult to capture and reflect in a lexicon.

The research literature on NS and non-native speaker (NNS) vocabulary size and knowledge suggests that NNS speakers may only rarely reach native standards of proficiency. Some evidence (see Case Study B on pages 98–104) indicates that, even at higher levels, candidate output does not contain much vocabulary beyond the first 2,000 words level. This falls a long way short of the 5,000 word families suggested by Nation (2001) as constituting general vocabulary use and even further from the 17,000 base words mentioned by Carter and McCarthy as being 'typically known by educated native speakers' (see Carter and McCarthy 2002, Goulden, Nation and Read 1990). It is clearly important to draw a distinction between 'known vocabulary' and 'vocabulary used'. There is also an indication that advanced learners' language may be of a different kind to native speaker language in as much as it makes less use of complex lexical units.

Lexical resources: Cambridge practice

KET input includes items which normally occur in the everyday vocabulary of native speakers using English today. Candidates should know the lexis appropriate to their personal requirements, for example, nationalities, hobbies, likes and dislikes. The consistent use of American spelling and lexis is acceptable.

Lexis of both the input text and the imagined output text is expected to be within the KET wordlist. The KET Vocabulary List (available on the website) comprises words from the Waystage Specification List (Van Ek and Trim 1991a) and other vocabulary relevant to the level (shown by corpus evidence to be high-frequency and salient). Certain lexical constraints placed upon KET language mean that it is not allowable to combine prefixes and suffixes freely with KET words to make other words. The only compound words and phrasal verbs which may be freely used in the input are the ones included in the KET wordlist.

PET tasks involve items which are expected to occur in the everyday vocabulary of native speakers using English today as laid out in Threshold 1990 (Van Ek and Trim 1991).

All lexis in the rubric and any input materials must be within the PET (2006) Vocabulary List (available on the website) which comprises words that candidates can be expected to understand. A list of allowable prefixes and suffixes is provided in the Vocabulary List. Compound words are allowable if the two words appear individually in the list providing the meaning of the compound phrase is either transparent or literal. Any phrasal verb in a fully literal sense is permitted, where the individual verb and particle appear on the list.

Cambridge ESOL's materials writers use wordlists to help them to produce realistic question paper materials which are accessible to the whole candidature taking an examination at a specific proficiency level. On a regular basis words are suggested for inclusion in such wordlists by the personnel involved in the exam (i.e. exam paper Chairs and Subject Officers). These words are explored in a range of corpora (receptive and productive language, business and general English, learner and native speaker) to reveal their frequency in L1 and L2 English and to provide contextualised examples for the specific sense of the word under investigation. A number of words are also removed from wordlists, usually due to being old-fashioned, taboo or no longer relevant to today's candidature. It is important to note that the quantitative corpus-informed evidence is always discussed by a panel of experts for each examination and it is this expertise which influences the ultimate decision of which words should be included or removed from item writer wordlists. (For more information, see Ball 2002.)

FCE input vocabulary in Parts 1 and 2 is designed to engender a large lexical resource in addition to generating the right number of words and appropriate FCE level language. The input lexis is common, general, and non-specialised, without cultural references, and is at a language level that is fully comprehensible to candidates – although a maximum of two words and/or expressions beyond this level in any one exam paper may be used, for reasons of authenticity, as long as they are glossed.

Item writers are expected to use their professional judgement of what an FCE candidate should be able to understand. Item writers also find it useful to refer to the PET Vocabulary List as all PET words are acceptable in the FCE paper. Widely used abbreviations which fall within the general frequency of words which are allowable for FCE would also be acceptable.

CAE is the first Main Suite level that does not involve use of a wordlist in the specifications for item writer guidance to constrain lexical content (though see ongoing work referred to in the Lexicon Project).

At CAE level the lexical range of the input will be close to FCE level, i.e. well within the reading competence of the candidates at this level. In addition it will be general, non-specialised, and without cultural references. Trialling of materials for all Cambridge ESOL papers ensures that, as far as possible, the language of the rubric is accessible to all candidates. In CAE Writing, more difficult lexical items are occasionally included in Part 1, if their meaning is either glossed or not essential for completion of the task. The lexical demands at this level relate less to the task input and more to the expected output from candidates. The main Part 1 task might, for example, require candidates to demonstrate control of register, e.g. being tactful or succinct in a situation where this demands some linguistic skill. Some task types (notices, personal notes and messages, instructions, announcements, directions) are less likely to generate CAE-level language and can only be included as a short second task in a Part 1 question.

Part 2 'letters' are very well exploited at FCE so there needs to be an extra 'dimension' to the task at CAE. This can often be achieved by selecting a lexically challenging topic area (e.g. the scientific world, traditions) and/or a diverse and demanding set of functions (e.g. prioritising and justifying, complaining, etc.).

At CPE, the lexical range of the input is once again general, non-specialised, without cultural references, and well within the reading competence of the candidates at this level (i.e. below CPE level). Candidates need to be familiar with the vocabulary relevant to the functions of the language of persuasion, description, comparison and recommendation. Trialling ensures that, as far as is possible, the language of the rubric is accessible to all candidates.

One of the main focuses of the Task Specific Mark Scheme (TSMS) for Part 1 is the range of language used. For example, in the TSMS range might capture the following criteria:

- language for expressing and supporting opinions
- language for making recommendations
- language for either attacking or defending arguments.

In Part 2, range of language used is also a main focus of the TSMS. Elements of the General Mark Scheme (GMS) include: sophisticated and/or fluent use of vocabulary, collocation and expression appropriate to the task.

Table 4.5 Lexical resources of March 2004 tasks

KET	PET
Part 9: Lexis of note as appropriate to the specified functions, i.e. answering request for information to meet, lexis of exchange of services, place, times, car parking details (location).	**Part 2**: Lexis of note as appropriate to the specified functions, i.e. evaluation of art gallery, rationale for choice of card, weather enquiry. **Part 3**: Lexis of story as appropriate to the specified functions, i.e. 'very unusual evening', recounting personal or imagined experiences, lexis of the first/third person. Lexis of letter as appropriate to the specified functions, i.e. answering request for information regarding suitable present.

Table 4.6 Lexical resources of December 2003 tasks

FCE	CAE	CPE
Lexis as appropriate to the specified functions, i.e. giving details, making plans, requesting details/ information, inviting suggestions. The better candidates were able to express a range of vocabulary and expression. The most common language error occurred for the second content point which was 'hair/hairs' ('my hairs are very short now').	Lexis as appropriate to the specified functions, i.e. rewording/paraphrasing input language, reporting appropriately; language of contrast and comparison; leisure and tourist vocabulary. Strong candidates successfully worded or paraphrased the language from the input. The weaker candidates, however, tended to use 'lifted' language directly from the question. In some cases, this lifted language was spelled incorrectly.	Lexis as appropriate to the specified functions, i.e. language of contrast and comparison; language of justification; language of opinion and recommendation; sporting competition vocabulary.

Finally, it is worth noting that at all levels candidates' written responses to tasks in the Cambridge ESOL examinations are acceptable in varieties of English which enable them to function in the widest range of international contexts; this includes American English spelling and usage.

The lexical expectations of tasks can be explored more closely by considering how candidates performed during the December 2003 and March 2004 administrations.

Although our understanding of the nature of lexical resources in tests across different levels/domains remains partial, it is nevertheless growing, and investigative work is ongoing on a number of fronts. In order to gain a better understanding of lexical progression in the Cambridge Main Suite examinations, and particularly what contributes to lexical difficulty, Cambridge ESOL commissioned a report from Norbert Schmitt, an acknowledged expert in the field of second language vocabulary and assessment at Nottingham University, UK (Schmitt 2005). The nature and findings from his lexical analysis of the Main Suite examinations is reported here as the second case study in this volume; it is presented to illustrate the type of investigation which examination boards may wish to conduct if they are to gain a better understanding of test takers' lexical resources across the proficiency continuum.

Case Study B: Lexical analysis of the Main Suite examinations

Background

The goal of this exploratory study was to examine and compare lexical features of both test input (the Writing task prompts) and test output (the candidates' written responses) across the five Main Suite examination levels, KET–CPE.

1. Analysis of the Writing task prompts (test input)

Schmitt based an analysis of test input on a representative sample of 27 test versions of KET (6), PET (6), FCE (6), CAE (5) and CPE (4) used in live test administrations between March 2003 and December 2004. The Writing components of all the test versions were scanned into electronic text files, with tests from the same exam level (e.g. PET) placed in a single file. The range of Writing tasks was considered typical for each level. For each of the five exams, the final files included the front page instructions for examinees (once) and all the prompt material for the Writing section.

An analysis of lexical content showed that the average number of words (tokens) test takers are required to read in the Writing prompts increases progressively up the levels. The marked exception is for CPE, but this can be explained by the item format in CPE Part 1, where the task prompts consist of very short texts, often in 'speech bubbles' (Table 4.7).

Table 4.7 Number of word tokens within Main Suite examinations

Level	KET	PET	FCE	CAE	CPE
Number of word tokens	71.33	380.33	591.17	709.80	568.50

Similarly, the number of different word types at each level increases steadily, except for CPE which can probably be explained once again by the effect of the length of the Part 1 task (see Table 4.8).

Table 4.8 Number of word types within Main Suite examinations

Level	KET	PET	FCE	CAE	CPE
Number of word types	23.50	73.33	104.50	165.60	148.50

(If a text is 1,000 words long, it is said to have 1,000 'tokens'. However, a lot of these words will be repeated, and there may be only, say, 400 different words in the text. 'Types', therefore, are the different words.)

Number of word tokens or types to be processed is one factor, but a more significant factor is likely to be the 'difficulty' of these words. Schmitt notes that the notion of word difficulty can depend on many contextual and co-textual factors, including qualities intrinsic to the lexical items of test input. Laufer (1997), for example, identifies the following as potential factors:

- whether phonemes (the minimal unit in the sound system) are familiar
- phonotactic regularity (the sequential arrangements or 'tactic' behaviour of phonological units)
- the variability of stress and vowel change
- consistency of sound-script relationship
- inflexional regularity (morphological reference to the processes of word formation)
- derivational regularity (as above – the result of a derivational process is a new word whereas the result of inflectional process is a different form of the same word)
- morphological transparency (the term 'transparency' is used to 'refer to an analysis which presents the relevant facts in a direct and perspicuous manner' Crystal 1996:360)
- amount of register marking on the word
- whether there are several meanings per word form.

Other factors include the similarity/dissimilarity of L2 words to the corresponding L1 words (see Swan 1997 for a review).

Clearly it is difficult or impossible to use the above criteria for word selection in an examination suite designed for candidates of multiple nationalities and first languages. Analysing every word in an examination paper according to such factors would not be practical for operational test construction. These factors will affect examinees from various L1 backgrounds differently, making it impossible to select words of equal difficulty for all of the candidates taking the tests.

Because it is so complex to decide upon the difficulty of a word, language specialists generally rely on a different measure to rank vocabulary: a word's frequency of occurrence. Although this does not measure difficulty directly, research has consistently shown that higher frequency vocabulary is generally learned before lower frequency vocabulary (e.g. Schmitt, Schmitt, and Clapham 2001). This means that L2 learners are more likely to know higher frequency words than lower frequency words, and since the number of exposures is also greater for the higher frequency vocabulary, learners are also likely to know these words to a higher level of mastery as well. It can be reasonably assumed therefore that, on average, test takers will know higher frequency words relatively better than lower frequency words, and that these words are therefore 'easier'. Studies of learner corpora can provide us with valuable insights towards determining word frequencies, though the original purpose and age of the corpus always needs to be borne in mind as vocabulary use, and therefore its frequency, changes over time as do the nature and topics of question papers.

Zipf's law (2006) states that shorter words tend to be more frequent than longer words (Field 2004, Read 2000). It is therefore possible to get an indirect indication of the frequency of the words in the input for Main Suite examinations by looking at word length. Mean word length (in number of letters) increases across the input in the suite (thus indicating decreasing frequency), except between CAE/CPE levels (see Table 4.9).

Table 4.9 Mean word length within Main Suite examinations

Level	KET	PET	FCE	CAE	CPE
Mean word length	4.02	4.08	4.35	4.78	4.50

Schmitt (2005) argues that we can derive a direct measure of frequency by comparing the words in the suite to frequency lists. There are a number of frequency lists available, deriving from a range of corpora, e.g. the early one million Brown corpus (Francis and Kucera 1979 and http://khnt.hit.uib.no/icame/manuals/brown/INDEX.HTM) to the current British National Corpus (BNC) (Aston and Burnard 1998) which is in excess of 100 million words. Although frequency lists vary, this is mainly at the lower frequency levels; the highest frequency words are fairly stable across the lists. Schmitt opted to use the frequency information provided by Paul Nation and adapted by Tom Cobb in his Lexical Tutor website (www.lextutor.ca). According to the Lexical Tutor, the lexical content of the Writing test prompts could be assigned to one of four bands in terms of its high/low frequency:

Band 1: the first 1,000 most frequent words of English – comparable to the Waystage Specification List which is used to write the KET tasks.

Band 2: the second 1,000 most frequent words – still considered high frequency basic vocabulary.

Band 3: words from the Academic Word List (AWL) (Coxhead 2000).

Band 4: all other words not on these three lists.

The categorisation of lexical items in the Writing task prompts according to these four bands resulted in the distribution shown in Table 4.10, expressed as a percentage of the total number of words.

Table 4.10 Frequency distribution of vocabulary within Main Suite examinations (%)

	KET	PET	FCE	CAE	CPE
Band 1: 1st 1,000 words	87.15	88.50	88.46	82.39	83.89
Band 2: 2nd 1,000 words	6.31	6.50	4.18	7.24	4.77
Band 3: Academic Word List	0.47	0.66	1.57	4.93	5.12
Band 4: Other words	6.07	4.35	5.78	5.44	6.23

Table 4.10 suggests that the main change in word frequency occurs between the FCE and CAE levels. Over 85% of the prompt words in KET, PET, and FCE are in the first 1,000 band; the figure drops slightly for CAE and CPE but is still over 80%. For KET and PET 6–7% of words come from the second most frequent 1,000 words (slightly fewer for FCE and CPE but not CAE). KET and PET contain few words from the AWL – only about 0.5%. The AWL figure is higher for FCE, and especially for CAE and CPE which is perhaps not surprising since both of these examinations are used for accessing academic study opportunities. The 4–6% of Band 4 words at each level represent mainly personal names, geographical locations and words necessary to write about a particular topic area (e.g. hobby, television, guitar). Although statistically these are lower frequency words, they are unlikely to cause many problems for test takers as they refer to common well-known things and places.

Comparisons can also be made across levels to identify those 'new' words which appear at the next level up (see Table 4.11), although the relatively small amount of data (4–6 test versions per level) makes these results somewhat tentative.

Table 4.11 New words in each subsequent level of Main Suite examinations (%)

	Words in PET not in KET	Words in FCE not in PET	Words in CAE not in FCE	Words in CPE not in CAE
Band 1: 1st 1,000	79.40	61.31	55.22	49.25
Band 2: 2nd 1,000	10.55	9.55	14.93	10.55
Band 3: Academic Word List	1.01	7.54	14.93	17.59
Band 4: Other word list	9.05	21.61	14.93	22.61

This analysis suggests that from KET to PET the new words are mainly still in the first 1,000 frequency band. There are relatively few new words in the lower frequency bands (AWL and Other). From PET to FCE, some academic words start to appear and there is a large increase in the 'Other words' category, as previously noted. Other words may be lower frequency but are not necessarily problematic. From FCE to CAE there is a significant increase in AWL words, and from CAE to CPE, a large portion (>40%) are in the lower frequency bands.

The approach described above is useful in helping us to gain a better understanding of the general increase in demands made on test takers' lexical resources across the exam suite – at least in terms of test input. A complementary approach is to compare the figures generated for the test input with frequency figures derived from the test output, so the second part of this case study analysed a sample of candidates' written responses.

2. Analysis of the candidates' written responses (test output)

A sample of 95 candidates' written responses to the tasks analysed above were selected from the Cambridge Learner Corpus (CLC). Though the number of performances at each level was relatively small – KET (20), PET (15), FCE (20), CAE (20), and CPE (20), the sample was considered sufficiently representative for at least an initial exploration. Each exam level had a range of four grades or levels of performance quality, except for PET which had three.

Schmitt (2005) notes that the rating of learner output in terms of lexis is one of the most problematic areas in vocabulary studies. With receptive measures such as Reading or Listening tests, it is possible to evaluate words selected in a principled manner based on frequency lists or other criteria. However, with learner output such as an extended written response, control of the target words produced by candidates is limited and evaluating the vocabulary produced is more problematic. Although no entirely satisfactory solution exists for this, several possible approaches are outlined in Read's *Assessing Vocabulary* (2000). For this analysis, Schmitt analysed the candidates' written responses using various measures reported by Read (lexical density, lexical variation, lexical sophistication, and lexical frequency) to explore whether such measures could detect and usefully describe the differences in ability between test takers at the different proficiency levels.

Lexical density is the percentage of content words in a text. Greater use of content words usually corresponds to a higher information load, thus higher lexical density figures usually correspond to more 'literate' texts. Table 4.12 suggests that the lexical density of test-taker output at the various levels is very similar, except for KET. KET's higher figure is likely to stem from the shorter answers, often with truncated grammar, i.e. fewer function words, such as articles and prepositions.

Table 4.12 Lexical density of examinee output across Main Suite examination levels (%)

	KET	PET	FCE	CAE	CPE
Lexical density (content words/total)	52	48	47	49	48

Lexical variation is better known as type/token analysis and gives an indication of how far a variety of words is used in a text, rather than a few familiar words being used over and over again. One drawback of the type/token formula is that text length has a strong effect on the result, regardless of the underlying variation. For this reason, it is important to either use texts of the same length, study the first 100 words say of each text to make texts of similar length or to use some standardised type/token measure. WordSmith Tools offers a standardised type/token measure which controls for text length and the results of this measure are illustrated in Table 4.13.

Table 4.13 Lexical variation of examinee output across Main Suite examination levels (%)

	KET	PET	FCE	CAE	CPE
Lexical variation (type/token)	31.50	38.58	45.92	46.94	46.64

The lexical variation increases from KET to PET and from PET to FCE, where it levels out. It seems that test takers do use progressively more lexical variation through the lower end of the suite, but a lexical variation measure cannot separate lexical mastery at the higher end of the suite. Schmitt notes that future analyses of test-taker output might benefit from the use of Malvern and Richards' D-measure – a recently developed type/token measure which cancels out the length factor (Duran et al 2004).

Lexical sophistication (rareness) refers to the number of relatively unusual or advanced words in a text. Although this can be operationalised in different ways, words above the most frequent 2,000 words of English were considered low-frequency enough to be advanced for this group of test takers. Such information relates closely to the notion of a learner's lexical frequency profile. It is generally recognised that learners learn more frequent words before less frequent words and that a typical learner has a vocabulary where they know the most words in the highest frequency band, the next highest number of words in the next band and so forth. This means they will know some relatively rare words while not knowing all of the more frequent

Table 4.14 Frequency distribution of examinee output across Main Suite examination levels (%)

	KET	PET	FCE	CAE	CPE
1st 1,000	86.32	90.97	85.26	85.94	86.51
2nd 1,000	5.50	3.86	5.71	6.09	5.12
Academic Word List	0.28	0.34	1.77	2.13	2.43
Other words	7.90	4.83	7.26	5.84	5.94

ones. With this in mind, Laufer and Nation (1995) suggest that the best way to describe a learner's vocabulary is with a profile, rather than a single number. The Lexical Tutor was used to analyse test-taker output according to their vocabulary profile.

Interestingly, a lexical profile of the vocabulary occurring in the five levels does not show any strong patterning to indicate increasing lexical mastery (Table 4.14).

At the different levels, test takers produce a very similar profile in terms of frequency. The possible exception concerns academic words, which showed a steady increase, and a significant shift between PET and FCE, but the percentage increase is still small. It seems that a frequency analysis, at least at this 1,000 banding level of analysis, cannot be used to discriminate test takers of different levels. Even a more detailed lexical analysis comparing candidates who performed relatively well or poorly within each level showed little evidence that those attracting higher marks are systematically using lower frequency vocabulary than poorer examinees. Overall it seems that a lexical profile analysis may be too crude a measure to differentiate between better and poorer performances; this is perhaps to be expected since raters use a range of criteria besides vocabulary.

Summary and implications for the Cambridge Main Suite examinations

Schmitt (2005) concludes that none of the above measures seems sufficiently sensitive to describe how test-takers' lexical performance differs across various levels. Similarly, they do not show the examinees' increasingly advanced lexis as indicated by their correspondingly higher marks. The quantitative measures currently available continue to struggle to adequately describe test-taker output. Instead, a more qualitative analysis may be preferable which takes into account how well the words are used. This qualitative approach is one adopted by the Cambridge ESOL examiners when rating Writing scripts. Some guidance for this is provided in the general and task specific mark schemes for Writing assessment. Examiners intuitively judge the vocabulary in each written response according to whether the correct meaning is used, whether the collocations and phraseology are natural, and whether each word is used with the expected register. Unfortunately, there are currently no automated procedures which can replicate the examiner's thorough individual attention and intuitions. Schmitt suggests some manual procedures which give an indication of increasing lexical mastery, but notes their shortcomings:

> *Collocation*: concordance lines of an individual test-taker's output can be generated and the collocations in that output compared to corpus results or to other test takers at other proficiency levels. However, this would have to be done on a word-by-word basis, which would limit it to words occurring in multiple texts across the levels (a time-consuming and labour-intensive process).

> *Error analysis*: this is another possible measure for assessing vocabulary mastery but this approach is beset by numerous problems, chief among them the difficulty in reliably identifying and categorising the lexical errors. This is being done by Cambridge University Press using a system of error-codes (Nicholls 2003).

Schmitt (2005) concludes his report on lexical progression in Cambridge Main Suite examinations with a useful review of the differences that can be noted between the levels. He argues that most of the criteria used in the summary table of lexical progression (Table 4.15) are functional in nature, and this is appropriate, as a straight frequency analysis did not differentiate either levels, or students within a level, very well. At the KET and PET levels, the main lexical feature seems to be how well vocabulary is used to realise functional language. This means that test takers can be expected to produce vocabulary which allows the effective use of the required functions. Although most of this vocabulary will be frequent, some of it will not be, which means that wordlists with a functional component are necessary, i.e. the Waystage and Threshold lists and wordlists derived from KET/PET lists.

At the FCE level candidates need enough vocabulary to go into topics in detail, and to be much more precise in stating and obtaining information than is the case at PET. This moves beyond the functional language of KET and PET, towards a more transactional language, requiring some lower frequency vocabulary (e.g. a greater range of adjectives for describing) necessary to state ideas with more precision. Matching the FCE requirements with a wordlist is difficult. In general frequency terms, Schmitt suspects that the vocabulary required will be beyond the most frequent 2,000 words, but less than the 5,000 frequency band, which is where he estimates CAE would lie.

The CAE level description ('ability to use English well in almost any situation, but perhaps not with the proficiency expected at CPE level') indicates that examinees need to know a lot of vocabulary. It is difficult to prescribe an existing vocabulary list which would satisfy this remit. Perhaps the way to approach this problem is to specify what a broad 'general' vocabulary entails.

Nation (2001) suggests that 5,000 word families is about the end of general use vocabulary, and that beyond this people need to start learning the technical vocabulary related to their field, or whatever topics they wish to be conversant in. This may be a useful guide for Writing items at this level though it is interesting to note that the candidate output does not appear to contain much vocabulary at the 'beyond 2,000' level.

Schmitt proposes that the more academic tasks are what distinguish the CAE level because they entail mastery (or developing mastery) of the Academic Word List (AWL), and the ability to communicate effectively in one's own field of expertise. One way this might be operationalised is according to cognitive level, for example:

- literal
- inferential
- analytical
- synthetic
- evaluative.

A literal description is less cognitively demanding than having to infer information which is not explicitly stated and cognitive demands increase up the hierarchy. KET and PET require language use which is mostly at the literal level, but at FCE and the higher levels the demands become greater. However, this impacts most at CAE where candidates are required to use the higher-level processes, and have the vocabulary available to allow these processes to operate. Although item writers do not have a specific vocabulary list to refer to, they are successful in writing items that require many more lexical resources than items at the FCE level. Language at a high level contains appropriate collocations and phraseology, idiomatic elements, and expected register marking. In Schmitt's experience, these are the aspects which most reliably distinguish between learners at the higher levels. At CPE level, the candidate is expected to have a vocabulary approximating to that of an educated native speaker. The real difference between the higher levels (and perhaps all levels) is how well the words are used, as indicated in the mark scheme: sophisticated and/or fluent use of vocabulary, collocation and expression appropriate to the task. These are qualitative variables, and at present there is no satisfactory way to quantify them, other than with an intensive corpus analysis of each individual word or phrase (see Hawkey and Barker 2004).

Schmitt concludes that the quantitative measures employed for his analysis of candidate output, i.e. lexical density, lexical variation, lexical frequency profiling are not particularly robust in describing how performance on the various proficiency levels differs. Lexical density of candidate output does not seem to vary significantly across the levels or distinguish meaningfully between the levels or the candidates at each level. This may reflect the general nature of the Writing tasks set, avoidance strategies used by candidates in examination settings or the inability of analysis programmes to pick up on multi-word use.

It may be that candidate use of vocabulary does not differ significantly across levels due to the influence of task, topic or conditions of output. The literature also suggests that topic may influence productive vocabulary use, not just in that it may constrain it to particular lexical fields but also because (lack of) engagement by a writer in a particular topic may produce varying levels of lexical density. Tasks may be generating language that is considered lower than the level. Further work is needed to investigate the effect of the attractiveness of topic on lexical variety and richness in exam scripts, and their implications for frequency counts.

Questions remain over whether frequency of occurrence is an adequate criterion for distinguishing between proficiency levels. 'Get' and 'set' and 'mean', for example, may be high-frequency words, but are also polysemous and it would be important to know which of their meanings learners can be expected to know at any given level. In addition, a functional criterion may be required, to distinguish between everyday, personalised and academic purposes for language use. At more advanced levels the influence of colloca-tion, phraseology, idiom and register may well be more significant in distin-guishing between levels, though automated rather than manual measures for confirming this are not readily available.

Despite these difficulties, efforts continue to address lexical progression in Cambridge ESOL examinations within the limitations of current knowledge and to engage in a longer term research agenda which will extend our under-standing of the nature and development of L2 learners' lexical resources.

Summary of lexical resources across Cambridge ESOL levels

At the KET and PET level lexical items normally occur in the everyday vocabulary of native speakers using English. At FCE topics need to be addressed in more detail and with greater lexical precision. For CAE and above the language expected is more sophisticated and the tasks more lexi-cally challenging than at FCE. Topics, tasks and functions which only require simple language are avoided at the higher levels. At FCE and above there is also an expectation that candidates are able to reformulate input lan-guage in their own words. Language associated with conative functions is needed for tasks at CAE and CPE. (See Table 4.15.)

Structural resources

The CEFR (Council of Europe 2001) provides no guidance on the structural range candidates might be expected to deploy in Writing tasks at various

Table 4.15 Lexical resources in Main Suite examinations

KET	PET	FCE	CAE	CPE
Basic everyday vocabulary of native speaker.	General vocabulary sufficient for most topics in everyday life.	Good range of vocabulary. Topics need to be addressed in more detail and with greater precision.	Broad range of vocabulary including idiomatic expressions and colloquialisms.	Very wide range of vocabulary including idiomatic expressions and colloquialisms.
Waystage (Van Ek and Trim 1991a) and other high-frequency words from corpus evidence.	**Threshold** (Van Ek and Trim 1991) and other high-frequency words from corpus evidence.	**Vantage** (Van Ek and Trim 2001) and other high-frequency words from corpus evidence.	Ability to use vocabulary appropriate to specific contexts demonstrating mastery of a particular domain.	As for CAE but with a range and appropriateness of vocabulary which could be expected for an educated native speaker.
Lexis appropriate to simple personal requirements.	Lexis appropriate to personal requirements.	Specified general lexis as appropriate to the specified functions, i.e. giving details, making plans, requesting details/ information, inviting suggestions.		Written output which could be used in real-world professional contexts without having to be substantially edited or rewritten (other than what might be expected if an educated native speaker wrote the piece).
Mainly literal use.	Mainly literal use.	Literal + some inferential evaluative/ synthesis/ analytical use.	Literal/inferential evaluative/ synthesis/ analytical use.	Literal/ evaluative/ synthesis/ analytical use.

levels of ability. This is inevitable given that the CEFR was not written as a language specific document but as one that would serve to guide the teaching and learning of a range of European languages. While the lexical domains and functions which the learner of English, Spanish, Danish or Hungarian needs to acquire will be equivalent, the structural patterns which the learner has to master will inevitably vary from language to language.

This has consequences for the use of the CEFR in schools. Keddle (2004:43–4) noted that the CEFR did not measure grammar-based progression and this was problematic in relating the descriptors to the students' achievements. She argued that as a course designer she would have been happier if there were more explicit guidance in relation to grammatical appropriateness at the various levels.

The structures which learners need in order to be able to cope appropriately with the functions identified at levels from A2 to B2 in the CEFR have been identified and are listed in the books describing the Waystage, Threshold and Vantage levels and in the handbooks for KET and PET. At higher levels in the CEFR there has as yet been no such systematic attempt to match structures with level. One of the main objectives of the English Profile Project (see Chapter 8) over the next decade is to provide such description. The taxonomy of stylistic markers provided by Biber (1991) should prove useful in this further research as will the work being done in relation to the ongoing development of a Common Scale for Writing at Cambridge (see the section on knowledge of criteria on pages 78–9 and the case study of the CSW in Chapter 5), and developments in our knowledge of structural progression from Second Language Acquisition research (Pienemann 1998).

By PET or B1 level, many of the basic structures of English have already been taught. B2 level students will have covered the full repertoire of verb forms and other key structures. Only a few major patterns – such as rhetorical uses of inversion or more sophisticated uses of modals remain. Most of the rest of the grammar work to be done with C1 and C2 learners is a matter of recycling as it will focus on improving the learners' accuracy and confidence in handling the structures they were taught at lower levels, allowing them to express themselves accurately and appropriately, using a range of structures and showing some sensitivity to register.

Structural resources: Cambridge practice

In general, in the Cambridge ESOL Main Suite examinations, the Writing tasks do not force the use of specific structures. They set tasks which give candidates the opportunity to demonstrate their structural resources to the best of their ability. The success with which they do so is assessed by the grading descriptors which become steadily more demanding as candidates progress up the levels (see the section on knowledge of criteria on pages 77–80). The extent of what candidates are expected to produce also rises steadily through the levels and this puts increasing demands on learners' structural resources (O'Dell 2005).

KET

All grammatical structures tested must fall within the KET Grammatical Specification, which itself relates to Waystage. The Writing tasks are therefore expressed so as to require candidates to use structures that they should be familiar with. As far as the one open-ended Writing task, Part 9, is concerned, the verb forms which students are most likely to be required to handle are the present simple or continuous, the past simple, future with 'will' and 'going to', the first conditional and the modals 'can', 'could', 'may', 'must' and 'should'.

The ability to produce other grammatical forms such as the past continuous, the present perfect, pronouns, demonstratives, quantifiers, comparatives, adverbs and prepositions may be observed through the open cloze exercise that constitutes Part 7 as well as through the candidates' responses to Part 9.

Parts 6 and 8 also involve the candidates in writing but they only have to produce lexical items. Of course, as in all other tasks in the paper, these tasks require students to understand grammatical forms of the types listed in the Specification.

The input for the tasks is carefully constructed to avoid ambiguity and to ensure that candidates are not prevented from showing their writing skills by a failure to understand what was expected of them. The content of what is to be written is tightly controlled by the wording of the task.

PET

All grammatical structures tested must fall within the PET Grammatical Specification, which itself relates to Threshold.

In Part 1, candidates might, for example, have to employ an appropriate adverb, adjective, preposition, conjunction or verb form in the structural transformation. The basic verb forms that they must be able to handle at this level are the same as for KET with the addition of the past continuous, past perfect simple, passives and the second conditional. Additional grammatical items which are introduced at PET level include 'used to', 'causative have/get', simple reported speech, and phrasal verb patterns.

Part 2 is less constrained but the content of what candidates write is tightly controlled by the bullet points they are provided with. Part 3 allows a degree of free writing of one of the genres which are likely to be most familiar to candidates, an informal letter or a story.

From PET level upwards, there is an element of choice as far as one of the Writing tasks is concerned. However, care is taken in the trialling process (see Appendix E) to ensure that the structural demands on the learner are at an equivalent level regardless of which task is selected.

The difference in grammatical ability between KET and PET levels lies not so much in there being an extended range of structures which students are expected to know as in the degree to which they are expected to be able to produce as well as understand them. The amount and scope of the writing that PET candidates are expected to produce (35–45 words in Part 2 and 100 words in Part 3) is significantly greater than the 25–35 words required of KET candidates.

FCE

At this point there ceases to be a Grammatical Specification. The tasks are designed to ensure that candidates demonstrate an ability to produce a range of structures. The assumption is that, at FCE (Vantage/B2) level, learners will have reasonable competence in handling all the basic verb forms and structural patterns of English. It can be assumed that the PET Grammatical Specifications would at FCE level be supplemented by such grammatical structures as the third conditional, past modal forms such as 'should have', 'might have', 'must have', more complex reported speech patterns and a fuller range of passive forms, including the present perfect passive, which is notably absent from the *Threshold* list.

FCE-level candidates tend either to write simply and accurately or to write in a somewhat more ambitious way but then to make more grammatical errors. Both of these approaches will allow a candidate to be considered 'minimally adequate' from the point of view of grammar.

CAE

Above FCE level there are relatively few new aspects of grammar to introduce. These include structures that are mainly used for rhetorical effect and are, therefore, not an essential part of the writer's repertoire; for example,

- aspects of inversion such as 'Had I known . . .', 'No sooner had she arrived home than . . . ', 'Up the hill rolled the carriage'
- complex sentences using less frequent connectors such as 'provided that', 'as long as', 'notwithstanding', 'lest'
- the use of ellipsis
- cleft sentences and fronting
- complex noun phrases
- more sophisticated uses of modals.

The tasks lend themselves to structural range in the CAE Writing paper and candidates who demonstrate their ability to use the new structures accurately and appropriately will be given credit for doing so. The part of the mark scheme that deals with range would account for candidates getting credit for this kind of language.

Similarly, understanding of the key features of the input does not depend on an appreciation of these more obscure aspects of grammar. Care is taken to ensure that the input is at a rather lower level than, say, the texts used in the CAE Reading paper. This is done to ensure that, as far as possible, the Writing paper tests the candidates' ability to write; candidates are not penalised in this paper by having weaker reading skills.

In terms of what students are expected to produce, all tasks are (as at other levels) appropriately stretching for the candidates. They are more demanding than FCE tasks in terms of the range of structures required for a good response. Although the successful CAE-level candidate may still make grammatical errors, these should not result in misunderstanding or in offence being taken.

The input does, however, provide a certain structure for the candidate. The issues which they have to address in their writing are spelled out clearly, often through the use of bullet points. In the compulsory Part 1 task relatively little invention is demanded of the candidate although there will be scope for more ambitious learners to show their greater proficiency skills.

Again the length of the Writing tasks demanded of candidates imposes demands on their grammatical knowledge. The marking criteria also determine what is expected of candidates' use of grammar at this level. As range is an important factor which markers take into account, candidates who are, say, required to give advice have to do so in a variety of ways, not just by writing 'you should . . .'.

CPE

The range of language structures available to candidates at C1 and C2 levels are ostensibly similar but there are a few differences as illustrated in Table 4.17 for the December 2003 tasks on page 113. The real difference lies in how well the C2 or CPE candidate can draw on the full range of structures and make appropriate use of them. The CEFR says that at this level learners 'can exploit a comprehensive and reliable mastery of a very wide range of language to formulate thoughts precisely, give emphasis, differentiate and eliminate ambiguity'. Clearly the ability to use structures effectively is one aspect of the mastery of the wide range of language expected at this level.

Once again, rather greater demands are placed on the extent of what candidates are expected to write. They must write answers to two tasks of 300–350 words. This is slightly more than is expected of CAE candidates in the same amount of time.

In terms of input, care is taken to ensure that the language will not cause any problems for candidates. Unduly complex structures are not used in the input. It does, however, provide rather less support for the candidate than at CAE level. Candidates are set a somewhat more open task (constructed so as to be accessible to the majority) and have to think rather more about how to structure and present their ideas.

Tasks at CPE level demand more than a straightforward presentation of information. Candidates have to make more decisions about what their content should be as well as how to structure their work than at CAE level. Tasks require candidates to present ideas and opinions with a degree of subtlety and with good organisational skills. This clearly puts demands on the structural resources available to the candidate. They cannot perform well unless they can effectively make use of, for example, linking devices, referencing words, modals and the language of hypothesising.

As with all the tasks in the suite, the descriptors used in marking scripts are of key importance. Range, organisation and accuracy are all taken into account when examiners are looking at grammatical use in CPE scripts and expectations are proportionately higher of candidates at this level. To demonstrate a more than adequate level of performance, a candidate must use a range of structures, demonstrate a high level of accuracy and present ideas and opinions in a well-organised fashion.

The structural resources of tasks can be viewed in light of what candidates were expected to produce during the December 2003 and March 2004 administrations of the Main Suite examinations as shown in the tables below. Although the precise structures required by the tasks set in any administration vary to some degree, these tables provide a typical picture of the range of structures that candidates at specific levels may be expected to write.

Table 4.16 Structural resources of March 2004 tasks

KET	PET
Part 9: Structures as appropriate to the specified functions and lexis e.g. future, present simple, progressive tenses, main and subordinate clauses, first conditional, polite command forms.	**Part 2:** Structures as appropriate to the specified functions and lexis e.g. past tense forms, present continuous, past simple, prepositions of location and event description; comparatives and superlatives; sequence of event linkers; interrogatives; modals.
	Part 3: Present continuous, past simple, past continuous, past perfect simple (narrative), future with present continuous and present simple; modals; interrogatives; conditional sentences.

Table 4.17 Structural resources of December 2003 tasks

FCE	CAE	CPE
Structures as appropriate to the specified functions and lexis, e.g. future, present simple, progressive tenses, statement and question forms, first conditional, polite command forms.	Structures as appropriate to the specified functions and lexis, e.g. present simple, present perfect, future tenses; reason and purpose structures; explaining structures; comparatives and superlatives; organising and linking devices; complex sentence structures.	Structures as appropriate to the specified functions and lexis, e.g. present perfect, future tense; coherent organisation; linking devices; reasoned argument; justification, developing arguments through complex structures.

Summary of structural resources across Cambridge ESOL levels

There is a gradual progression in the complexity of the grammatical constructions required by tasks. This is in line with the structural levels appearing in English Language Teaching (ELT) coursebooks aimed at language levels corresponding to the Council of Europe levels A1 (KET) through to C2 (CPE). At KET level candidates are expected to have control over only the simplest exponents for the Waystage functions at this level. The marker is tolerant of basic errors such as missing third person 's' and misuse of articles. At PET level candidates show a degree of ability to handle some of the exponents listed at Threshold level. Although the marker is primarily interested in the extent to which meaning is conveyed, control with regard to such basic structures as 'to be' agreement is expected. However, in PET Part 3 where candidates demonstrate ambition their writing may be judged adequate even if flawed. At FCE level candidates should have a good grasp of Vantage-level language. They should have mastered the main structures of the language and should not be prevented from communicating by a lack of structural resources. As long as the marker does not have to make an effort to understand the writer's meaning, errors with such aspects of language as gerunds/infinitives or some confusion between the past simple and present perfect will not be unduly penalised. At FCE level candidates tend to write either simply and accurately or more ambitiously but less accurately. Both types of candidates may achieve adequate performance if other aspects of their writing are satisfactory. By CAE candidates are expected to use the structures of the language with ease and fluency. There should be some evidence of range; very simple but accurate language is not enough at this level. Candidates must be able to demonstrate some ability to use complex structures even though they are not expected to write error-free prose. CAE candidates must also show that they have a grasp

Table 4.18 Structural resources of Main Suite examinations

KET	PET	FCE	CAE	CPE
Waystage level (Van Ek and Trim 1991a).	Threshold level (Van Ek and Trim 1991).	Vantage level (Van Ek and Trim 2001). Learners at this level are able to use all the main tense forms and structural patterns of English.	The writer is able to adjust his or her writing to suit the context and the target reader adopting a style that will convey the intended message in an appropriate way.	The writer is able to use grammar to organise writing effectively and to express subtle differences of meaning and attitude.

of structures which allow them to express opinions and feelings in an appropriate register. They can, for example, express dissatisfaction in a manner that does not sound aggressive by using appropriately tentative structures. By CPE level candidates should demonstrate a high degree of range and accuracy with regard to structures. They should have a mastery of the structures needed to present ideas and attitude in a well-organised and sophisticated manner. Some errors will be tolerated so long as they do not confuse the reader in any way; for example, an inappropriate use of a preposition after a verb or an omitted article will not in themselves cause the candidate to lose marks.

Discourse mode

Urquhart and Weir (1998:141ff) argued that test developers must generate evidence on which discourse modes are appropriate at each proficiency level. Investigating the nature and impact of discourse mode is, however, beset by two problems. First, there is little agreement in the literature on the terminology that should be used to classify different texts and second, the effect of texts required on the difficulty level of the task is not that well researched at the moment.

Alderson (n.d.) highlights the difficulty in determining the types of written and spoken texts that might be appropriate for each level in the CEFR. Part of the problem in addressing this deficiency is the plethora of different schemes for analysing discourse. We confine ourselves below to those that seem most helpful for analysing Cambridge examinations in accessible terms, and in particular we draw on the work of Weigle. According to Weigle (2002:62) discourse mode includes the categories of genre, rhetorical task, and patterns of exposition:

> The **genre** refers to the expected form and communicative function of the written product; for example, a letter, an essay, or a laboratory report. The **rhetorical task** is broadly defined as one of the traditional discourse modes of narration, description, exposition, and argument/persuasion, as specified in the prompt, while the **pattern of exposition** (Hale et al 1996) refers to subcategories of exposition or specific instructions to the test taker to make comparisons, outline causes and effects, and so on.

In relation to the 'prompt' or stimulus for a Writing task, Hamp-Lyons and Prochnow (1991; see also Hamp-Lyons and Mathias 1994) identified a range of prompts which they categorised according to five task types: expository/private; expository/public; argumentative/private; argumentative/public, and combined-type. They attempted to correlate task difficulty (as perceived by expert raters) with overall Writing scores. Postulating that the more difficult task types would engender weaker responses and hence lower Writing performance scores, they found to their surprise that this was not the case.

Hamp-Lyons and Prochnow's research thus seems to add to generally conflicting evidence from the L1 and L2 literature on perceived Writing task-type difficulty and its effect on Writing test results. Brossell and Ash (1984) and Hoetker and Brossell (1989), in their studies undertaken with L1 writers, observed no appreciable differences in the test scores awarded to essays employing differences in the wording of their prompts.

In the area of L2 writing, Carlson et al (1985) observed the influence of different topic types (comparison/contrast and iconic interpretation) on the rank-ordering of candidates sitting the Test of Written English (TWE). By analysing correlations of global scores they noted that correlations were similarly high both across, and within, the two topics.

Some researchers in contrast have found differences. In their L1 investigation of 11th and 12th graders, Quellmalz et al (1982) observed that, in the main, performance on expository tasks outweighed performance on narrative tasks. Hoetker (1982) attributed the lower scores observed in the California State University and Colleges Equivalency Examination for 1974 (compared to the previous year) to the different task requirements: the earlier task being more reflective and based upon personal experience; the later task demanding thinking of a more abstract nature.

In her comparative analysis of FCE and TOEFL, Weigle (2002:153) states that the construct being measured by the FCE examination is more difficult to define than its TOEFL counterpart:

> The FCE, with two tasks, samples the domain of interest somewhat more widely than the TOEFL, and the different rating scales reflect the fact that different genres and tasks make use of different dimensions of writing ability and thus may give a truer picture of the test takers' range of abilities in writing than does the TOEFL. On the other hand, the variety of possible test tasks in the FCE may make it difficult to say exactly what it is that the FCE is testing, as two test takers writing on very different tasks may arrive at similar scores through very different means (2002:153–4).

Weir (2005b:68–9) argues that:

> In writing tests, increasing the number of samples of a student's work that are taken can help reduce the variation in performance that might occur from task to task [a view supported by Jacobs et al (1981:15)]. . . . student performance will vary even on very similar tasks as well as when writing in different discourse modes. This argues for sampling students' writing ability over a number of tasks, typical and appropriate to their discourse community . . . [this] has obvious implications for test practicality, particularly in terms of time . . . The more samples of a student's writing in a test, the more reliable the assessment is likely to be [in terms of both

content coverage and reliability of score] and the more confidently we can generalize from performance on the test tasks [to real world behaviour].

In high stakes tests it would be imprudent to rely on a single sample if important decisions are going to be made on the basis of evidence provided by the test.

Discourse mode: Cambridge practice

In FCE, CAE and CPE examinations candidates are expected to complete tasks which differ in terms of genre, rhetorical task and patterns of exposition. In FCE, CAE and CPE Part 2 questions, test takers have a choice of different options from which to select. With two tasks, these Writing tests sample a wide domain of interest. The rationale for selection is based upon the expectation that test takers will find at least one of the available tasks relevant not only to their own particular background, but also to their specific objectives for learning English. 'The tasks themselves simulate genuine real-world tasks, and the fact that an audience and purpose are specified for each task adds to their authenticity' (Weigle 2002:154).

After each examination administration the uptake of optional questions is studied alongside the examiners' ratings of candidate scripts and the range of marks awarded for each question. The uptake of Part 2 questions is useful for determining suitable question formats and topics for future papers. Uptake figures are used by Cambridge ESOL to improve the face validity of future question papers for candidates and additionally to determine what factors in a question allow candidates to show their strengths. The interaction of how candidates score on each question is also analysed, as is the rating behaviour of examiners. While Cambridge ESOL does not publish detailed question paper statistics it does provide examination reports for the majority of its examinations, which describe how candidates responded to questions, gives the uptake of optional questions, lists Do's and Don'ts to help teachers to prepare candidates more effectively for each paper and provides substantial information on candidate preparation.

In the case of the CAE Writing paper, for example, a survey over a four-year period (2000–2003) covering 16 sessions (two per year for two versions) has been undertaken (Barker and Betts 2004). The investigation included 64 optional questions, each of which was selected by a minimum of 8% of candidates and a maximum of 64% in any one administration. The Part 2 questions covered a range of 16 topics, the most common ones being: work (30% of questions); language learning (10% of questions); social/national customs (10% of questions); people (8% of questions). A total of 13 task types were included in the CAE Writing paper. The most common format for optional

CAE Writing tasks has been an *article* (over 20% of questions), followed closely by *competition entries*, *proposals* and *reports* which together account for 40% of Writing tasks. Just under 10% of tasks required candidates to write *text for a leaflet*. In December 2003, for instance, Question 2 (article) was the most popular option in both versions, with 44% and 35% of candidates choosing this task. In version A there was a varied spread of question uptake, with Question 5 (work-related letter) being attempted by 30% of candidates and a smaller though similar number of candidates attempting Questions 3 (reference) and 4 (proposal – approximately 14%). In version B Questions 3 (reference) and 5 (work-related letter) were chosen by just under 30% of candidates with Question 4 (review) being the least popular, being attempted by only 7% of candidates. It is clear, therefore, that CAE candidates choose from the whole range of Part 2 questions available and this suggests that all of these choices are suitable for this candidature.

Table 4.19 illustrates types of discourse mode in relation to the levels of genre and rhetorical task across the Main Suite examinations.

Summary of discourse mode across Cambridge ESOL levels

There appears to be a clear distinction between PET and FCE. At FCE the rhetorical task of argument differentiates it from PET and discursive tasks are important throughout FCE, CAE and CPE. CAE is differentiated from FCE by the greater range of genres the candidate might have to address overall and in the compulsory Part 1 task having to deal with varying degrees of persuasion with the intended audience having to be convinced of the writer's point of view. At CPE candidates might have to write an essay (a genre not previously encountered at lower levels). (See Table 4.19.)

Functional resources

Weir (2005a:294) notes:

> Based on the foundations of the earlier functional-notional approach to language in Europe (Threshold Level, Waystage and Vantage studies) and the ground-breaking empirical work of North (2000) in calibrating functions on to a common scale, functional competence is well mapped out in the CEFR [Council of Europe 2001] and is one of its major strengths.

The work of North and his colleagues building on over 30 years' work in this area by the Council of Europe has resulted in functional requirements at the various levels being clearly defined in Cambridge examinations. With its focus on language as a means of communication, the Common

Table 4.19 Discourse modes in Main Suite examinations

Genre refers to 'the expected form and communicative function of the written product . . . essay, letter, informal note, advertisement' (Weigle 2002:62–3);
Rhetorical task refers to 'one of the traditional discourse models of narration, description, exposition, and argument/persuasion, as specified in the prompt' (Weigle 2002:62);
Pattern of exposition (Hale et al 1996): 'refers to subcategories of exposition or specific instructions to the test taker to make comparisons, outline causes and effects and so on' (Weigle 2002:62). Examples of patterns of exposition include '. . . process, comparison/ contrast, cause/effect, classification, definition' (Weigle 2002:63).

To comment meaningfully on patterns of exposition it is necessary to consider specific individual questions as this category analyses tasks in detailed rather than general terms. In effect, a consideration of patterns of exposition focuses on those aspects of language which are dealt with in the section of this chapter that looks at functional resources and so this aspect of a task is not explored further in this section.

KET	Part 9 **Genre**: note, postcard, email. **Rhetorical Task**: narration, description.
PET	Part 2 **Genre**: postcard, note, email. **Rhetorical Task**: description, expository. Part 3 **Genre**: informal letter or story. **Rhetorical Task**: narration, description, expository.
FCE	Part 1 (Q1) **Genre**: transactional letter (formal/informal). **Rhetorical Task**: narration, description, expository, argument. Part 2 **Genre**: an article, a non-transactional letter, a report, a discursive composition, a short story, a letter of application. **Rhetorical Task**: narration, description, expository, argument. *Q5 (prescribed background reading)* **Genre**: an article, an informal letter, a report, a composition. **Rhetorical Task**: narration, description, expository, argument.
CAE	Parts 1 and 2 **Genre**: informal/formal letter, article (newspaper and magazine), report, proposal, text for a leaflet, review, competition entry, contribution (to e.g. a guidebook, directory, brochure or similar document), application, information sheet, memo (Q5 only). **Rhetorical Task**: narration, description, exposition, and justification/persuasion.
CPE	Part 1 **Genre**: letter (formal or semi-formal), article, proposal, essay. **Rhetorical Task**: narration, description, exposition, and argument/persuasion. Part 2 *Q2–5* **Genre**: letter (formal or semi-formal), article, proposal, report, review. **Rhetorical Task**: narration, description, exposition, and argument/persuasion.

European Framework puts language functions in a central position and, consequently, language learners are graded in terms of what they can do with the language rather than on, say, an ability to handle specific grammatical structures or to translate increasingly complex texts. This is consistent with the communicative approach to language teaching and is reflected in most contemporary course materials; while usually retaining some degree of work on teaching and awareness of grammar, these materials also make a point of teaching learners how to cope with functional-notional demands such as giving advice, describing people or expressing preferences in the target language.

Functional resources: Cambridge practice

Given this central role for functions in language learning, it is appropriate that in the Cambridge examinations Writing tasks are usually explicitly presented to candidates in terms of the functions which they are required to demonstrate (O'Dell 2005a). A typical PET Part 2 task, for instance, asks candidates to write an email in which they:

'invite . . .'

'say when . . .'

'explain why . . .'

A key aspect of a functional approach to language learning is that many functions can appropriately be tested at a range of levels. There are some basic functions which candidates may be expected to perform at any level – candidates from KET level upwards may be asked to express opinions, for example talking about likes and dislikes at KET or expressing opinions in an argument at FCE. In such cases, learners show their level by the range of exponents which they can use to perform that function and by the degree of sophistication with which they can put across their views.

However, there are also other functions which will not be tested until the higher levels of examination. Hypothesising, for instance, is not a function which candidates at lower levels would be expected to be able to handle.

In considering functional resources as they relate to the different levels of the Cambridge ESOL Main Suite of examinations we need to consider both the tasks that candidates are set and also the approach to the assessment of candidate responses to the tasks.

KET

The functions which candidates are expected to handle at KET level are listed in Waystage and in the KET Handbook (2005g) under the heading: *Inventory of Functions, Notions and Communicative Tasks.*

As far as writing is concerned the most relevant of these functions are:

- asking for and giving personal details
- asking for and giving information about routines and habits

- giving information about everyday activities
- talking about past events, recent activities and completed actions
- talking about future plans or intentions
- asking for and giving simple information about places
- expressing purpose, cause and result and giving reasons
- making and responding to offers and suggestions
- expressing thanks
- giving and responding to invitations
- giving advice
- expressing preferences, likes and dislikes (especially about hobbies and leisure activities)
- expressing opinions and making choices.

Other functions listed in the handbook – such as asking and answering questions about personal possessions or giving directions – may occasionally be required of the candidates at KET level.

At KET level, communication of the message is paramount and so long as the message is conveyed lexical inaccuracies are tolerated. In other words, as far as functional resources are concerned, KET candidates are expected to be able to deal with a range of everyday basic functions but at a fairly minimal level.

PET

At PET level, too, a full list of language specifications is given in the handbook under the heading: *Inventory of Functions, Notions and Communicative Tasks* (2005). These reflect the functions outlined at the Threshold level of the CEFR.

As far as PET Writing tasks are concerned, the key new functions are:

- letters giving information about everyday activities
- producing simple narratives
- writing about future or imaginary situations
- describing simple processes
- drawing simple conclusions and making recommendations.

The essential changes at PET level, as far as functional resources are concerned, are that candidates are now expected to be able to handle the more demanding genre of the letter, in addition to the postcard, note or message. They are also expected to be able to move beyond the personal and informational into narrative and imaginary situations.

As well as the new functions indicated above, all the functions from the KET list are also included on the PET list. The difference at PET level is that candidates are expected to be able to demonstrate an ability to handle these functions at greater length and with a somewhat higher degree of accuracy.

In PET Part 3, the overarching function of the writing is provided by the genre candidates choose – writing a letter or producing a narrative – but other functions such as describing people and places or talking about feelings may also come into play.

Not only do PET candidates have to write more but they are also understandably expected to write rather better than at the lower level; they are, for example, expected to show ambition and range in terms of structure and vocabulary. In the story, for example, they are expected to use a range of tenses and variety of adjectives, etc.

To sum up, PET candidates have to demonstrate rather more breadth and also more depth as far as functional resources are concerned. This is demonstrated by looking at both the tasks candidates are set and at the criteria which assessors use when grading candidates' performance.

FCE

From FCE level upwards no list of specified functions is provided in the exam handbook. FCE, however, is at Vantage or B2 level and this determines the functions which learners at this level are expected to be able to handle. By this stage learners are considered to be 'independent users' able to operate in a range of personal and social situations in English.

The writing skills appropriate to the level can be summed up in functional Can Do statements in the ALTE Can Do project as:

- I can write clear, detailed text on a wide range of subjects related to my interests.
- I can write an essay or report, passing on information or giving reasons in support of or against a particular point of view.
- I can write letters highlighting the personal significance of events and experiences.

FCE Part 1 is always a transactional letter based on a substantial piece of input and tasks involve such functions as requesting, giving information, persuading, suggesting, making arrangements, complaining and criticising, correcting, expanding, describing, narrating, explaining and thanking. The main functions that tend to be tested in Part 2 are giving information, narrating, describing people and places, giving opinions and expressing attitudes, comparing, arguing a point of view, evaluating, giving instructions, recommending and drawing conclusions.

FCE, therefore, is more demanding than PET in that FCE candidates:

- have to write more, which inevitably means demonstrating more sophisticated functional skills

- have to process more input, which constrains how they approach the functions required by the task
- have to handle a wider range of genres
- have to handle a wider range of functions including in particular discursive functions such as arguing a point of view or evaluating a situation
- are assessed in terms of range and accuracy as well as how effectively they perform the functional demands of the task.

CAE

CAE candidates are at level C1 on the CEFR and are considered as 'competent users'. In functional terms C1 level students should be able to say:

- I can express myself in clear, well-structured text, expressing points of view at some length.
- I can write about complex subjects in a letter, an essay or a report, underlining what I consider to be the salient issues.
- I can select style appropriate to the reader in mind.

As at other levels, the rubrics for all tasks are explicit about the functions which students are required to fulfil in their writing. Functions tested at CAE level typically include comparing/contrasting, complaining, expressing attitude and giving opinions, evaluating, hypothesising, justifying, persuading, prioritising, summarising, advising, apologising, correcting, describing, expanding, explaining, inviting, recommending, requesting, thanking and suggesting. Some of these functions appear for the first time at this level; hypothesising, prioritising and summarising, for example, are functions that are not tested at lower levels. This is because these functions are most typical of writing in an academic or professional context and so are typically found in some of the genres new at this level of the Main Suite. They are also more likely to necessitate the kind of expected word output required at CAE.

Clearly, many of the other functions which are tested in the CAE Writing paper are also tested at lower levels too. The difference at CAE level is that – once again – candidates are expected to write both with more accuracy and using a richer variety of functional exponent. Particularly significant at this level is the fact that candidates are expected to be able to use an appropriate and consistent register of language when meeting the various functional requirements of the question. While an article reviewing a new film, for example, in an international magazine might be written in any of a variety of registers, it should not move from praising in a very formal language to criticising in very informal language unless it is clear this is done deliberately for effect.

CPE

By C2 level in the CEFR, learners have a very good command of written English. They will be able to operate comfortably in the contexts of work and of higher education.

The functional Can Do statements summing up a learner's writing skills at this level say:

- I can write clear, smoothly flowing text in an appropriate style.
- I can write complex letters, reports or articles which present a case with an effective logical structure which helps the recipient to notice and remember significant points.
- I can write summaries and reviews of professional or literary works.

In CPE, candidates are expected to do two pieces of writing of 300–350 words each. The Part 1 task is a response to an input text and the Part 2 task allows candidates to select one of six options (three of which relate to set texts). The only genre that is new to the level is that of the essay.

In Part 1 the writing functions that candidates are asked to demonstrate typically include defending or attacking an argument or opinion, comparing or contrasting aspects of an argument, summarising an argument, explaining a problem and suggesting a solution, or making recommendations having evaluated an idea.

From this list it is clear that functions that relate to aspects of presenting a reasoned argument are key at this level. Candidates may sometimes be expected to produce arguments for and against and sometimes one side of the argument will be what is required.

The functions that are tested in CPE Part 2 are typically drawn from the following: describing, narrating, persuading, complaining, reporting, presenting ideas, making proposals, evaluating, reviewing, outlining, analysing, comparing, contrasting, drawing conclusions, giving/requiring information, giving reasons/explanations, hypothesising, judging priorities, making proposals and recommendations, narrating, persuading and summarising. Table 4.22, showing functional resources in Main Suite examinations, indicates that there are only a few discernible differences in functions between the CPE and CAE Writing examinations. The distinction lies more in the quality of writing that is expected of candidates. Particularly significant is the fact that candidates are expected to write within an appropriate context in an appropriate register and demonstrate sensitivity to their audience. In other words, there are expectations of CPE candidates in terms of their stylistic proficiency in handling functions.

Again, the functional resource of Main Suite tasks can be viewed in light of what candidates were expected to produce during the December 2003

Table 4.20 Functional resources for the March 2004 tasks

KET	PET

Part 9
Note to a friend:
• suggest place to eat
• arrange a time to eat
• offer a suggestion as to where car can be parked.
Giving factual information, making arrangements, making suggestions.
	Part 2
	Postcard to a friend:
	• describe art gallery
	• offer an explanation for choice of postcard
	• enquire about weather in Australia.
	Describing information, providing explanation, requesting information.
	
	Part 3
	Question 7 Letter to penfriend:
	Answering a penfriend's question by offering a suggestion for a present suitable for a teenage boy.
	  Writing a letter, giving information, making suggestions.
	
	Question 8 Story for English teacher:
	Describe or narrate a very unusual evening from either personal experience or experience relating to others.
	  Writing a story, narrating past events, writing about imaginary situations.

and March 2004 administrations (see Tables 4.20 and 4.21, and Appendix A for copies of the papers). Table 4.22 tabulates our findings on the functional resources required by candidates in dealing with Main Suite examinations.

Summary of functional resources across Cambridge ESOL levels

There is a clear functional progression across the first three levels KET, PET and FCE in terms of complexity but also in the degree of precision in the structural exponents employed to fulfil the function(s). Functions associated with conative purposes and argumentative tasks for language appear at CAE. The functions at CAE and CPE are increasingly diverse and demanding and intended to produce more complex structures or collocations.

Content knowledge

Weir (2005b:75) draws attention to the critical importance of the interaction between the writer and the task topic in the writing process: 'The content knowledge required for completing a particular task will affect the way it is dealt with. The relationship between the content of the text and the

Table 4.21 Functional resources for the December 2003 tasks

FCE	CAE	CPE
Part 1 **Letter to penfriend about candidate's proposed visit:** Writing an informal letter Processing information Selecting relevant information Giving information Making suggestions Asking for information Describing people	**Part 1** **Report to club members about proposed trip:** Writing a report Processing information Selecting information Making comparisons Making recommendation Justifying a recommendation	**Part 1** **Essay about value of international sports competitions:** Writing an essay Processing information Selecting information Evaluating information Presenting and developing an argument
Part 2 **Composition on mobile phones:** Writing a composition Giving an opinion Arguing a case	**Part 2** **Article about the environment:** Writing an article Describing a problem Evaluating a situation Giving an opinion	**Part 2** **Article about role of machines in contemporary life:** Writing an article Describing a situation Evaluating a statement Giving and justifying an opinion
Letter of application for weekend job in café: Writing a formal letter Describing people – qualities Offering an explanation	**Reference for friend:** Writing a reference Describing people – character, skills, experience and suitability	**Review of a concert:** Writing a review Describing an event Commenting on an event Giving and justifying an opinion
Article about historical place: Writing an article Describing places Offering an explanation	**Proposal for exhibition stand about country:** Writing a proposal Making suggestions Justifying suggestions	**Report on visit investigating in set book:** Writing a report Giving information Evaluating a place Giving and justifying an opinion
Composition about characters: Writing a formal letter Writing a composition Describing people Expressing attitudes	**Letter about work experience:** Describing a company Describing work Describing people – skills and qualities	**Article about set book:** Writing an article Commenting on set book Giving and justifying an opinion
Article about events in set book: Writing an article Describing events Giving an opinion		**Report about set book:** Writing a report Commenting on character Describing change in character Giving and justifying an opinion
		Essay about set book: Writing an essay Describing a situation Evaluating a situation Giving and justifying an opinion

Table 4.22 Functional resources for all Main Suite examinations

KET	PET	FCE	CAE	CPE
Basic functions relating to personal information, everyday activities and simple social interaction.	As for KET but dealing with those functions with a degree of range and accuracy.	As for PET but dealing with those functions with a greater degree of range and accuracy.	As for FCE but dealing with those functions with a greater degree of range and accuracy.	As for CAE but dealing with those functions with a greater degree of range and accuracy.
Candidates are expected to handle these functions in a simple fashion.	Also some more demanding writing functions in terms of (a) length (b) genre (e.g. writing a letter, writing a narrative) and (c) language skills.	Also more demanding writing functions in terms of (a) length (b) genre (e.g. writing a report, writing a composition) and (c) language skills (e.g. arguing a case, correcting, recommending).	Also more demanding writing functions in terms of (a) length (b) genre (e.g. writing a proposal, writing a leaflet, writing a competition entry (c) language skills (e.g. summarising, hypothesising, prioritising, evaluating, justifying) and (d) register.	Also more demanding writing functions in terms of (a) length (b) genre (writing an essay) (c) language skills (e.g. In Part 1: attacking or defending an argument, explaining an argument and suggesting a solution) and (d) style.
See Handbook and Waystage for full listing of functions.	See Handbook and Threshold for full listing of functions.	See Vantage for listing of functions.		

candidate's *background knowledge* (general knowledge which may or may not be relevant to content of a particular text which includes cultural knowledge) and *subject matter knowledge* (specific knowledge directly relevant to text topic and content) needs to be considered (see Douglas 2000).'

The content knowledge variable is thought of as being a significant variable in test performance (Alderson and Urquhart 1984 and 1985, Park 1988, Clapham 1996, Douglas 2000). Read (1990) provides indisputable evidence that differing topics engender candidate responses that are measurably different. Empirical research by Papajohn (1999:52–81) employing interview, rater survey and test score data, suggests that topic does affect test scores. Read (1990:78) argues that it is a reasonable assumption that we would write better about a familiar topic than an unfamiliar one.

Providing input

There is obviously a good case for providing input in Writing tests where provision of stimulus texts reflects the real-life situation (e.g. writing university assignments). It also ensures equal access to content knowledge among candidates and reduces the potential bias that such internal knowledge can have (Horowitz 1991).

Reporting on the potential effect of task stimulus, Weigle cites an L1 study by Smith et al (1985). In this study, the researchers observed that 'students generally performed better on a task that involved reading several short excerpts on a topic than when they read only one such excerpt' (Weigle 2002:68). The Smith et al (1985) investigation demonstrates the efficacy of a number of short but thematically-linked input texts compared with a solitary, extended one.

The impact of background reading as task input on the quality of L2 written production has also been investigated by Lewkowicz (1997). While offering students a rich source of ideas, the provision of a background text did not appear to enhance quality of writing. Moreover, there was evidence of significant 'lifting' of the input task material by students. Weigle summarises the findings of the Lewkowicz study in the following way: 'writers who were given a text tended to develop their ideas less than students who were not given a text, and also tended to rely heavily on the language of the source text' (2002:68).

There is additional evidence that integrating reading into writing activities presents problems for markers in making decisions about what level of borrowing from these texts is permissible; being confident about what the candidate is capable of actually producing rather than just copying. The extent of borrowing can be reduced by ensuring that the Writing task demands a significant level of input language transformation from the candidate, i.e. the candidate has to do something more than simply lift input material. Weigle (2002:97) provides an example of a task for adult immigrant students taken from Butler et al (1996). Alternatively it may be necessary to make clear to candidates what is not permissible in terms of borrowing from text provided and also limits may have to be set on how much text can be quoted.

A further parameter that can potentially impact on candidate performance is the topic knowledge required for completing a particular task. The CEFR currently provides no guidance as to the topics which might be more or less suitable at differing levels of proficiency (Weir 2005a). We next describe how Cambridge ESOL has addressed the parameter of topic at different levels in its own examinations.

Content knowledge: Cambridge practice

Given the powerful effect that topic may have on performance, candidates should perceive task topics as suitable, realistic, reasonably familiar and feasible (Hamp-Lyons 1990:53). In Cambridge ESOL examinations, the *sine qua non* is that candidates, either through internal knowledge or external knowledge provided by the task input, should have sufficient knowledge of the topic to write to the length prescribed in accordance with the other specified contextual parameters.

In the writing of tasks, Cambridge ESOL considers the following issues:

- Are the topics appropriate for the level of candidature from all cultures, experiences and age groups?
- Is there any cultural/UK bias (urban/rural, boy/girl, etc.), i.e. does any task favour a candidate of a particular background, age or sex?
- Have any cultural knowledge assumptions been made in the topic?
- Are potentially distressing topics such as war, death, politics and religious beliefs avoided?
- Is each topic likely to appeal to a broad base of candidates?
- Will any topic 'date' too quickly?
- Is there a good range of options in terms of topic and functions?
- Are the topics likely to produce answers of the appropriate level and of the required length for the particular candidature, i.e. not too easy or too difficult?
- Will test takers have an existing schema (organised mental framework) for the topic even though the topic is unseen yet familiar?

Detailed lists of suitable and unsuitable topics for task input material are given in Section 3 of the *Information Common to All Papers* document for Main Suite examinations.

The topics or 'specific notions' covered in the Waystage document which are suitable for inclusion in the KET examination are as follows:

- personal identification
- personal feelings, opinions and experiences
- hobbies and leisure
- sport
- travel and holidays
- transport
- health, medicine and exercise
- shopping
- clothes
- services
- language
- house and home
- daily life
- entertainment and media
- social interaction
- school and study
- food and drink
- people
- places and buildings
- weather
- the natural world
- work and jobs

The topics or 'specific notions' covered in the Threshold document which are suitable for inclusion in the PET examination are as follows:

- clothes
- daily life
- education
- entertainment and media
- environment
- food and drink
- free time
- health, medicine and exercise
- hobbies and leisure
- house and home
- language
- people
- personal feelings, opinions and experiences
- personal identification
- places and buildings
- relations with other people
- transport
- services
- shopping
- social interaction
- sport
- the natural world
- travel and holidays
- weather
- work and jobs

The following are some suggested topics for the higher levels – FCE, CAE and CPE:

- business/commerce/industry
- education/training/learning
- entertainment/leisure
- fashion
- food/drink (non-alcoholic)
- health/fitness
- history/archaeology
- language/communication
- lifestyles/living conditions
- natural world/environment/ wildlife
- personal life/circumstances/ experiences
- places/architecture
- psychology
- relationships/family
- science/technology
- shopping/consumerism
- social and national customs
- social trends
- sports
- the arts
- the media
- travel/tourism
- weather
- work/jobs

In Cambridge ESOL examinations, test material does not contain anything that might offend or upset candidates, potentially affect their performance or distract them during the examination. Thus the following topics are considered unsuitable for use in Cambridge ESOL examinations in general:

- war
- politics
- racism (includes cultural clichés, stereotyping and what could be seen as patronising attitudes towards other countries, cultures or beliefs)
- sex and sexism (includes stereotyping)
- potentially distressing topics (examples include death, terminal illness, severe family/social problems, natural disasters and the object of common phobias such as spiders or snakes, where the treatment might be distasteful)
- examinations, passing and failing
- drugs
- national standpoints
- religion (includes aspects of daily life which are not acceptable to certain religions)
- anything historical likely to offend certain nations or groups
- gambling.

When considering whether a text on a certain topic is suitable to act as a prompt for one of the Main Suite Writing tasks, the treatment and language used is carefully taken into consideration. Care is taken to ensure that candidates come to the text equally, no matter where they are from, how old they are, what their background is, and so on (as far as it is possible to control for this). Precautions are also taken to ensure that material does not contain anything that might upset or distract candidates as this might affect their performance. Candidates who are angered, upset or mystified by a text are less likely to perform to their best or to provide a valid and reliable sample of their language skills in an examination situation.

The following information is given as general advice to those constructing the tasks:

- Specialised or technical material – material must not favour candidates with specialised knowledge of a particular subject or have content that would be too specialised or technical for the majority of candidates.
- Topicality – texts and topics with a short 'shelf-life' are avoided as they tend to be out-of-date by the time candidates take the examination.
- Real names – items testing facts about persons/products/organisations, etc. could be answered from general knowledge; facts about a product/person/organisation etc. need to be changed in order to facilitate items, so they are no longer accurate; facts given about the name would be likely to change before the material appears in an examination.

- Imperial measurements – are converted to metric, with the exception of fixed expressions. Monetary units are not changed, though amounts may need to be updated in older texts.

Topics are chosen to be accessible and of interest to the broad range of Main Suite candidates and are not intended to exclude any large group in terms of their standpoint or assumptions. Clearly, it is impossible to interest everybody, but subjects which appeal only to a minority are avoided.

CAE Item Writer Guidelines also provide a list of topics separated into two halves. The second half of each list represents topics which are well-covered at FCE level. These can of course, be used at CAE but care is taken to ensure that, for example, a topic which can be discussed with fairly simple vocabulary is matched with a more demanding function in order to generate an appropriately demanding task.

The topic should not be biased in favour of any particular section of the test population. In those situations where Writing tests are constructed for heterogeneous groups of students, there is a need to select texts with a wider appeal than may be the case when we have a more homogeneous group, for example, ESP tests. In the latter case, such as for the Cambridge BEC examinations (see O'Sullivan 2006) it may be easier to select topics with narrower or more targeted appeal.

The topic area should be sufficiently familiar so that candidates of a requisite level of ability have sufficient existing schemata to enable them to fulfil the requirements of the task. Cambridge ESOL attempts to identify and cover relevant content domains. Coverage of the appropriate domains of language use is attained through the employment of relevant topics, tasks, text types and contexts. The domains, therefore, need to be specified with reference to the characteristics of the test taker, and to the characteristics of the relevant language use contexts.

There is some evidence (Read 1990) that different topics may elicit different responses which are at different levels of performance thus allowing a degree of uncontrolled variance into the test (Jacobs et al 1981:1). Differences in scores may not then be due to real differences in writing proficiency but rather result from choice of different topics. This once again raises the issue of the relative advantages and disadvantages of allowing candidates a choice of topics in a Writing test; there may be a risk that different writing options are not measuring the same construct. Choice of tasks also raises the issue of whether there can be a sufficiently reliable basis for comparing test scores in situations where test takers have not responded to the same Writing task(s). Rater consistency in scoring (see pages 181–190) may also be affected if the tasks performed by candidates are on different topic(s).

Cambridge ESOL does allow a choice of topic in one part of the Writing test in an attempt to satisfy a varied candidature; however, all candidates have to write one task in common which means that it is then possible to calibrate performance on the tasks where there is a choice.

Summary of content knowledge across Cambridge ESOL levels

At KET level candidates need to have the language to deal with personal and daily life: basic everyday situations and communication needs (Van Ek and Trim 1991a). The focus tends to be on topics that are accessible to teenage candidates. AT PET level a broader range of general topics relating to the candidate's personal life and experience is covered; narrative topics also feature at PET level (Van Ek and Trim 1991a). FCE candidates may be expected to deal with a wide range of knowledge areas including any nonspecialist topic that has relevance for candidates worldwide (Van Ek and Trim 2001). CAE candidates are expected to be able to deal with topics that are more specialised and less personal than those that tend to feature at lower levels. The step up to CAE also involves coping with lexically challenging topic areas (e.g. the environment, the scientific world, traditions). At CPE level more abstract and academic topics appear and the candidate may be expected to be able to write on any non-specialist topic. CPE candidates are expected to be able to operate confidently in a wide variety of social, work-related and study-related situations. At all levels topics that might offend or otherwise unfairly disadvantage any group of candidates are avoided.

So far we have focused on the task in terms of both task setting and the demands it makes on candidates. Next we turn to a wider view of setting which looks at the conditions under which the examination as a whole is administered. The administrative conditions under which a task is set can heavily influence not only the cognitive processing involved in task completion but may also impact adversely on scoring validity if they deviate from the accepted norms.

Setting: administration of Writing tests

Primary considerations affecting validity are the circumstances under which the test takes place. These conditions need to be similar across sites or the processing will differ. If the test is not well administered unreliable results may occur. Precise steps should be laid down to ensure that the test is administered in exactly the same efficient way whoever is in charge or wherever it takes place. This requires that exam invigilators are provided with a clear and precise set of instructions and are familiar and comfortable with all aspects of the test before administering it; test conditions, should be of equivalent standards and suitably equipped (chairs, desks, clock etc.); test materials and equipment should be carefully screened for any problems before the test is administered; procedures for dealing with candidates' cheating should have been sorted out in advance with the invigilators; all administrative details should have been clearly worked out prior to the exam, in particular ground rules for late arrivals, the giving of clear test instructions, ensuring candidates have properly recorded names and other necessary details (see SATD Manual, Khalifa 2003, for a comprehensive approach to this aspect of test validity).

Within the Cambridge ESOL context, there are a number of publications dealing with the general requirements for the administration of standard Cambridge ESOL examinations:

- Cambridge ESOL Centre Registration Information Booklet explains the basis of authorisation, provides a definition and classification of Cambridge ESOL centres, and gives an outline of the responsibilities of centres in regard to the administration of Cambridge ESOL exams, particularly with new applicants in mind.

- Regulations for the relevant year (available on www.CambridgeESOL.org) contain brief information about entry procedures, results, etc., for the benefit of Local Secretaries, schools and candidates; they also include a summary of the content of particular examinations, plus details specific to the year in question, e.g. dates of sessions and the titles of any background reading texts. A copy of this document is made available to all applicant candidates.

- Handbook for Centres (available on CentreNet which is restricted to Local Secretaries and their support staff) provides detailed general information on the running of a centre and guidelines on the administration of the examinations. It provides a basis for detailed instructions and guidelines to supervisors and invigilators on the conduct of tests and is regularly updated by the Cambridge ESOL Centre Inspections Unit.

These publications – issued to Local Secretaries – contain general information on the administration of Cambridge ESOL examinations and are supplemented by handbooks and promotional materials for specific examinations (e.g. Cambridge ESOL KET/PET Instructions to Local Secretaries, Supervisors and Invigilators for Examination Administration 2004; Cambridge ESOL FCE/CAE/CPE Instructions to Local Secretaries, Supervisors and Invigilators for Examination Administration 2004).

The process of carrying out an assessment of language proficiency involves a combination of specialist and non-specialist elements. The specialist elements of the assessment cover syllabus and question paper content; professional requirements for conducting Cambridge ESOL examinations, marking and grading; providing a service to the users in areas such as the interpretation of results, examination reports, analysis of performance and the preparation of candidates. Responsibility for these specialist elements lies principally with Cambridge ESOL, but also involves a large number of item writers and examiners supervised by Cambridge ESOL.

The administrative elements of the assessment, which may be centralised (i.e. Cambridge ESOL) or local (i.e. centres), include: ensuring that the candidates have information on what to expect when they are examined; making all necessary arrangements for the administration of papers under secure, standardised or special conditions; providing the candidates with their results, with the means to interpret them and, if there are grounds, to have their results checked; and – to those candidates who have gained appropriate grades – issuing their certificates. Responsibility for these elements of carrying out assessment is shared between Cambridge ESOL administrative staff based in Cambridge and the centres where examinations take place (Local Secretaries, their supervisors, invigilators, etc.).

Cambridge ESOL also provides a Helpdesk facility which has specific responsibility for dealing with enquiries about the administration of Cambridge ESOL examinations.

Cambridge ESOL sets its own closing date for receipt of entries in Cambridge close to the date of the administration for the relevant examination, as this will allow all the necessary procedures to be completed and documentation, including test material, to be despatched in good time for centres. The precise closing dates for receipt of entries in Cambridge for each examination, or group of examinations, are clearly specified in the Regulations.

A number of Cambridge ESOL candidates have special requirements (including those with a permanent or long-term disability or those with short-term difficulties) which make it difficult for them to demonstrate their ability in English. In such cases the appropriate action is to make special arrangements for these candidates so that, insofar as possible, they are then able to take the examination on an equal footing with other candidates (see Chapter 2 on test-taker characteristics in relation to Special Arrangements made before the candidate sits the examination). Responsibilities for dealing with Special Requirements are distributed across a number of groups within Cambridge ESOL. One of those responsibilities is to give advice on the most appropriate arrangements for any given candidate. Special Arrangements fall into two main categories: those involving the provision of modified material (often in conjunction with administrative arrangements), and those involving administrative arrangements only.

Modifications to material may comprise the production of papers in Braille or enlarged print with associated changes to layout and rubrics to help candidates navigate them; or, in some cases, changes to content in order to, for example, make a task accessible to blind candidates. In all cases, changes are made such that the assessment objectives of the test in question are not compromised.

Administrative Special Arrangements include provisions such as allowing candidates extra time, or the use of an amanuensis or word processor, perhaps with assistive software, to record their answers.

The conditions related to minimum entry requirements and the specific minimum numbers for each examination are set down in the Regulations and Cambridge ESOL Centre Registration Information Booklet. Supplies of administration and information materials for the range of examinations are despatched to centres annually, and may be increased or decreased on request. All entries are submitted via ESOLCOMMS (although entries for Young Learners English tests (YLE) are optional). ESOLCOMMS is a comprehensive examinations administration system designed for the personal computer and Cambridge ESOL supplies IBM-compatible software on compact disc for entering candidates, accompanied by a detailed instruction guide. Separate computer-based administration packages exist for IELTS which are obtainable by IELTS centres on request from the Cambridge ESOL On Demand Unit. The entry data can then be sent to Cambridge on disc using the internet-based carrier system FUEL (File Upload from External Locations or by normal postal services.

It should be noted that open centres which have both internal and external candidates are encouraged to do everything possible to facilitate entries from external candidates. Furthermore, entries from candidates who wish to enter for more than one level of examination in the same session may be accepted provided that satisfactory arrangements can be made at the centre. Centres may also make reserve entries for candidates not identified at the time of entry. Cambridge ESOL will accept entries after the published closing dates on payment of a late entry fee and thereafter in accordance with a graduated scale of additional fees related to the lateness of the entry. Provisions for syllabus amendments, i.e. a change of examination sitting between, for example, FCE 0100 and FCE 0102 in the same centre in the same session, are also available. Changes between different examinations are not, however, permissible.

All candidates are provided with full timetable information, including venues, relating to the examination(s) for which entry has been made on their behalf. The responsibility for timetables and their circulation to candidates lies with the Local Secretary. For security reasons, requests to deviate from the published timetable are not normally sanctioned. However, should it be impossible for a candidate to sit an examination at the scheduled time, a request to vary the time of the paper(s) affected may be submitted by the Local Secretary utilising a form available on request from the Cambridge ESOL Centre Inspections Unit.

Checking procedures – before the day of an examination – exist for determining whether candidates are familiar with the concepts and use of computer answer sheets (OMRs).

Examination requirements and arrangements

Accommodation is such as to ensure that the range of Cambridge ESOL examinations is administered under secure conditions in circumstances conducive to the candidates performing to their best ability. To facilitate the carrying out of inspections, Local Secretaries must complete and return at the earliest opportunity, a Venue Details form to the Cambridge ESOL Centre Inspections Officer, giving details of examination venues where these differ from the centre's postal address.

Cambridge ESOL issues centres with a statement of entry for each candidate. This document confirms entry information and includes a timetable for the examination.

All candidates (except for the YLE tests) are informed that they are required to provide evidence of identity at each separate paper, by passport, identity card, etc. Ensuring that candidates' identities are checked against photographic evidence – a key responsibility for Local Secretaries – provides confidence regarding a candidate's true identification.

Supplies of a poster-sized Cambridge ESOL Notice to Candidates – presented so that it is clearly visible outside each examination room (inside for the YLE examination) – are sent to centres well before the examinations.

Candidates may be required to take a short written anchor test in addition to the examination. Anchor tests are an essential part of the monitoring of examination difficulty. Candidates' performance in the anchor test – which will normally last no more than 20 minutes – does not affect their examination results. Centres required to administer an anchor test may do so either on the day of the examination, or up to two weeks earlier. In any event, the anchor is administered under examination conditions.

Cambridge ESOL has clear rulings on examination supervision. The purpose of supervision and invigilation is to ensure that all candidates are under surveillance for every moment of each examination period. Supervision and invigilation arrangements for the examinations are entrusted to the Local Secretary, who ensures that these tasks are carried out by suitably qualified people. Relatives of candidates in the examination room are specifically not eligible to serve as a supervisor or invigilator.

The supervisor is the person appointed at each centre or separate hall to be responsible for overseeing the general conduct of the examination sessions. The invigilator is the person in the examination room responsible for the conduct of a particular paper. In large centres, for example, with 100 candidates or more, Cambridge ESOL advises that the supervisor has an assistant. Sufficient invigilators are appointed to ensure that each examination paper is conducted in accordance with certain requirements, including having at least one invigilator for every 30 candidates, being able to observe each candidate at all times, the facility for lone invigilators to be able to summon assistance easily and so on. In the case of external venues, Cambridge ESOL may request centres to appoint an external supervisor, i.e. one not connected with the venue.

Centres keep signed records of the invigilation arrangements for each examination paper which are made available to Cambridge ESOL on request. Supervisor and invigilator familiarity with the relevant notices, and requirements relating to the specific Writing examination is assured through a document entitled Instructions to Local Secretaries, Supervisors and Invigilators for Examination Administration (ILSSIEA) – a copy of which is kept in every examination room.

Physical conditions

Here we are concerned with actual place, background noise, lighting, air-conditioning, and power sources.

In Cambridge ESOL examinations the selection of venues must take into account a number of factors including general ambience, accessibility of location and suitability of rooms. Separate arrangements exist for the paper components.

Requirements for the written components

Cambridge ESOL ensures that any room in which the examination is conducted, whether on centre premises or in an external venue, provides candidates with appropriate conditions in which to take the examination. Matters such as general cleanliness, air temperature, lighting, ventilation and the level of external noise is taken into careful consideration.

Candidates who do not comply with instructions which prohibit eating, drinking, smoking, carrying of digital recording equipment and possession of mobile phones during the examination, may be disqualified from taking the examination. Incidents of disqualification and malpractice are reported to Cambridge ESOL on the Report on Suspected Malpractice During Examinations form.

Cambridge ESOL insists upon rooms offering certain facilities. A board must be visible to all candidates showing the centre number, the actual time that each component will start and the time at which it will finish. Moreover, the provision of a reliable clock – made visible to all candidates in the room – is regarded as essential.

The seating arrangements for all Cambridge ESOL examinations are such as to prevent candidates from overlooking, intentionally or otherwise, the work of others. Cambridge ESOL stipulates very exact seating arrangements. Each candidate is provided with adequate space for a Writing question paper and answer sheet and at least 1.25 metres must be allowed between the centre of the desk assigned to any candidate and the centre of the desk assigned to the next candidate in any direction. Special care is taken to ensure distances are adequate, and are increased as necessary, for example, where some candidates are sitting higher than others. The use of chairs with side flaps is not permitted where these impede the candidate from being able to work with Writing question papers and answer sheets side by side as in the case of full-size desks. The sharing of desks is discouraged. However, if desks are to be shared, the minimum distance between candidates is still observed. Candidates are seated in column layout in candidate number order, facing the same direction and their numbers are displayed clearly on each desk.

During the examination, a simple sketch plan is completed for each room which accompanies the answer sheets and/or question papers being returned to Cambridge ESOL. The plan indicates the position of each candidate by candidate number, the direction in which candidates are facing, and the distance between the rows of candidates and between the candidates in each row. The room plan also indicates the number and base position of invigilators. Each room plan is signed by the supervisor.

Uniformity of administration

A constant testing environment where the test is conducted according to detailed rules and specifications so that testing conditions are the same for all test takers is essential. If the uniformity rule is broken say by one centre giving extra time for planning, producing or monitoring a task, then the cognitive validity of the test is compromised because executive processing may differ markedly across testing sites as a result.

Examination conduct and associated regulations are provided in Part 5 of the Handbook for Centres 2004 and Section 2 of the ILSSIEA. General conduct (for all exams) covers starting the examination, supervision of candidates, completing the attendance register, late arrival of candidates, completing the room plan, leaving the examination room, irregular conduct, emergency procedures, Special Consideration (for candidates who have been disadvantaged), concluding the examination, collection of candidate answers, collection of question papers, collection of mark sheets for Speaking tests and inspection of centres.

In addition, detailed instructions for individual papers are provided in the ILSSIEA. Every supervisor in each centre is required to follow specific procedures for each of the respective examination papers.

The conduct of the Writing examinations

Cambridge ESOL question papers remain sealed so that they may be opened by the invigilator in the examination room in the presence of the candidates.

Papers are not normally opened more than 10 minutes before the time at which the test is set to begin. Before candidates are permitted to start, the invigilator ensures that candidates are seated according to prescribed arrangements and that they conform to the regulations of the examination. At this point candidates will have their attention drawn to any Writing test instructions and are helped to complete any administrative requirements such as entering their names, candidate numbers and so on. Candidates are also informed as to when they may begin to write their answers with the time allowed for the paper specified.

An attendance register is kept and completed by the supervisor or invigilator who ensures that an entry has been made for every candidate taking the examination. If a candidate is absent or has withdrawn, invigilators record the absence in the attendance column on the attendance register.

A candidate who arrives late for a Writing paper may be admitted at the discretion of the supervisor, though normally not later than halfway through the time allowed for the paper concerned. Late arrivals are given full instructions as issued to other candidates and are allowed the full schedule time for completion of the paper. However, if the candidate arrives for the Writing paper after any candidate has been released from the examination room, that candidate is not admitted nor accommodated in a separate sitting for the same paper but is recorded as an absentee.

According to the Handbook for Centres (University of Cambridge ESOL Examinations 2005i:19): 'In all cases where a candidate is admitted late into the examination . . . any work done after the scheduled finishing time must be indicated, taking care where questions may have been answered non-sequentially'. In cases where candidates are late for good reason, for example, sudden illness or transport difficulties, so long as Cambridge ESOL is satisfied that there has been no breach of examination security, the work completed in the whole of the examination period will normally be accepted. The same applies in cases where candidates are late because of negligence or oversight, including over-sleeping and misreading of the timetable. The work completed in any additional time allowed to compensate for the late arrival, however, is not normally accepted.

All cases of irregularity or misconduct in connection with the examination are reported to Cambridge ESOL Results (Special Circumstances) by the Local Secretary, who is empowered to exclude or expel a candidate. Any infringement of the regulations or any irregularity, misconduct or dishonesty may lead to the disqualification of the candidate. The decision on disqualification rests with Cambridge ESOL.

At the conclusion of the Writing test, candidates' scripts, rough paper, answer sheets, etc., whether being returned to Cambridge ESOL or retained at the centre, are collected and accounted for before candidates leave the examination room. After collation, the attendance register, room plan and all answer materials are handed immediately to the person responsible for packing and despatching them to Cambridge ESOL or ensuring their security. All question papers for the Writing test – used and unused – are returned to Cambridge ESOL. Scripts and answer sheets are packed in accordance with the instructions and despatched to Cambridge ESOL by the fastest means within five calendar days of the paper having been taken.

Cambridge ESOL reserves the right to visit centres unannounced during the period of the examinations to inspect the arrangements made for the security of confidential examination material and for the conduct of examinations. Inspections are intended to ensure that arrangements are in order, but can also offer opportunity to capture first-hand knowledge of any problems from the centre's point of view. Local Secretaries are expected to point out the security facilities and examination rooms to visiting inspectors who may visit any Writing test being conducted. A copy of the inspector's report is left with the centre and any shortcomings identified in the report are invariably rectified immediately. In the case of an adverse report which indicates cause for concern, the Cambridge ESOL Centre Inspections Officer will write to the centre requesting written assurance that appropriate remedial action is being taken.

Security

This involves limiting access to the specific content of a test to those who need to know it for test development, test scoring, and test evaluation. In particular, test items of secure tests are not published; unauthorised copying is forbidden by any test taker or anyone otherwise associated with the test. If tests are not secure then some candidates would be able to prepare their answers in advance and their processing will be of an entirely different nature, i.e. solely reliant on memory.

Examination writing materials

Confidential examination materials, at both pre- and post-examination stage, are locked away in a place of high security such as a safe or non-portable, lockable, reinforced metal cabinet or other similar container. Cambridge ESOL requests that the safe or container is held in a securely locked room with access restricted to a small number of authorised persons. The room should preferably be windowless and on an upper floor; windows, whether internal or external, should be fitted with safety devices. Moreover, the door to the room is expected to be of a solid construction, have secure hinges and be fitted with a secure lock. If the security of the question papers or confidential ancillary materials is put at risk by fire, theft, loss, damage, unauthorised disclosure, or any other circumstances, Cambridge ESOL is informed immediately.

All materials – packed separately to ensure that question paper packets do not need to be opened before the test date – required for Cambridge ESOL examinations are despatched to centres according to the dates listed in the relevant administrative calendar, which is sent automatically to Local Secretaries. On receipt of the materials, the Local Secretary is required to check the contents of the despatch carefully, giving particular attention to the question paper packets. This is done under strict security conditions. Question paper packets are checked against the timetable and arranged in timetable order so as to reduce the possibility of opening a packet of question papers at the wrong time.

Candidate answer sheets, pre-printed with each candidate's name and index number, are supplied for the appropriate Writing components for the range of ESOL examinations. Fully personalised CIS, also pre-printed with each candidate's name and index number, are provided. The data from the CIS is required for the purpose of research and validation of the examinations and anonymity is guaranteed. The CIS may be completed at any time during the examination period provided that it is done under supervision.

Postscript

Tasks which have generated adequate evidence of *a priori* validity according to expert scrutiny of their cognitive and context validity would next be trialled on a representative group of candidates before administration proper. Any final amendments would be made with reference to the results and feedback from the trialling. Writing examinations would be constructed from such tasks.

We have now discussed all aspects of the *a priori* validation of test tasks in terms of their cognitive- and context-based validity. Once scores are available on operational tasks we enter the stage of *a posteriori* validation. The first crucial aspect of post test validation we will deal with is the aspect of *scoring validity*. We have already addressed the importance of candidates being aware of the criteria by which they will be assessed and noted the implications of this for planning, monitoring and revision. In the next chapter we look at the issues relating to criteria and rating scale in more detail and examine the whole rating process from appointment and training of examiners through to post-examination adjustment procedures, all of which contribute to scoring validity and thereby to the overall validity of a test and its scores.

5 Scoring validity

Introduction

Scoring validity is concerned with all the aspects of the testing process that can impact on the reliability of test scores. It accounts for the extent to which test scores are based on appropriate criteria, exhibit consensual agreement in marking, are free as possible from measurement error, stable over time, consistent in terms of content sampling and engender confidence as reliable decision-making indicators.

In earlier chapters we looked at the test taker, cognitive validity and the parameters of context validity that need to be considered at the test-design stage; in so doing we identified a number of factors which can impact on the scoring validity of Writing tests such as inadequate sampling, too much choice, unclear and ambiguous rubrics, lack of familiarity with test structure, inconsistent administration, and breaches of test security (see also Hughes 2003, Chapter 5).

In this chapter we concentrate on the scoring process itself but earlier points made in relation to performance conditions with the potential to affect test reliability emphasise the interconnectedness of these components of the validity construct. Although for descriptive purposes the various elements of the model have been presented separately, we have emphasised throughout that there is a 'symbiotic' relationship between context validity, cognitive validity and scoring validity, which together constitute what is frequently referred to as construct validity. Decisions taken with regard to parameters of task context will impact on the processing that takes place in task completion. Likewise, where scoring criteria are made known to candidates in advance this will similarly affect cognitive processing in planning, monitoring and revision. The scoring criteria in writing are an important part of the construct as they describe the level of performance that is required. At the upper levels of writing ability in particular, it is the quality of the performance that enables distinctions to be made between levels of proficiency (Hawkey and Barker 2004).

Scoring validity is criterial because if we cannot depend on the rating of exam scripts it matters little that the tasks we develop are potentially valid in terms of both cognitive and contextual parameters. Faulty criteria or scales, unsuitable raters or procedures, lack of training and standardisation, poor or variable conditions for rating, inadequate provision for post exam statistical adjustment, and unsystematic or ill-conceived procedures for grading and awarding can all lead to a reduction in scoring validity and to the risk of construct irrelevant variance. If the marking is not reliable this may vitiate all the other work that has gone into creating a valid instrument (Alderson et al 1995:105). Exam boards need to devote attention and resources to each of these aspects of scoring validity.

Evidence for the lack of scoring validity in direct tests of writing has been accumulating since at least 1890. Edgeworth (1890:653) noted:

> I find the element of chance in these public examinations to be such that only a fraction – from a third to two-thirds – of the successful candidates can be regarded as safe, above the danger of coming out unsuccessfully if a different set of equally competent judges had happened to be appointed.

A seminal study undertaken by Diederich et al (1961) demonstrated huge variability in script ratings. Huot (1990) also observed that variability associated with raters is significant.

Weaknesses in rating reliability have long been a concern at Cambridge (see for example Roach 1945). Later studies, specifically in relation to Cambridge examinations, have all contributed to a greater understanding of the rating process leading to enhanced appreciation of writing performance assessment (Falvey and Shaw 2005, Furneaux and Rignall 2000, Jones and Shaw 2003, Milanovic and Saville 1994, Milanovic, Saville and Shuhong 1996, O'Sullivan 2000, O'Sullivan and Rignall 2002, Pollitt and Murray 1996, Shaw 2001, 2002, 2002a, 2002b, 2002c, 2003, 2003a, 2003b, 2003c, 2004, 2005, 2005a, 2005b, Shaw and Falvey forthcoming, Shaw and Geranpayeh 2005, Weir and Milanovic 2003).

Scoring validity parameters

In this section we briefly outline the parameters we are concerned with in this chapter before examining each in detail for what the literature has to say and how Cambridge ESOL deals with them in practice.

The first scoring validity parameter we will address is that of the *criteria and type of rating scale*. Weigle (2002:109) summarises McNamara (1996) on the centrality of the rating scale to the valid measurement of the writing construct:

> the scale that is used in assessing performance tasks such as writing tests represents, implicitly or explicitly, the theoretical basis upon which the test is founded; that is, it embodies the test (or scale) developer's notion of what skills or abilities are being measured by the test. For this reason the development of a scale (or set of scales) and the descriptors for each scale level are of critical importance for the validity of the assessment.

Three discrete and separate sources of rater variability in the direct assessment of writing have been identified by McNamara (1996:121). Variability associated with: *candidate* (relative abilities of candidates – that quality that causes candidates' performance on one task to be correlated with their performance on other tasks); *task* (particularly where the candidate is given a choice of tasks to select from – no two tasks, for example, measure exactly the same thing and so tasks may interact with candidate idiosyncrasies to make them appear slightly more or less difficult to different candidates or groups of candidates); and, *rater* (the greater the degree of judgement exercised by a rater, the greater the scope for the rater to exhibit severity or leniency – that quality that causes him or her to systematically under- or over-mark all similar tasks). *Rater* characteristics and the *processes* followed in rating will be the next concerns of this chapter. McNamara (1996:123–5) offers four ways in which raters may be at variance with one another:

1. A pair of raters may differ in terms of their tendency to overall leniency.

2. Raters may exhibit bias towards certain groups of candidates or types of task. Such bias may manifest itself in sub-patterns of either severe or generous marking giving rise to two kinds of interaction: *rater–item interactions* (the tendency for a rater to display consistent severity on one particular item type whilst simultaneously showing consistent generosity on another item type) and *rater–candidate interactions* (the tendency for a rater to over- or under-rate a candidate or a group of candidates).

3. Raters may reveal differences with regard to their consistency of rating behaviour. In other words, the degree of the random error related to their judgements.

4. Raters may display differences in how they interpret and apply the rating scale instrument. In their actual interpretation of the scale, raters do not behave in identical ways. Systematic variations may exist among raters in the manner in which they employ the available mark range. For example, some raters may exhibit central tendency (when a rater tends to give ratings clustered closely around the mid-point on the scale) whilst others may consciously restrict their use of the scale to its extremities, preferring instead to perceive differences between candidates 'more starkly and hedging their bets less' (1996:124) i.e. consistently rating higher or lower than the performance merits, or than other raters.

The *rating conditions* under which marking takes place (e.g. temporal, physical or psychological) are increasingly seen as having a potential impact on scoring and need to be standardised too. As Weir (2005b:200) notes, 'papers marked in the shady groves of academe may receive more considered treatment than those scored on the 5.30 rush hour tube out of London on a Friday afternoon'.

The importance of rater training has been stressed in the literature (Alderson, Clapham and Wall 1995, Bachman and Palmer 1996, Brown 1995, Lumley 2000, Weigle 1994, 1998, Weir 1988). Alderson et al (1995:105) argue that it is widely accepted in second language writing assessment circles that the training of examiners is crucial to validity in testing language performance and emphasise the vital role training has to play in the removal (or at least the reduction) of rater variability.

Statistical analysis of examiner performance normally takes place after marking is complete. Scaling of writing is one accepted statistical method for detecting errant Writing examiners and this is often used in post-exam adjustment to alter their marks to bring them in line with the population of markers as a whole. Multi-faceted Rasch analysis is a further possible procedure for ensuring fairness in marking that will be discussed below.

Generally, when examination papers have been marked and a series of checks to ensure that all candidates have been assessed accurately and to the same standards have been carried out, *grading* of examinations takes place.

We examine below all these dimensions of scoring validity in detail following the organisational structure outlined above (see Figure 5.1).

Criteria/rating scale

The choice of appropriate rating criteria and the consistent application of rating scales by trained examiners are regarded as key factors in the valid assessment of second language performance (Alderson, Clapham and Wall 1995, Bachman and Palmer 1996, McNamara 1996).

Writing standards are often written down in the form of assessment criteria, band level descriptors, mark schemes or other statements. However, the actual standard required of a candidate is not always entirely communicated by the

Figure 5.1 Aspects of scoring validity for writing (adapted from Weir 2005b:47)

Scoring validity
Rating
• Criteria/rating scale
• Rater characteristics
• Rating process
• Rating conditions
• Rater training
• Post-exam adjustment
• Grading and awarding

words and phrases embraced by these statements. In other words, written assessment criteria alone are not always sufficient to convey a standard.

Indeed, it is questionable whether any mark scheme can wholly capture the definition of a level in a way that examiners could reliably and consistently apply. The definition of a level is not captured merely on paper, but rather through the process of examiner training and standardisation. It depends crucially on exemplar scripts, that is, those scripts which have been identified as exemplifying the level by experienced examiners. Standards are, in this way, communicated by exemplar scripts.

Wolf (1995) draws attention to the potential importance for standards to be communicated by examples of students' work rather than by explicit assessment criteria alone because if assessment criteria were separated from students' work they could be interpreted as appropriate for many different levels of achievement. However, there is little research evidence on the extent to which exemplar scripts achieve a standardising effect (Wolf 1995:76).

Ideally, mark schemes are little more than mnemonic devices for use by examiners who have already internalised a representation of the levels. For those who do not share this internalised representation, mark schemes may be meaningless. In this respect there is no necessary difference between the holistic and analytic (global and profile) mark schemes we discuss below. First, holistic mark schemes may refer to the same features – register, accuracy, range, impact, task fulfilment etc. – which are separated out as subscales in an analytic approach. Second, analytic subscales, though they focus on an aspect of performance, are equally dependent on training and standardisation for appropriate interpretation of their meaning.

The primary function of rating scales is to attempt to equate a range of samples of written performance to very specific verbal or qualitative descriptions corresponding to these performances (Upshur and Turner 1995). Thus when either developing a new rating scale or revising an existing one, the construction of individual level descriptions should be afforded considerable care in the interests of validity.

Alderson (1991) points to several troublesome and perplexing issues associated with rating band-scale construction:

- settling on and defining appropriate assessment criteria for scale inclusion
- defining and representing band extremities and in particular band thresholds i.e. determining features that constitute the end of one band and the beginning of the next
- refraining from the use of needlessly verbose and awkward descriptors
- avoiding evaluative expressions such as 'unsatisfactory', 'adequate', 'good'.

Despite acknowledging such difficulties, Alderson recognises that rating scales have inherent worth in facilitating enhanced reliability in assessing

Writing through the provision of a common or universal standard and meaning for such judgements.

The co-ordination (or standardisation) meeting (see below) offers Writing examiners the opportunity to interpret Writing standards in accordance with the mark scheme. Mark schemes are widely perceived to derive from a criterion referencing approach to assessment in that qualitative criteria have to be met to gain marks. When examiners use mark schemes they invariably apply a principle of 'best fit'; in other words, they award a particular band of marks where a candidate's response fits the corresponding descriptor. For example, when an examiner reads a candidate's answer they decide which level descriptor best describes the answer and then choose an appropriate mark from the range available in that band depending upon the worthiness of the candidate's response.

The process upon which Writing examiners arrive at qualitative rating decisions is based upon the notion of shared interpretation of the rating instrument. It has been argued by Pollitt and Murray (1996) that any such process must be characterised by simplicity and transparency. What has become increasingly clear from the assessment reliability literature is that the shared interpretation and consensual assimilation of rating scale level descriptors cannot be taken for granted, and unless points across the rating scale clearly define differentiated levels or bands of proficiency, exact understanding by different audiences will differ (see Brindley 1998:63). Bachman (1990:36) similarly stresses the need for the rating scale to be precise so that examiners can clearly distinguish between the different levels defined.

Types of rating scales

Alderson's (1991) seminal paper on rating scale provides a useful account of the principles and practices of developing and operationalising scales.

Pollitt and Murray (1996:74) offer summary descriptions of three discrete kinds of rating scale, identified by Alderson (1991) and used in language testing, distinguished by their function and intended audience:

- User Oriented (UO) scales aim to describe to potential employers and others outside the education system the sorts of circumstances, in work or social life, in which the student will be able to operate adequately
- Constructor Oriented (CO) scales aim to describe the sorts of tasks that the student can do at each level, and so describe potential test items that might make up a discrete test for each level
- Assessor Oriented (AO) scales aim to describe the sort of performance that is typically observed in performance by a student at each level.

The forms of scale are readily differentiated by inspection, each offering different kinds of statement about the abilities of students.

In establishing scales for these different audiences the test developer needs to first establish appropriate criteria based on the purpose of the assessment and the construct being measured and then determine levels of performance in relation to these criteria. According to Weigle (2002:109), three main types of rating scales are discussed in the writing assessment literature: primary trait scales, holistic scales, analytic scales. Weigle argues that the three scales:

> can be characterised by two distinctive features: (1) whether the scale is intended to be specific to a single writing task or generalized to a class of tasks (broadly or narrowly defined), and (2) whether a single score or multiple scores are given to each script.

Whereas the primary trait scale is specific to an individual Writing task, holistic and analytic scales have undoubtedly gained widespread acceptance in teaching practices more generally (especially when employed for use when grading multiple tasks) and, more specifically, in second language testing (Canale 1981, Carroll 1980, Jacobs et al 1981, Perkins 1983). Furthermore, research in the field of writing assessment has reinforced the value offered by holistic and analytic rating instruments.

Primary trait scoring

Primary trait scoring involves the award of a holistic score to a stretch of discourse in relation to one principal trait – a feature specific to the writing, for example: structure, tone, or vocabulary. Perkins (1983:658) notes that such traits are criterial in the performance of specific rhetorical tasks.

A set of primary trait rating guidelines for use by examiners are developed separately for every Writing task. The guidelines comprise (a) the task (b) the statement of the primary rhetorical trait to be elicited (c) an interpretation of the task hypothesising writing performance to be expected (d) an explanation of how the task and primary trait are related (e) a scoring guide (f) sample papers, and (g) an explanation of scores on sample papers.

The assessment criteria used in this rating approach are restricted to a particular Writing task and assessment is not generalisable to other types of Writing task. Given the lack of generalisability and the requirement to produce detailed rating protocols for each task, the primary trait approach is regarded as time-consuming and expensive to implement. It is generally used only in research situations or in relation to a course of teaching where information is sought on learners' mastery of specific writing skills.

Weigle (2002:72) consequently narrows the choice down to two:

> most rating scales can be classified as either holistic (a single score is given to each writing sample) or analytic (separate scores are given to different aspects of writing, such as content, organization, language use and so on).
>
> While the literature is replete with arguments for or against various scale types for both L1 and L2 writers, there has been surprisingly little research on the effects of different scale types on outcomes.

Holistic scoring

Holistic scoring, often referred to as impressionistic marking, involves rating scripts impressionistically on a single rating scale according to their overall properties rather than providing separate scores on specified features of the language produced e.g. accuracy, lexical range (see Davies et al 1999:75, Stiggins and Bridgeford 1983:26).

A distinct advantage of holistic assessment is that, from a purely practical perspective, compositions can be assessed rapidly and are therefore more economical to mark. Holistic scoring focuses the mind of the rater on the respective strengths of the written text rather than drawing attention to its shortfalls.

Notable 'holistic' antagonists (such as Charney 1984, Gere 1980, Odell and Cooper 1980) have argued that a holistic approach to assessment is devoid of any real theoretical underpinning and this has led some researchers to challenge the foundations upon which conclusions about the method's validity have been constructed.

Holistic scoring has a number of significant disadvantages. In essence, holistic rating is a rank ordering process and as such is not appropriate for providing student correction or diagnostic feedback (Charney 1984). A global award, devoid of diagnostic information, does not permit examiners to distinguish between different features of writing such as determining the extent of lexical resource, aspects of rhetorical organisation, or control of grammatical structures and accuracy.

According to Weigle (2002:114) 'This is especially problematic for second-language writers, since different aspects of writing ability develop at different rates for different writers'.

Weir (1993:164) argues that in the past there was a major problem with most global impression band scales in that they were not empirically derived (except perhaps from rater judgements as in Hamp-Lyons 1986). They appear to represent levels of proficiency, but as yet, we do not have a clear idea of the order of acquisition of various skill attributes in writing or even whether there is such an order. Until adequate research is carried out, and scales are empirically founded on the scripts produced by real candidates, then they are at best tentative in their implications. For examples of such empirically driven scales, see Hawkey and Barker (2004) for writing and Hasselgren (1997) and Fulcher (2003) for speaking, as well as the discussion of the Common Scale for Writing Project (see Case Study C below) and the IELTS Writing Revision Project (see Case Study D below).

Analytic scoring

Analytic scoring is a form of assessment frequently used in the evaluation of writing, where a separate award is given for each of several nominated performance features of a particular task, for example relevance and adequacy of content, organisation, lexical breadth and depth, in contrast to awarding one global score. This involves the separating out of various textual aspects of a written text into 'rater-manageable' components for assessment purposes ensuring that the raters are all addressing the same features of the performance.

For our purposes we treat analytic scoring and multiple trait scoring as synonymous. Multiple trait scoring procedures aim to focus on the most salient criteria or traits relevant to the task, as identified during a careful iterative test development process, ideally by a group as opposed to a single 'expert'. The same multiple-trait method may be employed for a range of different Writing task prompts providing they have in common the same test specifications.

Multiple trait assessment is thought to be invaluable in the sense that it provides more information, for example, for diagnostic purposes and complex placement decisions, offering the researcher a host of details about textual features and the value raters ascribe to texts and text facets (Hamp-Lyons 1986, 1991a). 'When accompanied by proper rater training and multiple rating, they have the potential to improve the reliability of scores; they are also less costly than primary-trait instruments, although more expensive than holistic scoring' (Davies et al 1999:126).

An analytic scale has the effect of focusing the raters' judgements and thereby ensuring a reasonable degree of agreement among raters so that a reliable award can be derived from a set of summed, aggregated or 'averaged' multiple ratings. Multiple ratings awarded to the same script will tend to enhance the reliability of assessment of that script (Hamp-Lyons 1991, Huot 1996, Weir 1990). Analytic assessment, therefore, leads to improved reliability as each candidate is awarded a number of scores.

Furthermore, analytic assessment allows for more exact diagnostic reporting of literacy progress, particularly in the case of differential skills development as reflected in a marked or 'jagged' candidate profile. In this sense, analytic scales are more suitable for second-language writers as different features of writing develop at different rates. This method, therefore, lends itself more readily to full profile reporting and could well perform a certain diagnostic role in delineating students' respective strengths and weaknesses in overall written production. Analytic scores act as useful guides for providing feedback to students on their compositions and to formative evaluation. For example, since a Writing test must be related to a specific context in which the assessment is required for a particular purpose, analytic scoring is especially useful for informing the end-user of the test score (an employer, or a university admissions officer) whether a candidate has a flat profile or whether it is in any sense marked by particular strengths or weaknesses (Hamp-Lyons 1991:253–5). This information cannot be supplied through a global impression scheme.

Analytic scoring entails a presupposition that raters will indeed be able to realistically and reasonably differentiate between specific skills or textual features and some research does in fact imply that such discrimination is of value in the training of raters, especially inexperienced or 'new' raters, who are better placed to more readily assimilate the assessment criteria in individual subscales rather than in holistic scales (Adams 1981; Francis 1977).

Luoma's (2004:80) comments on the number of applicable analytic rating criteria should be noted. She cites the Common European Framework (Council of Europe 2001:193) as suggesting that at four or five categories the cognitive load begins to affect raters and that seven categories is a psychological upper limit. In order to maintain conceptual independence between criteria she argues for limiting criteria to five or six.

Marsh and Ireland (1987), however, doubt the ability of raters to effectively discriminate between certain performance attributes and add force to the argument against analytic scoring suggesting that it is too time-consuming and costly to be practical in large-scale operational testing contexts and that, furthermore, analytic scoring may even 'distort and misrepresent the writing process' (1987:8). Hughes (2003:103–4) also indicates some additional potential drawbacks associated with using such scales. He mentions that focusing on single aspects may divert from overall effect and potential discrepancies when linked to impression scoring.

Weigle (2002:121) provides a useful comparison of holistic and analytic scales on five qualities of test usefulness (Table 5.1).

Summarising his discussion on the rating scale tradition, McNamara (1996) claims that the development of rating scales has been considerably influenced by the original assumptions underlying the construction of the first scale for the Foreign Service Institute (FSI) Oral Proficiency Interview back in the 1950s and 'little empirical validation of them [successive rating scales] has been attempted' (1996:212). Faced with a surprising paucity of research in this area, McNamara calls for more concerted research effort into the validation of rating scales 'which are central to the construct validity of the instruments with which they are associated' (1996:212).

Table 5.1 Comparison of holistic and analytic scales according to Weigle (2002:121)

Quality	Holistic scale	Analytic scale
Reliability	Lower than analytic but still acceptable.	Higher than holistic.
Construct validity	Holistic scale assumes that all relevant aspects of writing ability develop at the same rate and can thus be captured in a single score; holistic scores correlate with superficial aspects such as length and handwriting.	Analytic scales more appropriate for L2 writers as different aspects of writing ability develop at different rates.
Practicality	Relatively fast and easy.	Time-consuming; expensive.
Impact	Single score may mask an uneven writing profile and may be misleading for placement.	More scales provide useful diagnostic information for placement and/or instruction; more useful for rater training.
Authenticity	White (1995) argues that reading holistically is a more natural process than reading analytically.	Raters may read holistically and adjust analytic scores to match holistic impression.

Types of rating scales: Cambridge practice

Cambridge ESOL employs both holistic and analytic rating scales in its performance assessment, although it is the holistic approach to assessment which predominates in the Writing test components. Shaw (2004) summarises the advantages of holistic assessment for Cambridge Writing tests as:

• appropriate for ranking candidates
• suitable for arriving at a rapid overall rating
• suitable for large-scale assessments – multiple markings (likely to enhance reliability)
• useful for discriminating across a narrow range of assessment bands.

Although the holistic approach is used more routinely across the Cambridge ESOL exams, the use of analytic marking schemes can also be found. For example, analytic marking schemes are used for Cambridge's Business Language Testing Service (BULATS) – where analytical scales are given as guidance to examiners (although no marks are given for each analytical scale) – and also for the IELTS Writing Modules (Academic and General Training). An analytic approach may be especially important in tests involving only one marker.

Rating scale development: Cambridge practice

Having mapped out the issues surrounding criteria and rating scales we next examine work conducted by Cambridge ESOL to develop criteria and rating scales which build on the procedures and evidence emerging from the discussion above. As in Chapters 2 and 4, this work is presented in the form of case studies to illustrate the type of projects which other examination boards may wish to conduct in this area.

Case Study C: The Common Scale for Writing Project

Background

The Common Scale for Writing Project (CSW) forms part of a much larger and long-term project at Cambridge ESOL to locate all the Cambridge ESOL examinations across different levels and domains within a comprehensive and coherent framework of reference. Construction of this interpretive framework was based in the first instance around the five established Cambridge proficiency levels – KET, PET, FCE, CAE and CPE – but is continually being extended to accommodate the other examinations in the Cambridge ESOL product range (for further detail, see Hawkey and Barker 2004, Hawkey and Shaw 2005, Taylor 2004b).

Rationale for the CSW project

The CSW project was an empirical corpus-based study which set out to answer the following questions:

- What are the distinguishing features in the writing performance of EFL/ESL learners or users taking the Cambridge ESOL English examinations?
- How can these distinguishing features be incorporated into a single scale of bands, that is, a 'common scale', describing different levels of L2 writing proficiency?

The methodology for the CSW research combined qualitative and quantitative approaches in order to corroborate and triangulate data synthesised from a variety of sources. In this sense, the approach aligns with suggestions made by Alderson (1989) that assessment criteria bands can be constructed through iterative drafting informed by feedback from markers; it involves the judicious selection of sample scripts corresponding to each band level, agreement on the salient characteristics of each script, identification of criteria for evaluation, and definition of these criteria in relation to levels of proficiency.

The CSW project was envisaged as a phased developmental and continuous process, reflecting the cyclical and iterative approach to test development favoured by Cambridge ESOL.

Phase 1: Preliminary exploration of performance levels

Phase 1 of the project (Saville et al 1995) adopted a two-fold approach: an experienced senior Cambridge ESOL examiner (Capel) and an applied linguist with a particular interest in writing (Hamp-Lyons) set about identifying writing criteria for different levels of proficiency but from different angles.

Capel reviewed existing Cambridge ESOL exam mark schemes for writing; she then used these to draft a set of 'pass-level' descriptors of the writing proficiencies of candidates from CEF A2 (Basic user, Waystage) through to C2 (Proficient user, Mastery) levels (see Chapter 1 for description of these levels) by modifying the descriptors for the levels represented by the Main Suite of Cambridge exams. The first draft was analytical in orientation focusing on individual assessment criteria; a second draft was developed based on holistic impression marking principles: 'Pass level' descriptors. A new draft general mark scheme for the FCE Revision Project (0–5 scale) was also developed at this time. This resulted in a draft five-band Common Scale for Writing characterised by criteria such as: operational command of written language; length, complexity and organisation of texts; register and appropriacy; range of structures and vocabulary, and accuracy errors (Saville et al 1995).

In parallel with the work undertaken by Capel on existing Cambridge mark schemes, Hamp-Lyons analysed a corpus of PET, FCE, CAE and CPE exam candidate scripts. The scripts were candidate responses to a range of communicative tasks in Writing tests at the different exam levels. The following criteria were applied in the script selection:

- a range of candidate nationalities and L1s were represented (scripts came from test centres in the UK, Spain, Poland, Turkey, Brazil, Germany, France, Greece, and Japan)
- a variety of task types was represented
- a minimum of five scripts per task (and ideally 10) were selected
- all scripts were within the 'C' pass boundary.

The aim of this part of the research was to characterise the proficiency levels of the scripts through 'can do', 'can sometimes do', and 'cannot do' statements for which Hamp-Lyons identified the following assessment criteria: task completion; communicative effectiveness; syntactic accuracy and range; lexical appropriacy; chunking, paragraphing and organisation; register control; and personal stance and perspective (Hamp-Lyons 1995).

Attempts to create a common scale proved difficult. Hamp-Lyons expected to find different aspects salient in judging Writing from task to task, and indeed this appeared to be the case. This was not so much a problem for scoring, taking into account rater training and the scoring of each item independently, but it was perceived to be a great problem for developing a 'common' scale. Not only were different aspects of writing ability salient for different tasks, but the apparent ability level of the answer sets seemed to vary from task to task even after appropriate salient features had been used for making judgements. Scale development for any test assumes that writing performance is the same regardless of the task, and can be described by the same scale features. When task type becomes too significant an influence, different scales are necessary for each task type. When individual tasks within the same apparent task type behave too differently, there is a test design problem.

Hamp-Lyons noted, however, that the wide range of Cambridge ESOL exams and tasks covered by the script sample made it difficult to identify consistent features of writing at different levels. To avoid this, it was necessary to control the task variable by ensuring that all candidates, from whatever level, responded to the same task.

The approaches and findings of Phase 1 led to the following decisions on the methodology for Phase 2 of the project:

- control the task effect variable, i.e. gather a corpus of candidates' writing performance which were all responses to the same communicative task
- have all sample scripts scored by at least three raters, including the script analyst, with inter rater-reliability analyses carried out across all scores
- support the manual script analyses, where feasible, by computer analyses of the corpus.

Phase 2: Developing corpus-informed performance level descriptors

Phase 2 of the CSW project set out to identify distinguishing features in the writing performance of ESOL learners across three Cambridge English examination levels (FCE, CAE and CPE) and to incorporate these features into a scale of band descriptors common to these three levels. After consideration of the report from a senior examiner, an 'argumentative/public' task was selected from the live test paper used in the December 1998 FCE exam session; this type of task was regarded as likely to satisfy face validity criteria for candidates at the three levels concerned, and unlikely to present any unforeseen difficulties of task topic or type. A corpus of 288 candidate writing performances (108 FCE scripts and 180 CAE and CPE scripts) was obtained on the Writing task and each script was graded by more than one experienced and trained rater, using the FCE assessment scale (as used by FCE markers for the same task in the live FCE exam).

As a first step in the drafting of band descriptors common to the three levels of writing performance, each of the 288 scripts was read and described qualitatively in terms of its salient features. The script analyst wrote brief comments on the distinguishing characteristics of each performance. The four most common features noted were: 'fluency' (referring not only to length of text but also to the apparent ease of use of the target language); 'organisation' (covering the overall structure and coherence of the writing, and its use of links, or cohesive devices); 'accuracy' (of vocabulary, grammatical structure – a feature referred to more than any other in the text analyst's initial rating of all the scripts); and 'impact' (on the reader – originally seen as reflecting the communicative writing construct, but also perceived as a criterion for assessment).

All ratings of the corpus of 288 scripts, including those of the script analyst, were then used to select four sub-corpora of scripts. The first sub-corpus (n=29 scripts) consisted of scripts to which *all* raters had assigned a Band 5 (including scores of 5.3, 5.2 and 5.1) according to the FCE scale which had been used; the second sub-corpus (n=18) were scripts banded at 4 by all raters; the third (n=43) were those banded at 3 by all raters; and the fourth sub-corpus (n=8 only) consisted of scripts banded at 2. Since these scripts had attracted unanimous rating agreements, the four sub-corpora were regarded as representing discrete *high*, *fairly high*, *medium*, and *lower* proficiency levels. These four sub-corpora of scripts were subjected to closer analysis and specification of their typical features: the analysis and specification were cross-checked for agreement through expert consultation. Detailed re-examination of the four groups of scripts involved:

- re-reading of each script
- characterisation according to main communicative descriptors, i.e. features of the script that had a favourable or less favourable impact on the reader
- classification of counts of error using conventional marker error categorisations
- selection of script extracts considered 'typical' of communicative characteristics of the sub-corpus.

This qualitative analysis of the scripts in the four sub-corpora was supplemented with computer analyses of certain 'typical' features as well as additional related features of potential relevance. The characteristics and criteria identified were then 'rationalised into a draft scale of band descriptions for the proficiency levels specified, this scale to be proposed as a draft common scale for writing' (Hawkey and Barker 2004), using descriptors with a focus on three criteria:

- sophistication of language
- organisation and cohesion
- accuracy.

Phase 3: Extending the analysis to other examinations

Phase 3 of the CSW project extended the analysis beyond the Main Suite examinations to explore how successfully the newly developed draft Common Scale for Writing could be applied to samples of candidate writing performance from other Cambridge ESOL exams targeting similar proficiency levels. Using a similar approach to that applied to the CPE, CAE and FCE corpora in Phase 2, qualitative analyses were performed on corpora of IELTS, BEC and CELS candidate scripts, this time over a range of levels and tasks (Hawkey and Shaw 2005). This exercise made it possible to trial and validate the draft common scale band descriptors; following their application to each new corpus of candidate writing samples, the descriptors were progressively modified.

A particular focus in Phase 3 was the alignment of the emerging common scale band descriptors with performance levels on IELTS Writing tasks. Work to compare IELTS bands and the Main Suite levels explored two research hypotheses:

• that ratings of IELTS Writing performances using the draft common scale will correlate satisfactorily with ratings assigned by trained IELTS raters using IELTS mark schemes
• that comparisons between the performance levels of candidates across different exams will be facilitated by the use of a common scale for writing.

The data for analysis was 79 IELTS Writing performances representing a wide range of IELTS band scores. They included: Academic Writing Task 1 scripts (description of iconic data); General Training Writing Task 1 scripts (letter writing); and Academic Writing and General Training Task 2 scripts (both argumentative tasks). All the scripts used in this analysis were selected from IELTS *certification* scripts used for examiner training purposes between 1995 and 2000; this means they had already been multiply marked and identified as benchmark examples of particular levels. They had also been reproduced as word-processed text files to make them amenable to statistical software packages such as Wordsmith Tools (www.oup.com/elt/catalogue/isbn/6890?cc=gb). Text files also have the advantage of removing the potential impact of handwriting and photocopying.

Qualitative analysis of the individual IELTS Writing performances included their description and rating according to the criteria and band levels of the draft Common Scale for Writing (sophistication of language, organisation and cohesion, accuracy). An initial, impressionistic overview of the 79 IELTS scripts was followed by a more detailed descriptive analysis of the features which emerged from each script. These descriptions and ratings were then compared with the original IELTS profile and global ratings given to the performances.

Finally, a comparison was made of the levels of IELTS Writing performance with the common scale bands previously identified (see also Chapter 7 for further discussion of this in terms of the aspect of criterion-related validity).

The IELTS:CSW comparisons proved to be neither neat nor proportional; nevertheless, they provided initial indications of the nature of the relationship between IELTS band scores and CSW levels as follows:

- CSW level 2 (linked to CEF level B1) could extend from the upper reaches of IELTS Band 3 to the lower reaches of IELTS Band 5
- CSW levels 3 and 4 (B2 and C1) relates to IELTS Band 6
- CSW level 4 reaches from around IELTS Band 6.5 to 7 and 8
- CSW level 5 (C2) extends from high IELTS Band 8 into Band 9.

The wide band of performance apparently represented by CSW level 4 (CEF level C1) and described by the Common European Framework (Council of Europe 2001:2) as 'an advanced level of competence suitable for more complex work and study tasks' extends from around IELTS Band 6.5 (a common university cut-off band) to Band 7 and even the beginnings of Band 8; this suggests that C1 or a successful performance at CAE level may be a strong qualification for English-medium university course entrance.

High performance at IELTS Bands 8 and 9 appears to be at the level of CEF C2, or CPE. Indications from the study are also that CSW level 5 (CEF C2) stretches from high IELTS Band 8 to 9.

The inferences made here on the relationship between IELTS Writing band scores and the draft CSW levels remain tentative. Further validation studies are needed, with larger samples and on different candidate test populations to confirm these findings. For this reason, a study was also made of Cambridge ESOL BEC scripts at the three levels – Preliminary (B1), Intermediate (B2) and Higher (C1). The data was drawn from the set of BEC Writing co-ordination (standardisation) scripts used in 2002. They comprised a small corpus of 56 'live' Writing scripts from BEC Preliminary (15 scripts), Vantage (25 scripts) and Higher (16 scripts) and included a mix of Task 1 and Task 2 scripts. All scripts had been multiply marked and identified as benchmark examples of writing performance levels within the BEC suite. The scripts had also been reproduced as word-processed text files.

The BEC mark scheme scales have five bands for each level (Preliminary, Vantage and Higher) and, in most instances, identically worded criterial descriptors are used across the three exam levels, even though the descriptors are being applied to distinctly different levels of performance/proficiency. The BEC Handbook reminds users that 'This mark scheme should be interpreted at BEC Preliminary (or Vantage or Higher) level. N.B. a Band 5 may be far from perfect in most instances.'

Once again, each script in the BEC corpus was described qualitatively and assigned CSW band scores for the three criteria (sophistication of language; organisation and cohesion, accuracy). In terms of the mean CSW band scores assigned to the 56 scripts, there appeared to be some fit, albeit limited, between the draft CSW band scale scores and the BEC levels.

The CSW ratings of all 56 BEC scripts were then compared with the 'live' band ratings assigned to the same scripts using the BEC mark scheme. All but four of the 56 ratings demonstrated middling correlations. Further investigation indicated that in three of the four cases this was because the CSW scale did not penalise the scripts concerned as strictly as the BEC mark schemes for missing or misunderstood information; this was a task-specific factor in the context of otherwise higher communicative performance. In the fourth case the candidate had written too few words for the three CSW criteria to be validly applied.

Analyses of the three BEC corpora appeared in general to support the hypothesised relationship between the draft CSW, CEF levels and the BEC levels.

Summary

Findings from the CSW project are contributing to the development of a scale of meaningful, criteria-focused performance descriptors that are relevant to the assessment of writing across different exams at CEF-specified levels. A scale of this nature can help comparisons of candidate writing performance across different exams, enabling inferences to be made about what a Band 3 on an FCE task might mean at CAE level, or what a Pass at BEC Vantage might mean in terms of IELTS band scores. The draft Common Scale for Writing derived from the research described here (see pages 78–9) functions as a user-oriented scale to assist with the process of locating and interpreting performance levels associated with particular exams within a wider framework of reference.

It should be emphasised, however, that any inferences made so far across Cambridge ESOL exam bands and the draft CSW remain provisional. Further CSW validation studies are still needed, with larger samples and on different candidate test populations. Ongoing research continues to refine our understanding of the relationship between the Cambridge ESOL examination levels and the CEF levels (see Chapter 1 and Chapter 7 for further details).

Case Study D: Revising the IELTS assessment criteria and rating scales

Background

Several of the issues about criteria and rating scales which were discussed in Case Study C above were uppermost in the minds of the Cambridge ESOL team responsible for revising the IELTS Writing assessment criteria and band level descriptors. Although the major focus of this book is on the Cambridge ESOL Main Suite examinations, a brief overview of the IELTS Writing Assessment Revision Project is included here as a practical illustration of how criteria and rating scales for a specific test can be developed. This overview may be particularly helpful to other examination boards and test developers in understanding the sorts of activities and timescales which can be involved in the revision of large-scale tests. (For more details of the IELTS test see Chapter 1. A full description of the IELTS Writing Revision Project, including the purpose, activities and results of each phase, can be found in the project report published by Shaw and Falvey, forthcoming.)

The IELTS Writing Assessment Revision Project followed the management model successfully adopted when revising the IELTS Speaking test (1998–2001) (See also the discussion of Cambridge ESOL's approach to test development and revision in Chapter 2 of Weir and Milanovic 2003). Although the IELTS Speaking test revision had included redesign of the test content and format, revision of the Writing test was limited to:

1. Redesign of the assessment procedures, i.e. scales, criteria and bands.
2. The implementation of new training systems, i.e. the production of a new and comprehensive set of materials and procedures for the systematic (re)training of IELTS raters.

As with the CSW project, IELTS scale re-construction was an iterative process involving:

- expert/stakeholder evaluation of draft descriptions
- identification by highly experienced markers of performances at different levels and agreement on 'salient' features
- discussion and identification of criteria for assessment, defined in terms of performance levels
- 'fine-tuning' from feedback data obtained through Writing examiner trials.

The project plan allowed for five distinct phases between June 2001 and January 2005; each of these is summarised below.

Phase 1: Consultation, initial planning and design (June – December 2001)

Phase 1 involved a review of routinely collected score and performance data for the operational Writing test, as well as a survey of commissioned and non-commissioned studies relating to IELTS Writing (including studies funded under the IELTS Joint-funded Research Program); this was supplemented with a review of the literature on holistic and analytic approaches to writing assessment. Another key component of Phase 1 was a stakeholder survey to investigate IELTS rater attitudes and behaviour with a view to highlighting theoretical and practical factors that could inform redevelopment of the writing assessment criteria and scales. Phase 1 activity revealed several important issues from the perspective of the assessor, in particular individual approaches and attitudes to IELTS Writing assessment, differing domains (Academic and General Training) and differing task genres (Task 1 and Task 2); these provided a valuable focus for the re-development of the existing rating scale criteria. (See Shaw 2002a for more details.)

Phase 2: Development (January 2002–May 2003)

The development phase comprised a two-fold approach to re-developing the existing rating scales (Shaw 2004). Traditionally, the design and development of rating scales for direct tests of Writing have tended to rely upon an *a priori* measuring approach in which development of criteria and scale descriptions is based on the intuitive judgement and experience of 'experts' (Fulcher 1996). The panel of external 'experts' convened for this project included academic consultants and senior IELTS examiners with a particular interest in Academic Writing and with a background in language pedagogy, applied linguistics and language testing. Together with Cambridge ESOL staff, the team set about re-developing the existing IELTS criteria and rating scales. Scale (re)construction is widely believed to be both an expert and complex process and Lumley's view that revision must be accompanied by 'the involvement of a great many people' (2000:49) is well-illustrated by Cambridge ESOL's approach in this project.

In addition to an *a priori* approach, however, several writers have advocated a more empirically-oriented approach to the construction of rating scales (Fulcher 1987, Milanovic, Saville, Pollitt and Cook 1996, Shohamy 1990, Weir 1993). An empirically-based approach involves analysing samples of actual language performance in an attempt to construct (or reconstruct) assessment criteria and rating scale descriptors; it also involves investigating the way in which scale descriptors are likely to be interpreted and applied by human raters. For this reason, quantitative and qualitative analyses of writing performances by IELTS candidates also played a central role in the Development Phase, just as it had done in the CSW Project described above in Case Study C.

Phase 2 thus combined use of quantitative methodologies (application of draft criteria and scales to language performances) and qualitative methodologies (insightful and intuitive judgements derived from 'expert' participants) to inform the reconstruction of IELTS assessment criteria and scales (Shaw 2002b).

The five revised analytical criteria for both Modules and both Tasks are shown in Table 5.2.

Table 5.2 Revised IELTS Writing criteria for Tasks 1 and 2

TASK 1 assessment criteria (Academic and General Training Modules)	TASK 2 assessment criteria (Academic and General Training Modules)
Task Achievement	Task Response
Coherence and Cohesion	Coherence and Cohesion
Lexical Resource	Lexical Resource
Grammatical Range and Accuracy	Grammatical Range and Accuracy

Phase 3: Validation (June 2003–May 2004)

Phase 3 sought validation evidence for the revised assessment criteria and band level descriptors which emerged from the multiple drafting and redrafting activity in Phase 2 (Shaw 2003a). Once again, both qualitative and quantitative methods were used to establish their validity, reliability, impact and practicality; these four aspects have been identified by Cambridge ESOL as four essential qualities of test or examination usefulness and are known collectively by the acronym VRIP (see Weir and Milanovic 2003). Senior IELTS examiners in the UK and Australia took part in a multiple rating trial of a set of benchmarked IELTS scripts. Examiner scores and questionnaire responses collected from the multiple rating exercise were analysed using multi-faceted Rasch (FACETS) and Generalisability theory to explore answers to questions such as:

- Do the scales measure different aspects of language proficiency?
- Do they contribute consistently to the candidate's final score?
- Do raters use and interpret the mark scheme in the same way?
- Do candidates score in the same range on the current and revised rating schemes?

In addition, focus group techniques and verbal protocol analysis were used with examiners as they actually applied the draft criteria and scales to sample performances; this provided additional insights into what raters apparently paid attention to in their rating, how they reached their final judgement, and whether they found certain criteria more difficult to identify and scale than others.

Evidence gathered from a variety of sources, and derived from both quantitative and qualitative methodologies, confirmed that the revised criteria and scales were functioning as expected and were suitable for release into operational mode. Full details of all the studies conducted during the Validation Phase, together with their outcomes, can be found in the IELTS Writing Assessment Revision Project Report (Shaw and Falvey, forthcoming).

Phase 4: Implementation (June – December 2004)

Phase 4 required that the global cadre of IELTS examiners be fully trained and standardised in preparation for introducing the revised approach to IELTS Writing assessment in January 2005 (Bridges and Shaw 2004). Considerable resources were therefore allocated to developing a comprehensive examiner training and standardisation programme, including a set of materials and a system of procedures for delivering the programme to trainers and examiners worldwide. Any decision to retrain and re-standardise a large and geographically dispersed community of examiners, such as that which operates for IELTS, has major practical and logistic implications in terms of time, expertise and other resources. One issue which needs to be noted, for example, is that once examiners have been trained and are ready to use the new criteria and scales, they may well have to continue with the existing system for an interim period until the new approach becomes operational. In the case of IELTS, the new training package was first trialled with senior examiners and then amended in light of the feedback received; it was trialled again with experienced raters who, once they had satisfactorily completed the training exercise, cascaded the training and standardisation programme out to the rest of the rater cadre worldwide.

Phase 5: Operational (January 2005 onwards)

The revised IELTS Writing assessment criteria and rating scales were used operationally for the first time in January 2005. Shortly after their introduction, a small-scale trial was undertaken with a group of IELTS examiners in a UK centre to ascertain how well the criteria and scales were functioning in the live context (Falvey and Shaw 2005). This trial involved: a preliminary discussion of examiners' thoughts prior to script marking; verbal protocols, where an examiner was asked to think aloud while marking; and a focus group discussion after marking to capture examiner reactions and attitudes to the new scale. The trial was designed to provide insights into how well the revised rating scale was being interpreted and applied by examiners and to gather further validation evidence together with any issues raised by the new assessment approach. Throughout the trial analysis, findings were related to observations, reports and concerns which had been articulated by examiners during the 2001 global survey conducted in Phase 1 of the project. Comparisons were also made with findings from a validation trial undertaken in 2003 when the revised scale was used by senior examiners for the first time. Once again, full details of this phase are reported in Shaw and Falvey (forthcoming).

Undertaken four months into the operational life of the revised rating scale, the small-scale trial involved asking a group of experienced examiners from Anglia Ruskin University (ARU) to articulate their thoughts about the revised scale. A semi-structured, facilitated discussion covered areas relating to initial script management, approach to assessment, use of band descriptors, paragraphing, old and new scale comparability, formulaic language, training, guidelines for word counts, and script legibility. In addition, concurrent 'think-aloud' protocols with examiners as they individually rated tasks provided immediate and explicit explanations of:

- what examiners do as they mark
- how examiners' thought processes are structured during the marking process
- what particular information examiners heed when judging candidates' answers.

Retrospective data was captured by an examiner questionnaire. Examiners found the revised rating scale a marked improvement on the old scale and welcomed the greater clarity and additional explanatory text in the new descriptors. Examiners also believed the revised rating scale provided a more comprehensive description of the key features of writing at each band level. The separation of *Lexical Resource* and *Grammatical Range and Accuracy* was perceived to be extremely valuable.

Examiners confirmed they understood the revised criteria for Task 1 and Task 2 and seemed to have acquired confidence in their ratings after using the scale for four months. There was a general satisfaction with the accuracy of final awards. Moreover, the subscales seemed to work well for each of the two writing domains. Additionally, the revised *Task Achievement/Task Response* criterion was effective for rating Task 1 and Task 2 across the differing domains.

Encouragingly, the revised, prescribed method of assessment was being adopted. The revised approach is depicted as a flow diagram in the Instructions to IELTS Examiners booklet (see also Appendix C) and is now a prominent feature of examiner training.

It was evident from the protocols that examiners were generally adhering to the revised and prescribed method of assessment (described in Bridges and Shaw, 2004 and shown as Appendix C). The protocols also indicated that raters were processing several assessment criteria simultaneously and that all four assessment criteria were uppermost in the minds of raters when evaluating either Task 1 or Task 2. Additionally, protocols revealed:

- that examiners analysed the task requirements before attempting to rate responses
- that examiners tended to revisit the task throughout their marking
- that examiners tended to base their assessments on a detailed study of the features of the candidate's response in relation to the task
- that examiners appeared to employ different marking approaches for different criteria
- that examiners generally adopted one of two marking approaches: a 'principled two-scan/read' and a 'pragmatic two-scan/read'. (See pages 172–73.)

For the final study in Phase 5, two questionnaires (revised in the light of the ARU pilot trial) were constructed: an examiner questionnaire and a centre administrator's feedback form (in order to elicit views on the new scales from an assessment, administrative and practical point of view). The questionnaire was completed by 211 examiners at the top 30 IELTS test centres based on candidate entries. Centres were located in several continents including Europe, Australasia and Asia.

Feedback from examiners

It was clear that an overwhelming majority of examiners appreciated the revised rating scale believing it to be a considerable improvement overall on the former one. General feedback from examiners was very positive. IELTS examiners acknowledged that the revision project had been well researched and empirically grounded. Moreover, use of the new writing criteria engendered a positive washback effect on assessment. The new scale, it is believed, now offers examiners a better indication of where to place candidates on the IELTS proficiency continuum. The scale is perceived to be more helpful than the previous one, offering better guidance to examiners, and is considered to be fairer to the candidate. According to qualitative examiner feedback, the changes have facilitated more efficient and effective marking and engendered greater confidence among examiners. Examiners were appreciative of the increased explanatory text accompanying the new descriptors as the revised text has allowed for 'greater delicacy of assessment'. The descriptors are seen as clearer, more comprehensive, easier to follow and achieving a greater precision than before. Examiners also felt that the new criteria helped a great deal with the problem of marking memorised or potentially memorised scripts though this still remains an area of some concern. The revised scale appears to deal very effectively with the problem of candidates supplying 'off topic' responses. The introduction of ceilings and penalties and the inclusion of descriptors legislating for the use of formulaic language, appropriate paragraphing and punctuation seem to be positive. Overarching statements are also felt to make marking simpler. The new scale seems to have eliminated some areas of doubt which previously existed in the minds of examiners such as the nature and degree of underlength script penalization, poor topic exposition and the extent to which credit should be given for aspects of lexical resource in the face of poor grammar.

Feedback from Test Administrators

From the Test Administrator perspective, the introduction of the new scale appears to have been relatively smooth. There was a fairly widespread perception that sufficient time had been given to retraining examiners. Several centres were favourably disposed to the new administrative procedures although not all centres echoed this sentiment. One administrative change relates to the input requirements for ESOLCOMMS (Cambridge ESOL's administrative system used for the processing of IELTS). All eight criteria (compared to the original single entry) now require keying. The problems associated with entering additional scores have been widely acknowledged and in the majority of cases managed both quickly and efficiently. Nevertheless, centres observed that increased keying engendered significant extra workload for clerical administration staff. An increase in data processing time has added to the workload. However, the need for manually computed overall writing band scores has been removed which was previously a potential source of error in the rating process.

Summary

A particular feature of the IELTS Writing Assessment Revision Project was its iterative nature, i.e. regular refinement of IELTS criteria and descriptors for the Writing module was continually undertaken, issues were constantly revisited, and fresh studies were carried out when deeper insights were required. The fine-tuning of descriptors to reach Draft 12 after multiple inputs and the careful reading and assessing of descriptors by different stakeholders exemplifies this approach.

The compelling need for examination boards to have in place a systematic set of procedures for rating is attested to by the literature on rater performance and in the practical experience of projects such as that discussed in this case study. The need for test developers and examination boards to devote considerable resources to selecting appropriate raters, establishing satisfactory conditions for rating, training raters, and monitoring their performance is clear.

The Cambridge approach to these essentials of scoring validity will be examined in detail after the following review of the research on rater characteristics.

Rater characteristics

A crucial factor which influences the manner in which raters evaluate written performance is the characteristics of the raters themselves. In examining test-taker characteristics in Chapter 2 we noted that a number of facets might impact on test-taker behaviour. Those facets taken from O'Sullivan (2000), which, *mutatis mutandis*, may also impact on rater performance are revisited and listed in Table 5.3.

Table 5.3 Rater characteristics (based on O'Sullivan 2000)

Physical/Physiological	Psychological	Experiential
Short term ailments *(toothache, cold etc.)*	Personality	Education
	Memory	Examination preparedness
Longer term disabilities *(speaking, hearing, vision)*	Cognitive style	Examination experience
	Affective schemata	Communication experience
Age	Concentration	Target language –
Sex	Motivation	Country residence
	Emotional state	

Some of the physical/physiological or psychological conditions may not lend themselves to future investigation or not be considered worth the effort, but the effects of others might be more interesting and could in principle be looked at as part of an ongoing, long-term research agenda. Only limited evidence is available on their effects on rating at the moment and this is an area in need of further comprehensive research. Experiential factors have received the most attention in the literature and we will focus on these in our discussion below not least because it may be possible to address these in selection and recruitment procedures and through the training process (see Appendices D and F).

The significant role of both personal and professional experience in the rating event has been verified in a number of studies of L2 performance contexts (Elder 1993, Hamp-Lyons 1990, 1996, Hill 1998, Odell 1981, O'Loughlin 1992). Results from previous studies show that marker behaviour and rater response varies with different groups in ways that can be partially attributed to variables such as professional, cultural and linguistic background, extent of training in the use of assessment instruments, gender, amount of exposure to L2 writing (Hamp-Lyons 1990, Vann et al 1991), and disparate and external pressures (circumstantial, emotional, psychological: Hamp-Lyons 1990).

Two experiential features which appear to be particularly salient are briefly considered below.

Effect of language experience: Language background is particularly influential in terms of rater behaviour and values. Examiners conversant with first language rhetorical patterns undoubtedly demonstrate a tendency to be more sympathetic to L2 compositions, manifesting identical patterns unlike raters who are less familiar with these patterns (Hinkel 1994, Kobayashi and Rinnert 1996, Land and Whiteley 1989).

Effect of professional experience: Comparisons are often made between how language proficiency exam raters and subject specialists rate essays. This research is important in considering tests of EAP but the same concerns do not necessarily pertain to tests of general proficiency for example, to KET, PET, etc.

Subject specialists and language-trained EFL teachers demonstrate a tendency to employ rating instruments differently (Elder 1992). Brown (1995) observed individual differences in rater behaviour according to the linguistic background and occupational experience of the raters during her development of an occupation-specific language performance test. The marking scheme was banded and was developed through negotiation between examiners from a number of different occupational and linguistic groups. She found that no group as a whole was unsuitable to develop and examine an occupation-specific language performance test. The test consisted of a 30-minute interview. The candidates were assessed on linguistic skills and task fulfilment. Linguistic skill was assessed using a range of criteria, e.g. vocabulary on a scale of 1–6 using descriptive band scales. Task fulfilment was assessed on a scale of 1–6 for each of five phases in the interview. There were no differences overall between the groups in terms of the grades awarded to candidates' performance. However, there were group differences in terms of the application of individual assessment criteria. Brown (1995) argued that had the different groups been allowed to develop their own tests they might have been very different. This statement illustrates that norms of judgement can be formed at the item level within tightly knit groups.

Bridgeman and Carlson (1983) developed and employed the use of questionnaires in mainstream English university departments and EFL programmes. In one particular survey of 190 departments involving 34 universities in America and Canada, responses from staff in English departments demonstrated more generally 'the most disagreement with other departments'. It was clear that the notion of 'audience' was regarded as significantly more important as an assessment criterion by staff within the English departments than staff elsewhere. Moreover, English staff were more dismissive of 'content' in terms of its hierarchical importance as an assessment criterion than their subject-specific counterparts (1983:37). (See also Santos 1988, Weir 1983 below.) Conversely, sentence structuring assumed a greater degree of prominence by the English staff compared with other staff. Results from the Bridgeman and Carlson (1983) survey suggests that a significant number of university staff across the entire range of departments were adopting differing and disparate standards and focusing on different aspects of writing while rating (1983:2). Mechanical and orthographic features of text such as spelling, punctuation and the structuring of sentences, the use and extent of lexis, 'appropriateness to audience' together with 'overall writing ability' were, it was observed, assessed less harshly for non-native speakers (1983:30).

Weir (1983) details the differences in marking by university staff in the UK depending on whether the writer was a non-native speaker or not, noting that standards may vary markedly even between tutors on the same course. He concluded that English language tutors teaching on university pre-sessional programmes were overly preoccupied with the mechanics of writing. In contrast, subject specialists were primarily concerned with content and organisation and did not appear to be unduly concerned by mechanics as they regarded native speakers to be worse in these respects. Hamp-Lyons (1991a), in a further comparison of the responses of language-trained specialists with teachers in other disciplines, investigated the approaches teachers employed when attending to certain textual characteristics such as rhetorical features and content. She observed that EFL teachers 'attended to rhetorical criteria foremost', whereas the specialists emphasised content (1991a:134).

A similar investigation undertaken by O'Loughlin (1992) attempted to compare the respective behaviours of examiners responsible for rating essays produced by native-speaker students and EFL students. Findings revealed that (a) language teachers were less interested in content than their counterparts in other academic subject areas, and (b) EFL teachers ascribed greater importance to grammar and cohesion than mainstream English teachers.

We would want to be sure that the scores awarded by trained language proficiency raters are similar to those that would be awarded by subject specialists where our target situation is academic performance. These researchers make it clear that the broad sample of academic subject staff surveyed regard relevance and adequacy of content and organisation as criterial rather than linguistic aspects of spelling, grammar and punctuation *per se*. This has serious implications for the importance of planning, organisation, monitoring, editing and revision of content and coherence in writing which we saw as key cognitive processes in Chapter 3. The saliency of organisation and content must be reflected in the nature of the processing required for successful task completion and in the criteria used in rating to ensure this. Language proficiency raters must be carefully trained in this respect since it may run counter to their previous practices.

Further evidence of variability occasioned by rater preferences

Other L1 and L2 research suggests that this simple dichotomy between language and subject specialists may only be the 'tip of a variability iceberg'. A wide variety of studies have been conducted in this area and they indicate a host of additional complexities attributable to the behaviour of raters in language examinations and the lack of any real consensus with regard to the importance of individual criteria for assessing written production.

A brief survey of the relevant literature illustrates the lack of consensus. According to Diederich (1974), mechanics exerts a far more powerful influence than organisation on overall rater assessment. Stewart and Grobe (1979) concluded that markers were most influenced by length and accuracy. Freedman (1979) in contrast demonstrated that content was uppermost in the minds of the rater when making a final judgement on an essay. Freedman found a hierarchy of assessment criteria, for example raters rating content higher than organisation and that features like mechanics are less important (1979:161). In a later study conducted by Grobe (1981) markers were found to be principally influenced by diversity of vocabulary. Raforth and Rubin (1984) support the notion that mechanics is a predominant consideration in the (L2) assessment process though they expressed some doubt about raters' ability to distinguish between content and mechanics (1984:456) thus casting serious doubt on the degree to which judgements are indeed influenced by mechanics.

Freedman (1979) and Breland and Jones (1984) discovered through empirical investigation of actual L1 ratings that examiner claims and examiner reality are not always entirely synonymous. Vaughan concluded that each examiner relied upon their own method for making L2 judgements (1991:121). This suggests that there are considerable individual differences between raters particularly in the areas of how raters perceive script content and organisation, and in regard to specific rater characteristics.

Milanovic and Saville (1996) examined the decision-making behaviour of L2 composition markers by investigating the judgements made by 16 raters of FCE and CPE scripts. They noted that with the higher levels (CPE), markers tended to focus more on vocabulary and content, while with the intermediate level scripts (FCE), markers focused more on communicative effectiveness and task realisation. The researchers also commented on the striking diversity of the composition elements referred to by raters in explaining their assessments. In terms of rater background, it appeared to be the case that different experiential backgrounds can affect the way in which markers assess compositions, despite the fact that special training has been given to the rater for the specific marking exercise. According to Milanovic et al, FCE markers frequently noted *length* when marking both FCE and CPE scripts, whereas CPE markers tended to note *content* in the FCE scripts and mother-tongue teachers were more concerned with *tone*.

All these studies testify to the need to establish clear and explicit rating criteria appropriate to the Writing task (see previous section) and the pressing need to train examiners and standardise them to these criteria (as discussed later in this chapter).

As well as variability occasioned by the differing views on the salience of various criteria, examiners may also vary in their ratings as a result of differing expectations of a task.

Rating process

According to Weigle (2002:71) rater expectations have been shown to have an effect on overall rater judgement. She cites Stock and Robinson (1987) and the strong claim that 'expectations may be as important as the quality of the text itself in determining composition scores'.

We noted earlier in the section on context validity the importance of the interaction between the test taker and the Writing task. A second, related and potentially problematic type of interaction involves the rater and the task. The rater's interaction is complicated as it is essentially two-fold in nature: not only does the rater interact with the text produced by the candidate, but the rater must necessarily interact with the task also. This raises the issue of task difficulty. Raters may attempt to compensate for perceived task difficulty in applying the rating to the written response (Polio and Glew 1996 make mention of this as do Weigle, Lamison and Peters 2000).

The interest is in the decision-making processes that are used by examiners. Research has become increasingly more concerned with recommending that investigating the cognitive processes of raters in arriving at judgements is one specific way in which a greater understanding of rater behaviour may be accomplished (Brown 1995, Hamp-Lyons 1990, Huot 1990, Lumley 2000, Milanovic, Saville and Shuhong 1996, Tedick and Mathison 1995). Some examples of research in this area on Cambridge ESOL examinations are provided next.

Cambridge ESOL research

Milanovic et al (1996) employed a range of qualitative methodologies: group interviews, introspective verbal reports, and retrospective written reports to investigate the judgements made by 16 experienced (stronger) and less experienced (weaker) raters of Cambridge FCE/CPE compositions. The aims of their study were to investigate the range of approaches used by examiners to evaluate compositions and the elements markers focused on while marking those compositions; and to investigate whether examiners adjust their marking behaviour according to the level of the script.

The data revealed four discernible approaches to composition marking: *principled* and *pragmatic two-scan approaches*, *read through approach* and *provisional mark approach.* Markers adopting a principled two-scan/read approach scan or read the script twice before deciding on a final mark. The second reading is 'principled', being undertaken indiscriminately with all scripts, hence the term 'principled two-scan/read'. Markers adopting the pragmatic two-scan/read approach to the process of marking also read the scripts twice before assigning a mark to the script. What distinguishes this marking approach from the principled two-scan/read approach is the motivation behind the second reading of the composition. The pragmatic two-scan/read occurred only when the marker encountered difficulties in the script or in the marking environment and had to re-read to determine a mark. That is to say, markers only had recourse to this approach in the event of the failure of another method to generate a confident mark.

Milanovic et al (1996) identified two further approaches: 'Read through' is the least sophisticated of the marking approaches and consists of reading a script through once to pick up its good and bad points. The provisional mark approach is also characterised by a single reading of the script, but with a break in the marking flow, usually imposed towards the start of a candidate's effort, which prompts an initial assessment of its merits before reading is resumed to discover whether the rest of the answer confirms or denies that assessment.

The study also revealed the remarkable diversity of the composition elements (see section on rater characteristics on pages 168–70) referred to by the trial examiners in attempting to provide a rationale for their overall judgements.

Stronger, experienced examiners appeared to attend less to the analytical activities and spend more time gaining an overall impression of the composition. The weaker, less experienced examiners attended more frequently to analytical activities. The weaker examiners tended to be more positive in their comments, but this was at the cost of questioning and neutral comments, two strategies that the strong examiners may have employed as a check on their marking behaviour.

A detailed analysis of the protocols indicated that different script levels do appear to elicit different marking behaviour. In higher-level scripts (CPE), markers focused more on vocabulary and content. With intermediate-level scripts (FCE), markers focused more on communicative effectiveness and task realisation.

Furneaux and Rignall (2000) investigated the awards given by trainee examiners on IELTS scripts over a period of time during training, a study described in more detail below. Asked to make notes regarding how they had reached final decisions for some of their ratings, the differences in the decision-making processes between trainee and senior examiners were analysed. The trainee examiners' reports (reproduced as written notes) initially tended to refer to using accuracy of language as the main criterion for awarding marks but their later notes implied that examiners began to use the other criteria as well. This would suggest that the trainee examiners' decision-making process evolved to conform to the prescribed method.

Group effects on examiner reliability

It has long been known in psychology that group dynamics can influence individual judgements. Sherif (1935) studied the effects of group norms on the formation of judgements by bringing together a group of participants and asking them to make judgements (about how far a light had moved) in the presence of other participants. After two or three sessions their judgements rapidly converged. The same participants were called in for further sessions where they were asked to make judgements when no other participants were present. Their judgements were similar to the judgements that they had made in the group. These participants initially formed a group frame of reference which was then used to make judgements when the participants made individual judgements. This suggests that if examiners are required to make judgements publicly in a group they will form a group frame of reference and their judgements will converge. After such a meeting they should make judgements which are similar to those of the other members of the group. That is, there should be an increase in the agreement between the examiners.

Sherif (1935) also varied the experiment to explore the effects of adding a group member who conspired with the experimenter and took an extreme opinion in order to identify whether the group moved towards their view. Such extreme opinions can affect the group norm even for a while after the group member with the extreme opinion has left the group. This suggests that one 'rogue' examiner meeting with other examiners could unfortunately influence the judgements of other examiners.

Orr and Nuttall (1983) argue that examiner meetings for English GCSE and GCE examinations are important for promoting reliability. Wolf (1995) adds that the differences in reliability between different subjects reflect the degree to which markers are socialised into the assessment model during examiners' meetings where different examinations are discussed. Discussion in groups goes further than the simple public declaration of judgements reported to affect other judges' decisions by Sheriff (1935). Wolf (1995) also argues that examiner networks or discussion between examiners is needed for reliability. She states that: 'Also marker reliability is lower the less the markers concerned form part of a group in constant contact and discussion with each other' (1995:77).

Freedman (1981) argues that examiners could be trained to be more or less severe in their judgements. It has been found that examiner behaviour varies with different groups, such as professional background, subject specialism and gender (Hamp-Lyons 1990, Vann, Lorenz and Meyer 1991). This is presumably due to each group having a unique frame of reference. Brown's (1995) study to develop an occupation-specific language performance test (see earlier discussion) also suggests that norms of judgement can be formed at the question level within tightly knit groups.

Weigle (1994) studied the scores and verbal protocols of four inexperienced examiners both prior to, and following, training. The training process brought the initially aberrant inexperienced examiners more or less in line with other examiners in terms of scores. The 'training clarified the intended scoring criteria for raters, modified their expectations of student writing and provided a reference group of other raters with which raters could compare themselves' (1994:197). However, agreement between peers was not a major concern for Weigle (1994).

Weigle (1998) states that a focus on rater consensus may compel raters to ignore their own expertise and experience (essential components of the process of reading the candidates' answers) in assessing Writing. Rating essays is often based on the premise that the essay is measuring a defined trait which can be measured accurately and that raters can be trained to agree on the definition of the trait. Detractors have argued, however, that by adopting the agreed interpretation of the mark scheme the examiners have inadvertently forsaken their own respective subject experiences. Alternatively, it might be that in a group situation examiners learn from one another by a process of 'osmosis' and may agree on the interpretation of the mark scheme thereby improving reliability.

All the variables identified above may impact on the scoring validity of a test. There is one further critical variable: the conditions under which the scripts are rated, which may also influence the interaction between the exam script and the rater.

Rating conditions

Setting

To date, there has been no empirical research into the effect on rater performance of factors associated with the environment or contextual setting of the rating process. Such marking settings include:

- rating of written performances at test venue (often a university or private language school) – this can be familiar or unfamiliar to the rater
- raters attending examination boards to award ratings to written performances
- raters receiving written performances to score at home.

It seems clear that variation in the above settings may lead to systematic variability in the scores awarded in the rating process. For instance, familiarity with one's work conditions may result in a more settled and therefore less erratic performance. In addition, variations in the physical characteristics of the setting may have a similar effect. Examples of this might be the provision of air conditioning (or heating) where the climate requires it, or the presence (or absence) of noise – e.g. some raters like to have music playing in the background as they rate, others require silence.

With the second pair of conditions, it is not unusual to find that examination boards can allow raters to work in either (or both) of the situations described. Within Cambridge ESOL two marking models predominate: 'On-site' marking and 'At Home' marking. While there may not be a problem with this, it might be worth investigating the issue, to ensure that there is no systematic effect on rater performance (see Appendix D for an overview of marking procedures and models adopted by Cambridge ESOL). The basic question here is 'Do raters behave differently when they rate written performances under different conditions?'

New technology and the possibility of 'online' marking 'At Home' or 'On-site' raises further issues of rater performance in relation to a new medium. This will be taken up again in the later sections on new technologies (pages 199–217).

This development will of course introduce a further performance condition for raters, namely the format in which the script is presented to the rater.

Handwritten and word-processed writing

Studies have found that handwriting, neatness and layout contribute to the basis of legibility (Brown 2004, Bull and Stevens 1979, McGuire 1995, Marshall and Powers 1969, Sloan and McGinnis 1978). Evidence also suggests that handwriting affects the assessment of a piece of extended writing. Hughes et al (1983) have argued that raters with neat and presentable handwriting significantly underrate untidy and illegible written responses. Other things being equal, it is thought that well-presented constructed responses tend to receive higher scores than their poorly-presented counterparts (Briggs 1970, Chase 1986, Markham 1976).

The introduction of computer-administered direct tests of Writing – in which examinees can choose to word-process their responses – has raised fundamental questions regarding salience of legibility and the rating of second language writing. Clearly, in translating a test from one medium to another medium it is crucial to ascertain to what extent the new medium may alter the nature of the underlying test construct, or change the scale. Theoretical studies of writing and testing suggest that there are important differences between writing by hand and word-processing. Some of the specific research considerations include:

- the impact of composition medium on essay raters in second language writing assessment

- the significance and impact of the role of legibility in the assessment of word-processed scripts

- whether raters rate handwritten and word-processed responses differently and, if they do, whether any differences interact with gender, ethnicity or socioeconomic background.

Brown (2004) argues that we have known for a long time about the possible contaminating effect of handwriting and neatness in rating written scripts. Several L1 writing assessment studies have explored the impact of legibility on the general evaluation of writing quality. In the main, the quality of handwriting has an effect on the scoring of essays with improved legibility resulting in higher awards.

In contrast, however, there exists a paucity of studies examining the effect of handwriting in the assessment of second language writing.

Assessment constraints in the language testing context – multiple assessment focuses and restricted time – have, according to Charney (1984), resulted in handwriting playing a more significant role in assessment than it perhaps should (as compared to more construct valid criteria) because it is easily identifiable while rating rapidly.

Chou et al (1982) have suggested that essays are easier to read if presented neatly and that it is not merely handwriting *per se* that creates a favourable impression in the mind of the rater but that severe text editing may produce an unfavourable effect. Not only is poor handwriting difficult to process but, on the basis of poorly presented text, raters may formulate a somewhat pejorative picture of the author's disposition. Dramatic examples of script revision may be negatively interpreted by raters as being indicative of a candidate wholly ill-prepared for writing and devoid of any sense of effective textual organisation.

Huot (1993) puts forward the argument that fast reading during examination marking would be expected to be impacted by the quality and presentation of handwriting: untidy and illegible handwriting is likely to hamper flowing, rapid reading especially from a second language perspective where focus on 'fluency' is considered a major component of communicative effectiveness. Vaughan (1991), investigating protocol analysis as a means of identifying factors which influence the assessment of second language writing, surmised that handwriting and overall presentation is especially important to examiners. Whilst content was uppermost in the minds of the trial protocollers, the number of direct references to handwriting followed closely behind. Milanovic et al (1996) corroborate this finding by suggesting that layout appears to engender particular prejudices in certain raters before even considering the content of a response.

In a recent IELTS research study, Brown (2003) investigated the differences between handwritten and word-processed versions of the same IELTS Task 2 essays giving consideration to the effects of handwriting on legibility and assessment. She hypothesised that legibility – judged by examiners on a five-point scale – has a significant but small impact on scores. Moreover, the size of the impact is relative to the 'quality of handwriting and neatness of presentation' (2003:141). Contrary to her hypotheses, the handwritten versions of the same script were assessed higher than the word-processed versions: the worse the handwriting – the higher the comparative assessment. This finding echoes an earlier observation gleaned from a study of L1 handwritten versus word-processed study (Powers et al 1994). Higher handwritten scores observed in this particular investigation were attributed to the greater examiner expectations of typewritten texts (format, grammar, spelling). Errors occurring in word-processed responses tend to be more readily discernible.

Protocol analyses of the raters in Brown's study revealed that raters may well have been compensating for poor handwriting in their assessment. Interestingly, as script illegibility became more pronounced, the number of pejorative examiner comments increased (in accordance with expectations). However, and somewhat surprisingly, scores awarded to the responses also increased (as opposed to decreasing as might be predicted).

A study by Whitehead (2003) investigated differences in the assessment of Writing scripts across formats. The study sought to investigate whether candidates taking IELTS Academic Writing tests in computer-based mode (CB) would receive the same marks as in pen-and-paper mode (P and P), and whether examiners would approach the assessment of computer-based scripts in the same way as for pen-and-paper scripts. A sample of 50 candidates' scripts was collected from six centres which had been involved in the 2001 trialling phase of computer-based IELTS. Candidates in the 2001 trial took a CB version of IELTS followed soon afterwards by their pen-and-paper IELTS: this meant that for each candidate a handwritten and a computer-generated writing response was available for analysis. In Whitehead's study, six trained and certificated IELTS examiners were recruited to mark approximately 60 scripts each; these consisted of handwritten scripts, computer-based scripts and some handwritten scripts typed up to resemble computer-based scripts. The examiners for the study also completed a questionnaire about the scripts, assessment process and their experiences of, and attitudes to, assessing handwritten and word-processed performance. Whitehead found no significant differences between scores awarded to handwritten and typed scripts. Although CB scripts yielded slightly lower scores and higher variance, Whitehead suggests that these differences could be attributable to a motivation effect with candidates performing better on official rather than trial tests.

An investigation of FCE (syllabus 0100, from the June 2002 administration) handwritten and typed versions of the same scripts revealed insights into how examiners approach and rate different forms of candidate writing (Shaw 2003b). The study aimed to deduce whether salience of legibility, as realised through quality of handwriting, contributes to an understanding of examiner bias by focusing on two key questions:

- What is the impact of legibility on ratings awarded to FCE handwritten and word-processed Writing tasks?
- How are examiners affected by aspects of legibility and presentation as manifested by handwritten and word-processed responses?

Three highly experienced and current FCE examiners participated in the study. Each examiner independently re-rated 75 scripts typed up from their original handwritten forms. Examiners were additionally asked to comment on the marking experience by completing a questionnaire. Details of candidate name and centre were removed from the scripts so as not to unduly influence the examiners and the remaining text word processed. Keyers typed exactly what appeared on the original responses including all errors. The examiners were, therefore, provided with an exact representation of each script. Letter case was keyed as in the original script as was the punctuation used and the format of the script as far as possible. Each script was presented separately, by task, on several pieces of paper. These versions, minus the front cover, were given to each of the three examiners. It should be noted that the typed up scripts were not 'authentic', in the sense that they were not produced on a keyboard by the candidates under examination conditions.

The study revealed that the impact of rating typed versions of the original handwritten scripts is to deflate the mean – a finding which is in line with previous research (Brown 2003). In both Task 1 and Task 2, the mean was lower for the typed texts than for their handwritten counterparts. At first glance, the direction of this effect might be unexpected, i.e. increased script legibility might be thought to produce higher scores and poor legibility thought of as leading to lower scores – as is the case for first language assessment.

Mechanical aspects of writing such as mastery of orthographic and iconic conventions and handwriting neatness may not be particularly significant assessment focuses in L1 (Cumming 1998). In second language writing assessment however, greater stress is often put on certain linguistic features such as grammatical accuracy and range, lexical resource, syntactical structures and a focus on mechanical aspects of writing. Poor legibility might in fact serve to distract from mechanical errors of L2 writers.

All three examiners were enthusiastic about the marking trial, claiming it to be a positive experience. FCE examiners, it was believed, would appreciate not having to read poor handwriting. Despite initial difficulties, once examiners had gained familiarity with the typed responses they became increasingly comfortable assessing them. Furthermore, the speed of scripts assessed increased with time and examiners achieved their normal marking rates. Whilst examiners feel that it is difficult not to be influenced by bad handwriting they also consider that consistent format aids assessment of language and task and that a typed response can engender an objective approach to rating. Examiners were unanimous in their belief that typed scripts were easier to read than handwritten scripts, paragraphs were more readily located and spelling/punctuation errors were accentuated permitting their immediate recognition.

To summarise, although response format seemed to have relatively little impact on scores, Brown (2003), Shaw (2003b) and Whitehead (2003) all identify differences in the way that examiners approach typed and handwritten scripts.

Other rating conditions

Evidence is emerging that other conditions may also have the potential to impact on the rating process.

Time

Vaughan (1991) indicates that the time spent by raters on reading a script may have an impact on the reliability of scoring. The recommendation is that they should not take too long as this could influence their decisions. It may not be just a question of the temporal aspect however but rather one of personal characteristics also. Anecdotal evidence suggests that raters who reach a decision quickly and stick to it tend to be more internally consistent raters than those who take a long time and vacillate. Shaw et al (2001) found that for CAE impression marking on-screen, examiners with the highest script throughput turned out to be the most consistent. Further research is needed into this potentially important rating condition.

Scaffolding

The way that Principal Examiners or Team Leaders prime the raters may vary and accordingly have a good or bad effect. The procedures used by Cambridge are outlined in Appendices D and F but more attention might need to be paid to any differences in ways in which examiners are advised. Again further research is needed in this area.

For all the reasons laid out in the above sections on rating criteria and scales, rater characteristics, rating processes and rating conditions, the potential for variability in marking is considerable and it clearly needs to be addressed in order to enhance the scoring validity aspect of examinations. As well as the work on establishing appropriate and usable criteria discussed earlier, Cambridge ESOL devotes considerable time and resources to procedural matters:

• selecting and employing rating personnel
• rating procedures
• optimising rating conditions.

Cambridge has developed a two-pronged practical approach to these in an attempt to ensure that examiner accuracy and consistency can be realised. The approach is based on:

- a network of professionals (Principal Examiner (PE)/Team Leader (TL)/Assistant Examiner (AE)), with various levels of responsibility
- a set of established procedures which apply to each professional level known as RITCME: *Recruitment, Induction, Training, Co-ordination, Monitoring* and *Evaluation.*

More details of the selection of rating personnel and administrative procedures are located at Appendix F and an overview of marking procedures and models is provided in Appendix D.

We next turn to two key elements of scoring validity that are essential for further reducing potential rater variability discussed so far in this chapter:

- rater training (including standardisation/co-ordination)
- monitoring rater performance.

Rater training

The effects of training: research

There is a strong plea for attention to training in the testing literature (Alderson, Clapham and Wall 1995, Bachman and Palmer 1996, McNamara 1996, Weir 1988). The practical experience of projects such as the IELTS rating scale revision project discussed above and the evidence from our discussion of raters and rating processes also point to the need for this.

A review of the literature indicates that the effects of training on scoring validity may not be as positive as might be expected (Lumley and McNamara 1995, Weigle 1998). Differences in the severity and leniency of different examiners were not eradicated during standardisation according to Black (1962) who found that some examiners' level of leniency was affected by the task that the candidate had been asked to perform e.g. writing an essay and a letter. Lunz, Wright and Linacre (1990) and Stahl and Lunz (1991) found that training can:

- bring examiners' differences in severity to a tolerably acceptable level but that it cannot wholly eradicate differences in severity
- make examiners more consistent in their individual approach to marking.

This is echoed in other research which found that leniency and severity are fixed traits of examiners. Lumley and McNamara (1995) and Weigle (1998) found that training had not eliminated variation in the harshness of the examiners' marking. Lunz and O'Neill (1997) found that retraining did not affect the leniency and severity of examiners.

In a later investigation Weigle (1998) – using FACETS to model rater training effects – analysed the ratings of 16 raters (8 new and 8 experienced) both before and after training. The study was undertaken with a view to trying to gain a better understanding of the processes that an examiner uses to arrive at a score and explored the differences in severity manifest across the rater group and the extent to which raters were consistent. Ratings were based on a sample of 60 essays in the context of the English as a Second Language Placement Examination (ESLPE) administered by the University of California at Los Angeles (UCLA). Multi-faceted Rasch analysis was employed in order to analyse ratings. Weigle observed that, despite the success of training in enabling raters to be self-consistent, training was clearly less valuable in accomplishing desired levels of inter-rater reliability (similarity of the marks awarded by different examiners as opposed to intra-rater reliability, i.e. the consistency in the severity of an examiner's marking). She also found that prior to training inexperienced examiners were both more inconsistent and severe in their individual marking compared to their experienced counterparts – a finding also derived from the research of Ruth and Murphy (1988). Following training, significant differences in rater harshness remained. The less-experienced examiners exhibited a tendency to be both harsher and less consistent than their experienced counterparts. Although important differences in severity remained across the rater group, the effect was decidedly less marked following training and, perhaps more significantly, greater consistency existed for the majority of raters. Post-training, all but one of the inexperienced examiners appeared to improve in terms of the consistency of their own individual marking (without necessarily becoming less consistent). Weigle's findings fortify the belief that the efficacy of training may be restricted to promoting intra- rather than inter-rater reliability.

McNamara contends that the traditional objective of rater training (to eradicate any differences between raters) may be 'unachievable and possibly undesirable' (1996:232). Instead he argues that the fitting aim of training is to get raters to become more focused and to encourage new examiners to be self-consistent. This is the view adopted by Cambridge ESOL.

Research into effects of training for marking Cambridge ESOL exams

In relation to FCE and CPE monitoring, Jones and Shaw (2003) examined the effects of rater training and, in particular, the nature and quality of rater feedback. The study attempted to ascertain whether feedback is capable in practice of engendering the required change in rater behaviour. More details of rating personnel and rating procedures in Cambridge ESOL are located at Appendices C and F and the reader is referred to them for detailed coverage.

Assistant Examiner (AE) marking trends for the December 2002 sessions of FCE (syllabuses 0100/0101/0102) and CPE (syllabuses 0300/0301) – were constructed. It was hoped that by subjecting the trends to a quantitative and qualitative analysis, the approach to the assessment of examiner behaviour during the Team Leader (TL) monitoring phase of the marking process would offer greater insights into:

- the efficacy of TL intervention
- the type of feedback given by the TL (and Principal Examiner (PE)) to AEs
- the nature of any AE modified marking behaviour in response to TL feedback.

For each exam, AEs were identified where the difference between their raw and scaled mean mark overall was greater than one. The direction of the scaling was compared with the direction of the trend in mean score over the three batches (see Appendix D for further details). It was hoped that such an approach might provide a rough idea of whether AEs were modifying their marking to reflect the probable feedback they would have received (assuming the monitoring was successful in picking up the AE's degree of severity). A quantitative comparison was made, therefore, between the direction of examiner scaling and the direction of the trend in mean mark over three monitored batches of scripts. From the findings it was hard to conclude that feedback was having a predictable effect on the raters' marking behaviour.

The qualitative strand, undertaken by two experienced FCE/CAE/CPE examiners, involved an attempt to associate apparent trends manifest in the data with TL observations noted during the marking experience. This was accomplished by examining information captured by the Batch Monitoring Form (BMF) – see Appendix D. The form provides two types of information:

- discrepancies in the marks awarded by the AE/TL, either reflecting a trend upwards or downwards or sometimes inconclusive
- accompanying written feedback/guidance by the TL (or occasionally the PE) in the form of text in a comment box.

The qualitative reports considered examiner trends in light of information provided by the three stages of BMFs. Findings revealed some evidence of:

- examiner over-compensation – there was evidence of this, both between Batch 1 and Batch 2 but also as late as Batch 3
- TL desire to agree with AEs – the 'expert' FCE examiner involved in the study noticed in discussion at the June 0101 Team Leader meeting how far TLs strive to agree with their team members. This spirit comes

across on many of the forms, even when there is clear disagreement on
the marks awarded by each person. Obviously there is a desire to
reassure and encourage, but sometimes this can result in a rather mixed
message. This is something to be borne in mind when deciding long-
term about the efficacy of the monitoring process
- Team Leader effect – many TLs appear in the lists of scaled markers.

These findings constitute areas of concern that many senior examiners
have been conscious of during the marking process. In terms of *over-compensation*, there is an argument for giving only minimal feedback to examiners in order to avoid its effects. This could be trialled with a pilot group of
examiners, guided by one or two well-established 'definitive' TLs. As for
the *Team Leader effect* itself, whilst it is possible to continue to improve
standardisation by regular training and rigorous PE monitoring, there will
always be some TLs who appear on the scaling lists. In the final analysis,
marking is a huge operation and will always comprise a trace of subjectiv-
ity. If this is the case, then attempts should be made to minimise any tendency to influence an examiner in the wrong direction. The emergence of
Electronic Script Management (ESM) will have implications for the future
nature and role of the TL (see below for further discussion of the potential
impact of ESM).

Although some of the observations gleaned from this study were quite fas-
cinating in themselves, they contributed very little to an explanation of how
the TL/AE relationship is working and how the value of the feedback given
can be improved. Nevertheless, some valuable insights were noted. It is
evident that some aspects of TL feedback are more reliable than others –
direct reference to particular scripts is usually more successful than generalised comment – but it is widely held by senior examiners that it is often very
difficult indeed to get certain raters to assess scripts consistently when factors
other than accuracy are concerned.

The training process itself: research

Although there has been considerable investigation into the effectiveness of
examiner training in terms of standardising raters, Weigle (1998) observed
that little is known about what happens during examiner training and how it
affects examiners. In an earlier study Weigle (1994) presented the outcome of
'think aloud' verbal protocol analyses conducted on four inexperienced
raters in the context of the ESLPE which is administered quarterly at the
University of California, Los Angeles (UCLA). Students are expected to
produce a 50-minute essay on one of two prompts: interpreting graphical
information (GRAPH prompt), and making and justifying a decision based
on information presented within a chart or table (CHOICE prompt).

Examiners were asked to rate the same compositions both before and after rater training.

Weigle concluded that the training procedures employed were effective in creating a consensual understanding among the four new and initially aberrant raters who appeared to be 'more or less in line with the rest' with regard to their judgements and the decision-making process by which they converged on those judgements. This fits well with the notion that examiners learn the mark scheme from peers and contemporaries, that is, group members and discussion.

The verbal protocols showed that training:

- clarified marking criteria for raters
- modified their expectations of candidate scripts
- provided a comparative reference group of other raters (Weigle 1994).

In a refinement of previous research and as a part of a continuing investigation into the effects of training of raters of ESL compositions, Weigle (1999) investigated rater/prompt interactions in the assessment of ESLP essays using quantitative and qualitative methodologies. Again, she examined the rating behaviour of experienced and inexperienced examiners in the context of essays produced by ESL students responding to either a 'choice' or 'graph' prompt. Multi-faceted Rasch Measurement (MFRM) identified that inexperienced examiners were more harsh than experienced examiners on one prompt but not on the other. Training appeared to eradicate any differences between the experienced and inexperienced examiners on the different prompts. A qualitative line of enquiry accompanied and buttressed the quantitative strand of the study which entailed the capture and investigation – through the analysis of raters' think-aloud protocols whilst rating – of the decision-making processes raters undergo. Protocol analysis offered valuable and rich insights essential to the understanding and rationalisation of any differences in rater behaviour observed during the trial. Individual rater differences stemmed from the straightforwardness with which the scoring rubric could be applied to the prompts and to differing perceptions of the suitability of the prompts (1999).

Lumley and O'Sullivan (2000) found that inexperienced and newly trained examiners tended to be severe, but consistent, in their judgements. In contrast, in this study experienced raters with many years of examining tended to demonstrate a propensity for leniency with occasional bouts of inconsistency. In one sense, these observations are broadly in line with Weigle's findings that experienced raters are more generous than perhaps inexperienced ones (1998) but to some degree contradict Weigle's findings that inexperienced examiners tend to manifest inconsistency.

The training process: Cambridge ESOL research and practice

Cambridge ESOL researchers have also argued for a better understanding of the processes that an examiner uses to arrive at a rating: 'lack of knowledge in this area makes it difficult to train markers to make valid and reliable assessments' (Milanovic, Saville and Shuhong 1996:93). In addition they have continued investigations into the effects of training, and more particularly whether training is capable in practice of engendering the required change in rater behaviour (Furneaux and Rignall 2000, Shaw 2002). Research linked to ESOL examinations in which Cambridge is involved is discussed next.

Wigglesworth (1993) investigated the complex variables or 'facets' (see Appendix H for a discussion of how the assessment setting may be conceptualised in terms of the facets of the setting) associated with inter-rater reliability (similarity of the marks awarded by different examiners) and intra-rater reliability (the consistency in the severity of an examiner's marking). In her IELTS study, a group of 13 raters was monitored throughout a rating event. She was able to offer feedback to raters through the generation of individual 'performance maps' by employing MFR bias interaction analysis. By doing this, Wigglesworth was able to demonstrate how it was feasible to restrict the effects of rater bias during marking. This study is unusual in that it signifies a rare investigation of the effect on rater behaviour and performance of systematic feedback awarded throughout the entire rating process.

Wigglesworth's (1993) investigation was paralleled by O'Sullivan and Rignall (2002) within the context of the IELTS General Training Writing examination. The results of this investigation, however, were not as immediately apparent or as readily interpretable as those gleaned from the original. Feedback, it seemed, engendered a tendency among raters to become increasingly more reflective of their cognitive processes during marking. It was not found that rater judgements were necessarily more accurate or consistent. O'Sullivan and Rignall (2002) evaluated the value of bias analysis feedback to raters for the IELTS Writing Module. It sought to explore and corroborate Wigglesworth's (1993) hypothesis that formal feedback based on bias interaction analysis (MFRM) could improve rater consistency (O'Sullivan and Rignall 2002). 20 trained IELTS examiners and scripts from more than 80 candidates were used in the study. The study aimed to determine the effect MFR-based feedback has on rating performance; the usefulness of MFR-based feedback on rating and its effect on approach to rating. The design of the study comprised two groups of 10 examiners: one group receiving feedback reports with additional commentaries on their performance, the other group receiving no feedback. This procedure was reproduced for a second rating exercise. Empirical analysis indicated that feedback exhibited only a marginal effect on rater performance despite contradictory findings from a questionnaire distributed to the feedback group. One outcome of the qualitative analysis was that the contribution of feedback was perceived by examiners to be beneficial to their marking of the examination.

While clear differences exist, what these studies reveal is the value of training beyond the initial standardisation phase. This raises the issue of rater stability which has undoubted implications, on a very practical level, in relation to the 'accreditation' of raters and the requirements of data analysis following test administration sessions.

Other studies which explore the possibility of rater training throughout the marking process include the effect of *standardisation* training on rater judgements for the IELTS Writing Module (Furneaux and Rignall 2000) and the effect of successive standardisation iterations on inter-rater reliability for the revised CPE Writing Paper 2 (Shaw 2002c).

Furneaux and Rignall (2000) investigated the ratings awarded by 12 trainee examiners on eight IELTS scripts from the Academic Writing Module on four separate occasions over a period of six months during training. The IELTS mark scheme at that time comprised three assessment criteria and nine-band level descriptors. IELTS examiner training routinely involves marking scripts and discussing marks and differences between marks with other examiners – a process which is repeated for a number of different scripts. Using training materials produced centrally by Cambridge ESOL, the examiners are trained locally at their particular centre before they can apply to be certificated. Certification is a process that occurs after examiner training and consists of a rating exercise. It is designed to ensure that new examiners rate to standard. In their study Furneaux and Rignall analysed the differences between the marks awarded by the trainee examiners and senior examiners and they concluded that the mark scheme itself has some standardising effect even without training. However, there was a gain in standardisation of rating between the first and last occasion on which marking took place; the number of marks that were on (equal to) the standard rose from 4% to 35% over the four occasions. The percentage on or within one band of the standard rose from 83% to 92%. The examiners became less severe during training, a phenomenon also found by Ruth and Murphy (1988) and Weigle (1998).

Shaw (2002c) observed that an iterative standardisation process of training and successively delivered feedback to CPE examiners did not enhance inter-rater reliability but this was perhaps affected by the fact that inter-rater reliability was already encouragingly high. This study focused on the standardisation process as the variable most critical to improving the assessment of Writing and aimed to find ways of improving inter-rater agreement.

Shaw's study tested the hypothesis that a steady improvement in inter-rater correlation would take place with each successive iteration of the standardisation exercise. However, results revealed that whilst the inter-rater reliabilities are high (0.75–0.85), they do not improve with time and standardisation but remain roughly constant. The study revealed that the scores awarded by examiners became less harsh after standardisation training. It additionally revealed that there was a modest gain in standardisation over the first four iterations, that is, the percentage of ratings 'on-track' rose and the percentage of aberrant ratings (more than one band from the standard) fell. Like Furneaux and Rignall (2000), Shaw argued that the mark scheme itself has a powerful standardising impact on raters.

Interestingly, the data from Shaw's study showed evidence of examiners modifying their behaviour with successive standardisation exercises. The scores by the raters in Iteration 1 (IT1), i.e. before standardisation training, did not differ grossly from the standard. Initial results may well reflect examiner experience despite the fact that half the AEs were unfamiliar with the revised mark scheme. It is possible that the mark scheme, comprising a set of detailed and explicit descriptors, engenders a standardising effect even in the absence of a formalised training programme. The group had a tendency to harshness with roughly equal severity on the compulsory and optional questions although the examiners were nearly twice as generous on the optional question. The mark scheme applied to the compulsory question is both more rigid and more clearly defined than its optional question counterpart. Additionally, the range of language required by the compulsory task is less wide and its focus is discursive whereas the optional task permits more scope for invention and a variety of interpretation. Consequently, examiners are allowed greater freedom in their assessment of the optional response which may account for increased leniency.

The evidence from the scores for Iteration 2 (IT2) suggested that standardisation prompted some adjustment in the severity of examiner rating. There was a trend to increased leniency. The group rated significantly less severely in IT2 which may be a consequence of the greater attention given to the revised mark scheme. For both tasks, the group was more generous in their awards. As far as changes in relative severity/leniency are concerned, the results of this study are broadly in line with Weigle's finding that experienced raters are more generous than perhaps inexperienced ones (1998). 'On Standard' scores show a marginal decrease for the compulsory task and a slight increase for the optional question.

Significant improvement was manifest for Iteration 3 (IT3) for both 'On Standard' and 'Within+/−One Band of Standard' for both the compulsory and optional questions. For the compulsory task, examiners were less harsh and less lenient for 'On Standard' and 'Within+/−One Band of Standard' respectively than for IT2. However, more interestingly, examiners assessing the optional question reversed the trend of IT2 where there had been more generous marking. A pattern was beginning to be established which reflects alternating trends between low and high marking over the various standardi-sations creating a 'see-saw' effect.

Iteration 4 (IT4), including a batch of scripts which constituted optional questions only, reinforced the emerging 'see-saw' pattern. The percentage of ratings 'On Standard' remained roughly constant and the percentage 'Within+/−One Band of Standard' is virtually unaltered. However, a significant shift from harshness towards leniency was manifest, reflecting the earlier trend at IT2. Over the first four iterations, the percentage of aberrant ratings i.e. more than one band from standard, fell for both compulsory and optional questions.

The results for Iteration 5 (IT5), however, were erratic. Batch 5 consisted of only 10 scripts and was a collection of different tasks: Revision Task B, Task M and Set Text 2. Moreover, the marking of Batch 5 scripts coincided with 'live' marking of the June administration. It may be that examiners at this point in the trial were experiencing 'participation fatigue' and 'divided loyalty'.

Evidence for the rater 'see-saw' effect is demonstrated graphically in Figure 5.2.

Figure 5.2 Rater performance over five iterations: low, high and on-track marking optional question

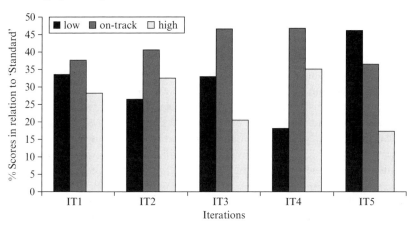

Despite the fact that more examiner ratings were increasingly 'on-track', the extent of examiner over-compensation appeared to be increasing as the trial continued. It would appear that some examiners were becoming increas-ingly concerned by their lack of consistency with 'standard' ratings.

According to interviews conducted with AEs after the trial, examiner confidence throughout was affected in varying degrees. Many examiners were worried by the frequency with which they appeared to be 'off-track' when their ratings were compared with 'standard' ratings, especially when their ratings were greater than one band score from 'standard'. Discrepancies were thought to be related to training issues and rater variation attributed to limited training opportunities with the revised mark scheme. Whenever it was perceived that AEs were 'off-track' some corrective action was considered. The nature of this action was symptomatic of the extent of any variation and examiner personality. Examiners were provoked into making a range of adjustments to their individual assessment approach. For certain examiners, however, no adjustments were made. Peer pressure to rate in a similar manner is a training factor thought to be an influence in assisting, even enhancing, inter-rater reliability (Cooper 1977).

On balance the literature suggests that benefits of training for improving intra-rater consistency outweigh those for improving inter-rater consistency but additional benefits accrue if intra-rater consistency can be established because then it is possible through statistical programmes such as MFRM to take account of inter-rater variation and also to compensate for differing levels of severity (see the section on post-exam adjustment on pages 192–95). MFRM can also guard against bias, e.g. from different tasks or markers, and inform any decisions to be made concerning score adjustment before grade setting.

Post-exam adjustment: Cambridge practice

Statistical analysis of examiner performance takes place after marking is complete. Scaling of Writing is an effective statistical method that is used to detect errant Writing examiners and to alter their marks to bring them in line with the population of markers as a whole. The main purpose of such scaling is to transform a distribution of marks to a specific mean and standard deviation. This may result in the addition or subtraction of marks for candidates.

In order to justify scaling, it is necessary that the intervention will produce a more equitable result for candidates overall. Obviously, the majority of candidates marked by an examiner deemed harsh will be thought of as disadvantaged. The estimated overall disadvantage is an arithmetic average across all the candidates although there will very likely be individual candidates who are disadvantaged more and perhaps others who are not disadvantaged in any way. The primary intent of scaling is that the influence of variable examiner severity is progressively reduced and the true rank order of candidates thus better represented.

Cambridge ESOL uses scaling to correct for certain individual examiner effects. In broad terms, the approach is to scale each examiner's mark distribution to the global distribution of all examiners. The key assumption applied to the act of scaling is that the global distribution is the correct one to set each examiner's marks to. This is of course true if allocations are sufficiently large and randomly apportioned, thus engendering confidence that the examiner's group is totally representative in ability. These conditions are met in Cambridge ESOL's application of scaling.

To be reasonably confident that adjustments made to candidates' marks are accurate, scaling of Writing requires a minimum number of candidates marked by each examiner. Individual Cambridge ESOL examiner allocations are typically of the order of 500–600 scripts per examiner (a sample deemed representative of the test-taker population) which far exceeds Jones' (2002a) recommendation of 40 candidates as the minimum number per examiner.

For FCE, CPE and BEC the scaling procedure is modified by a judgement as to whether a group is in fact of average ability, via a comparison with performance on Papers 1 (Reading) and 3 (Use of English for Main Suite and Listening for BEC).

Automated scaling through the Examination Processing System (EPS) is already in operation for FCE, CPE and BEC. It scales from a given examiner group's mean and standard deviation to a new mean and new standard deviation, where these include a comparison with Papers 1 and 3.

Examiner scaling is also translated as 'comments'. Examiners are given feedback on their marking in the form of a marking tendency for the scripts assessed. The summary is based on conclusions reached after comparing the performance of those candidates on Paper 2 scripts marked ('examiner group') with their performance on other papers, and a comparison of the examiner group performance on Paper 2 compared to the performance of all the candidates who took the same paper. The summary table given to examiners as feedback indicates whether the candidates the examiner placed in the different bands were correctly placed, or whether there was evidence that the examiner was overmarking (being too generous) or undermarking (being too severe).

Where scaling identifies instances of individual erratic performance, all scripts assigned to the examiner identified are routinely re-marked.

In contrast to FCE and CPE examinations, CAE and PET marks are not scaled in the manner described above. Cambridge ESOL uses 'on-site' double marking for CAE and targeted second marking for PET to identify questionable marking, the analysis being undertaken between marking weekends to allow re-marking where required the following weekend. The check on discrepant marking in the double-marking approach deals satisfactorily with differences in marker severity. This approach is not easily scalable as it is limited by the availability of a suitable examiner cadre large enough to cope with the number of candidates entering in any session of the exam. Its viability is, therefore, reviewed regularly.

During the first and second double-marking CAE weekend, the first examiner assesses a script. No mark or comment is placed on the scripts and the second rater is unaware of the first mark given. The script is then passed to the second examiner who also assesses it. If the marks are within the required tolerance of each other and the examiners agree the candidate has answered the same question then the two marks are added together and doubled to give a weighted mark out of 40.

If the first and second markings for the script differ by more than 20%, the script is marked by a third rater (usually the PE or a TL) at a subsequent weekend. The script will be awarded a final mark if the TL's mark is within tolerance of one of the original examiner's marks. The TL's mark is combined with the closest of the other two marks to produce the final mark. If the third mark is not within tolerance of one of the original examiners, for example if the TL's total mark is in the middle of the other two marks, the script will go to fourth marking by the PE.

One method for resolving differences between marks is to take the mean of the differences. This may be done for all differences or for relatively small differences. However, in the double-marking literature, there are studies that suggest that taking the average of two marks is not the best way to reconcile the differences. For example, Massey and Foulkes (1994) suggested that the average of two blind marks may not always be a sound estimate. It remains at least arguable that the greater the difference between two markers the more likely it is that one has seen something the other has not. Logically, averaging will, in some cases, involve combining a correct mark with an incorrect mark. This means that the magnitude of errors is reduced but the number of errors increased.

Fourth-marking generally involves a situation where two examiners have marked at the extreme ends of the range and a third marker (normally a TL) has come down in the middle. In this case, the PE's mark is the final mark. Scripts are heavily scrutinised at this stage to ensure that marking has been fair. The PE's mark is non-negotiable. The final mark is subsequently loaded on to EPS where it is collated with the marks for the other four CAE papers in preparation for grading.

Using Rasch measurement: a way forward?

Rasch advocates argue that training helps raters to develop a common understanding of the mark scheme but that the training cannot overcome this unique personal experience by requiring examiners to conform to the agreed application of the mark scheme. Using Rasch and a system where a proportion of essays are double-marked it becomes unnecessary for all examiners to award the same marks. Rather if the relative severity and leniency of examiners is known then the true score of each candidate can be calculated. Newstead and Dennis (1994) say that marker severity could be seen as a systematic bias in the marking. However, it can only be a bias if the severity or leniency is intolerable and cannot be overcome with the Rasch system. Given this, examiners only need to be trained to be consistent in their own individual marking, not to conform to reproduce one another's' marking. When an examiner appears to be particularly lenient or severe their marking is scaled.

Research at Cambridge ESOL has recently employed an MFRM approach for detecting and measuring rater effects for CAE Writing examiners (Shaw 2005a, Shaw and Geranpayeh 2005)

FACETS was employed to study three rater effects: *leniency/severity* (the attitude shown by a rater towards a performance by a test taker), *central tendency* (the rater tendency to give ratings clustered closely around the midpoint on the scale) and *randomness* (the inconsistency in rater behaviour).

The study set out to evaluate the reliability of the existing double-marking CAE Writing model. It aimed to investigate:

- examiner performance effects (at group level and individual level)
- the ability of the CAE model to reliably distinguish different levels of examiner severity
- examiner behaviour in terms of leniency/severity, central tendency and randomness.

The CAE Writing Examiner Behaviour study comprised two phases. The first phase of the project – reported in Shaw and Geranpayeh (2005) – attempted to evaluate the reliability of the existing double-marking CAE Writing model by investigating the rating behaviour of examiners during the first/second marking stage of the assessment process for the December 2003 (0150/2) administration of CAE Writing Paper 2. The participant rater set consisted of four teams of highly experienced CAE examiners (36 examiners in total) marking at a centre in Southampton. Candidate data comprised 3,070 performances.

FACETS analyses during Phase 1 revealed the following about each of the three rater behaviour effects: in terms of *examiner severity* it is clear that the raters did not all manifest the same degree of severity when making judgements about candidate performance. In relation to *central tendency*, there was no group-level central tendency effect present in the rater data; all of the raters were operating within an acceptable range of consistency of performance and the suggestion that CAE Writing examiners are consciously or unconsciously exercising excessive caution when rating CAE scripts was not supported by the MFRM approach adopted for this analysis. Finally, investigation of the *randomness* suggested that there was probably no group-level randomness effect manifest in the data.

Using the same Phase 1 data and adopting a similar MFRM methodological approach, Phase 2 extended the analysis to embrace third markings and sought to assess the behaviour of examiners at this second stage in the CAE assessment event (Shaw 2005a).

Again, data for analysis comprised ratings awarded during the December 2003 session of the paper. The Phase 2 rater set comprised the original 36 examiners and a further 12 senior third-marking examiners: a total of 48 markers. 210 performances were third-marked.

Findings indicated that third-rating examiners do not all manifest the same degree of severity. Moreover, the most generous and the most severe examiners were both third markers. All third raters were operating within an acceptable range of consistency of performance although the rating behaviour of one examiner appeared somewhat different from the others. The severity measure for this marker was over 13.79 standard errors under the mean severity of the group. Candidates awarded scores by this examiner might well receive higher than average ratings. There was a strong suggestion that the examiner was rank ordering candidate performance in a manner inconsistent with other third-rating examiners. Despite this, third raters are clearly differentiated in terms of the levels of severity they exhibit. Third ratings reduce the script estimate (abilities) range marginally, enlarge the rater severity range for the entire data set by approximately 1 logit, and have minimal effect on the task measurement scale (optional Question 2 – article – was the most difficult task to rate whilst the optional – work-related task – was the least difficult to rate). Group-level and individual-level statistical indicators suggested that there was no central tendency effect present in the third-rater data. There was no evidence of a randomness effect either.

It is envisaged that the next stage of the work will comprise an investigation of bias interaction (e.g. rater/ratee gender). Methods for estimating and reporting reliability will also be explored.

MFRM has also been used by Sudweeks et al (2005) in conjunction with Generalisability Theory (G theory) in an attempt to assess and enhance the procedures for evaluating the essay writing ability of college sophomores. Studies which compare and contrast the use of the two measurement approaches are not uncommon and in this study were used to estimate potential sources of rating error, to produce reliability estimates, and to offer suggestions for improving upon current rating practice. The researchers deduced that G theory and MFRM (with their common and unique characteristics) have their relative merits and although each method may be more appropriate than the other in certain measurement scenarios, information from each type of analysis may be employed to complement the other (see also Lumley and McNamara 1995, as well as the section on the discussion of these two methods in the Validation Phase of the IELTS Writing Assessment Revision Project above).

McNamara (1996) attests to the feasibility of employing multi-faceted measurement procedures under operational test conditions for certain high-stakes performance tests. He refers to a number of conditions that need to be met in carrying out such studies. Data sets need to be large implying that great care needs to be taken in the design to ensure that the data set is sufficient for the number of facets that are under investigation (de Jong and Stoyanova 1994). Second, given the transient nature of rater behaviour across test administrations, there is a need for fresh analyses to be undertaken on a periodic basis perhaps at the beginning of each marking episode. However, McNamara (1996) also argues that the overall cost and viability of applying multi-faceted measurement procedures on a routine basis are not entirely dissimilar to those where more conventional approaches are implemented.

Grading and awarding: Cambridge practice

Once the procedures described above are completed, grading and awarding can take place. Wood (1991:134) notes:

> The reliability of grades is, in an important sense, the bottom line of the examining system; all other reliabilities, of markers . . . feed in to produce outcomes which are more or less reliable, and therefore just. There exist direct relationships between the reliability of the examination, which usually means the reliability of the overall marks, the number of grades on the scale, the reliability of the grades and the severity of the consequences of misclassification.

Weir and Milanovic (2003) describe how once all examination papers have been marked and a series of checks to ensure that all candidates have been assessed accurately and to the same standards have been carried out, grading takes place. Certificated exams report results as passing and failing grades, rather than a score on a continuous scale. Grading is therefore a process of setting the cut-off score for the various grades – A, B, C 'Passing', D and E 'Failing'.

The Cambridge ESOL Subject Officers (SOs) who are responsible for a particular examination hold a Grading Meeting to review the performance of candidates and to set the boundaries for each grade, according to the performance criteria defined for that grade. At this meeting, reports and analyses which have been carried out on the score data, and in relation to various groups of candidates, are reviewed according to an established procedure. Checks are also carried out to ensure that scaling procedures have been applied accurately.

The SOs review the item analysis and descriptive statistics and this enables them to confirm whether the examination materials 'performed' as predicted by the pretesting and standards fixing activities which were carried out during the question paper production cycle. (See Appendix E for an overview of the standard procedures for the production of Writing examination materials).

They also compare the performance of the entire candidature and large groups of candidates (or cohorts) with performance in previous years. In combination, this ensures that the standards being applied are consistent and fair to all candidates, and that a particular grade 'means' the same thing from year to year and throughout the world. Any requests for special consideration are reviewed at this stage, together with any reports from centres about specific problems that may have arisen during the examination.

The grade boundaries recommended by the Subject Officers are scrutinised and approved by Senior Management. There then follows a series of activities designed to ensure fairness of candidates' results.

Grade Review follows on immediately after the internal grading procedure for exams has been completed. The purpose of Grade Review is to be a final check on the performance of candidates who have just failed to reach the pass boundary. Candidates are selected for consideration at Grade Review according to specified criteria.

Cases where a candidate was absent for all or part of a component, or who have been affected by adverse circumstances immediately before or during the examination are referred to the Awards Committee. This may be informed by statistical evidence, as relevant.

The Cambridge ESOL Malpractice Committee convenes to make recommendations relating to the action to be taken in cases of malpractice or dishonesty by candidates. The following are examples of dishonesty and malpractice by candidates. The list is not exhaustive and other instances of dishonesty and malpractice may be considered by Cambridge ESOL at its sole discretion:

- obtaining unauthorised access to examination material
- using or attempting to use unauthorised material, for example, notes, study guides, dictionaries (where prohibited), personal stereos, mobile phones or other similar electronic devices in the examination room
- collusion or copying, or attempted collusion or copying (including the misuse of information and communication technology to do so)
- disruptive behaviour/failure to abide by the instructions of an invigilator, supervisor or Local Secretary, including not switching off mobile phones
- impersonation
- the alteration of any results document, including certificates.

The Committee will make recommendations on what action to take based on its conclusions. The final decision on what action should be taken rests with Cambridge ESOL. Decisions are not taken without giving the candidate the opportunity to make a statement.

Reporting results and certification: Cambridge practice

Weir and Milanovic (2003) describe how, once the award procedure is complete, centres are sent individual Statements of Results for each candidate. These results are still subject to a final quality check, e.g. to ensure that the candidate's name is spelled in the correct or preferred way before certificates are printed.

The Statement of Results provides the candidates with a 'graphical profile' which shows the profile of performance in relative terms across the various components of the exams. Approximately three months after the examination, certificates are issued (via the centre) to successful candidates. These documents incorporate a number of security features to make them extremely difficult to forge. Cambridge ESOL keeps detailed records of the certificates awarded to candidates, so that it can verify any claim about which an employer or university, for example, is dubious.

In addition, the Results Online service was launched in 2006 for the March administrations of KET, PET, FCE, CAE and BEC. This service enables candidates to access their results online, which reduces the time between their sitting an examination and receiving their result. They will see both their overall grade and their profile.

Once results have been issued, Cambridge ESOL certificates remain valid for an indefinite period, i.e. they do not have a limited 'shelf-life' and do not expire (the only exception being IELTS). The certificates attest to the fact that, at the time when the examination was taken, the candidate achieved and demonstrated a specified level of English proficiency. The length of time since the certificate was obtained is a factor that potential employers, universities, and so on, need to take into account, and Cambridge ESOL provides a number of additional services for institutions to check, quickly and economically, whether the holder still has the required skills. As a general rule it is recommended that a Test Report Form (for reporting IELTS results to candidates) that is more than two years old should only be accepted as evidence of present level of ability if accompanied by proof that a candidate has actively maintained or tried to improve their English language proficiency.

While the users of the Cambridge ESOL Main Suite exams are still overwhelmingly in favour of the current approach to grading, with a single exam grade, there is at the same time a demand for more information concerning how this overall grade was arrived at. This reflects the pedagogical context in which Cambridge ESOL exams are generally taken – more diagnostic feedback on performance in each test component is seen as a useful guide for further study, particularly in the case of failing candidates who may wish to re-take the exam.

Cambridge ESOL Statement of Results have been developed in the course of various test revision projects. The Statements of Results are designed to make the reporting of final grades and component-level performance as clear as possible to test users. The latest Statements of Results were introduced in 2000 and the following explanatory notes were issued to accompany them:

> Every candidate is provided with a Statement of Results which includes a graphical display of the candidate's performance in each component. These are shown against the scale Exceptional – Good – Borderline – Weak and indicate the candidate's relative performance in each paper.
>
> In looking at this graphical display it is important to remember that the candidates are NOT required to reach a specific level in any component, i.e. there are NO pass/fail levels in individual components. Thus different strengths and weaknesses may add up to the same overall result.
>
> We recommend that fail candidates planning to resit an examination, or pass candidates who plan to continue their studies, do not focus only on those areas where they have a performance which is less than Borderline, but try to improve their general level of English across all language skills.
>
> The profile indicates a candidate's performance on the specific occasion when they sat the exam – this may be influenced by a number of different factors, and candidates can find that they have a somewhat different profile on another occasion. Evidence of candidates who resit exams indicates that in some cases performance declines overall and in other cases declines in some papers while improving in others.
>
> The information on these new-style Statements of Results replaces the indications of High Performance/Particularly Weak Performance provided previously.

The purpose of the profiled result slips is to give useful information about performance in each paper. The information plotted in the result slip is not the candidate's raw marks, but marks which are scaled to implement the normative frame of reference which has been presented above. A candidate with a borderline pass, if their skills profile was completely flat, would be shown as having all papers just above the 'borderline' boundary. A very good candidate, achieving an A grade, would most probably have at least one paper in the 'exceptional' band. In each paper a similar proportion of candidates fall into the 'exceptional' and 'weak' bands.

The profiled result slips attempt to achieve a balance between the need to provide more information about performance in components, and a full-blown system of component-level grading. This latter option, as explained above, is not wholly appropriate for the construct of English language proficiency embodied in the Cambridge ESOL Main Suite exams. Feedback from consultative exercises with stakeholders on the use of the result slips has generally been extremely positive.

In the next section we turn to new scoring validity developments in Cambridge ESOL: computer-based test versions, electronic script management (ESM), and e-rating, all of which may radically affect the way examinations are both delivered and assessed. As with all new technologies, the progression of development is often striking. We are only able to describe the situation at the time of writing in the full knowledge that things may well move on quickly in each of these areas.

New technologies and their impact on the rating of written scripts at Cambridge ESOL

New technology has provided opportunities to improve the manner in which education is delivered and assessed (Maughan 2001). Bennett (2002) argues that the inexorable advance of technology will force fundamental changes in the format and content of assessment and therefore that the incorporation of technological expertise into assessment is inevitable.

Hyland (2002) argues there is little doubt that the rapid emergence of new technologies and increased global communication have engendered substantial changes in the nature of writing itself in terms of the ways in which writing is composed, the genres created, the authorial identities assumed, the forms finished products take and the ways in which the reader is engaged. Concomitant with these changes is the impact of technology on the assessment of writing (Weigle 2002).

Research into pencil and paper versus computer-based tests of writing

Despite some of the tangible advantages of the computer over pen and paper in the composition of texts, in regard to flexibility, automation, and cognitive demands, the results of research on the quality of writing generated in a computer context are not all entirely favourable; only some studies have yielded beneficial effects for student compositions produced by word processing in contrast to pen and paper (Pennington 1996). From the L2 perspective, mixed findings have been reported. In some studies, word processing gave writers an advantage in terms of the quality of their writing (Lam and Pennington 1995, McGarrell 1993); in others, word processing appeared to offer no advantage over pen and paper (Benesch 1987, Chadwick and Bruce 1989).

In our earlier discussion of the features of candidate scripts that affect raters (see section on criteria/rating scale above) we examined the effect of handwriting on markers and noted how fully edited and highly polished computer-generated products may engender higher rater expectations; handwritten text may provoke an enhanced reader-writer relationship; the construction of handwritten responses may convey to the rater a greater sense of effort on the part of the writer; and while allowances might be made for handwritten responses, the same may not be true for those that are word processed. Making raters aware of a tendency to downgrade word-processed essays has been shown to be, to some extent, an effective strategy.

Writing on word processors

A literature review by Shaw (2005b) revealed evidence of some interesting findings emerging from studies of writing using a word processor. It has been found that writing on computer has the greatest positive effect on the quality of writing for learning disabled students (Kerchner and Kistinger 1984, MacArthur 1988, Sitko and Crealock 1986), early elementary and low-achieving students (Phoenix and Hannan 1984, Williamson and Pence 1989), and college-aged students (Haas and Hayes 1986). Any differences between the two media are far less frequent for more able students. It would also seem that the overall effects of word processing on the composing process vary considerably between writers and with general factors related to the teacher and the class (Bangert-Drowns 1993, Cochran-Smith 1991, Pennington 1996).

In comparison with composing on paper, writing on screen appears to involve less attention to macro-planning as an initial activity, though the ability to cut and paste makes editing at both the micro and macro level easier in this medium. Micro-planning appears to assume more importance than macro-planning when composing on computer as writing is developed more on the basis of concrete text already created rather than on the initial plan (Haas 1989). Computer writers tend to plan as they write as opposed to writing to accommodate a plan (Haas 1989). This phenomenon has been documented for L2 writers as well as L1 writers (Akyel and Kamisli 1989, Li and Cumming 2001). Distributing the cognitive load in this way across the whole word-processing experience appears to be helpful for L2 writers (Akyel and Kamisli 1989, Jones and Tetro 1987, Li and Cumming 2001).

Advantages of writing on word processors

Word processors may be helpful to L2 writers who, perhaps more than inexperienced L1 writers, lack confidence in their ability to write in a second language (Betancourt and Phinney 1988). There is also evidence to suggest that the use of word processors can lead to an improved sense of audience (MacArthur 1988).

Findings from a large proportion of L1 studies (largely conducted in academic settings where virtually all writing is done on computer) suggest that computer writing may in fact lead to measurable increases in students' motivation to write, the amount of their work and the number of revisions made throughout the composing process (Bangert-Drowns 1993). L2 writers have also been shown to revise more when composing on computer (Chadwick and Bruce 1989, Li and Cumming 2001, Phinney and Khouri 1993), to revise in a more dynamic and continuous manner (Phinney and Khouri 1993), and to spend more time revising in a computer context where they may 'continue revising after planned changes [have] been made' (Phinney and Khouri 1993:271). L2 writers additionally demonstrate a tendency to make more revisions beyond the surface level (Brock and Pennington 1999, Daiute 1985, Pennington and Brock 1992, Susser 1993).

Studies conducted with L2 writers (Cochran-Smith 1991) report positive attitudes associated with word processing. Phinney (1989) and Pennington (1999) contend that word processors can alleviate the anxiety certain L2 writers experience when writing the L2 script, when producing academic texts in their L2, and when writing in a more general context. Moreover, word-processed essays are invariably longer than their handwritten counterparts once students have acquired a mastery of typing skills and are given sufficient time to familiarise themselves with various commands. A number of studies undertaken with L2 writers (Brock and Penington 1999, Chadwick and Bruce 1989, Pennington and Brock 1992) report that a general effect of word processing is the production of longer texts. When both experienced and inexperienced writers use word processors for composing, the experienced writers tend to make more revisions (Chadwick and Bruce 1989, Hult 1986, Li and Cumming 2001, MacArthur 1988, Phinney and Khouri 1993).

Disadvantages of writing on word processors

Examinees with limited word processing skills might be distracted from the Writing task at hand because of the additive cognitive demands of familiarising themselves with the layout and functions of the keyboard and of composing on a keyboard. Moreover, additional demands may impact negatively, intruding on the composing process (Dalton and Hannafin 1987, Porter 1986).

While computer proficiency and concomitant familiarity do not necessarily affect computer-based test scores, researchers nevertheless warn of the need to cater for a possible relationship when comparing with paper-and-pencil assessment tests (McDonald 2002, Weir et al 2005). Recent research demonstrates that items which test writing directly when administered via paper and pencil yield underestimates of students' skills when compared with the same items administered via computer (Russell 1999, Russell and Haney 1997) and that levels of word-processing experience reduce any difference between the two formats (Wolfe, Bolton, Feltovich and Bangert 1996).

Research at Cambridge into pencil and paper versus computer-based tests of writing

In this section we will look at developments in computer-based (CB) approaches to examining at Cambridge with specific reference to IELTS and Cambridge Main Suite examinations (see Appendix G for detailed discussion of the issues relating to the delivery of computer-based tests). We will deal with these developments in the order in which they became operationally available starting with IELTS.

Over a number of years, Cambridge ESOL worked to develop a computer-based version of IELTS and a linear computer-based version of the IELTS test was launched in 2005. The test development phase involved a series of research and validation comparability studies designed to investigate differences between computer-based (CB) tests and the more familiar paper-based (PB) tests and findings indicated that the two modes of administration do not appear to affect levels of candidate performance to any meaningful or significant degree.

Candidates taking the IELTS test are presented with different options depending on whether they choose the paper-based or computer-based mode of test administration; this impacts specifically on the type and nature of their response in the Writing Module.

The 2003/04 Cambridge ESOL Live CB IELTS Trial was split into two parts: Trials A and B. Three Writing versions were used in each trial. It was intended that approximately 500 candidates would take part in each trial. In Trial A (Maycock 2004a), 423 candidates – representative of the global IELTS test-taking community – sat one of three CB Writing versions. Each candidate sat the computer-based version of the test within one week of sitting a live paper-based test. Approximately half of the candidates were administered the CB test first, whilst the remaining half took the PB test first. Candidates were offered the choice as to whether they wished to word process their answers to the CB Writing tasks or to write them in the conventional manner. Both candidate and Writing examiner were oblivious to which form would be employed to generate official scores. It was assumed, therefore, that they would react to both tests as live.

Candidates were additionally asked to complete a questionnaire, which was administered after the second test, in order to examine candidate opinions and attitudes towards CB IELTS and their experience with and confidence in using computers generally.

Results from Trial A indicate that the use of a different test format has only a marginal effect on agreement rates across the two forms with half of the candidature obtaining an identical band score for the test on both occasions. Moreover, a further 45% obtained a score that differed by just half a band on the nine-band IELTS scale. The findings of Trial A indicated that the equivalence of the paper-based and computer-based formats of IELTS is similar to that of two paper-based versions.

The results of CB IELTS Trial B corroborate the positive findings of Trial A in that they indicate test mode comparability, i.e. paper-based and computer-based IELTS versions are as comparable as two paper-based versions (Maycock 2004b). For Writing, there was no significant difference in the mean scores on the paper-based and computer-based test format. This echoes findings from the Whitehead (2003) study. Although there was some evidence that reflected Brown's (2004) concern that legibility may impact on rating, the actual impact on scores appeared minimal.

Correlations between scores in different modes of the same skill were of the level expected and the agreement in band scores was in line with what the estimated standard error of IELTS band scores would predict. The correlation between Writing on the different modes was lower than those for the objective skills, replicating the Trial A findings. Green (2005) deduced, however, that any Trial A differences could be attributed to differences in rater marking approaches, irrespective of the mode of administration or the format of the response, i.e. typed or handwritten.

Results on the Writing test were further investigated, using repeated measures analyses of covariance (ANCOVA), with PB Writing test scores as the dependent variable, to explore differences between groups in the relationship between paper- and computer-based scores. Groups were defined by gender (male or female); age (five different age groups) and first language (Chinese or non-Chinese). Handwritten responses to the CB test were separated from word-processed responses for the purpose of the analysis.

ANCOVA revealed no significant inter-group differences by gender, age or first language either where CB scripts had been typed or handwritten. This suggests that the relationship between CB and PB scores is not meaningfully affected by these differences between candidates. No significant differences between scores on the CB and PB tests, when responding on paper or on-screen were indicated by t-tests for repeated measures, either for the Chinese L1 or non-Chinese L1 groups. These results suggest that the CB and PB versions of the IELTS Writing test yielded comparable scores across groups.

Candidate feedback through questionnaire survey indicated that candidates who opted to write their responses using the keyboard encountered very few problems in managing the Writing tasks on computer and found the range of facilities available (cut, copy, paste and word count) useful. The candidates taking part in the trials were reasonably confident in their own ability to use computers, but the majority felt that candidates with more advanced computer skills would perform better on CB IELTS than those with only basic skills. This was not, however, borne out in the analyses. As Weir et al (2005) and Taylor et al (1998) before them found, candidate proficiency and experience in using computers was not shown to have any significant effect on the difference between paper-based and computer-based scores for any of the tested skills.

The evidence accumulated thus far would imply that PB IELTS can be used interchangeably with CB IELTS (Blackhurst 2005:16). Furthermore, providing candidates possess suitable word-processing skills and adequate computer familiarity, they should realise their potential equally well on either version of the test.

Building on the methodology of this earlier work, Green (2005) argues that particular thought will need to be given to implications for the training of examiners, the treatment of scripts and the treatment of spelling errors and typos in the light of CB IELTS and that further research in the following areas would be desirable:

1. Comparison of candidate performance on the same tasks on PB and CB tests involving the new IELTS Writing scoring criteria.
2. More extensive investigation of rater responses to typed and handwritten scripts through a wider questionnaire study involving larger numbers of examiners and a more intensive detailed protocol study with a small group.
3. An audit of procedures for ensuring that consistent standards are being applied across contexts in the scoring of Writing scripts.

Since the live trials were conducted, the revised Writing assessment criteria and band level descriptors have been introduced for IELTS Writing (see Case Study D). Further studies will be undertaken to assess the impact of these changes on the marking of typewritten scripts, and there will be a need to seek feedback from examiners involved in marking typewritten scripts from the live test.

Weir et al (2005) investigated whether there are meaningful differences in candidates' internal cognitive processing and their test scores where an IELTS Writing test is presented in two modes – pencil-and-paper and computer. A total of 262 participants aged between 18 and 22 in China, Turkey and Britain performed two comparable Writing tasks under the two different conditions. Analysis of the test data provided strong evidence to support the claim that there were no significant differences between the scores awarded by two independent raters for candidates' performances on the tests taken under two conditions. Analysis of the computer familiarity and anxiety questionnaire data showed that these students in general are familiar with computer usage and their overall reactions towards working with a computer are positive. Candidates' reactions to the computer were also examined with respect to fair mean average scores in the tests and it was found that the effect of computer familiarity on their performances in the two modes was negligible for most of the items in the questionnaire. However differences of up to half a band were detected in two areas: accessibility of public computers and frequency of word-processing activity. Analysis of candidates' responses to a cognitive questionnaire survey, which inquired about the internal processing undertaken during the two task performances, indicated a similar pattern between the cognitive processes involved in writing on a computer and writing with paper and pencil. Overall results of the study are, in general, encouraging for the computerisation of the Writing test, though further replication or expansion of this study using a larger and more balanced population is necessary.

In addition to the introduction of a computer-based version of IELTS, a computerised version of PET is now available based on research undertaken by Cambridge ESOL in 2005 which we now describe.

Candidates who took part in the CB PET comparability trial in 2005 (Maycock and Green 2005) were asked to complete a questionnaire regarding their attitudes towards the test and their levels of computer familiarity. The aim of the study was to address issues such as whether candidates preferred taking PET on paper or computer and how user-friendly they found the navigation of the test, and to discover any aspects which might cause problems for candidates on the launch of CB PET in late 2005.

Analysis of the questionnaire data indicated that:

- in general, the candidates were very familiar with using computers for word processing, with the majority using computers and the internet either most days or every day
- CB PET was very popular with candidates – 63% preferred the Reading and Writing component on computer as opposed to on paper
- a greater proportion – over two-thirds (67%) indicated a preference for typing their answers
- the tutorials for both components were found to be of value, with 68% for Reading and Writing agreeing that they were helpful.

Further detail of the development of a CB version of PET is provided in Appendix G including issues of trialling and equivalence.

Research into Electronic Script Management

An Electronic Script Management (ESM) programme is intended to take advantage of new technologies to modernise the conduct of examinations and to support human examiners in the assessment of paper scripts (see Appendices G and H for further information). ESM has been described as the 'industrialisation' of the examination process (Lebus, ESM Communications Meeting 2005), impacting every activity from test production to awarding.

The research programme constitutes two major sets of objectives (Palmer and Raikes 2000):

1. To investigate practical possibilities and the impact on process quality and time.
2. To provide data for research to enable an evaluation of the impact on assessment reliability of handling documents on-screen rather than on paper.

ESM defines the process by which scripts are scanned at pre-determined locations under Cambridge ESOL control, this being related to their imaging and capture strategy, and the relevant images transmitted electronically to an image server at Cambridge ESOL. Copies of these images are then distributed electronically and marked on-screen by examiners. Question level marks and examiners' annotations are also captured electronically throughout the marking process, without manual intervention, for onward processing by existing supporting systems.

ESM requires a number of technologies to be adopted in order to support high volumes whilst ensuring data integrity. Reliable management of the assessment process is dependent upon a central system capable of tracking and auditing all items throughout the process (an item is a response to a single question or part of a question). It is envisaged, therefore, that a core management system would provide a number of vital functions: the core being the workflow management (i.e. an auditing and workflow engine) tracking progress of all items being processed, and a database (i.e. an operation data store) holding all of the data. A workflow engine allows alerts to be automatically raised at each stage of the process, immediately identifying when an issue arises or when actions are expected but not completed. For example, tracking could monitor expected script arrival at a scanning company, completion of the scanning, entry to e-marking and return of marks. This enables reports to be generated showing where any item is at any point in time. It also allows alerts to trigger immediate action to be taken if, for example, an expected script does not arrive at the scanning company. The heart of the operation will be the database which will provide secure storage of all data generated during the marking process, including backup and archiving. Initially set up with detailed requirements information from Cambridge ESOL (including question paper and mark scheme information, candidate entry data, etc.) it will also contain all of the audit tracking information, images of the whole scanned scripts (or other data to be marked), images of the item-level questions to be marked, mark return data and other examiner/performance data.

Prior to an examination session, the management system and database would be pre-populated with the appropriate ESOL information which defines the exact requirements for processing. For example, this could include information on the Writing components to be processed in a given session, the type of marking required (ERM, MFI, single or partial double/full double-marking) and the examiner apportionment for the session.

The ability for examiners to mark a script from an 'on-screen' image will be provided via scoris – an on-screen marking application. On-screen marking using scoris is the marking solution that Cambridge Assessment is currently pursuing with its technology partner to enable examiners to mark candidates' test responses 'online'. The application displays digital images of the scripts 'on-screen' through a web-based system and enables examiners' marks and notations to be recorded and the marks automatically returned to Cambridge Assessment.

It is expected that ESM will deliver significant improvements in terms of quality and operational efficiency to the marking, awarding and post-results processes for Cambridge Assessment. The key areas of benefit for ESOL are in the areas of quality, operational efficiency and computer-based testing, and are listed in greater detail below.

Increased operational efficiency

- Expanded examiner pool (since marking could be location-independent).
- Improved script tracking and monitoring.
- Reduced marking and grading time: ESM enables faster and more flexible assessment and script management processes by:

    – dynamic apportionment of scripts to offsite examiners ensuring that scripts are only allocated and distributed to examiners when they are ready to receive them thus ensuring that no examiner is without work while others are over-loaded (see Appendix H for further details)

    – improved script monitoring enabling the status of a script to be identified at any point throughout the process, thereby ensuring tighter management and rapid identification of bottlenecks.

Enhanced scoring validity

- ESM permits effective double-marking by allowing the same script to be marked by two examiners simultaneously. Moreover, as ESM is web-based and could potentially support online co-ordination (see below), there is no restriction on recruiting examiners from beyond the UK, thereby greatly augmenting the future examiner base.
- ESM ensures greater consistency between teams. Currently, assessment quality is very much dependent upon the calibre of the Team Leader and any inconsistency which may exist across teams can be difficult to detect. The widespread use of comparative performance data and standardised scripts should improve the consistency of marking

between teams (see Appendix H for discussion of a marking model for ESM).

- ESM provides the potential for an online mechanism for more effective examiner co-ordination. Satisfactorily performing examiners, whose competence has been proven, may be released to engage in the marking process whilst those of unacceptable or doubtful quality may be given further assistance by comparing their marks with definitive marks and annotations. Data on performance may be collated throughout the marking process in order to observe trends.

- ESM facilitates effective interaction between examiners and their supervisors on the quality of their marking. Automatic generation of statistics, based on direct comparisons between examiner marks and definitively marked scripts, provide immediate information on the quality of examiner marking. Tighter feedback mechanisms will enhance training, improve examiner standards quickly and provide assurance that such standards are being consistently maintained (see Appendix H for further details).

- ESM increases fairness in all aspects of assessment through random script allocation and by anonymisation of script origin – both of which are already features of Cambridge ESOL practice.

- ESM is able to supplement existing feedback mechanisms which presently include item pretesting and post-marking performance grading for analysis of question/item and examiner performance.

More effective training

- ESM would allow greater freedom of discussion through the establishment of electronic or virtual communities of practice to promote consistency of assessment. Reliable marking is purported to be produced by having an effective community of practice (Wolf 1995). Communities of practice are groups of people who share similar goals and interests. In pursuit of these goals and interests, they employ common practices, work with the same tools and express themselves in a common language. Through such common activity, they come to hold similar beliefs and value systems.

- Cambridge ESOL has a strong interest in the potential of technology to improve communication between examiners within the Cambridge examining process and has been investigating the use of email discussion networks to facilitate the creation of 'online communities' of examiners, focused on Cambridge ESOL Writing qualifications, specifically FCE and CELS. These networks are able to foster conditions in which collegiate, reflective, practice-based development can occur, allowing examiners to share experience, information and good practice (Lieberman 2000).

- Email discussion lists comprise a set of features that make them especially suitable for building examiner communities. They support many-to-many communication (facilitating inter-group communication); are asynchronous (participants are not required to be online simultaneously; asynchronous discussion also engenders contemplative thought which can lead to richer contributions); are 'push' rather than 'pull' (the information comes to the user rather than the user having to retrieve it); are text-based (text allows structured discussion and, in conjunction with asynchronicity, can promote reflection and increasingly articulate messages); allow the creation of searchable archives such that messages and discussions can be retained for future reference and research.

- The discussion lists initiated by Cambridge ESOL generate lively debate and foster the conditions in which Writing examiners can share experience, information and good practice. Moreover, they promote professional development which should, among other things: be ongoing; include opportunities to put individual reflection and group enquiry into practice; be collaborative and allow Writing examiners to interact with peers; be rooted in the knowledge base of examining; and, be accessible and inclusive. Such communities might facilitate the reliability of marking if they are utilised in the co-ordination process of electronic marking. This would be achieved by examiners posting queries on a secure discussion website. TLs and PEs would be able to answer the queries to the benefit of all examiners as all examiners for the Writing paper would be able to read the website.

Piloting ESM

Cambridge ESOL's first major test of on-screen marking of scanned paper scripts was conducted in Spring 2001 (Shaw et al 2001). The principal aims of the trial were to:

- investigate alternative methods of marking scripts
- establish the practical possibility of the scanning and electronic movement of scripts
- give Cambridge ESOL the opportunity to evaluate the procedure by comparing examiner experience with the actuality of the on-site marking exercise
- compare marking throughput and marks awarded
- uncover issues, both technical and human, to be investigated in later stages of the development of a productive system
- provide research data concerning examiner reliability.

For this purpose approximately 1,500 CAE Greek and Portuguese scripts (0151/02) from the December 2000 administration were scanned and double-marked on-screen by examiners who had not marked that paper. Examiners were given a training session in the use of the latest version of PaperView (an online marking software package) on the Friday evening of the marking weekend. Both the pre-marking and on-the-day co-ordination were paper-based. Following a co-ordination meeting on the Saturday morning, examiners marked scripts throughout the remainder of the weekend. Examiners were apportioned scripts as they appeared in the batch queue and the scripts were double-marked and, where appropriate, third-marked. Conclusions (Shaw 2003c) were:

- The pilot demonstrated that examiners found the system user-friendly and were, in general, favourably disposed towards this style of marking, conscious of its great potential.
- In terms of examiner productivity, the overall rate of marking for the trial was approximately half of what would have been expected from conventional marking. However, the number of first and second markings during the trial was the same, indicating that the work flow system was allocating work correctly.
- Initial marking speeds were slower than with conventional paper marking but this was attributed to the novelty value of the system. Statistics for both the first day afternoon and the second day morning showed a substantially higher marking rate.
- Statistical analysis of the marking indicated that examiners awarded marginally higher marks on-screen for both the compulsory and optional Writing questions and over a slightly narrower range of scores than on paper. The difference in marking medium, however, did not appear to have a significant impact on marks.

Cambridge ESOL is engaged in a programme of research and development to identify the refinements needed for a production quality system and the contexts in which screen-based marking is fully valid and reliable. Pilot findings would suggest that ESM is promising from a number of different aspects, including reliability. Cambridge ESOL ESM Working Groups are proposing further trials to be undertaken with a view to introducing ESM to Cambridge ESOL examiner-marked papers. Cambridge ESOL plans to trial ESM within the following key areas:

- traditional paper-and-pencil Main Suite tests (on EPS)
- IELTS: exploration of IELTS-specific requirements for ESM on IBASE (IBASE is the internal database for managing IELTS data. It contains both the electronic records returned from centres via ESOLCOMMS – for example, names, candidate information, band scores, versions used –

and also the item level data from the scanning of candidate OMRs).

- computer-based (CB) products
- LIBS development: changes required to make question papers and mark schemes 'ESM-able'.

Further information on ESM is included in Appendices G and H. Appendix H provides further detail of some issues and directions in the future use of ESM in Cambridge ESOL and explores a potential scoring model for ESM. Appendix G details some of the issues and directions in computer-based testing at Cambridge ESOL and in particular it provides a description of a pilot to evaluate on-screen marking of extended Writing assignments for CB PET.

Electronic rating: research

Another emerging area of increasing interest is the automatic assessment of writing known as electronic rating, or e-rating.

With the advent of a burgeoning testing candidature, the increased demand placed upon large-scale assessment programmes in evaluating responses to direct tests of Writing is widely recognised.

Cambridge ESOL is investigating the feasibility of automatically grading essays using a computer. In this context an essay is simply a textual response to a question which is typed into a computer and can be any number of words from a few sentences upward. The aim of these studies is to investigate a number of possible approaches to the automatic assessment of natural language essays. Human-assigned grades represent an overall judgement of the quality of language form, structure and content in the essay. The research question raised by such studies is whether automatic techniques can simulate human judgement.

Clearly, the practical implications of either automated or partially-automated rating are obvious – not simply in terms of money saved but also in terms of the automatic generation of valuable diagnostic feedback for learners, teachers and testers alike.

Cambridge ESOL's primary interest in automated writing evaluation of 'free' or extended text was engendered by the development and implementation of computerised systems capable of assessing essays automatically. Described here is a review of the theoretical models of four of the most prominent implemented systems. An attempt to appraise their respective strengths and weaknesses is also given.

Automated assessment

Traditionally, open-ended items have been widely perceived to be unsuitable for machine marking because of the difficulty of handling the multiform ways in which credit worthy responses may be expressed. The extent of successful automatic marking of free text answers would seem to presuppose, at least in part, a sophisticated level of performance in automated natural language understanding. More recently, however, advances in Natural Language Processing (NLP) techniques have revealed potential for automatic assessment of free-text responses keyed into a computer without the need to create system software that fully comprehends the responses. In essence, NLP is the application of computational methods to analyse characteristics of electronic files of text (or speech). NLP applications utilise tools such as syntactic parsers which analyse the discourse structure/organisation of a response (Marcu 2000) and lexical similarity measures which analyse word use in a text (Salton 1989).

Perceptions of automated assessment

Despite understandable scepticism regarding the potential value of automated essay assessment (Wresch 1993), some reactions have been decidedly favourable. Apart from being cost effective, computerised scoring is unfailingly consistent, highly objective and almost wholly impartial (Schwartz 1998). There are those, however, who regard the concept of computer-assisted evaluation as being incompatible with current notions of communicative writing proficiency, which stress, among other things, the writer's ability to communicate, or engage, a specific readership.

It is the view of some critics that, unlike human raters, computers are incapable of differentiating between inspirational and creatively exceptional essays and their technically correct but ordinary counterparts (DeLoughry 1995, Mitchell 1998). This recognised shortcoming originates, it would seem, from the presumption that automated scoring emphasises linguistic rules and grammatical conventions at the expense of less tangible or demonstrable qualities, such as textual clarity and overall coherence. In accordance with this view, computers may be able to investigate writing for the presence or the absence of certain words, phrases or structures, but they cannot be expected to appreciate a writer's communicative purpose in the same way that human raters can. Even the developers of automated systems readily acknowledge that (although such systems can be useful tools in assessment) they are unable to adequately replace effective writing assessors.

Four conceptual models for automated essay assessment

Project Essay Grader (PEG) can trace its beginnings to work undertaken during the 1960s by Page (1966) and is widely regarded as the first and most enduring implementation of automated writing evaluation. It depends, principally, on the linguistic features of an essay. Beginning with an established corpus of pre-rated student compositions, by experimenting with a combination of automatically extractable textual features, Page applied multiple linear regression techniques to ascertain an optimal permutation of weighted features that most accurately predicted the teachers' ratings. The system was then able to rate (by adopting the same set of identified weighted features) other student essays. In their developmental work, Page and his research associates adopted two explanatory terms:

> *Trins* were the in*trin*sic variables of interest – fluency, diction, grammar, punctuation, and many others. We had no direct measures of these, so began with substitutes: *Proxes* were ap*prox*imations, or possible corre-lates, of these trins. All the computer variables (the actual counts in the essays) were proxes. For example, the trin of fluency was correlated with the prox of the number of words (Page 1994:130).

Multiple regression techniques employed by the PEG model are used in the computation, derived from the proxes, of an algorithm to predict a rating for each essay.

However, the use of proxes and trins and the multiple regression method-ology has been criticised in a number of ways, not least because of its lack of attention towards actual essay content. It is claimed that meaning and coher-ence cannot be reliably judged by such techniques, which focus on surface features of writing (Miller 2003).

Latent Semantic Analysis: The Intelligent Essay Assessor (IEA) was first patented in 1989 and uses techniques designed to address Miller's concern. It uses Latent Semantic Analysis (LSA), a natural language processing technique for comparing the semantic similarity of documents and is based on word doc-ument co-occurrence statistics represented as a matrix, which is subsequently decomposed and then subjected to a dimensionality reduction technique.

LSA is often referred to as the 'bag of words' approach because it neglects word order and has been criticised because it will assign an equally high rating to a scrambled version of a good essay. However, Landauer et al (2003) argue that this is a positive aspect because it can be taken as a measure of content alone, while grammar, discourse and so on can be measured separately.

The IEA uses LSA to measure content as one of three components in the model (alongside style and mechanics). It is 'trained' by using an extensive background text to represent the meaning of words as used in the domain of the test (for example, using text books from the same field). In this way, LSA does more than just match keywords; it is trained to recognise words which have similar meaning. The similarity between each essay to be graded and each of a previously scored batch of essays is computed, and a grade pre-dicted based on which pre-scored essays the new essay is most similar to.

E-rater (or essay-rater) is a system developed by ETS (Attali and Burstein 2005, Burstein et al 1998a, Burstein et al 1998b, Burstein, Leacock and Swartz 2001) and has been used for automated essay scoring since 1999. The system (which uses shallow parsing techniques to identify syntactic and discourse features) employs a hybrid approach of combining both statistical tools and linguistic features derived by using NLP techniques to model the decision of a human assessor. The original operational version of e-rater, version 1.3, was trained on a sample of essays which had been rated by humans and were all on the same topic. More than 50 aspects of the writing, designed to capture surface, structural, and content features, were measured and used in a stepwise linear regression procedure in order to identify those features significantly contributing to the prediction of scores. The result would be a regression equation typically consisting of around 8 to 12 of the original 50 variables.

E-rater version 2.0 was unveiled in the autumn of 2005 (Attali and Burstein, 2005) and improves on version 1.3 in a number of ways. First, the feature set was reduced to 12 and the features were standardised for essay length. Many of the models used in automated scoring engines, including the first version of e-rater, are prompt specific, so a different model would need to be calibrated for each new topic. This would require a considerable, ongoing requirement for human ratings to provide data for calibrating new models. However, for e-rater version 2.0 the models are uniform across prompts. This uniformity has been made possible due to the fixed, reduced feature set. ETS took this further, by not only fixing the features to be included in the regression model, but by fixing the parameters for some of the features in advance. This was the first step towards controlling the weighting of features based on theoretical considerations as opposed to simply statistical optimisation (Attali and Burstein 2005). The final major change in the new version of e-rater is how grades are assigned. Previously, the continuous score resulting from the application of the regression equation would simply be rounded to the nearest whole number. However, research has shown that this is not necessarily the best cut-off point for optimising human-computer agreement. Attali and Burstein (2005) detail a new method for finding the optimal cut-off point, which is based on signal detection theory and also takes into account the benefit and loss associated with each decision (to round up or down). They find that the resulting cut-offs between two adjacent scores tend to fall midway between the average unrounded e-rater score for those essays assigned the lower grade by humans, and the average unrounded e-rater score for those essays assigned the higher grade by humans.

An additional but related strand of research activity currently being undertaken by ETS Technologies is an investigation into the feasibility of automating the rating of short answer content-based questions. The *C-rater* prototype, again using NLP technology, is being evaluated for its effectiveness at producing 'credit/no credit' ratings.

Text Categorisation Techniques (TCT), developed by Larkey (University of Massachusetts, 1998), utilise a combination of modified key words and linguistic features. Text categorisation is the process of grouping text documents into one or more predefined categories based on their content. Several machine learning methods and statistical classifications have been applied to text categorisation including Bayesian classifiers, nearest neighbour classifiers, decision trees, neural networks and support vector machines.

A feature of a great many Cambridge Assessment examinations (including Cambridge ESOL tests) is the widespread use of questions requiring one or two sentences from candidates as a response. Any system that could either partially or completely automate the valid marking of short, free text answers would, therefore, be of great value. Until comparatively recently this has been considered either impossible or impractical. However, recent innovations in computational linguistics, together with an increasing emergence of computers in the classroom, have triggered a number of assessment organisations including Cambridge Assessment to explore the possibility of automatic marking and its application to high or low-stakes tests. Cambridge Assessment funded a three-year study at Oxford University which began in summer 2002 (Raikes 2006, Sukkarieh et al 2005). The project employs information extraction and retrieval techniques to mark GCSE biology answers using an automatic short answer assessor called *Automark 3*.

Automark 3 has been developed by Intelligent Assessment Technologies (Mitchell et al 2002) and employs information extraction techniques in the sense that the content of a correct response is specified in the form of a number of mark scheme templates. The stretch of text to be rated is fed into a parser – in this case the Link Grammar parser (Sleator and Temperley 1991) and the resulting parsed text is then compared to the already-defined templates or mark scheme. Mitchell et al (2002) claim about 95% agreement with human markers in blind testing. Callear, Jerrams-Smith and Soh (2001) at the University of Portsmouth also use pattern-matching techniques to mark short answers in programming languages, psychology and biology-related fields.

In essence the pattern-matching technique matches answers to be marked against pre-written patterns to extract pertinent information previously judged by human examiners to warrant the award or forfeiture of a mark. The patterns can include syntactic information to specify parts of speech, verb groups and noun phrases, and essentially a pattern covers the synonyms for each pertinent piece of information. A pattern is essentially all the paraphrases discovered for a particular entry in the mark scheme and includes both linguistic features as well as keywords. Patterns are written by hand and based on the marking scheme used by human examiners, together with sample training data – a set of human marked answers. The sample answers are annotated by the human examiners to indicate precisely the part(s) of each answer which gained or forfeited marks – this annotation is done to minimise the need for the person writing the patterns to make these judgements.

The automatic marker was evaluated at Cambridge using eight 1-mark items and five 2-mark items. The items were all taken from a GCSE Biology question paper, and answers from a sample of paper scripts were keyed into a computer file for automatic marking. The automatic marker marked all but two of the 1-mark items with a high degree of correctness; more than 90% of the answers for which there was a definitive (undisputed) human mark were marked correctly. Agreement levels between the automatic marker and human markers were also broadly similar, for these items, to those found between human markers. No simple explanation for why the remaining two 1-mark items were marked less well by the system can be offered; suitability for automatic marking does not appear to depend simply on item difficulty or the number of alternatives given in the examiners' written marking scheme. However, the 200 sample answers used for pattern-writing appear likely to be sufficient for screening 1-mark items for automatic marking. The system was generally less often correct, and there were greater differences between auto–human and human–human agreement levels, for 2-mark items.

Patterns were written for three of the items by a temporary examiner highly qualified in psychology and computing, but with no previous exposure to the project or computational linguistics. The correctness and inter-marker agreement levels were similar for both sets of patterns, implying that it is possible to transfer pattern-writing skills from the developers to new staff. This is an important step for the commercialisation of the system.

It is concluded that automatic marking is promising for 1-mark items requiring a short, textual response. More work is needed to see how the findings generalise to subjects and qualifications other than GCSE biology, and to investigate why some items are less suitable for automatic marking using this system than others.

Clearly, findings demonstrate that information extraction techniques can be successfully employed for the task of marking GCSE biology scripts. It has also been shown that a relatively naïve text classification method can rate better than a simple baseline grading technique. There are still many refinements to the approach that can be usefully made: the final aim is to attempt to approach the accuracy of the information extraction method but using completely automatic machine learning techniques.

Information extraction and retrieval techniques have some potential for certain Cambridge ESOL Writing tests. The CB PET Writing test comprises three parts. Two are clerically marked (Parts 1 and 2), while one is examiner marked (Part 3). The two clerically marked parts often trigger only a few sentences as a response. The use of a system that could be restricted to the auto-marking of these short text answers has clear benefit. Cambridge ESOL is currently giving consideration to the possibility of the electronic assessment of CB PET Writing Parts 1 and 2.

The operationalisation of automatic essay scoring in testing environments would reduce both the time and the significant costs associated with having multiple human raters manually assess essay responses. The agreement between two human raters, and between the conceptual models described above and a human rater is very favourable. Automated essay scoring would, therefore, appear to be a potential solution that would allow introduction of more Writing assessments on certain high-stakes standardised tests, and also in a lower-stakes context, for example, for the purposes of classroom instruction. Moreover, the increased availability of these technologies may well provide incentives for making a greater quantity and range of assessment and instructional materials available online.

In the final analysis, human involvement will not of course be rendered redundant in the rating event. Activities such as the preparation of exemplar scripts and the need for some face-to-face interaction will still be required. It is also difficult to conceive at present how a computer can make judgements on the relevance and adequacy of content, the overall coherence of a text or the effect on the audience of the way a text is written. Scoring validity must always be a more critical requirement than practical expediency.

So far we have looked at those 'internal' elements of our validity framework that affect the candidates, the test task and the raters, and which make a direct contribution to the construct validity of our tests. The other elements of validity we now turn to are 'external' to the test process itself; they relate to the effects and impact of test scores, and how these scores compare with other measures of the same construct in the world external to the test.

6 Consequential validity

Language test impact and washback

In the language teaching and testing literature, the concept of impact co-occurs frequently with the term 'washback' (or 'backwash') and it is the distinction between the two that is often an issue of debate. Impact is generally considered to include test washback (or, for some, its synonym backwash e.g. Green 2003, Hughes 2003). Hamp-Lyons (2000) advises washback is now normally used specifically for influences on teaching, teachers, and learning (including curriculum and materials) whereas in the mainstream educational literature wider influences of tests on the community at large are referred to by the term 'impact' (McNamara 2000, Wall 1997). Washback and impact are clearly matters of major importance to examination boards because their examinations have such widespread currency and recognition.

The impact concept covers in part what Messick (1989) terms consequential validity, arguing that it is necessary in validity studies to ascertain whether the social consequences of test use and interpretation support the intended testing purpose(s) and are consistent with other social values. Messick emphasises that the appropriateness, meaningfulness, and usefulness of score-based inferences are a function of the external social consequences of the testing as well as the aspects of internal construct validity described earlier in this volume.

Green (2003) provides a useful review of the interpretations of washback in the language testing literature:

> There is now a clear consensus on the need for concern with, if not agreement on the effects of what has been termed 'washback/backwash'. Washback is considered a 'neutral' term (Alderson and Wall 1993 and 1996) which may refer to both (intended) positive (Bachman and Palmer, 1996; Davies et al. 1999) or beneficial (Buck 1988; Hughes, 2003) effects and to (unintended) harmful (Buck, 1988) or negative effects (Bachman and Palmer, 1996; Davies et al. 1999; Hughes, 1989).
>
> Backwash is broadly defined as 'the effect of a test on teaching' (Richards, Platt and Platt, 1992) and often also on learning (Hughes, 2003; Shohamy, 2001). It has also been variously associated with effects on teachers, learners (Buck, 1988; Messick, 1994; Shohamy, 2001), parents (Pearson, 1988), administrators, textbook writers (Hughes, 2003), instruction (Bachman, 1990; Chapelle and Douglas, 1993;

Weigle, 2002), the classroom (Buck, 1988), classroom practice (Berry, 1994), educational practices and beliefs (Cohen, 1994) and curricula (Cheng, 1997; Weigle, 2002), although for Hughes (2003) and Bailey (1999), the ultimate effects on learning outcomes are of primary concern.

There is the difficulty, however, in the multi-faceted area of impact and washback studies, of establishing clear-cut cause and effect between a test and developments apparently associated with it. Hawkey (2006), among others, reminds us that Washback is complex, with a great many independent, intervening and dependent variables. Alderson and Wall (1993) state 15 washback hypotheses, covering a test's influence on: the teacher, the learner, what and how teachers teach, and learners learn, the rate and sequence of learning, and attitudes to teaching and learning methods. Milanovic and Saville (1996:2) note the scope and intricacy of the washback concept, including as it does the complex interactions between the factors which make up the teaching / learning context (including the individual learner, the teacher, the classroom environment, the choice and use of materials etc.).

Tests have important effects on people's lives and are thus potentially an instrument of power and control. Shohamy (2001) argues that, the above difficulties notwithstanding, we must be aware of the social and political dimensions of tests as well as their technical qualities and accordingly we need to include within the validation process studies of the use of tests.

Following Messick (1989), consequential validity might be viewed from three criterial perspectives:

Figure 6.1 Consequential validity (adapted from Weir 2005b:47)

Consequential validity
• Washback on individuals in classroom/workplace • Impact on institutions and society • Avoidance of test bias

Impact and washback: research

A number of early studies have examined the impact of testing innovations (Burrows 1998, Cheng 1997, Wall and Alderson 1993). Yang and Weir (1998) described a comprehensive validation study of the College English Test in China (CET) and detailed how one examination board attempted to generate empirical evidence on the value of its tests as perceived by a variety of its stakeholders, e.g. end users of results in universities and the business world. Other early studies compared test preparation and general English courses (Alderson and Hamp-Lyons 1996).

In his introduction to Cheng and Watanabe (2004), Alderson (2004) draws attention to the fact that test washback and impact have become a central area of concern in educational research. Eight new projects are described in this volume including Saville and Hawkey's IELTS Impact Study (2004) conducted for Cambridge ESOL. The centrality of test washback and impact in language testing is also reflected in the publication of several recent titles in the Studies in Language Testing series (SiLT) published jointly by Cambridge ESOL and Cambridge University Press. Between 2005 and 2007 four new volumes appeared focusing on major washback and impact studies carried out by Liying Cheng, Dianne Wall, Roger Hawkey and Tony Green.

Rather than undertake *post hoc* investigations of the results of change, other researchers have focused more proactively on how tests might become instruments of desirable positive change. Hughes (2003) offers some suggestions for achieving beneficial backwash:

- test the abilities whose development you want to encourage
- sample widely and unpredictably
- use direct testing
- make the testing criterion-referenced
- ensure the test is known and understood by students and teachers
- where necessary provide assistance to teachers.

Weir (2005b) emphasises that the major washback research studies carried out by Wall (2005) and Cheng (2005) argue for the centrality of Hughes' criterion of necessary provision of assistance to teachers if beneficial washback is to occur. Training teachers in the new content and methodology required for a high-stakes test is essential. If teachers are untrained in the new knowledge, skills and attitudes required for effective teaching towards the examination, why should we expect positive backwash? Support in the form of appropriate teaching materials must also be readily available.

Green (2003) offers a number of other conditions that need to be in place:

- there needs to be a considerable overlap between test and target situation demands on language abilities
- success on the test is perceived to be important
- success on the test is perceived to be difficult (but both attainable and amenable to preparation)
- candidates operate in a context where these perceptions are shared by other participants.

Cambridge ESOL: impact and washback research

Concomitant with the growing importance of high-stakes language tests is the increasing demand for preparation courses for international English language tests, and for accompanying coursebooks and associated materials. As candidature rises for language tests such as those in and beyond the Cambridge Main Suite, so does the importance of the study of the washback of preparation courses for international English language tests, and of the textbooks designed for use on such courses (e.g. Saville and Hawkey 2004, Smith 2004). Green's study on IELTS washback (2003), for example, compares practices and outcomes on IELTS examination preparation courses with EAP courses such as university pre-sessional courses.

The CPE Textbook Washback Study (Hawkey 2004) is a good example of an exam board's concern for the effect that changes in an examination might have on the textbooks used in preparation for the test.

The principal objective of the study was to test the hypothesis that the constructs and content of a test have washback effects on test preparation textbooks. The primary research questions which the study sought to explore included:

- To what extent did the revision of the CPE examination in 2002 impact on textbooks designed for use with CPE students?
- In what way were the changes in the exam reflected in the textbooks?

Ten CPE-related textbooks were identified as being suitable for the study. They included four books written for the preparation of CPE candidates prior to 2002, four books revised for the post-revision CPE exam, and two totally new CPE-oriented books. Each of the 10 chosen books was independently assessed by two language-teaching specialists, selected on the basis of their background with the CPE exam and other relevant experience. In total, 20 textbook evaluations were produced.

The instrument used for making evaluations was the Instrument for the Analysis of Textbook Materials (IATM). This particular instrument had its origins in an initial version developed by Bonkowski (1996) at Lancaster University under the supervision of Charles Alderson and had previously been refined and used in the study of IELTS impact described below (Hawkey 2006, Saville and Hawkey 2004). The IATM was further adapted – from suggestions made by members of the Cambridge ESOL Main Suite team – to make it suitable for the CPE washback investigation. The IATM gathers both quantitative and qualitative information on: the evaluator; the evaluator's view of the CPE exam; textbook type; units of organisation; language features; enabling skills; task types; genre; media; communicative activities and opportunities; text topics; text and task authenticity. The instrument further elicits qualitative comment on a textbook's treatment of language skills and use of English, the overall quality of the textbook, and its relationship with the CPE exam.

The hypothesis that the pre-revision and revised CPE exams washback strongly on the evaluated textbooks in their respective treatment of English language skills, micro-skills, task types, language elements and topics was supported by the study. Other main conclusions gleaned from the data are:

- evaluators deem it appropriate that the textbooks concerned reflect the content (text topics), approaches (enabling skills), activities and tasks of the exam directly
- evaluators consider that the textbooks should additionally offer opportunities and materials to aid the development of learners to enhance their overall language knowledge and ability
- both the revised and new versions of course preparation books mirror significantly the changes in the revised CPE exam.

The IELTS Impact Study (IIS) constitutes a major long-term programme of research by Cambridge ESOL into the impact of IELTS, one of the most widely-used language tests for those needing to study or train in the medium of English. Given its high-stakes nature, a lot of impact study work has been conducted in relation to IELTS and this is reflected in the prominence given to it in the remainder of this chapter.

Describing the study from its inception in 1995, Saville (2001:5) remarks: 'It was agreed that procedures would be developed to monitor the impact of the test and to contribute to the next revision cycle'. He explains the rationale for this study as follows:

> In order to understand the test impact better and to conduct effective surveys to monitor it, it was decided that a range of standardised instruments and procedures should be developed to focus on the following aspects of the test:
>
> - the content and nature of classroom activity in IELTS-related classes
> - the content and nature of IELTS teaching materials, including textbooks
> - the views and attitudes of user groups towards IELTS
> - the IELTS test-taking population and the use of results.

The first two of these points concern washback in the sense accepted above, (i.e. the effect of the test on teaching and learning). The second two are concerned with the *impact* of the test, its effects on other systems in the administrative and academic contexts of the tests, and on the attitudes and behaviour of the stakeholders in these contexts.

The study included three phases: Identification of areas to be targeted and the development of instrumentation to collect information which allows impact to be measured (Phase 1); validation of the instruments prior to full-scale implementation (Phase 2); and implementation of the instruments as part of a major survey (Phase 3).

Phase 1 was undertaken in the mid-1990s by Alderson and his research team at the University of Lancaster (see Alderson and Banerjee 1996, Banerjee 1996, Bonkowski 1996, Herrington 1996, Horak 1996, Milanovic and Saville 1996, Winetroube 1997, Yue 1997).

Phase 2 entailed analyses and pretesting of the draft data collection instruments by the Validation Group (Cambridge ESOL) in conjunction with external consultants including Bachman, Purpura, Kunnan and Hawkey. As Phase 2 developed, the original 13 data collection instruments (draft questionnaires, schedules or summary sheets intended for use in investigating the characteristics and attitudes of key IELTS stakeholders) were streamlined to five:

- a modular student questionnaire on pre- and post- IELTS candidate language learning background, objectives and strategies
- a language teacher questionnaire embracing teacher background and experience, attitudes towards IELTS, experience of and ideas on IELTS-preparation programmes
- an instrument for the evaluation of IELTS-related textbooks and other materials (the IATM described above)
- a classroom observation instrument for the analysis of IELTS-preparation lessons
- a pro forma for receiving institute IELTS administrators on their IELTS experiences and attitudes.

More than 300 university, British Council and IDP Education, Australia and other IELTS test centres globally were included in a pre-survey in 2001. Responses were received from 41 countries and contained information on: the language tests for which each centre runs courses; the frequency, length and dates of such courses; numbers and nationalities of students; textbooks and other materials used. The findings from the questionnaire informed the subsequent phase of the project: 30 IELTS centres were identified and selected for the main data-collecting Phase 3. These centres, which constituted a case study sample, reflected the IELTS nationality population (including teachers and candidates). A total of 572 test takers, 83 IELTS preparation course teachers, and 45 textbook evaluators responded through the questionnaires. 120 students, 21 teachers and 15 receiving institution administrators participated in face-to-face interviews and focus groups to enhance and triangulate questionnaire data from student and teacher participants.

Findings from this study are presented in Tables 6.1 and 6.2, under selected areas of principal interest, including the teaching and testing of writing.

Test module difficulty

Very similar perceptions of the relative difficulties of the IELTS macro skill modules (Reading, Writing, Speaking, and Listening) were held by both teachers and candidates in the study.

Hawkey (2006) notes that Writing skills are tested in IELTS in accordance with a strong communicative construct, involving candidates in tasks related as closely as is feasible to the skills required in their target language domains. Further statistical investigation of the relatively high level of perceived difficulty for the IELTS Writing Module revealed that test takers saw time pressures and topics as the main source for this.

Table 6.1 IELTS Impact Study student and teacher perceptions of IELTS module difficulty

Most difficult IELTS Module? (%)		
	Students	Teachers
Reading	49	45
Writing	24	26
Listening	18	20
Speaking	9	9

Source: Hawkey 2006:122.

IELTS impact on preparation courses

Teacher questionnaires, triangulated with observations gleaned from video recordings of IELTS preparation classes, yielded interesting results in relation to IELTS washback on language teaching and learning approaches. 90% of teachers believed the test influenced the content of their lessons with a further 63% claiming that it impacted their methodology. This has inevitable implications for preparation programmes which, according to findings of the study of IELTS impact, become: 'more focused, mainly test-oriented, aimed at developing relevant communicative micro-skills, encouraging discussion and brainstorming, and using authentic texts, including a wide range of multi-media target language materials from beyond the textbooks' (Hawkey 2004a:14). In response to open-ended student questionnaire items such as 'Do you think you were/are successful on the preparation course(s)?', analysis indicated a balance in students' perceptions of success between target language proficiency gain and improved familiarity with the test.

Overall findings imply that the impact on preparation courses by IELTS is significant. However, it is generally perceived by IIS participants that the resultant programmes of study/preparation are suitable for both students preparing for tertiary level education and for those who are not.

Test perceptions and pressures

Critical language testers (for example Shohamy 2001) suggest that one aspect of high-stakes test impact needing investigation is the pressures felt by candidates; such pressures might constitute an aspect of consequential validity that distorts scores and reduces test fairness. Of the 190 test-taker respondents, 70% considered IELTS to be a reasonable way of testing their English language proficiency and whilst 53% of teachers believed that IELTS was responsible for contributing to additional candidate stress, 94% were adamant that the test provided positive motivation for candidates. 54% of the IIS post-IELTS participants suggested that they had not performed to the very best of their ability on the test. When asked which factors affected their performance, post-IELTS candidates cited the pressures of time (40%) and topic unfamiliarity (21%) as constituting the two most significant aspects.

The test takers themselves responded to the item 'Did you worry about taking the IELTS test?' as in Table 6.2.

Table 6.2 IELTS test-taker anxiety

Did you worry about taking the IELTS test?

	Number	%
Very much	78	41
⇓	58	31
	36	19
Very little	18	9

Source: Hawkey 2006:119.

IELTS clearly causes some anxiety, with 72% of the post-test participants claiming to have been worried or very worried by the test. Such levels of stated concern are perhaps predictable in relation to high-stakes tests. The study pursued this observation through triangulation with other evidence; findings suggested that 49% of the participants claimed they normally felt positive about their performance compared with their potential after any high-stakes test, and 46% of those who had taken IELTS felt that they had performed to the best of their ability; the similarity of these two percentage figures suggests that the IELTS experience was no more anxiety-provoking in relative terms than any other high-stakes test.

Responses from the participating IELTS preparation course teachers suggest a strong perceived relationship between test anxiety and motivation. Whereas 53% of the teachers considered that IELTS caused stress to their students, 84 % also felt that the test provided these students with motivation.

This is an interesting and typical example of the complex relationships between factors encountered in consequential validity research.

Test fairness is, as we have been reminded frequently throughout this volume, the key aim of test validation. It is an aim that is also supported by the study of impact. In the IELTS research, for example, the post-test takers were asked whether they thought the IELTS was a fair way to test their proficiency in English: 72% replied 'Yes', 28% 'No'. This split could be considered a positive response, especially when follow-up explanations from the candidates revealed opposition to *all* tests as the most frequently mentioned reason for a negative view. Once again the need for probing research into the complex variables of impact is emphasised.

Impact research analyses to date imply perceptions that IELTS:

- is a suitable direct communicative performance test for candidates embarking on both undergraduate and postgraduate studies, or for those seeking English language accreditation in the professional domain
- has content which is largely relevant to target communicative activities. It was noted, however, that the Writing tasks are thought of by some as being 'too general' and/or may not have relevance for all candidates.

This latter view on content relevance is in large part supported by Green in his important study of the washback of IELTS (2003) in relation to what occurs in courses specifically designed for students preparing for the test.

Washback and impact: Cambridge practice

Cambridge ESOL fully recognises that, as a central part of the test validation process, there is a need for extensive research to be undertaken into the washback and impact of high-stakes tests on stakeholders.

High-stakes tests are so called because they are employed to determine admission or otherwise of candidates to specific programmes of study, professions or places. They are also instrumental in shaping educational goals and processes, and society generally. Cambridge ESOL (see, for example, Saville and Hawkey 2004, Taylor 1999) sees itself as answerable to a broad range of stakeholders, from test takers and their parents, test-preparation teachers, to test centre administrators, education policy makers, as well as test-taker receiving institutions and employers.

The importance ascribed by Cambridge ESOL to impact studies is well documented (e.g. Hawkey 2006, Weir and Milanovic 2003). Saville (2003) describes the procedures that need to be put into place after a Cambridge examination becomes operational to collect information that allows impact to be estimated. This should involve collecting data on the following:

- who is taking the examination (i.e. a profile of the candidates)
- who is using the examination results and for what purpose

- who is teaching towards the examination and under what circumstances
- what kinds of courses and materials are being designed and used to prepare candidates
- what effect the examination has on public perceptions generally (e.g. regarding educational standards)
- how the examination is viewed by those directly involved in educational processes (e.g. by students, examination takers, teachers, parents, etc.)
- how the examination is viewed by members of society outside education (e.g. by politicians, those working in business, etc.).

The need to monitor the test's effects on language materials and on class-room activity (see, for example, Green 2003, Hawkey 2004), as well as to seek information on and views of a full range of stakeholders (see Taylor 1999), is now accepted by most serious examination boards and it has been the hall-mark of Cambridge ESOL examinations since the modern revisions commenced in the 1980s. In the CPE 2002 revision conscious efforts were made to elicit feedback on the existing test from participants and a wide variety of stakeholders contributed to the decisions that were taken concerning changes in the examination (see Weir and Milanovic 2003 for a full account of the CPE revision and Hawkey 2004b for a description of the CELS examination change process). At the time of writing, a similar process of extensive stakeholder consultation is underway as part of the FCE/CAE modifications project.

Differential validity: research

The area of differential validity takes us back to the place we started from in this volume: the test taker. Test bias can result from either construct under-representation or the inclusion of construct-irrelevant components of test scores that differentially affect the performance of different groups of test takers (American Educational Research Association et al 1999). Bachman (1990) identifies four potential sources of test bias:

- cultural background
- background knowledge
- cognitive characteristics
- native language/ethnicity/age and gender.

Weir (2005b:265) reports on a number of studies which deal in more detail with these areas where bias may occur:

> Alderman and Holland (1981) looked at item performance on TOEFL across native language groups as did Oltman et al (1988). Chen and Henning [1985] looked at linguistic and cultural bias in proficiency tests. Kunnan (1990, 1994) and Ryan and Bachman (1992), Brown and Iwashita (1998) and Hill (1998) looked at differential item functioning

(DIF) in terms of a number of background variables. Tittle (1990) discusses the contexts in which test bias can happen and details various methodologies for establishing whether it has occurred or not.

Examination boards have to take steps to ensure that the potential sources of bias identified by Bachman and these other researchers are guarded against.

Differential validity: Cambridge practice

Before the test is administered it is obviously necessary to establish evidence of the context and cognitive validity of test tasks to try and ensure that no potential sources of bias are allowed to interfere with measurement. After the test it is useful to check up on this statistically in relation to candidate biodata such as that collected by Cambridge ESOL at the time of test implementation on the CIS (which are routinely administered to all ESOL candidates enabling Cambridge ESOL to gather a large amount of demographic data such as age, gender, nationality, first language etc. for research purposes). An example of the CIS form is supplied in Appendix B. Such candidate information is valuable as it can be collected and electronically recorded and later compared to test scores. Weir and Milanovic (2003:103) describe how at Cambridge ESOL Grade Review and Awards meetings:

> The performance of large groups of candidates (or cohorts) is compared with cohorts from previous years, and performance is also compared by country, by first language, by age and a number of other factors, to ensure that the standards being applied are consistently fair to all candidates, and that a particular grade 'means' the same thing from year to year and throughout the world.

This notwithstanding, it is important to remember Bachman's (1990:278) caveat that group differences must be treated with some caution as they may be an indication of differences in actual language ability rather than an indication of bias.

In this chapter we have argued that three parameters in consequential validity need to be addressed in considering a test's validity:

- the need for washback evidence that the effects of the test on learning and teaching is positive
- the need for evidence that the impact on society, individuals and institutions, is beneficial
- the need to demonstrate that bias has been avoided.

In the next chapter we turn to the final set of parameters that exam boards need to consider in generating evidence on the validity of their tests, namely those of criterion-related validity.

7 Criterion-related validity

Definitions

We have seen in earlier chapters how the internal cognitive, context and scoring dimensions of a test all contribute validity evidence in support of claims about the construct the test is measuring. Weir's validation framework also includes criterion-related validity as an evidence-based requirement which is external rather than internal to the test. This is described by Weir as 'a predominantly quantitative and *a posteriori* concept, concerned with the extent to which test scores correlate with a suitable external criterion of performance with established properties' (2005b:35).

The ALTE Handbook of European Language Examinations and Examination Systems (1998a) also advocates the value of establishing suitable external criteria for test validation. It notes that a test is said to have criterion-related validity if a relationship can be demonstrated between test scores and an external criterion which is believed to be a measure of the same ability (ALTE 1998). Criterion-related validity may be either concurrent or predictive in nature. Concurrent validity involves comparing scores from a given test with some other measure of the same ability of the candidates taken at the same time as that test. Predictive validity entails the comparison of test scores with a measure for the same candidates taken some time after the test (Alderson et al 1995; Davies 1990). This other, external measure may consist, for instance, of other test scores, ratings by teachers or other informants (Alderson et al 1995), or candidate language ability self-assessments. It may not necessarily be language based, e.g., for predictive purposes it may be content-based degree course results (see Alderson et al 1995 and Criper and Davies 1988 for exemplification of this).

The comparison between scores from a test and from another, external measure – whether for purposes of concurrent or predictive validation – is normally expressed in terms of a correlation coefficient. Correlations above 0.9 between the two sets of scores from the test of interest and the concurrent or predictive criteria would indicate a strong relationship between the two measures; with over 80% of the variance being shared (i.e. squaring the correlation indicates that, for a correlation of 0.9, around 20% of the information is not accounted for).

Weir (2005b) sounds a note of caution in relation to predictive validity arguing that predictive and concurrent studies are insufficient evidence of validity by themselves, especially given the problematic nature of examining these. Establishing predictive validity through correlating language performance against later job/academic performance is hampered by practical difficulties in mounting tracer studies and the problems associated with confounding intervening variables. Banerjee (2003) provides a critique of such approaches to establishing predictive validity and proposes an alternative approach taking into account the cost to individuals and institutions; she explores a practical exemplification of this in relation to IELTS.

These difficulties notwithstanding, Taylor (2004a) emphasises that test providers are being challenged to pay greater attention to issues of test comparability – both in terms of the relationships between their own assessment products and those offered by competitor examination boards. The reason for this, Taylor continues, is the increasing importance attached by test users to test comparability information. The ability to relate different tests to one another in useful and meaningful ways provides testers with criterion-related evidence to put to use for both test validation and test comparability purposes.

Taylor (2004a) develops this, arguing that test users seek firm statements concerning the 'equivalence' or otherwise of different tests. University admissions officers want to know how to deal with students who present them with TOEFL, IELTS or CPE scores; employers need to know how to interpret different language qualifications previously achieved by potential employees; schools, teachers and students have to make choices about which test to take and they want to be clear about the relative merits of those on offer (e.g. FCE or BEC Vantage).

The parameters of criterion-related validity in Figure 7.1 will be discussed in the next section.

Figure 7.1 Criterion-related validity parameters in writing

Criterion-related validity
• cross-test comparability • comparison with different versions of the same test • comparison with external standards

Cross-test comparability studies: Cambridge practice

Taylor (2004a) points out that there have always been informal as well as formal attempts to compare language proficiency measures; traditionally, comparisons have tended to focus on the notion of 'score equivalences', i.e.

how do the scores or grades from two different tests relate to one another, and to what extent can they be considered 'equivalent'? She draws attention to a formal attempt which took place in 1987 when Cambridge was involved in the three-year Cambridge–TOEFL Comparability Study, set up at the instigation of Cambridge ESOL and carried out under the direction of Lyle Bachman (see Bachman et al 1995 in this series for full details of this). In the preface to the volume Bachman reminds readers that any comparability study needs to take account of more than just score equivalences; it must also investigate comparability of test content and performance. It is also important to distinguish the activity of comparing scores across skills-focused subtests or components (e.g. a Writing subtest or a Reading Module) either from the same test or from different tests, and the activity of comparing whole test scores from at least two different tests. The following discussion begins with a consideration of score comparability at the level of the exam syllabus (or whole test battery); later on, the focus moves to the subtest or component level, with particular reference to writing.

The conceptual framework mapping exams onto a comparison scale presented by Taylor in Research Notes 15 (2004a) describes the links between Cambridge ESOL suites of level-based tests or syllabuses, i.e. Main Suite, BEC, CELS and YLE. These suites are targeted at similar ability levels as defined by a common measurement scale (based on latent trait methods); many are also similar in terms of test content and design (multiple skills components, similar task/item-types, etc.).

In a later article focusing on IELTS, Taylor (2004b) argues that the relationship of IELTS with the other Cambridge ESOL tests and with the Common European Framework of Reference is rather complex; IELTS is not a level-based test (like FCE or CPE) but is designed to stretch across a much broader proficiency continuum. So when seeking to compare IELTS band scores with scores on other tests, it is important to bear in mind the differences in purpose, measurement scale, test format and test-taker populations for which IELTS was originally designed.

She describes how from the late 1990s onwards, Cambridge ESOL has conducted a number of research projects to explore how IELTS band scores align with the CEFR levels. In 1998 and 1999 internal studies examined the relationship between IELTS and the Cambridge Main Suite Examinations, specifically CAE (C1 level) and FCE (B2 level). Under test conditions, candidates took experimental Reading tests containing both IELTS and CAE or FCE tasks. Although the studies were limited in scope, results indicated that a candidate who achieves a Band 6.5 in IELTS would be likely to achieve a passing grade at CAE (C1 level). Further research was conducted in 2000 as part of the ALTE Can Do Project (see below) in which Can Do responses by IELTS candidates were collected over the year and matched to grades; this enabled Can Do self-ratings of IELTS and Main Suite candidates to be compared. The results, in terms of mean 'Can Do self-ratings', further supported placing IELTS Band 6.5 at the C1 level of the CEFR alongside CAE.

A further source of evidence for the alignment of IELTS with other Cambridge ESOL examinations, international examinations and with the CEFR comes from the internal use made of IELTS, CPE, CAE and BEC Higher test scores by educational and other institutions for admissions purposes (for more details see www.CambridgeESOL.org/recognition).

The conceptual framework presented in early 2004 was subsequently revised to accommodate IELTS more closely within its frame of reference. Figure 7.2 illustrates how the IELTS band scores, Cambridge Main Suite, BEC and CELS examinations align with one another and with the levels of the CEFR.

Figure 7.2 Alignment of IELTS, Main Suite, BEC and CELS examinations with the Common European Framework of Reference

IELTS bands	Main Suite	BEC	CELS	CEF
9.0				
8.0				
	CPE			C2
7.0				
	CAE	BEC H	CELS H	C1
6.0				
	FCE	BEC V	CELS V	B2
5.0				
4.0	PET	BEC P	CELS P	B1
3.0	KET			A2
				A1

Figure 7.3 indicates the overall IELTS band scores that test takers might reasonably be expected to achieve at a particular CEFR level. Note that the IELTS band scores referred to in both figures are the overall scores, not the individual module scores.

Figure 7.3 IELTS band scores and CEFR levels

Corresponding CEFR level	IELTS approximate band score
C2	7.5+
C1	6.5/7.0
B2	5.0/5.5/6.0
B1	3.5/4.0/4.5
A2	3.0

This alignment is based not only on the internal research at Cambridge ESOL referred to above, but also the long-established experience of test use within education and society, as well as feedback from a range of test stakeholders regarding the uses of test results for particular purposes. It will continue to be refined as further evidence is generated.

The purpose of these figures is to provide a framework of how tests and levels relate to each other in broad terms within a common frame of reference. As Taylor (2004a) emphasises, comparative frameworks are primarily designed to function as communicative tools, summarising in an accessible and transparent manner those features which two or more tests are considered to share. They do not, for the most part, represent strong claims about exact equivalence between exam performances since, even though two different test scores may be used in a similar way, the actual content, length, format, availability, etc. of two tests may be different in ways that are significant. For this reason, comparative frameworks should not be over-interpreted.

The discussion so far has focused on comparing overall test scores, including the caveats which can apply when drawing such comparisons. Comparisons across individual skills subtests (e.g. Writing) and the scores these generate may be easier to make and may offer more meaningful insights. Recent research compares IELTS candidates' writing performance with that of Main Suite, BEC and CELS candidates. This work forms part of Cambridge ESOL's Common Scale for Writing project – a long-term research project which has been in progress since the mid-1990s (see description of this project as Case Study C in Chapter 5 and for fuller details see Hawkey and Barker 2004, Hawkey and Shaw 2005). A common scale, according to the Common European Framework of Reference for Languages (CEFR), may cover 'the whole conceptual range of proficiency' (Council of Europe 2001:40). The location on a common scale of proficiency of examinations for candidates at different levels should, the CEFR continues, make it 'possible, over a period of time, to establish the relationship between the grades on one examination in the series with the grades of another' (2001:41).

Hawkey and Shaw (2005) describe how the Cambridge ESOL Common Scale for Writing (CSW) project has derived, from empirical investigation, a scale of descriptors of writing proficiency levels to appear alongside the Common Scale for Speaking in the Handbooks for the Main Suite and other Cambridge ESOL international exams (see Case Study C in Chapter 5 for details). The scale is intended to assist test users in interpreting levels of performance across exams and locating the level of one examination in relation to another. They report that it is clear that candidates for tests representing particular language proficiency levels (for example Common European Framework Level B2 or ALTE Level 3) actually perform at a range of levels, some falling below the benchmark adequate performance level for the exam concerned, some appearing to reach levels higher than the exam's top performance grade, (for example 'pass with merit'). Candidates may in fact be reaching a level normally associated with the exam one higher on the level hierarchy (e.g. CAE at CEFR Level C1 rather than FCE at Level B2). Figure 7.4 (see also Hawkey 2001, Hawkey and Barker 2004) conceptualises the relationship between a Common Scale for Writing (intended to provide descriptor bands for levels from elementary to advanced) and the levels typically covered by candidates for

Figure 7.4 Conceptual diagram of a common scale across examination levels and ranges

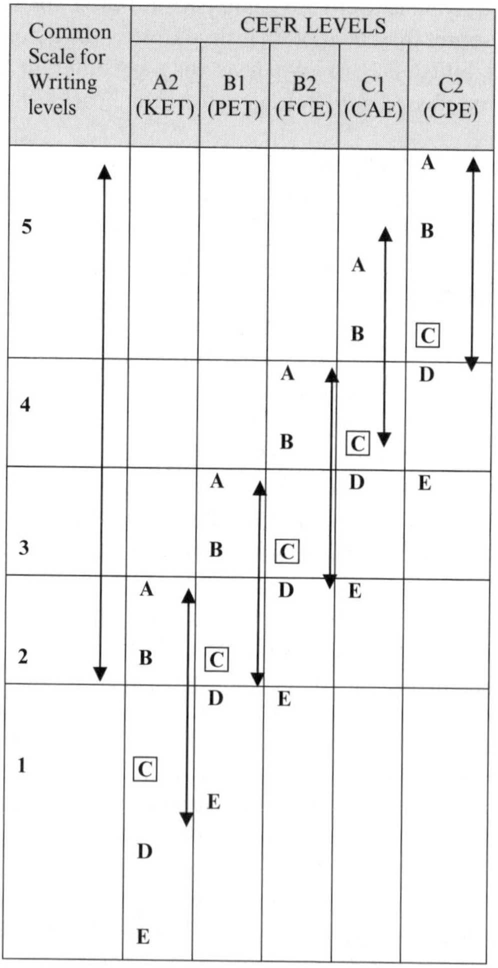

Common Scale for Writing levels	CEFR LEVELS				
	A2 (KET)	B1 (PET)	B2 (FCE)	C1 (CAE)	C2 (CPE)
5				A B	A B C D
4			A B	C	
3		A B	C	D	E
2	A B	C	D	E	
1	C D E	D E	E		

Source: Hawkey and Shaw 2005:20.

Cambridge ESOL examinations, the Key English Test (KET), the Preliminary English Test (PET), the First Certificate in English (FCE), the Certificate in Advanced English (CAE) and the Certificate of Proficiency in English (CPE), each of which has its own pass level (the 'C' in Figure 7.4).

The process of placing exams on a common scale or within a common frame of reference is no easy matter. Conceptually it may be possible and even desirable to be able to co-locate different tests at shared proficiency levels (e.g. B2 on the CEFR) or along common dimensions (e.g. social and tourist, study, work) but of course the different design, purpose, intended audience, methods of assessing language traits, mark schemes and formats of examinations under review make it difficult to give exact comparisons across tests and test scores. As we have noted in Chapters 3 and 4, where tests differ in terms of the contextual or cognitive parameters operationalised, differences in performance are likely.

Comparison with different versions of the same test

Test *equivalence*, also used in criterion-related test validation, is established if 'a relationship can be demonstrated between test scores obtained from different versions of a test administered to the same candidates in the same conditions on two different occasions' (Weir 2005b:208). The ALTE *Multilingual Glossary of Language Testing Terms* (1998:144) offers the following definition of equivalence in test forms:

> Different versions of the same test, which are regarded as equivalent to each other in that they are based on the same specifications and measure the same competence. To meet the strict requirements of equivalence under classical test theory, different forms of a test must have the same mean difficulty, variance, and covariance, when administered to the same persons.

The American Educational Research Association (1999) further refines the test equivalence definition. It distinguishes between: parallel forms, which should demonstrate equivalence in raw score means, standard deviations, error structures, and correlations with other measures for a stated population; equivalent forms, where score conversion techniques or 'form-specific norm tables' are used to compensate for differences in raw score statistics between test versions; and comparable forms, which are very close in terms of content but where the extent of statistical similarity remains unproven. For test providers, of course, it is vital to achieve as complete as possible equivalence across alternate forms of the same test which are produced on different session dates to meet the needs of test users. Taylor (2004a:2) notes that Cambridge ESOL produces different versions – also known as 'alternate' or 'parallel' forms – of the same test to be taken on different session dates throughout the year; tests must clearly be equivalent from session to session in terms of their content coverage and measurement characteristics. The glossary notes that equivalence is very difficult to achieve in practice and it is fair to say that considerable effort and expertise goes into ensuring test equivalence through the implementation of a comprehensive set of standard procedures applied at each stage of test production (see Saville 2003).

The *Dictionary of Language Testing* by Davies et al (1999) offers a similar definition for equivalence to the one given above and goes on to mention the increasingly common use of IRT analysis and item banking to help with the process of creating equivalent forms.

However, following our discussion of context and cognitive aspects of validity above, it must be stressed that high indices of alternate-form reliability alone do not necessarily yield a significant meaning unless supported by evidence of comparability in other aspects of validity as well. For example, inconsistent context validity across test forms may impact on test scores, resulting in bias against particular cohorts as a consequence and affecting test fairness.

A search of the research literature failed to produce any parallel form studies for Writing tests. We did, however locate a few studies that had been done in the area of Speaking and *mutatis mutandis* the methodology would seem appropriate for Writing tests and provide a possible research agenda for carrying out similar studies in this area. We have accordingly included a review of these Speaking studies below.

Weir and Wu (2006) attempted to measure a number of aspects of the parallel-form reliability of three trial proficiency test forms both quantitatively at the form and task level and qualitatively at the task level. In addition to more conventional statistical procedures, such as correlation and ANOVA, MFRM was also employed to process candidates' score data to account for the effect of variables associated with raters' severity and form/task difficulty.

Apart from measuring parallel form reliability statistically in a conventional quantitative way, the assistance of raters' judgements also helped to investigate such parallelness qualitatively. Their study employed the use of checklists to investigate the parallelness of content of the three trial forms from the viewpoints of raters. An individual checklist was specifically developed for each of the three task types in which potential variables affecting difficulty of the task were detailed for raters' judgements. Such a procedure would seem equally relevant and feasible for investigating parallelness in Writing tasks and might provide interesting insights across a range of contextual parameters in Writing identified in Chapter 4.

In addition to the use of checklists eliciting raters' views on task difficulty, this study also adopted the use of observation checklists to validate Speaking tests as proposed by O'Sullivan, Weir and Saville (2002) based on their research with Cambridge ESOL examinations. Through raters' observations, a comparison of the intended functions in Task B (Answering Questions) of the three trial test forms was made so that the extent to which the tasks across different test forms are similar in the area of test content coverage was also measured. It was reported that the language functions covered in the tasks of answering questions in these three tests were similar. Moreover, *a posteriori* studies on content coverage by way of a limited number of candidates' transcripts were carried out, in which raters were asked to map the language functions which they observed from candidates' actual performance, so that the previous findings in equivalent coverage of language functions in the three trial test forms can therefore be substantiated. *Mutatis mutandis*, raters might be asked to predict the intended functions of Writing tasks and an inspection of the scripts produced could be made to check if these intentions were realised

Weir and Wu's study (2006) sounds a warning for all those involved in intra-task variability research and producing equivalent forms. The results show that without taking the necessary steps to control context variables affecting test difficulty, test quality may fluctuate over tasks in different test forms. Weir and Wu argue that high correlations in themselves do not provide sufficient evidence that two tests are equivalent in validity. When evidence of context comparability in both test forms is also provided, this still only constitutes a partial equivalence argument. We need further evidence of their cognitive validity and consequential validity to be confident of the equivalence of the test forms.

Where for security reasons examination boards have to provide multiple versions of examinations for each administration as well as across annual administrations, providing such evidence may prove to be impractical. They may be limited to generating *a priori* statistical and context evidence through pilot studies and expert inspection. Secure tests such as IELTS or TOEFL might be expected to meet more comprehensive validity requirements.

Comparison with external standards

Each Cambridge ESOL examination is benchmarked to a specific criterion level and can be interpreted within the context of an overall framework of levels. In the context of the Association of Language Testers in Europe (ALTE), these levels are interpretable internationally and have been empirically linked to the Common European Framework of Reference (see discussion of this in Chapter 9 and Appendix D of the Council of Europe's *Common European Framework of Reference* 2001 – Jones and Hirtzel 2001). Saville (2003) details how Cambridge ESOL has linked its examinations closely to the levels laid out in the CEFR and the ALTE framework.

This level system provides an interpretative frame of reference for all the exams in the suite. A criterion referenced approach allows individual results on any one examination to be situated in relation to the total 'criterion space', i.e. the much wider continuum of ability. These European levels have the advantage of according with what have been termed the 'natural' proficiency levels familiar to teachers and are supported by the work of the Council of Europe over the last 30 years which is based on a consensus view that adequate coverage is afforded by six broad levels for the purposes of organising language teaching and learning in the European Community (Council of Europe 2001).

In the 1990s Cambridge ESOL contributed to the work of ALTE in developing a framework to establish common levels of proficiency in order to promote the transnational recognition of certification in Europe. ALTE members fitted their exams to this framework through an analytic process including comparison of test tasks and content (available on the ALTE website at www.alte.org). After the release of the first draft of the CEFR, ALTE conducted several studies to verify the alignment of the ALTE Framework with the CEFR, and a major project was carried out in 1999–2000 using the ALTE Can Do scales (Jones 2000, 2001, 2002), providing an empirical link between test performance and perceived real-world language skills, as well as between the ALTE Framework and the CEFR scales. The two frameworks had entirely complementary aims, and thus following the publication of the CEFR in 2001 during the European Year of Languages, ALTE members adopted the CEFR levels – A1 to C2.

Referencing to the criterion levels is undertaken by means of scalar analyses using the Rasch model to relate the results from the whole range of Cambridge examinations to the global scale of common reference levels of the CEFR (Council of Europe 2001). In addition, the ALTE Can Do scales provide criterion-related statements at each level in relation to the specified domains which are covered in the examinations (situated language use for social, tourist, work and study purposes). The criterion scale and the Can Do descriptors provide representations of the external reality, which helps to ensure that the test results are relevant and meaningful to the key stakeholders (the candidates, their sponsors and other users of examination results).

Considerable work has been undertaken to locate the examination systems of ALTE members in this framework, based on an analysis of examination content and task types, and candidate profiles. The Can Do scales consist currently of about 400 statements, organised into three general areas: social and tourist, work, and study. These are the three main areas of interest for most language learners. Each includes a number of more particular areas, e.g. the social and tourist area has sections on shopping, eating out, and accommodation etc. Each of these includes up to three scales, for the skills of Listening/Speaking, Reading and Writing. Each such scale includes statements covering a range of levels. Some scales cover only a part of the proficiency range, as there are many situations of use which require only basic proficiency to deal with successfully.

The scales have been subjected to an extended process of empirical validation aimed at transforming the Can Do statements from an essentially subjective set of level descriptions into a calibrated measuring instrument. Data
collection has been based chiefly on self-report, the Can Do scales being presented to respondents as a set of linked questionnaires (around 10,000
respondents have so far completed questionnaires). It is these response patterns which define the meaning of a given level in Can Do terms. In other
words, the definition of a level is not based on *a priori* prescriptive, absolute
criteria, but rather is descriptive of the experience of a large number of
foreign language users.

Taylor (2004b) argues for a cautious approach in using any comparative
framework. She argues that while they promise certain benefits they can also
carry inherent risks. This is because all frameworks, by definition, seek to
summarise and simplify, highlighting those features which are held in
common across tests in order to provide a convenient point of reference for
users and situations of use. Since the driving motivation behind them is usefulness or ease of interpretation, comparative frameworks cannot easily
accommodate the multidimensional complexity of a thorough comparative
analysis; the framework will focus on shared elements but may have to ignore
significant differentiating features. The result is that while a framework
can look elegant and convincing, it may fail to communicate some key
differences between the elements co-located within it. The result is likely to be
an over simplification and may even encourage misinterpretation on the part
of users about the relative merits or value of different exams.

Taylor (2004b) concludes that there is no doubt that comparative frameworks can serve a useful function for a wide variety of test stakeholders: for
test users – such as admissions officers, employers, teachers, learners – frameworks make it easier to understand the range of assessment options available
and help users to make appropriate choices for their needs; for applied linguists and language testers frameworks can help define a research agenda
and identify research hypotheses for investigation; for test providers frameworks not only help with product definition and promotion, but also with
planning for future test design and development. But we need to understand that they have their limitations too: they risk masking significant
differentiating features, they tend to encourage oversimplification and misinterpretation, and there is always a danger that they are adopted as prescriptive rather than informative tools. They need to come with the appropriate
health warnings!

To demonstrate that their tests are fair measurements of a specified level
of proficiency, providers need to furnish evidence that they adequately
address context, cognitive and scoring parameters of validity appropriate to
the level of language ability under consideration. Since the CEFR fails in its
current form to sufficiently explicate these dimensions across the proficiency

range it is perhaps not surprising that a number of studies have experienced difficulty in attempting to use the CEFR for test development or comparability purposes (see Alderson et al 2004, Huhta et al 1997, Jones 2002, Little et al 2002, Morrow 2004). The current descriptor scales are by definition generalised, thus taking no account of how variation in terms of contextual parameters may affect performances by raising or lowering the actual difficulty level of carrying out the target Can Do statement. In addition, a test's cognitive validity, a function of the processing involved in carrying out these Can Do statements, must also be addressed by any specification on which a test is based.

In response to these deficiencies, the aim of the construct volumes in the SiLT series (of which this volume focusing on the Writing construct is the first) is to establish a framework of contextual, cognitive and scoring validity parameters that can be described at various levels. Chapters 3–5 in this volume represent the first attempt at doing this for the construct of writing. Work will continue on this over the next decade in the English Profile Project being undertaken by a group composed of the British Council, Cambridge University, English UK and Cambridge University Press, a group of organisations with unrivalled knowledge and expertise in language education and assessment worldwide. Over the next decade the group will produce the English Profile – a set of Reference Level Descriptions for English, a ground breaking project which will define levels of proficiency in English more comprehensively than has ever been achieved before. The Profile will be a fundamental tool for language teaching, materials development, assessment and research for many years to come. The project will attempt to more closely define all the parameters listed in this volume as well as those for other constructs at each level of the Common European Framework of Reference.

We have now looked at all the parameters exam boards need to consider in generating evidence on the validity of their examinations. In the final chapter we attempt to summarise our findings in applying the whole of our validity framework to Cambridge ESOL Writing examinations. We suggest where enhancements and modifications might be considered and implemented over time in order to improve existing Writing tests in terms of each of these validity components. We also indicate where further research into elements of the validity framework might be necessary before such enhancements and modifications can be introduced to the operational testing context. There is no doubt that the identification of such a research agenda could be of considerable value to the wider language testing community as well as to Cambridge ESOL.

8 Conclusions and recommendations

Cambridge ESOL has a good track record of responding to advances in the field of language assessment and to developing knowledge in the wider area of Applied Linguistics (see Weir 2003 for a history of this over the last century). This volume represents a stock taking of the organisation's approach to the assessment of writing through an attempt to define more closely, in the light of current theory, the construct of Writing upon which its examinations are based.

To achieve this we have developed a socio-cognitive framework, building on Weir (2005b), which views language testing and validation within a contemporary evidence-based paradigm (see Chapter 1). We have used this framework to carry out a comprehensive evaluation of Cambridge ESOL's current approach to examining the skill area of Writing. This approach has shown itself able to accommodate and strengthen Cambridge ESOL's existing Validity, Reliability, Impact and Practicality (VRIP) approach (see Saville 2003). The new framework seeks to establish similar evidence, but in addition it attempts to reconfigure validity to show how its constituent parts interact with each other.

In reviewing the contribution of the socio-cognitive framework to research and practice in examining second language writing, Lynda Taylor (personal communication, 2006) on behalf of Cambridge ESOL Research and Validation comments that:

> it helps to clarify, both theoretically and practically, the various constituent parts of the testing endeavour as far as 'validity' is concerned. So the socio-cognitive framework gives us all a valuable opportunity to revisit many of our 'traditional' terms and concepts, to redefine them more clearly and to grow in our understanding.

The importance of the symbiotic relationship between the contextual parameters laid out in the task and the cognitive processing involved in task performance has been emphasised throughout this volume. Taylor believes it is important in language testing that we give both the socio and the cognitive elements:

an appropriate place and emphasis within the whole, and do not privilege one over another. The framework reminds us of language use – and also language assessment – as both a socially situated and a cognitively processed phenomenon. The socio-cognitive framework seeks to marry up the individual psycholinguistic perspective with the individual and group sociolinguistic perspective (personal communication, 2006).

Taylor further argues that the socio-cognitive approach:

> helps promote a more 'person-oriented' than 'instrument-oriented' view of the testing/assessment process than earlier models/frameworks. It implies a strong focus on the language learner or test-taker as being at the centre of the assessment process, rather than the test or measurement instrument being the central focus (personal communication, 2006).

This humanistic tradition has been a key feature of the Cambridge ESOL examinations since their inception in 1913 (see Weir 2003).

In this volume we have felt it helpful to conceptualise the validation process in a temporal frame thereby identifying the various types of validity evidence that need to be collected at each stage in the test development and post-implementation cycle. Within each of these, criterial individual parameters for helping distinguish between adjacent proficiency levels have also been identified and are summarised at the end of each chapter. According to Taylor (personal communication, 2006) the socio-cognitive framework:

> looks like being the first model/framework which allows for serious theoretical consideration of the issues but is also capable of being applied practically; it therefore has direct relevance and value to an operational language testing/assessment context – especially when that testing is taking place on a large, industrial scale such as in Cambridge ESOL . . . other frameworks (e.g. Bachman 1990) were helpful in provoking us to think about key issues from a theoretical perspective but they generally proved very difficult for practitioners to operationalise in a manageable and meaningful way.

The results from developing and operationalising the framework in this volume with regard to second language writing ability are encouraging, and evidence to date suggests that where it has been applied to other examinations/tests it has proved useful in generating validity evidence in those cases too, e.g. in the International Legal English Certificate (ILEC), TKT, and BEC and BULATS (see O'Sullivan 2006).

It would be illuminating for other examination boards offering English language tests at a variety of proficiency levels to compare their exams in terms of the validity parameters mapped out in this volume. In this way the nature of language proficiency across 'natural' levels in terms of how it is operationalised through examinations/tests may be better grounded. Similar comparisons across languages may also be worth considering but are likely to be more problematic with regard to certain parameters, for example structural progression (Alderson et al 2004).

In any evidence-based approach to validation it is essential to clearly specify each of the parameters of the validity model first and generate the data appropriate to each of these categories of description. Such data provides the evidential basis for inferential 'interpretative argument' logic. Useful contributions to the conceptualisation of the broad nature of such argument are provided by Toulmin (1958), Kane (1992), Mislevy et al (2002, 2003), Bachman (2004) and Chapelle et al (2004). These researchers all make a case (in slightly differing ways) for the need for clear, coherent, plausible and logical argument in support of validity claims based on evidence. Saville (2004) argues that this systematic approach to the reporting of a validity argument enables Cambridge ESOL 'to set out our claims relating to the usefulness of the test for its intended purpose, explain why each claim is appropriate by giving reasons and justifications, and provide adequate evidence to support the claims and the reasoning'.

At the heart of any validity argument, though, is the evidence. One potential problem with a number of these logical argument models is that the nature of the evidence to support claims and reasoning is not always clearly, explicitly, or comprehensively specified. This volume has sought to meet this deficiency by establishing and focusing in detail on the elements of validity evidence examination providers need to address, and attempting to begin to explain their inter-relationships.

Much of the substantial validity evidence generated in the past by Cambridge ESOL research into its Writing examinations has been brought together in this volume. The synthesis of this body of research in Chapters 1–7 helped clarify a number of areas in examining writing where further research would be beneficial.

In the remainder of this chapter we summarise the evidence that supports the claims and the reasoning for the validity of Cambridge Writing examinations in terms of each element of our socio-cognitive model of validity (cognitive, context, scoring, consequential and criterion-related). In addition we indicate some areas where research will take place in Cambridge ESOL to inform judgements on future revisions to its Writing examinations.

As Messick (1989) has pointed out, validity is a question of degree, not an all or nothing concept. Validity should be seen as a relative concept which examination boards need to work on continually.

Cognitive validity

There has been limited L2 research to date addressing the cognitive processing dimension and surprisingly almost none in L2 testing, despite the fervour over the criticality of construct validity in the last 30 years. Given our desire to extrapolate from our test tasks to real-world behaviour, it is felt to be sensible to carry out research to establish with greater certainty that the test tasks we employ do indeed activate the types of mental operations that are viewed in the cognitive psychology literature as essential elements of the writing process. To the extent that this is not the case, extrapolation is threatened.

Writing tasks in the Cambridge ESOL examinations are already specified in a number of different ways for the purposes of test writing and construction; nevertheless, it is acknowledged that there can be improvements with more comprehensive task specification, particularly in terms of purpose, readership, genre, length and known assessment criteria. These would undoubtedly help encourage the critical stages of macro-planning, organisation, micro-planning, and monitoring/editing/revision (see Chapter 3), and this is likely to be true for all tasks at all levels in the examinations.

From PET Paper 1, Part 3, candidates are provided with some autonomy and responsibility for shaping and planning the structure and outcome of their discourse. The activities of planning, monitoring and revising written work for content and organisation become increasingly relevant in FCE, CAE and CPE, particularly at CAE and CPE levels. In the current Writing tests no dedicated time is allocated for this and no explicit advice to do this is provided in the task rubric, so ways of making provision for both these will be explored.

From FCE upwards it is reasonable to expect candidates to demonstrate the skill of knowledge transforming as well as knowledge telling. This is not always required in the current FCE test but ways of building this in more systematically will be explored. The current possibility of candidates being able to choose between tasks in Part 2 of FCE creates something of a dilemma since it allows them to potentially avoid demonstrating knowledge transforming skills altogether at this level. In order to determine whether or not all candidates from this B2 level upwards should be required to write a knowledge transforming task, Cambridge ESOL will investigate further the work carried out so far (see Scardamalia and Bereiter 1987) into whether alternative choices (knowledge telling versus knowledge transforming tasks) make similar demands on candidates and result in equivalent performances.

In Part 3 of PET Paper 1, candidates are expected for the first time in the story option to provide an organisational structure for the task, and the narrative task is believed to be a sufficiently familiar rhetorical task for the candidature to be able to do this. In the compulsory task in Part 1 of the FCE Writing paper, however, candidates are provided with an organisational structure; this means that the requirement for them to demonstrate organisational skill is relatively limited – they simply have to present ideas logically. This partial anomaly across the two levels will be subject to empirical investigation to ensure that appropriate demands in terms of this level of processing are being made on test takers in each examination.

Recent research by Ellis and Yuan (2004) indicates that the addition of a planning condition can lead to improvements in written performance and research on planning in spoken language also reports similar outcomes (Mehnert 1998, Skehan and Foster 1997, 1999, 2001, Wigglesworth 1997). It would be reasonable to assume that similar benefits would accrue if planning activity was proactively encouraged in a test of Writing. Further research in this area is therefore acknowledged to be a priority.

For example, there may be an investigation into the effects of incorporating both a planning stage before candidates start writing and a monitoring and revision phase at the end of each task at FCE and higher levels, with dedicated time made available for these. The criteria of content and organisation at CAE and CPE levels might also be considered, particularly in regard to stronger weighting, given their importance in the real world (see Weir 1983). The benefits and drawbacks of making this weighting clear to candidates on the paper itself may also be explored.

If positive outcomes result from such research, then future revisions to the higher level test components might look into structuring and manipulating tasks so that they activate more systematically these critical planning, monitoring and revision processes. Since these are seen to be the hallmarks of the skilled writer attempts will need to be made to ensure that successful candidates are carrying out these activities to an appropriate extent.

Control of timing for planning and for monitoring phases in a test event clearly presents logistical challenges in large-scale paper-based (i.e. traditional) assessment contexts, though such developments are already beginning to appear in a number of international examinations. Such differentiated phases of the writing process might be more easily achieved through a computer-based mode where timing for individual phases or processing activities within the testing event can be more easily controlled (see Chapter 5 and Appendix G for details of computer-based testing advances at Cambridge ESOL).

Preliminary studies by Xiu Xudong (forthcoming) of the relationship between self perceptions of the cognitive processes employed in Writing test tasks and levels of performance in terms of specified analytic marking criteria indicate a close connection between what happens in terms of cognitive processing and the scores that result when completing a Writing task. His research suggests that, in general, the more the candidates claim to perform these activities the higher the scores they achieve. Encouraging appropriate cognitive processing is thus likely to enhance students' scores as well as improve the validity of a Writing task.

Context validity

Response format

An issue to which examining boards will need to give increasing attention in the near future is that of dealing with typewritten as well as or instead of handwritten responses in their Writing tests. In contemporary life, fewer personal letters are now written by hand; word processing is more common, and as email is often the modern means of communication for correspondence, it could be more realistic to ask candidates to respond to email. Emails have been used in PET and BEC and Skills for Life Writing tests, for some time and Cambridge ESOL plans to use email as input and require email as output for FCE and CAE when modifications are introduced from 2008.

These days, in the world of work and increasingly among students in full-time education, relatively few people write without access to a spell check facility, nor do they edit and revise by rewriting whole scripts. Conventional Writing tests, therefore, often ask candidates to perform in a way that is far less typical of the real-world context than it once was. The issue of email and other electronic communication genres, therefore, has to be addressed. A computer-based version of PET is already available. Computerisation of a number of Cambridge ESOL examinations is currently under consideration and this will allow email to be used in a more authentic way for these examinations. A computerised version will also facilitate editing and revision at all levels as it is obviously easier to move text around on computer to improve organisation and the foregrounding of key ideas.

In relation to the issue of gradation from controlled to uncontrolled tasks, KET is characterised by controlled tasks at the word level and limited semi-controlled tasks at the text level. PET Part 1 is controlled, Part 2 and the Part 3 letter are semi-controlled, but the Part 3 story is not controlled. At FCE, CAE and CPE there is a mixture of semi-controlled tasks where the task is framed by the rubric and/or input texts but candidates are expected to make their own contribution. For example, at FCE, CAE and CPE a number of tasks may involve responding to input provided, usually in the form of a number of short texts. Variation in the length and nature of these input texts might be one way in the future of further differentiating the higher level tests from one another.

Another issue for attention is the role of integrated Reading and Writing tasks. CAE and CPE are recognised for university entrance purposes in the UK but in their present format only include tasks which integrate reading and writing in a limited way; such tasks would better reflect reading to learn and writing in that target discourse community and are more likely to activate knowledge transformation which, as we have already seen, is the hall mark of writing at this level (see Weir 1983, 2005b).

Integrated tasks are not without their disadvantages however, not least in how to deal with candidates 'lifting' from the input texts provided; ways will have to be sought to eliminate this in preparing candidates for such an examination task. Punitive sanctions might also be considered to discourage 'lifting', e.g. candidates will be penalised if more than X number of continuous words are lifted from the source text(s). The whole area of integrating reading and writing activities is in need of further research but the potential positive washback of such integrated tasks should encourage further research of this nature (see Belcher and Hirvela 2001, Esmaeili 2002, Tierney and Shanahan 1991, Weigle 2004, Weir 1983, 2005b).

Task purpose

In terms of task purpose there is some progression from KET to CPE, for example the possibility of having to deal with conative purposes appears from the FCE level upwards. However, within these higher levels (FCE, CAE, CPE) the same broad range of purposes for writing may occur at each of the three levels and there is relatively little differentiation. Only at CPE is the discursive task compulsory.

The implication of offering a choice of Writing tasks emerges once again here. At the moment allowing a choice makes differentiation between levels difficult; and if the tasks are not equivalent in complexity and result in differential performance then this invariably raises issues of fairness. Research will be undertaken to explore whether writing for conative purposes poses the same level of difficulty for candidates and results in a similar level of performance as the current alternative purposes for writing that are available to candidates in the other task choices in FCE, CAE and CPE.

If it was then felt appropriate for candidates to complete a conative task as a compulsory requirement, at FCE we might be more certain that an additional criterial distinguishing feature was available for discriminating between the adjacent levels PET and FCE. Such a distinction might be made between FCE and CAE if this was felt to be appropriate. Again research is needed to confirm this.

Knowledge of criteria

Only at CAE and CPE is there an expectation that an adequate response will have an impact on the reader through the candidate's sophisticated use of language resources. At FCE a positive effect on the reader is expected and although meaning is always communicated, language use is far less sophisticated. At PET and KET there is no expectation of sophisticated use of language but an adequate response would be one where the candidate can use simple language flexibly to express much of what he or she wants to.

However, in PET and KET, in those cases where more complex use of language is attempted, written output may sometimes be difficult to follow owing to a number of linguistic and/or organisational weaknesses.

The stress on content and organisation at the upper levels is in accord with our discussion of L2 processing loads in Chapter 3. As we have seen, below B2 level there simply may not be enough attentional space available for any real planning and organisation as candidates have enough problems in coping with the demands of generating adequate grammar and lexis.

Candidates may need to be reminded of the criteria of assessment before embarking on a Writing task as this facilitates not only planning and organisation but also monitoring and revising, which are key processing elements in Writing tasks. Attention is drawn to marking criteria elsewhere, particularly in handbooks, but consideration will be given in future to repeating a synopsis of them on the paper itself. Currently the expectations of the reader in terms of marking criteria are not explicitly spelled out for the candidate on Cambridge Writing papers, but an investigation of the effects of doing this will be considered.

Length and time available

There is in general an increase of about 100 words between each of the first three levels if one takes the minimum amount required as the benchmark. The upper word limit at FCE is substantially greater than that which is expected of KET and PET candidates. There is also substantial difference between the amount required at FCE and at CAE. Longer pieces of writing will in themselves add to the cognitive pressures on the writer.

The upper and lower limits for the number of words a candidate must produce are set quite widely and this possible variation in length may be a matter for investigation. Variation in the acceptable length of responses could be addressed (FCE and CPE) to see whether candidates profit (or not) by writing substantially less (though still within the limits allowed) than their peers.

At FCE the time available is dedicated time for the Writing tasks alone rather than time being shared with the Reading tasks as in KET and PET. There is a substantial increase in the amount of time available at CAE and CPE. This increase in time allocation matches the increase in length of writing output.

It is important to remember that a symbiotic relationship exists between the various construct validity components of our socio-cognitive framework: context validity, cognitive validity and scoring validity. Clearly, the contextual parameters of the task setting, such as length of output or time allocation, will impact on the actual processing undertaken by the test taker. The linguistic and content knowledge required of the test taker in order to undertake the task, i.e. the executive resources, is instantiated by the task setting (the linguistic and content demands intended by the developer of the test are communicated through the task instructions). This means that any decisions which are taken with regard to task context, such as the time available to the candidate, will have potential implications for any subsequent processing needed for task completion. For example, it might be imprudent to reduce significantly the time available until the potential ramifications of this on performance are investigated not least the knock-on effect of the other parameters discussed in this volume.

If research findings were to suggest that dedicated macro-planning and monitoring enhanced performance when proactively encouraged and dedicated time were made available for promoting these critical aspects of cognitive processing, and if such measures were found to be administratively practical, it might in fact be necessary in the future to contemplate even longer Writing tests at FCE, CAE and CPE levels.

The time to be spent on each individual Writing task might also be clearly specified on the paper (and Reading and Writing separated into two papers at KET/PET) if the candidate is to devote appropriate time to each task in the test.

Writer–reader relationship

There is a gradual progression through the levels from personally known (e.g. friend or teacher) to specified audiences with whom candidates are not personally acquainted (e.g. an editor or magazine readers). Addressing a broader range of audience is required between PET and FCE as candidates only write to people they know personally in KET and PET. By PET, the candidates also need to take greater account of their audience by considering what the potential reader is likely to know about the subject, the amount of explanation required and what can be left implicit. By CAE, candidates are no longer writing to people they know personally. A slightly wider range of unacquainted audience distinguishes CAE and CPE. At these two levels candidates must decide what sorts of evidence the reader is likely to find persuasive. With the exception of KET, the effect of the writing on the reader is taken into account in the marking.

The effect of audience on performance in writing is a seriously underresearched area (see O'Sullivan and Porter 1995) and the ways in which this parameter might help to further ground distinctions between FCE, CAE and CPE is worth investigating further. The variety in audiences which results from the task choices available to candidates is also an area which Cambridge ESOL will be considering.

Lexical resources

At the KET and PET level, lexical items normally occur in the everyday vocabulary of native speakers using English. At FCE level, topics need to be addressed in more detail and with greater lexical precision. For CAE and above, the language expected is more sophisticated and the tasks more lexically challenging than at FCE. Topics, tasks and functions which only require simple language are avoided at the higher levels. At FCE and above there is also an expectation that candidates are able to reformulate input language in their own words. Language associated with conative functions is needed for tasks at CAE and CPE.

The research on lexis in Cambridge ESOL examinations by Schmitt (2005) reported in this volume is illustrative of the value of, the complexities involved and the effort required for the better grounding of our knowledge of progression in terms of each of our parameters. This work is long-term and details of Cambridge ESOL's commitment to such future enquiry are provided in the section on the English Profile Project described below.

Structural resources

There is a gradual progression in the complexity of the grammatical constructions required by tasks. This is in line with the structural levels appearing in ELT coursebooks aimed at language levels corresponding to the Council of Europe levels A1 (KET) through to C2 (CPE).

At KET level, candidates are expected to have control over only the simplest exponents for the Waystage functions at this level; the marker is tolerant of basic errors such as missing third person 's'. At PET level, candidates show a degree of ability to handle some of the exponents listed at Threshold level. Although the marker is primarily interested in the extent to which meaning is conveyed, control of such basic structures as 'to be' agreement is expected. However, in PET Part 3, where candidates demonstrate ambition, their writing may still be judged adequate even if grammatically flawed. At FCE level, candidates should have a good grasp of Vantage-level language. They should have mastered the main structures of the language and should not be prevented from communicating by a lack of structural resources. As long as the marker does not have to make an effort to understand the writer's meaning, errors with such aspects of language as gerunds, infinitives or some confusion between the past simple and present perfect will not be unduly penalised. At FCE level, candidates tend to write either simply and accurately or more ambitiously but less accurately. Both types of candidate may achieve adequate performance if other aspects of their writing are satisfactory. By CAE candidates are expected to use the structures of the language with ease and fluency. There should be some evidence of range; very simple but accurate language is not enough at this level. Candidates must be able to demonstrate some ability to use complex structures even though they are not expected to write error-free prose. CAE candidates must also show that they have a grasp of structures which allow them to express opinions and feelings in an appropriate register. They can, for example, express dissatisfaction in a manner that does not sound aggressive by using appropriately tentative structures. By CPE level candidates should demonstrate a high degree of range and accuracy with regard to structures. They should have a mastery of the structures needed to present ideas and attitude in a well-organised and sophisticated manner. Some errors will be tolerated if these do not confuse the reader in any way; for example, an inappropriate use of a preposition after a verb or an omitted article will not in themselves cause the writer to lose marks.

Discourse mode

There is a clear distinction between PET and FCE. At FCE the rhetorical task of argument differentiates it from PET and discursive tasks are important throughout FCE, CAE and CPE. CAE is differentiated from FCE by the greater range of genres the candidate might have to address overall and having to deal in the compulsory Part 1 task with varying degrees of persuasion to convince the intended audience of the writer's point of view. At CPE candidates might have to write an essay.

The effect of discourse mode on performance in writing is very much an under-researched area and the ways in which this parameter might contribute to further grounding of distinctions between levels in FCE, CAE and CPE needs investigating. As previously discussed, the variety of modes which result from the choices available to candidates needs to be looked at to ensure they present candidates with an equally difficult task and lead to equivalent performances.

Functional resources

There is a clear functional progression across the first three levels (KET, PET and FCE) in terms of complexity but also in the degree of precision in the structural exponents employed to fulfil the function(s). Functions associated with conative purposes and argumentative tasks for language appear at CAE. The functions at CAE and CPE are increasingly diverse and demanding and intended to produce more complex structures or collocations.

Systematic work has been conducted on this key parameter for nearly 40 years by the Council of Europe (Council of Europe 2001) and groundbreaking empirical studies of functional progression have been carried out by North and his associates (North 2000, 2002, 2004). Coursebook writers (in a more subjective fashion) have similarly operationalised what might be a suitable progression in terms of functions across the range of language ability. As a result we can perhaps be more confident that our examinations are better grounded in terms of this parameter than most others. The functional parameter is obviously not a stand-alone element as the structural exponents and the lexis chosen to achieve it will also vary from level to level in those cases where the same functions are being deployed. Research however has indicated a number of functions which seem to occur uniquely for the first time at a particular level. Cambridge ESOL is keen to pursue this research to better ground whether any of these functions is truly implicational, i.e. candidates at the next level down are not capable of realising them adequately even by using less complex structures and lexis.

Content

At KET level, candidates need to have the language to deal with personal and daily life, i.e. basic everyday situations and communication needs (Van Ek and Trim 1991a). The focus tends to be on topics that are likely to have relevance for teenage candidates since this has traditionally been the predominant age-span of the population to study for and take the KET exam following its introduction in the early 1990s. At PET level, a broader range of general topics relating to the candidate's personal life and experience is covered; narrative topics also feature at PET level (Van Ek and Trim 1991). FCE candidates may be expected to deal with a wide range of knowledge areas including any non-specialist topic that has relevance for candidates worldwide (Van Ek and Trim 2001). CAE candidates are expected to be able to deal with topics that are more specialised and less personal than those that tend to feature at lower levels. The step up to CAE also involves coping with lexically challenging topic areas (e.g. the environment, the scientific world, traditions). At CPE level more abstract and academic topics appear and the candidate may be expected to be able to write on any non-specialist topic. CPE candidates are expected to be able to operate confidently in a wide variety of social, work-related and study-related situations. At all levels topics that might offend or otherwise unfairly disadvantage any group of candidates are avoided.

Empirical research on the effect of topic on performance across levels is noticeably lacking and almost no guidance is available from research on what topics are appropriate as one progresses through proficiency levels. Exam board experience is not to be discounted but Cambridge ESOL will be adding to this with more empirically-grounded evidence.

Setting: administration

Cambridge ESOL takes considerable care to ensure appropriate physical conditions for taking its exams, to maintain uniform administration across centres and to achieve complete security of tests. The procedures which are currently in place and which were discussed at length in Chapter 4 will continue to be monitored, evaluated and enhanced to ensure that they do not pose a threat to test reliability and that they safeguard valid measurement of the construct in Writing tests.

Scoring validity

As this volume attests, scoring validity parameters seem to be far better researched than context validity with research into cognitive validity a long way behind in third place. This imbalance might need to be redressed in the future.

A consensus is developing in our field that all scripts should be double-marked or at least calibrated through IRT methods through some sort of overlap in batches of scripts marked (see Taylor and Falvey 2007 for a balanced discussion of this). Although this has cost implications, test fairness demands it. With the exciting developments in electronic script management reported in Chapter 5, this is becoming easier to operationalise.

Weir (2003) reports on the choices available to candidates in Writing tests as far back as the first CPE examination in 1913. The effect on scoring validity of allowing a choice in Writing tasks needs to be addressed, however, to determine whether or not task choice is introducing construct-irrelevant variance into the system. Using the common compulsory task already required of candidates and calibrating performance on a second alternative task against this as is the practice in FCE, CAE and CPE might be a way of ensuring test fairness.

The validity implications of having only one longer task need revisiting, especially given the importance of ensuring cognitive validity attested to in the literature (see Chapter 3).

Should the future be analytic? The report on the recent IELTS Writing Scale Revision Project (see Chapter 5) indicated that an analytic approach to marking had advantages over an impression banded approach for marking IELTS not least because of the enhanced marker reliability it led to and the possibilities of more detailed profiling. Research suggests that an analytic approach, double or targeted marking and the employment of multi-faceted Rasch analysis and calibration might serve to further increase the scoring validity of Cambridge ESOL examinations (see Chapter 5 and Appendix H).

Consequential validity

As mentioned in Chapter 7, the need to monitor a test's effects on language materials and on classroom activity (see, for example, Green 2003, Hawkey 2004, and Chapter 6 above) and to seek information on the views of a full range of stakeholders (see Taylor 1999) is now accepted by most serious examination boards and it has been the hallmark of Cambridge ESOL examinations at least since the modern revisions commenced in the 1980s, and in the case of stakeholder consultation since much earlier according to Weir (2003). In the recent CPE revision, conscious efforts were made to elicit feedback on the existing test from test takers and a wide variety of stakeholders contributed to the decisions that were taken concerning changes in the examination (see Weir and Milanovic 2003 for a full account of the CPE revision and Hawkey 2004b for a description of the CELS examination change process).

Establishing *a priori* evidence for context and cognitive validity is essential before candidates sit an examination to ensure that no potential sources of bias are allowed to interfere with measurement. Following the test, it is important in post-examination procedures to check that no bias has occurred. As we describe in Chapter 5, this is done statistically in relation to candidate bio data.

It would be useful to see evidence of a lack of bias in all examinations being researched and reported in the public domain.

Criterion-related validity

Evidence of criterion-related validity is routinely generated by Cambridge ESOL. The studies discussed in Chapter 7 show strong links between Cambridge ESOL suites of level-based tests, i.e. Main Suite, BEC, and YLE. These suites are targeted at similar ability levels as defined by a common measurement scale.

Chapter 7 detailed how Cambridge ESOL has linked its examinations closely to the levels laid out in external internationally accepted frameworks such as the CEFR and the ALTE framework. It is this level system which provides an interpretative frame of reference for all the exams in the suite. These European levels (though currently underspecified for testing purposes; see Weir 2005a) have the advantage of according with the 'natural' proficiency levels familiar to teachers and are supported by the work of the Council of Europe over the last 30 years; this important work is based on a consensus view that adequate coverage is afforded by six broad levels for the purposes of organising language learning, teaching and assessment in the European context (Council of Europe 2001:22–3).

The scale of levels which is used by Cambridge ESOL provides a set of common standards and is the basis of the *criterion-referenced approach* to the interpretation of examination results (see Introduction for linking of Cambridge ESOL Main Suite examinations to the CEFR Scale for Writing, and Chapter 7 for details of this).

Referencing to the criterion is undertaken by means of scalar analyses using the Rasch model to relate the results from the whole range of

Cambridge ESOL examinations to the global scale of common reference levels of the CEFR (2001:24). In addition, the ALTE Can Do scales provide criterion-related statements at each level in relation to the specified domains which are covered in the examinations (situated language use for social, tourist, work and study purposes). The criterion scale and the Can Do descriptors provide representations of the external reality, which helps to ensure that the test results are as meaningful and as useful as possible to the key stakeholders (the candidates, their sponsors and other users of examination results). Work to date in this area will be supplemented by the English Profile Project which was officially launched in 2006.

The English Profile Project

The English Profile Project is a consortium effort set up to provide a core reference document for English as a foreign or additional language linked to the general principles and approaches of the Common European Framework of Reference (Council of Europe 2001). The project is to complement and supplement the existing materials – *Waystage-Threshold-Vantage* series primarily (Van Ek and Trim 1991, 1991a, 2001) as well as other relevant documents, with the intention to be registered as the *Reference Level Description Project for English* with the Council of Europe (www.coe.int/T/E/Cultural_Co-operation/education/Languages/Language_Policy/Reference_levels/index.asp). It will incorporate both theoretical and empirical input while identifying criterial features that characterise individual language proficiency levels (A1–C2, as defined by CEFR) and translate the results into pedagogically appropriate materials. The project results are thus expected to have an important impact on a variety of study fields, primarily language pedagogy (e.g. curriculum development, teacher training, self-directed learning and certification) and contrastive linguistics.

The development team working on the project includes experts from three departments of the University of Cambridge – Cambridge ESOL Examinations, Cambridge University Press and the Research Centre for English and Applied Linguistics (RCEAL) – together with the British Council, English UK, University of Bedfordshire and several well-known academic advisors, including Dr John Trim, Professor John Hawkins (RCEAL) and Professor Cyril Weir (Centre for Research in English Language Learning and Assessment (CRELLA), University of Bedford shire). In addition, as the project develops over the coming years, the central project team will seek wider participation of teachers and other stakeholder groups (including curriculum planners, different L1 learners, etc.).

The project is still at the early stages of planning, but it has already been agreed that the new Reference Level Description for English should have a number of innovative features:

- All six levels (A1–C2) will be covered and the final document will integrate print and other media to make the descriptions as user-friendly as possible.
- The existing notional/functional approach, based around contexts of use and Can Do descriptors, will be a starting point but this will be revised and extended to identify criterial features at each level.
- The grammatical exponents and lexis will be handled more flexibly with greater exemplification and thus more impact for different user groups.
- Use of empirical evidence from corpora will be exploited. For example, the words specified at each level for receptive and productive use will, in part, be derived from analysis of corpora, including the Cambridge Learner Corpus (Cambridge University Press/Cambridge ESOL).
- The linking of specified contexts to real-life situations will be incorporated, for example using benchmarked samples for speaking and writing skills (e.g. with typical examples of performances at different levels as recommended by the CEFR Manual for Guidance).

The use of the CEFR is now a significant factor in language teaching and learning and the need for a description of English to update the well-known Threshold, Vantage and Waystage series is seen as an important requirement. In particular, there is a need to extend the description of English to take into account all six levels of the CEFR. While being standalone and comprehensive in its own right, the new profile description should also link with other key developments such as the European Language Portfolio (cf. EAQUALS/ALTE e-ELP) and other aspects of the 'CEFR toolkit'.

Endnote

The issues of what a language construct is and whether it is possible to identify and measure developmental stages leading towards its mastery are critical for all aspects of language learning, teaching and assessment. Exam boards and other institutions offering high-stakes tests need to demonstrate evidence of the context, cognitive and scoring validity of the test tasks they create to represent the underlying real-life construct. They also need to be explicit as to how they operationalise criterial distinctions between levels in their tests in terms of the various validity parameters discussed above.

This volume marks the first comprehensive attempt by any examination board to expose the totality of its practice to such scrutiny in the public arena. As we have demonstrated, much has already been achieved by Cambridge and other researchers towards a better understanding of the nature of second language writing proficiency and how it can be assessed; nevertheless, this volume also shows that there are many questions still to be answered and a great deal of work remains to be done. Future research needs to investigate whether further work on refining the parameters discussed in this volume, either singly or in configuration, can help better ground the distinctions in proficiency in writing represented by levels in Cambridge ESOL examinations and its external referent the CEFR, as well as in the level-based tests produced by other language examination boards. This will be a long and challenging road but an essential journey for all of us who are members of the worldwide language testing community.

APPENDIX A
Sample Writing tasks from Main Suite examinations

KET Writing (March 2004)

Part 6

Questions 36–40

Read the descriptions of some things you can read.
What is the word for each one?

The first letter is already there. There is one space for each other letter in the word.

For questions **36–40**, write the words on your answer sheet.
Example:

0 When your friends go on holiday, they send you this. **p** _ _ _ _ _ _ _

Answer:	0	*postcard*

---

36 If you don't understand a word, you can look in this. **d** _ _ _ _ _ _ _

37 You can buy this every week and read about many interesting subjects in it. **m** _ _ _ _ _ _ _

38 If you write about your daily life in this, you may not want anyone to read it. **d** _ _ _ _ _ _ _

39 You write this for your mother when you answer the phone for her. **m** _ _ _ _ _ _ _

40 People buy this every morning to read about what has happened in the world. **n** _ _ _ _ _ _ _

Part 7

Questions 41–50

Complete the letter.
Write ONE word for each space.
For questions **41–50**, write the words on your answer sheet.

Example: | **0** | be |

Paris

Dear Maria,

It's good to **(0)** .... back home in my country but I still think **(41)** .... all the friends I made in our English class, especially you. I cried **(42)** .... I left England because my visit **(43)** .... too short. I would **(44)** .... to return to England but **(45)** .... time I will stay in a different city.

I have started English classes again here. I learnt a **(46)** .... of things in England but I know I **(47)** .... to study even harder.

(48) .... about you? **(49)** .... you still looking for a job? I hope you find **(50)** .... soon.

Love,
Sophie

Part 8

Questions 51–55

Read the letter from Jane Harvey.
Fill in the information on the Lost Property Report Form.
For questions **51–55**, write the information on your answer sheet.

The Manager   16 March
North Line Trains
London

Dear Sir,

On 14 March, I got on the 12.45 train to London at Manchester station. I had a suitcase and a handbag with me. When I got off the train at 14.50, I did not have my handbag.

Has anyone found it? Please phone me on 723419 or, after 6 p.m., on 796327.

Jane Harvey

Lost Property Report Form

Name of passenger: Jane Harvey

Travelling from: **51** [   ]

Date of journey: **52** [   ]

Time journey started: **53** [   ]

What did you lose?   **54** [   ]

Daytime phone number: **55** [   ]

Part 9

Question 56
Read this note from your friend, Spencer.

Let's meet for dinner near your house on Saturday.
Where shall we eat? What time can you come? Where can I park my car?
     Spencer

Write Spencer a note. Answer the questions.

Write **25–35** words.
Write the note on your answer sheet.

PET Writing (March 2004)

Part 1

Questions 1–5

Here are some sentences about the pop star Madonna.

For each question, complete the second sentence so that it means the same as the first.

Use no more than three words.

Write only the missing words on your answer sheet.

You may use this page for any rough work.

Example:

0 As a child in Michigan, Madonna took ballet and singing lessons.

As a child in Michigan, Madonna took lessons in ballet .... **as singing.**

Answer:

0	as well

1   Madonna was the eldest of eight children.
Madonna had seven .... **brothers and sisters.**

2   She moved to New York in order to find singing work.
She moved to New York .... **wanted to find singing work.**

3   It didn't take her long to become famous.
She .... **famous very quickly.**

4   She has had a long and successful career in singing.
She has been a successful .... **for a long time.**

5   Madonna is possibly the most famous woman in the world.
Madonna is possibly .... **than any other woman in the world.**

Part 2

Question 6

You visit an art gallery and buy this postcard. You decide to send the postcard to your friend Chris, who lives in Australia.

In your postcard, you must

- say something about the art gallery
- explain why you have chosen to send Chris this postcard
- ask Chris about the weather in Australia.

Write **35–45 words** on your answer sheet.

Part 3

Write an answer to **one** of the questions (**7** or **8**) in this part.
Write your answer in about **100 words** on your answer sheet.
Mark the question number in the box at the top of your answer sheet.

Question 7

- This is part of a letter you receive from your penfriend.

> Help! It's my brother's 14th birthday next month and I can't think of a present to give him. What do teenage boys like getting as presents in your country?

- Now write a letter, answering your penfriend's question.
- Write your letter on your answer sheet.

Question 8

- Your English teacher has asked you to write a story.
- Your story must have this title:

A very unusual evening

- Write your **story** on your answer sheet.

FCE Writing (December 2003)

Part 1

You **must** answer this question.

---

1 You have recently received this letter from your English penfriend, Maria, who you're going to visit soon. Read Maria's letter and the notes you have made on it. Then write a letter to Maria. You must use all your notes.

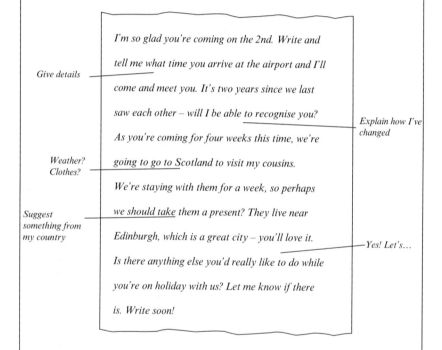

Give details

I'm so glad you're coming on the 2nd. Write and tell me what time you arrive at the airport and I'll come and meet you. It's two years since we last saw each other – will I be able to recognise you?

Explain how I've changed

As you're coming for four weeks this time, we're

Weather? Clothes?

going to go to Scotland to visit my cousins.

We're staying with them for a week, so perhaps

Suggest something from my country

we should take them a present? They live near Edinburgh, which is a great city – you'll love it.

Yes! Let's...

Is there anything else you'd really like to do while you're on holiday with us? Let me know if there is. Write soon!

Write a **letter** of between **120** and **180** words in an appropriate style on the opposite page. Do not write any postal addresses.

Part 2

Write an answer to **one** of the questions 2–5 in this part. Write your answer in **120–180** words in an appropriate style on the opposite page. Put the question number in the box at the top of page **5**.

2 You have had a class discussion about mobile phones. Now your teacher has asked you to write a composition, giving your views on the following statement:

There are both advantages and disadvantages to having a mobile phone.

Write your **composition**.

3 You have seen this advertisement for a job near your home.

WEEKEND WORK IN OUR CAFE

We want an enthusiastic English-speaking person to work at weekends in our cafe. You need to be:

* interested in different kinds of food
* good at dealing with people
* prepared to work long hours

Write explaining why you would be suitable for the job to:
Mrs Kate Ashby, Manager of Green Pepper Cafe.

Write your **letter of application**. Do not write any postal addresses.

4 A magazine giving tourist information is looking for articles on the history of your country. You have been asked to write an article about an important historical place. Describe the place briefly and explain why it is important in the history of your country.

Write your **article**.

5 Answer one of the following two questions based on your reading of one of these set books. Write the letter (a) or (b) as well as the number 5 in the question box, and the title of the book next to the box. Your answer must be about one of the books below.

Round the World in Eighty Days – Jules Verne
Animal Farm – George Orwell
A Tale of Two Cities – Charles Dickens
Deadlock – Sara Paretsky
Ghost Stories – retold by Rosemary Border

Either (a) Your teacher has asked you to write a composition saying what one of the characters in the book thinks of another character in the book. Write the **composition** with reference to characters in the book or one of the short stories you have read.

Or (b) 'In stories, events are sometimes outside the characters' control.' Is this true of the book you have read? Write an **article** for your college magazine, giving your opinion with reference to the book or one of the short stories you have read.

CAE Writing (December 2003)

Part 1

1   You are studying at a language school in England and have been asked to help organise a three-day trip for the English Language Club. You have decided to visit an area in north-west England.

The Club Secretary has asked you to write a report for the club members on accommodation in the area. Read the note from The Club Secretary below, and on page **3**, the information about accommodation which she has sent to you. Then, **using the information appropriately**, write a **report** for the club members, comparing the two hotels, recommending one of them and explaining the reasons for your choice of hotel.

Here are some final details for this year's trip:

- Final number going on trip now 10
- Breakfast, dinner, and picnic lunch each day
- 3 vegetarians

This is what some members have said that they want to do and see while they're there:

- long walks (2 people)
- live music (3 people)
- water sports (1 person)
- sightseeing and history (2 people)

I've found two hotels which might be suitable – Lawson House Hotel and Arnewood Hotel. Can you decide which of the two hotels would be better and write a report to send to the club members? It would be great if you could compare the two hotels, and explain which hotel would be best for everyone and why.

Thanks

Trudi
Club Secretary

Lawson House Hotel
Craniston

- In quiet valley, good views of Lake Craniston and hills, Semkirk Castle and 12th-century church ruins nearby
- Craniston village 3km – shops & regular folk music evenings
- Twelve single, six double bedrooms, comfortable, traditional decor
- Bed and breakfast, 3-course evening meal, packed lunches on request, special diets catered for.

Arnewood Hotel
Location: Tarnshaw

- 45 bedrooms, all with colour TV
- Meals: full board (picnic lunches if required) or bed and breakfast only
- Mountain bikes and canoes can be hired from hotel.

Local attractions include:

- scenic walking route to Lake Hawksmere
- Tarnshaw's excellent shops
- discount for Music Festival
- Langholm Gardens
- Local History Museum

Now write your **report** to the club members (approximately 250 words) as outlined on page **2**.

You should use your own words as far as possible.

Part 2

Choose **one** of the following writing tasks. Your answer should follow exactly the instructions given. Write approximately 250 words.

2 You see the following announcement in an international environmental magazine.

Help save the environment.

Today, the environment is under greater threat than ever before. Scientists say that we will face major problems in the future if we don't act now. Write and tell us about how people **in your country** are trying to solve environmental problems that exist there, and explain how successful they have been so far. We will publish the most interesting articles.

Write your **article**.

3 The director of an international youth centre has asked you to provide a reference for a friend of yours who has applied for a summer job as a supervisor of children's activities at the centre. The reference for your friend should include relevant information about your friend's:

- character
- previous experience
- skills and interests
- suitability for working with children.

Write the **reference**.

4 You see this advertisement in an international travel magazine.

We are a travel organisation and we are planning to hold an

International Exhibition in London

This exhibition will give information about different countries to visitors. Tell us what the display for **your** country should include. Write us a proposal:
- suggesting what should be included in your country's display
- explaining why your choice for the display best represents your country.

Write your **proposal**.

5 The principal of an international business school has contacted your company and asked if it would be possible to send one or more of its students to your company for work experience. Your manager has agreed to this and has asked you to reply to the principal, including:

- a brief profile of your company
- an explanation of the sort of experience your company could provide
- a description of the skills and qualities the student or students should have.

Write your **letter**.

CPE Writing (December 2003)

Part 1

You **must** answer this question. Write your answer in **300–350** words in an appropriate style on pages 3 and 4.

1   A major international sports competition is about to take place and your class has been talking about the advantages of such events. During the discussion the points below were made. Your tutor has asked you to write an essay evaluating the advantages of major international sports competitions and expressing your views on the comments made during the discussion.

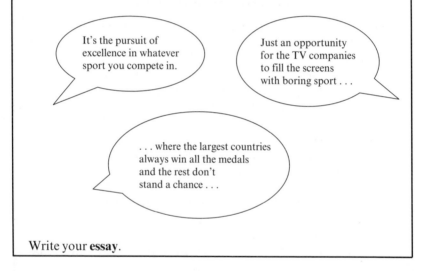

It's the pursuit of excellence in whatever sport you compete in.

Just an opportunity for the TV companies to fill the screens with boring sport . . .

. . . where the largest countries always win all the medals and the rest don't stand a chance . . .

Write your **essay**.

Part 2

Write an answer to **one** of the questions **2–5** in this part. Write your answer in **300–350** words in an appropriate style on pages **7** and **8**. Put the question number in the box at the top of page **7**.

2   Your local newspaper has invited readers to send in articles entitled

'Humans and machines – who is in control?'

You decide to write an article describing the role that machines such as computers and robots play in our lives, and saying whether you think there are any long-term dangers in our dependence on machines.

Write your **article**.

3   The music magazine, High Notes, has asked readers to write a review of a concert of their favourite kind of music: for example, classical, jazz, rock or pop. You recently attended such an event. You decide to write a review of the concert focusing on what made the music so memorable.

Write your **review**.

4   You work as a journalist for the travel section of a newspaper. You have recently visited a holiday resort to find out more about it. Write a report of your visit which will be printed in the newspaper. Within your report you should include information on the hotel you stayed in, local restaurants and entertainment facilities. You should also describe the suitability of the resort as a family holiday destination.

Write your **report**.

5   Based on your reading of one of these books, write on one of the following:

(a)   Anne Tyler: *The Accidental Tourist*

Your local newspaper has invited readers to contribute an article to their literature column entitled 'Sad, but funny'.

Write an article about *The Accidental Tourist*, mentioning what aspects of the novel you find sad and how humour is reflected in the characters and their actions.

Write your **article**.

(b)   Brian Moore: *The Colour of Blood*

You belong to a book club which has asked members to submit reports on books which portray strong leaders. You decide to write a report on *The Colour of Blood*. You should focus on the character of Cardinal Bem, and say how far you think he develops as a leader during the book.

Write your **report**.

(c)   L.P. Hartley: *The Go-Between*

'It did not occur to me that they had treated me badly.' Write an essay for your tutor briefly describing Leo's relationship with Marian Maudsley and Ted Burgess and saying how you feel he was treated by these two adults.

Write your **essay**.

APPENDIX B
Candidate Information Sheet

Candidate Name
If not already printed, write name
in CAPITALS and complete the
Candidate No. grid (in pencil).

Candidate Signature

Examination Title

Centre

Supervisor:

If the candidate is ABSENT or has WITHDRAWN shade here

Centre No.

Candidate No.

Examination
Details

0	0	0	0
1	1	1	1
2	2	2	2
3	3	3	3
4	4	4	4
5	5	5	5
6	6	6	6
7	7	7	7
8	8	8	8
9	9	9	9

Candidate Information Sheet

1 What is your age?

9 or under   10   11   12   13   14   15

16   17   18   19   20   21   22

23   24   25   26-30   31-40   41-50   51 or over

2 Are you: Female?   Male?

3 Are you:

studying at:

Primary school?

Secondary school?

College/university?

and/or working in:

Agriculture, forestry, fishing?

Construction?

Education?

Financial services?

Health and social work?

Hotels, restaurants?

Mining, manufacturing, utilities?

Public administration, defence?

Transport, communications?

Wholesale or retail trade?

Other business activities?

Other service activities?

4 How many years have you been studying English?

1 or less   2   3   4   5   6 or more

5 Did you attend classes to prepare for this exam?

No

Yes, at my school, college or university

Yes, at a language school

Yes, at my work

6 Have you taken this exam before?

Yes, once   Yes, twice or more   No

7 What other Cambridge examinations have you taken?

KET	FCE	BEC1/P	CELS P
PET	CAE	BEC2/V	CELS V
	CPE	BEC3/H	CELS H
YLE	IELTS		Other

8 Why are you taking this exam?
(mark one or two reasons)

For further study of English

To use English in studying other subjects

To help in my job or career

My college/university recognises it

For personal reasons

My company organised it

Company name (optional)*:

* The information provided will be added to our list of corporate users
available in information material and on the Cambridge ESOL website

Now please turn over ▶

CIS   The answers you give on this sheet will not affect your result in any way.   DP408/351

272

Candidate Information Sheet

⑨ Where do you come from?
If it is not listed, please complete the box 'other'.

001. Afghanistan	074. Guatemala	148. Poland
002. Albania	075. Guinea	149. Portugal
003. Algeria	076. Guinea-Bissau	150. Puerto Rico
004. American Samoa	077. Guyana	151. Qatar
005. Andorra	078. Haiti	152. Reunion
006. Angola	079. Honduras	153. Romania
007. Antigua	080. Hong Kong	154. Russia
008. Argentina	081. Hungary	155. Rwanda
009. Armenia	082. Iceland	156. San Marino
010. Australia	083. India	157. Sao Tome and Principe
011. Austria	084. Indonesia	158. Saudi Arabia
012. Azerbaijan	085. Iran	159. Senegal
013. Bahamas	086. Iraq	160. Seychelles
014. Bahrain	087. Ireland	161. Sierra Leone
015. Bangladesh	088. Israel	162. Singapore
016. Barbados	089. Italy	163. Slovakia
017. Belarus	090. Ivory Coast	164. Slovenia
018. Belgium	091. Jamaica	165. Solomon Islands
019. Belize	092. Japan	166. Somalia
020. Benin	093. Jordan	167. South Africa
021. Bermuda	094. Kampuchea (Cambodia)	168. Spain
022. Bhutan	095. Kazakhstan	169. Sri Lanka
023. Bolivia	096. Kenya	170. St.Helena
024. Bosnia-Herzegovina	097. Korea, North	171. St. Kitts-Nevis-Anguilla
025. Botswana	098. Korea, South	172. St.Lucia
026. Brazil	099. Kuwait	173. St.Pierre and Miquelon
027. British Virgin Islands	100. Laos	174. St.Vincent and the Grenadines
028. Brunei	101. Latvia	175. Sudan
029. Bulgaria	102. Lebanon	176. Surinam
030. Burkina Faso	103. Lesotho	177. Swaziland
031. Burundi	104. Liberia	178. Sweden
032. Cameroon	105. Libya	179. Switzerland
033. Canada	106. Liechtenstein	180. Syria
034. Cape Verde	107. Lithuania	181. Tahiti
035. Cayman Islands	108. Luxembourg	182. Taiwan
036. Central African Republic	109. Macao	183. Tanzania
037. Chad	110. Madagascar	184. Thailand
038. Chile	111. Malawi	185. Togo
039. China (People's Republic)	112. Malaysia	186. Tokelau
040. Colombia	113. Maldives	187. Tonga
041. Comoros	114. Mali	188. Trinidad and Tobago
042. Congo	115. Malta	189. Tunisia
043. Costa Rica	116. Marshall Islands	190. Turkey
044. Croatia	117. Martinique	191. Turks and Caicos Islands
045. Cuba	118. Mauritania	192. Tuvalu
046. Cyprus	119. Mauritius	193. Uganda
047. Czech Republic	120. Mexico	194. United Arab Emirates
048. Denmark	121. Moldova	195. Ukraine
049. Djibouti	122. Monaco	196. United Kingdom
050. Dominica	123. Mongolia	197. Uruguay
051. Dominican Republic	124. Montserrat	198. US Virgin Islands
052. Ecuador	125. Morocco	199. USA
053. Egypt	126. Mozambique	200. Uzbekhistan
054. El Salvador	127. Myanmar	201. Vanuatu
055. Equatorial Guinea	128. Namibia	202. Vatican
056. Estonia	129. Nauru	203. Venezuela
057. Ethiopia	130. Nepal	204. Vietnam
058. Faeroe Islands	131. Netherlands	205. Wallis and Futuna Islands
059. Fiji	132. Netherlands Antilles	206. Western Samoa
060. Finland	133. New Caledonia	207. Yemen, Republic of
061. France	134. New Zealand	208. Yugoslavia
062. French Guiana	135. Nicaragua	210. Zaire
063. French Polynesia	136. Niger	211. Zambia
064. Gabon	137. Nigeria	212. Zimbabwe
065. Gambia	138. Niue (Cook Island)	
066. Georgia	139. Norway	000. Other (please write below)
067. Germany	140. Oman	
068. Ghana	141. Pakistan	
069. Gibraltar	142. Palestine	
070. Greece	143. Panama	
071. Greenland	144. Papua New Guinea	
072. Grenada	145. Paraguay	
073. Guadaloupe	146. Peru	
	147. Philippines	

⑩ Which is your first language?
(i.e. your mother tongue).
If it is not listed, please complete the box 'other'.

001. Afrikaans	075. Mongolian
002. Akan	076. Nepali
003. Albanian	077. Norwegian
004. Amharic	078. Oriya
005. Arabic	079. Palauan
006. Armenian	080. Panjabi
007. Assamese	081. Pashto
008. Aymara	082. Polish
009. Azerbaijani	083. Ponapean
010. Baluchi	084. Portuguese
011. Bambara	085. Quechua
012. Basque	086. Rajasthani
013. Bemba	087. Riff
014. Bengali	088. Romanian
015. Bihari	089. Romansch
016. Breton	090. Russian
017. Bulgarian	091. Samoan
018. Burmese	092. Serbian
019. Byelorussian	093. Shona
020. Catalan	094. Sindhi
021. Chinese	095. Singhalese
022. Croatian	096. Slovak
023. Czech	097. Slovene
024. Danish	098. Somali
025. Dutch	099. Spanish
026. Efik	100. Swahili
027. Estonian	101. Swazi
028. Ewe	102. Swedish
029. Faeroese	103. Swiss German
030. Farsi	104. Tagalog
031. Fijian	105. Tahitian
032. Finnish	106. Tamil
033. Flemish	107. Tatar
034. French	108. Telugu
035. Fulani	109. Thai
036. Ga	110. Tibetan
037. Georgian	111. Tigrinya
038. German	112. Tongan
039. Gilbertese	113. Trukese
040. Greek	114. Tulu
041. Gujarati	115. Tupi/Guarani
042. Haitian Creole	116. Turkish
043. Hausa	117. Uighur
044. Hebrew	118. Ukrainian
045. Hindi	119. Ulithian
046. Hungarian	120. Urdu
047. Ibo/Igbo	121. Uzbek
048. Icelandic	122. Vietnamese
049. Igala	123. Wolof
050. Indonesian	124. Xhosa
051. Italian	125. Yao
052. Japanese	126. Yapese
053. Javanese	127. Yiddish
054. Kannada	128. Yoruba
055. Kashmiri	129. Zulu
056. Kazakh	
057. Khmer	000. Other (please write below)
058. Korean	
059. Lao	
060. Latvian	
061. Lithuanian	
062. Luba	
063. Luo	
064. Luxemburgish	
065. Malagasy	
066. Malay	
067. Malayalam	
068. Malinka	
069. Maltese	
070. Maori	
071. Marathi	
072. Marshallese	
073. Masai	
074. Mende	

This listing of places implies no view regarding questions of sovereignty or status.

273

APPENDIX C
Revised method of assessment for IELTS Writing

Work through the four criteria in order, starting with Task Assessment or Task Response, noting length requirements

For each criterion start with the over-arching statement that most closely matches the appropriate features of the script

Read through the more detailed features of performance at that band and match these to the script

Check that all positive features of that band are evident in the script

Check through the descriptors BELOW the band to ensure that there are no penalties/ceilings that are relevant

Check through the descriptors ABOVE the band to ensure that the rating is accurate

Where necessary, check the number of words and note the necessary penalty on the Answer Sheet

Write the band for the criterion in the appropriate box on the Answer Sheet and ensure that any other relevant boxes are completed

Rate all T1 and T2 responses together

APPENDIX D
Current Cambridge ESOL rating procedures and marking models

Current Cambridge ESOL rating procedures in practice

Appendix D reviews a number of Writing component assessment procedures for Main Suite Writing tests. The assessment of second language writing ability raises a number of important issues and the intention of this section is to compare and contrast features of marking associated with four types of assessment:

1. Home marking.
2. On-site, table-top, impression full double-marking.
3. On-site, table-top, partial second-marking.
4. Clerical marking.

Practicality considerations influence the choice of marking model adopted. Detailed descriptions of the marking procedures and models depicted in flow diagrammatic form are provided in Shaw (2003d).

1 At home, supervisor 'review marking' model

Scripts for certain exams are distributed to examiners at home. Their marks are returned to Cambridge ESOL for subsequent monitoring and processing. Scripts allocated to examiners marking at home are randomly apportioned with the aim of ensuring that there is no concentration of good or weak scripts, or scripts from one large centre, included in the allocation of any one examiner. Issues of apportionment, presented as options and accompanied by arguments outlining respective strengths and weaknesses, are given in Shaw (2005c).

Correlational monitoring of examiner marks is used to identify any anomalous trends among markers. The scripts of markers who fall into this category are sample monitored by a senior examiner, which may result in re-marking as required. In cases where examiners are identified as being either consistently harsh or lenient, marks are adjusted by the automatic process of scaling. Cambridge ESOL has perceived scaling to be a vital part of the assessment toolkit. Scaling is justified to the extent that the intervention will produce a more equitable result for candidates overall. Scaling is based on random script apportionment, modified by a check on overall performance in other papers, which indicates whether a particular group is stronger or weaker overall (see Chapter 5). Arguments for the retention or elimination of scaling in an Electronic Script Management (ESM) environment are given in Shaw (2004a).

Pre-rating procedures

Marking is undertaken by trained and experienced examiners. Scripts are marked at home by panels of examiners divided into small teams. Each team has an experienced examiner as Team Leader (TL) and each panel has a Principal Examiner (PE). There is one panel for each syllabus. The PE guides and monitors the marking process, beginning with a meeting comprising the PE for the paper, the TLs and the Subject Officer (SO). This is held immediately after the examination and establishes a common standard of assessment based on the selection of sample scripts for all the questions in the Writing paper.

Before the meeting the PE receives 200 scripts from which they select a range of scripts to be considered for standardisation purposes at a co-ordination meeting. The scripts are chosen to illustrate a range of responses and different levels of competence. The main co-ordination meeting for Assistant Examiners (AEs) follows the TL meeting. At this co-ordination meeting the scripts from the TL meeting are discussed and marked to standardise the marking of all examiners.

Rating procedures

After the co-ordination meeting, AEs receive their scripts in three consignments, or batches, which they mark at home. In advance of batch return deadlines, AEs post scripts to their TLs for monitoring. They do not return their final marks for a batch until any issues arising from the monitoring have been addressed. TLs are monitored by the PEs and the PEs attend each other's TL meetings so that there is standardisation across panels.

A rigorous process of checking is carried out throughout the marking process. The marking of each AE is sampled in three batches. The purpose of the sampling is to check that examiners are correctly and consistently applying the mark scheme. The TL keeps in close consultation with the PE throughout the marking period. For all batches, TLs are required to send a number of scripts to their PE for checking. During marking, the final decision remains with the PE.

Where it has become apparent that an examiner is not consistently follow-ing the mark scheme, remedial action is taken. The type of action taken depends upon the severity of the problem. Where there is disagreement between the TL and the AE, the TL's marks supersede the AE's marks. If marking is not satisfactory, further scripts are again chosen at random to be marked. In the event of continued dissatisfaction with AE marking, the PE is consulted and the scripts forwarded for further inspection: in extreme cases, an AE will be removed from the team and all the scripts re-marked. If marks are satisfactory, the scripts are returned to the AE and marking continues.

The TL in the 'At home, supervisor "review marking" model' monitors AEs on such things as:

- the timeliness of the co-ordination exchange, i.e. sufficiently early in batch marking for advice to be given and acted upon
- examiner accessibility for telephone co-ordination
- recognition and marking of errors
- thoroughness of marking
- mark sheet completion
- the making of appropriate comments
- accuracy in applying the mark scheme
- consistency in marking
- correct decisions relating to relevant/irrelevant candidate responses.

The TL provides feedback to the AE to guide him/her in the application of the mark scheme and to modify or stop aberrant marking.

Post-rating procedures

Examiners are graded by TLs at the end of the marking process and are given feedback on their marking trends by means of a standard letter. PEs also monitor each other by sending a number of scripts to each other for each batch.

In addition, the PE contributes to a report for the session which is pro-duced by the Chair of the paper. Examples of these reports can be found on the Cambridge ESOL website: www.CambridgeESOL.org

2 Full double-marking model

For some examinations, examiners meet at selected venues to mark the papers over the course of two weekends rather than individually at home. There are clear advantages for this style of marking providing the candida-ture is manageable and sufficient resources are available. It is much easier to standardise what is being done in a satisfactory way and there are senior examiners directly on hand when problems arise.

Analysis is undertaken to identify questionable marking between the marking weekends to allow re-marking where required during the second weekend. It is held that the check on discrepant marking in this double-marking approach deals satisfactorily with differences in marker severity.

In the Cambridge ESOL double-marking model, the candidate's final mark is based upon two independent ratings which are closely related. The two marks for the paper are compared by computer and if they differ by more than two marks, the paper is marked by a third marker who is always a highly experienced senior examiner (either a TL or PE). The TL's mark is then combined with the closest of the other two marks. If the mark awarded by the third marker differs by more than one mark from both the original marks, the script is fourth-marked by the PE. At Cambridge ESOL, the level of agreement between markers is high enough to enable the majority of scripts to be double-marked without further intervention (typically about 4% of scripts are sent for third-marking).

Double-marking is less feasible where there is a particularly large candidature.

There are three important elements to this type of marking: *table top*, *double-marking* and *impression marking*.

Table top: a group of markers work individually at a venue rather than individually at home.

Double-marking: every candidate's work is marked by at least two examiners. No mark or comment is put on the scripts so the second marker is unaware of the first mark given.

Impression marking: is employed so that the paper can be marked holistically. This means that the marker simply notes down an impression mark based on a combination of task achievement, accuracy and appropriate language.

Pre-rating procedures

Immediately after the paper set date, there is a meeting with the PE and their TLs. Before the meeting, the PE receives about 200 scripts from which they select a range of scripts for standardisation purposes at a co-ordination meeting for the AEs. The scripts are chosen to illustrate a range of responses and different levels of competence. PEs attend each other's TL meetings, so that there is standardisation across panels.

The main co-ordination exercise follows the TL meeting. This is conducted by telephone between the TL and the individual AEs on their team and takes place approximately one week before the first marking weekend.

Rating procedures

Marking is undertaken by trained and experienced examiners. Each syllabus has a PE and a panel of teams of examiners, each team of examiners has an experienced examiner as TL (selected on the basis of accuracy in previous sessions), and each marking venue has a Regional Team Leader (RTL).

PEs meet with TLs immediately after the examination and begin the process of establishing a common standard of assessment by the selection of sample scripts for all the questions in the Writing paper. These are chosen according to the same criteria adopted for the 'At home, supervisor "review marking model" ' (described above).

The marking weekend opens with further co-ordination of AEs. Once this is completed, marking commences. Each script is marked by two different examiners: a mark is awarded by an AE to each question and the question is then marked by a second AE. In order to ensure that the second marker's judgement is not influenced by the first, no marks or comments are written on scripts.

Marks awarded are recorded on machine-markable answer sheets (known as Optical Mark Reader (OMR) sheets) and the completed mark sheets are then scanned.

Post-rating procedures

RTLs provide the PE with reports from the session, which include AE feedback on the questions. These feed into the Examiner's Report which is made available for released papers on the Cambridge ESOL website.

Once any necessary third and fourth-marking has been completed all the final marks are processed by computer and collated with the marks for the other papers in the examination.

AEs are graded by TLs and TLs by PEs each session. AEs then receive feedback relating to their speed of marking and the accuracy and range of their assessments. In addition, TLs and above receive more detailed feedback on examiner marking behaviour as soon as all the statistics are available.

3 Partial or targeted 'second-marking' model

In some exams, a form of marking is used, where only a percentage of the scripts are second-marked. Scripts are targeted and second-marked, on-site and over one weekend. Unlike the double-marking model, the first mark awarded to a script is visible to the second examiner (usually a PE, TL or trusted senior examiner). TLs, or even AEs, identify packs of scripts which they feel would benefit from further scrutiny. AEs unsure about their marking on any particular packet are encouraged to refer their scripts to the TL for second-marking. Additionally, AEs are expected to regularly check the TL's monitoring sheets to see if their marking is 'on track'. In all cases where a discrepancy exists between first and second marks, the second mark takes precedence. Totally erratic examiners are prevented from continuing to mark. The decision to withdraw an examiner is based on the consensus from the PE (and where appropriate Assistant PE), and the relevant TL. All scripts from erratic examiners are re-marked.

Pre-rating procedures

The PE goes through a number of live scripts to identify scripts which are suitable for standardisation purposes. A meeting then takes place to discuss and confirm these.

AEs are sent 12 scripts, of which six are marked and six unmarked. The TL then contacts the AE to arrange a time, before the marking weekend, to carry out telephone co-ordination of the six unmarked scripts.

During the telephone co-ordination AEs give their marks and reasons for those marks to the TL. These are discussed and the agreed marks revealed. Commentaries for these scripts are available during the marking weekend for those examiners who wish to see them.

Rating procedures

AEs sit in a group with their team and TL and award marks to and discuss scripts which have been selected to cover a range of abilities. The TL answers any queries that the AE has about marks/mark scheme or marking process.

Once marking has commenced, TLs, PEs (and Assistant PEs where appropriate) monitor the first packet of each examiner. If they find a tendency to over or under mark they give the AE feedback. A further session of co-ordination takes place during Saturday and again on the Sunday morning.

At the end of the session AEs are expected to complete a questionnaire, covering their impressions of the marking weekend. This is considered to be valuable information by Cambridge ESOL as it feeds back into question paper production and administration procedures.

Post-rating procedures

Feedback letters are subsequently sent to AEs based on a report from the TL and data on the AE's marking history.

4 Clerical marking

Some exams contain short response items which can be marked by Clerical Markers (CMs). In this case, candidates indicate their answers by writing them on an OMR sheet. Once marked the OMRs are scanned.

Pre-rating procedures

A co-ordinating examiner (Co-Ex) is appointed to act as the representative of the SO during the clerical marking of a particular paper. Following the exam administration, the Co-Ex goes through 200–300 OMRs to identify:

a) possible answers not on the mark scheme but which are correct

b) any mark scheme issues

c) potential standardisation scripts.

Details and responsibilities vary from level to level and paper to paper.

This is followed by a meeting between the Co-Ex and the SO to review the representative sample and to make any additions to the mark scheme in light of these responses. A number of OMRs are chosen from this sample to be used for CM training and co-ordination. OMRs are also selected to exemplify marking points which may prove a source of difficulty to CMs.

Rating procedures

The precise procedure for training CMs is at the discretion of the Co-Ex but is discussed with the SO or the Clerical Marking Supervisor (CMS), who is responsible for the administration of the marking session. CMs are given a clear idea of the level of the examination, the focus of the particular paper and how it relates to other papers that make up the examination. Most of the general points are covered by the *Marking instructions and mark scheme* for the paper (which contains precise paper-specific information). It is the role of the Co-Ex to ensure that CMs understand the basic principles of the marking process i.e., the mark scheme should be adhered to at all times and that CMs should not make their own decisions about what is right or wrong. If a CM believes that he or she has come across a correct answer which is not included on the mark scheme, the CM refers the answer immediately to the Co-Ex for a decision on whether it is to be accepted as correct or not. The SO is then advised if additions are to be made to the mark scheme.

Following co-ordination, CMs collect a pack of scripts for marking from a rack. On completion of the marking the pack is signed in green by the CM responsible. The pack is then returned to the rack and a new set of scripts collected. This constitutes the first phase of marking. It is not unusual for CMs to have a large number of questions at the beginning of marking on the first day, and these queries are dealt with jointly by the Co-Ex and the SO/Chair.

During this phase the Co-Ex conducts a continuous and random check on the standard of clerical marking, noting in particular any incidence of high error rates amongst CMs. This monitoring ensures that marking is both accurate and consistent and that the lozenging of OMRs is satisfactory.

Based on the experiences of first marking and in collaboration with the SO, the Co-Ex produces a finalised and definitive version of the marking key.

A second marking phase – the 'checking' phase – is then conducted. Each CM marks a script a second time, carefully avoiding any scripts they had previously marked during the first phase. This time marked scripts are signed in red. Any issues encountered by CMs during the rating of this item are discussed immediately with the Co-Ex. The Co-Ex also monitors those CMs who appeared to exhibit a higher than usual error rate during the first phase of marking.

The checking of completed OMRs constitutes an important part of the clerical marking process since it serves to check that:

* the quality of the lozenging is sufficient for OMR scanning to take place
* all clerically-marked items have been correctly marked and that any errors found are corrected
* items affected by changes or additions to the mark scheme during first marking have been correctly marked.

Post-rating procedures

The Co-Ex is required to produce a report on each clerical marking session. Reports include points relating to: preparation for marking; documentation; the mark scheme; induction and training of markers; personnel; academic and administrative aspects of the marking operation; quality control; the examination paper in detail; the final mark scheme; a list of rejected answers; and if appropriate, recommendations for future sessions.

Assessment

Candidates' answers are assessed with reference to two mark schemes: one based on the examiner's overall impression (the General Mark Scheme), the other on the requirements of the particular task (the Task Specific Mark Scheme). The General Mark Scheme summarises the content, organisation and cohesion, range of structures and vocabulary, register and format, and target reader indicated in the task. The accuracy of language, including spelling and punctuation, is also assessed on the general impression scale for all tasks. The Task Specific Mark Scheme focuses on criteria specific to each particular task.

Depending on the level of the examination, certain other factors are taken into consideration:

- Length – Writing approximately the correct number of words is an integral part of task achievement. Significantly fewer words are likely to mean that the task has not been completed, whereas over-long pieces of writing may involve irrelevance or have a negative effect on the target reader. If this is the case, over-length will be penalised.

- Spelling and punctuation – These are important aspects of accuracy and for some levels are always taken into account. American spelling is acceptable, but there should be consistency.

- Handwriting – If handwriting interferes with communication, the candidate will be penalised. Totally illegible scripts receive Band 0.

- Irrelevance – The examiner's first priority is to give credit for the candidates' efforts at communication, but candidates are penalised for content irrelevant to the task set.

- Layout – Following the conventions of the various task types (writing letters, reports, instructions, etc.) is part of task achievement. Any acceptable modern layout may be used. Paragraphs should be clearly laid out either by indenting or by leaving a space between each paragraph.

- Paragraphing – This is a function of organisation and format. The Task Specific Mark Scheme will give an indication to examiners of what is expected.

Specific details of how these apply to each level can be found in the Handbooks for each examination.

APPENDIX E
Standard procedures for the production of Writing examination materials

Cambridge ESOL employs a set of standard procedures for the generation of high quality test materials for its Writing examinations. The procedures outlined below relate to the stages of the Question Paper Production (QPP) process which are the responsibility of Cambridge ESOL. Seven main stages can be identified that make up the production process:

- commissioning
- pre-editing
- editing
- trialling
- trial review
- test construction
- examination overview.

Cambridge ESOL believes that it is important for Chairs, Principal/Assistant Principal Examiners (PE/APE) and item writers to be fully aware of the importance of following standard procedures, of the requirements of each stage and of the role that they are expected to play as material progresses through each stage so that the thoroughness, fairness and consistency of all examinations can be ensured.

Commissioning

Commissioning of item writers is the first stage of the QPP process and is a task that has been centralised for Cambridge ESOL exams. The aims of centralised commissioning are:

- to co-ordinate the timing of commissions
- to plan well in advance across all Cambridge ESOL examinations
- to co-ordinate and utilise effectively the item writer resource
- to standardise commissioning procedures across examinations.

Once a year, the Subject Officer (SO) for each paper, in consultation with the Chair, determines the number of commissions required for the forthcoming period in accordance with current banks of material and future requirements. The item writing team for each paper is also reviewed at this stage.

The Cambridge ESOL database stores information on all commissions in addition to general information on item writers.

Pre-editing

Pre-editing takes place when commissioned tasks are received by Cambridge ESOL for the first time.

The pre-editing stage is intended to select material which will progress in the production process and to improve the quality and maximise the quantity of writing material available for editing.

The aims of pre-editing are:

- to suggest appropriate changes to material requiring amendments or re-writing
- by reference to the Item Writer Guidelines, to reject unsuitable, problematic or weak material
- to decide if a text is suitable before items are written in full (where appropriate)
- to comment on the item writer's proposed exploitation of a text and suggest possible alternatives (where appropriate); however, it is not intended that material is edited or re-written by the pre-editing team, as this is not a function of this stage
- by reference to the Item Writer Guidelines, to action the appropriate payment
- to carry out an initial check on the descriptive information provided for each task
- to speed up the editing process (i.e. item writers will not have to spend time working on unsuitable material)
- to increase the efficiency of editing since rejection at editing of tasks accepted at pre-editing is not normally an option.

Participants in pre-editing include the Chair; the SO; plus either a PE or an experienced item writer who is not currently on the team but has experience of a similar paper at the same level.

The pre-editing meeting considers material, decides on the outcome, and prepares feedback for the item writers.

Editing

Materials which successfully pass the pre-editing stage are re-submitted for editing. The editing stage ensures that, as far as possible, material is of an acceptable standard for inclusion in trials. The aims of editing are:

* to check or re-check the quality of material against specifications
* to make any changes necessary to submitted materials so that they are of an acceptable standard for trialling
* to ensure that the rubrics are appropriate and comprehensive
* to further develop the skills of item writers in order to improve the quality of materials submitted and the input of item writers to future editing sessions.

Editing meetings consist of the Chair, the SO and members of the item writing team.

Materials to be edited are sent in advance of the editing meeting to all participants. The expectation at the meeting is that material should require minimal changes only although re-writing of items will sometimes be necessary, and may be an important part of training. Material is not usually rejected at editing on the grounds that it is of unacceptable quality or does not correspond with current guidelines relating to quantity, length, subject matter, level, etc. as these aspects should have been dealt with at pre-editing.

Trialling

After the editing meeting the edited materials are checked by the Chair in readiness for trialling.

Trialling is intended to confirm that material is of a suitable quality to be used in a live examination. The aims of trialling are:

* to fine-tune rubrics
* to check that visual prompts are clear and accessible (where appropriate)
* to ensure that tasks are at an appropriate level, and as far as possible, equivalent in terms of difficulty of the question and output (vocabulary, functions and structures that candidates will need to use).

Trialling takes place at selected centres/schools around the world.

Trial review

After trialling, a meeting is held to review the performance of materials. Trial review aims:

- to review trialled material in the light of candidate performance and feedback from examiners, candidates and centres, as appropriate
- to finalise and ensure material is acceptable for use in test construction
- to make essential adjustments to tasks so that, as far as possible, no editing will need to take place at the test construction stage
- to finalise the mark scheme (where appropriate).

The trial review meeting takes place as soon as possible after the trialling session. The Chair, the SO, and an experienced item writer participate in the meeting. A PE may also attend.

Before the meeting, the scripts will have been marked by AEs who complete a feedback form for each of the candidates and assign a score to each performance. AEs complete an evaluation sheet for each task and, if appropriate, comment on the draft Task Specific Mark Scheme.

At the trial review meeting each task is reviewed in the light of information from the evaluation sheet completed by AEs, sample scripts and feedback from candidates and centres. Amendments to tasks and mark schemes are made, if appropriate, and recorded on a meeting copy of the task or mark scheme. Decisions on materials are categorised in the following ways:

1. Ready for test construction.
2. Amended at the meeting and requiring retrialling.
3. To be re-written and re-trialled.
4. To be given to another examination on the grounds of task difficulty.
5. Material is rejected – this material may be used for item writer training.

After the meeting, materials and relevant descriptive information are updated.

Systematic feedback to item writers is provided either in writing after trialling review or as part of a separate item writer training/feedback day.

Test construction

The test construction stage is a key activity in the production of question papers to ensure that they meet required standards in terms of level, coverage and content.

Test construction aims to construct sufficient question papers to meet ongoing requirements and to ensure that question papers meet required standards in terms of level, coverage, content and comparability.

Depending on the nature of the paper concerned, the Chair may make a proposal for paper content and draft papers may be produced at least two weeks in advance of a test construction meeting. The Chair checks that:

- a range of topics/tasks is maintained on each paper, bearing in mind the range of cultural perspectives desirable
- there is no obvious overlap in content either within a paper or historically
- the test(s) is/are at the right level.

Draft papers are prepared by the Paper Administrator (PA) using the information from the Chair's test construction form. The draft papers are circulated to those attending in advance of the test construction meeting for preliminary consideration of content, and range of items.

The test construction meeting usually consists of the SO, the Chair, and an experienced item writer. Again the same checks are made at the meeting as described above. Draft papers are amended by the Paper Administrator and checked by the SO.

Examination overview

The aims of examination overview are:

- to review content of the paper as a whole in order to confirm earlier decisions made at test construction
- to ensure the examination as a whole possesses the required continuity
- to check topics across the examination and historically.

The examination overview meeting includes all SOs working on the examination as a whole and the Examinations Manager (EM). Chaired by the EM, draft question papers are circulated and reviewed at the meeting. Decisions taken at test construction are looked at again and decisions are made on remedial action to be taken (where necessary).

After the meeting, the EM checks any remedial action taken by the SOs. Final copies of question papers are passed to the QPP Unit. These are accompanied by a checklist which is completed by the PA. Papers are sent out by secure post to the appropriate Chairs and content vetters for content checking. Following this, SOs review papers in the light of the feedback from Chairs and content vetters. The papers are given a final check by two proof readers before being signed off for print.

The procedures described here are reported in greater detail in the Handbook for Chairs and Item Writer Guidelines for each paper.

APPENDIX F
Minimum Professional Requirements for examiners of ESOL Writing tests

The descriptions given here are based on an internal Cambridge ESOL policy document for use by those involved in the supervision and deployment of Cambridge ESOL Writing examiners. The document aims to provide a broad outline of the professional procedures at each level; it does not attempt to provide a comprehensive list of duties or to cover paper-specific details.

Markers of Writing components of ESOL examinations are appointed by Cambridge ESOL Examiners Unit based on agreed Minimum Professional Requirements. The generic word for these markers is examiner. For each writing component, a panel is created from the list of approved examiners for each session. A panel is a hierarchical structure consisting of Assistant Examiners (AEs), Team Leaders (TLs) and a Principal Examiner (PE).

A set of six procedures is applied to each level of the examiner hierarchy (AE, TL, PE) to ensure that each person meets the requirements for carrying out their role, and that the role is carried out in accordance with Cambridge ESOL standards. The procedures go under the acronym of RITCME: *Recruitment, Induction, Training, Co-ordination, Monitoring* and *Evaluation*.

The structure of the document is the same for each RITCME component. RITCME descriptions conform to a standard set of overarching terms which include: *Objectives*; *Minimum Requirements*; *Implementation*; and *Outcome(s)*. An example set of descriptions for the *Objectives* and *Minimum Requirements* sections, for each of the six procedures and across all three examiner levels, is given below.

Objectives

Recruitment

To ensure that the background, experience, language competencies, availability and, where appropriate, location of AEs meet the minimum eligibility requirements.

To ensure that, in addition to the above, TLs and PEs have the interpersonal and administrative skills to meet the minimum eligibility requirements for the specified examination.

Induction

To familiarise new AEs with what is required of a Cambridge ESOL examiner for Writing components both professionally and administratively.

To ensure that, in addition to the above, new TLs or PEs are familiar with their roles and responsibilities for specific writing components.

Training

To develop the assessment skills which are required of an AE for a specific Writing component.

To ensure that, in addition to the above, new TLs are aware of the specific duties of the TL role.

To develop the professional skills of the PE in line with Cambridge ESOL procedures.

Co-ordination

To ensure that all AEs can make assessments according to general and task specific marking criteria right from the start of the marking period.

To ensure that TLs assess to the Cambridge ESOL standards and are confident in supporting the agreed assessments and script commentaries during AE co-ordination.

To ensure the PE maintains consistency of approach to marking and to marking standards over time.

Monitoring

To ensure that: AEs assess according to the marking criteria and the Cambridge ESOL standards throughout the marking period and, in the case of 'at home' marking, keep to deadlines; any AEs who fall significantly below the minimum professional or administrative standards are identified at an early stage; potential future TLs are identified.

To ensure that TLs are effective in carrying out their duties and that they maintain the Cambridge ESOL standards of assessment throughout the marking period.

To ensure that the PEs are consistently effective and have adequate support in carrying out their duties.

Evaluation

To provide Cambridge ESOL with a performance record of each AE and TL, which ensures that only AEs and TLs who meet the minimum professional and administrative requirements of the role are invited in the future; and to provide AEs and TLs with feedback which will help them to maintain and develop their role.

To provide Cambridge ESOL with a performance record of the PEs which will inform decisions on re-invitation and further co-ordination and training priorities.

Minimum requirements

Recruitment

For AEs, minimum requirements relate to aspects such as educational background (including teaching qualifications), teaching and/or examining experience, age, overall language proficiency relevant to the examination level, aptitude to fulfil the administrative aspects of the examiner role, and availability.

TLs must meet all the requirements of an AE and additionally have at least three years' experience as an AE for the specified Writing component (or similar Writing component in the case of a new examination). They must have demonstrated consistently accurate marking and have the necessary interpersonal and administrative skills.

A PE must meet all the requirements of the TL and additionally have significant experience as a TL for the specified component. PEs must have knowledge of other Cambridge ESOL examinations and of the Cambridge ESOL approach to writing assessment. They must also be able to lead meetings effectively, make professional decisions and write and revise mark schemes.

Induction

Newly invited AEs are expected to have: a good understanding of the importance of meeting deadlines and dealing efficiently with administrative documents; the need for confidentiality; the amount of work to expect; the training/co-ordination/marking process; the administration process; and the evaluation of their own performance.

A new TL must have a good understanding of: the objectives of the RITCME of AEs; the role of the PE; the nature of the relationship with AEs; and the importance of efficient administration.

The new PE must have: a thorough understanding of and willingness to deal with the nature of their relationship with Cambridge ESOL and also with TLs and other PEs; the RITCME procedures as applied to AEs and to TLs; the specialised input required in ensuring the integrity of examination results, such as grade review and re-marking procedures, and their contribution towards the production of examination reports for both internal and external audiences.

Training

All AEs must have a good grasp of assessment standards, test format, general marking instructions and administrative procedures for the component.

In addition, new TLs must be available to take part in any training events and must respond promptly and effectively to feedback.

New PEs should also take part in any training events arranged by Cambridge ESOL.

Co-ordination

All AEs must participate in a process of co-ordination before the start of each marking period.

Before every marking period, all TLs must take part in a TL co-ordination meeting where marks are agreed for a range of scripts selected by the PE and the TSMS is agreed.

The PE must collaborate with the Subject Officer (SO)/colleagues on a regular basis and refer to appropriate ranges of sample scripts whenever appropriate.

Monitoring

All AEs must be monitored by TLs and by Examiners Unit staff throughout the marking period. The monitoring process covers the requirements for accuracy and consistency of marking and all aspects of administration.

All TLs must be monitored by PEs throughout the marking period for accuracy and consistency of marking and all aspects of administration. They should be able to demonstrate effective guidance and monitoring of team members and respond efficiently to the directions of their PE.

The PE must be able: to meet the requirements for reliable assessment over time; to demonstrate the ability to manage a panel of examiners; to satisfy the expectations of Cambridge ESOL.

Evaluation

AEs and TLs must be evaluated at the end of each marking period in respect of their reliability/consistency of marking. Their ability to meet administrative requirements is also evaluated.

In addition, the PE is evaluated on a session-by-session basis with reference to the criteria in the Provision of Services document.

APPENDIX G
Computer-based (CB) exam versions: Issues and directions

With the development of new technology, many tests that have previously been available on paper are being adapted for computer administration. This has advantages in:

- allowing for innovative test formats: integrating audio, dynamic task types and manipulating text on screen
- allowing for greater control over aspects of administration such as timing
- enabling more efficient (and detailed) capture and scoring of candidate responses. It is possible, for example, to record the precise timing of candidate responses and to score them instantly
- providing the potential for greater test security – no need to ship papers to test centres.

Computer-based testing (CBT) raises issues in relation to item design and marking strategy:

- What special constraints does a CBT interface place on item design? (e.g. limitations on dimensions of questions and answer spaces; limitations on methods of responding).
- What novel opportunities does a CBT interface offer item design? (e.g. interaction; movies; sound).
- Might CBT affect costs in ways making them a factor in item design?
- Will CBT technology (e.g. interfaces) restrict or expand the range of marking strategies available and will any such change affect test or item design?
- Could/should CBT affect the mix of marking strategies used in large scale examining and hence test or item design?
- How do any novel constraints or opportunities arising from the CBT interface etc. affect the design of specifications?

In recent years, Cambridge ESOL has been involved in the development of a new Online Test Delivery Engine. The Engine comprises a series of separate components each responsible for different functions collectively known as Cambridge Connect. Apart from delivering computer-based tests at test venues, Connect also ties in to the 'backend' systems that drive Cambridge ESOL examinations and assessments, including LIBS and EPS, as well as Online Entries, Online Speaking Marks Capture and Online Return of Results initiatives.

Cambridge Connect is shown diagrammatically in Figure 1G. The Engine itself is generic enabling Cambridge Assessment to map a range of assessments onto the same CB Delivery System; the first assessment utilising this platform is a computer version of the Preliminary English Test (PET). It is envisaged that CB PET will shortly be followed by other ESOL examinations in which the Writing components will also be taken on computer.

Figure 1G Cambridge Assessment's Online Delivery Engine (Cambridge Connect)

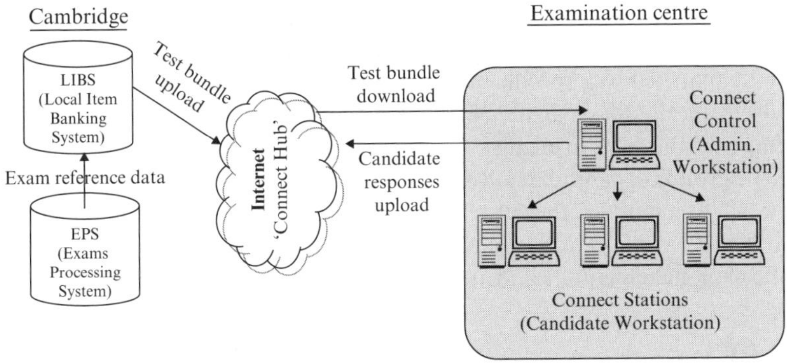

Cambridge Connect provides obvious benefits both to the candidates and to the test centre as it offers improved flexibility and greater frequency of test dates. Presently, there are six fixed date exam sessions for the paper-based version of the PET exam; however, with Connect many more test sessions can be administered in any one year, with sessions in months not already covered by the paper-based examination. With the addition of Online Entries, the lead-in time for entries can be shortened considerably – up to two weeks before the day of the examination providing both candidates and the centre greater opportunity to make entries much closer to the exam date. In addition the results can be returned to the candidate online within three weeks of taking the exam, therefore, ensuring that a candidate can enter for an exam, take the exam and receive their results within five weeks.

The requirement for centres to receive exam materials and to ensure their security will no longer be necessary as this will be accomplished automatically. Immediately following the test, centres need only to upload candidate responses back to Cambridge making the entire process faster, more robust and less prone to error. Recent trialling of the assessment and its delivery mechanisms has produced a favourable reaction from both centres and the candidates involved (see Chapter 5).

LIBS

LIBS was developed to construct ESOL examinations, store examination material at all stages of development and store all relevant related information. LIBS has been used comprehensively in ESOL since 2000 and is now an integral part of pretesting, standards fixing, test construction and grading. A large database, LIBS is organised as a series of 'banks'. Each examination component has a set of banks and examination material moves through these banks in a prescribed order. Each bank has a specific purpose and position in the sequence of banks. By looking at which bank a piece of material is in, it is possible to see which stage of development it has reached. An item bank is a large collection of test items from which we can draw high quality calibrated items that are matched to a specific measurement need or purpose. When stored as an electronic database, an item bank greatly enhances the practice of language testing as it allows us to create tests of known difficulty, tailored to the needs of specific groups of candidates. Tests created using classical methods need to be pretested as a unit: i.e. the entire test must be used in the pilot. Items analysed through IRT methods can, in contrast, be pretested at different times, be added to the bank incrementally and assembled into tests when required.

CB PET

CB PET, the first Main Suite examination to be delivered online, was officially launched in November 2005 and will be offered as an alternative to the paper-based format. The reasons for its introduction are clear. The candidature for PET has grown rapidly throughout the last five years (up by 45% since 2000) and there has been demand for PET sessions outside the standard exam timetable. Moreover, over 70% of PET candidates are aged 20 or under, and this is an age group likely to cope well with keyboard technology. It is also believed that the format of the PET examination is comparatively well-suited to on-screen display.

Online administration will involve many more sessions and test versions than are currently required by the pen-and-paper test and, as such, can only be supported by a test construction methodology based mainly on the recycling of materials. It is not possible to grade each version judgementally in isolation due to the practical difficulty of grading a large number of small sessions and because overlap of test material means judgements based on one version would have knock-on effects across other versions. Thus, CB PET will be pre-graded.

In an attempt to determine how specific elements of Electronic Script Management (ESM) will benefit CB exam processing, the Cambridge ESOL CBT Development Unit has been engaged in a series of trials relating to the CB PET project. The first task in the project was to assess the suitability of PET task types for use in a computer test and to identify any potential problems and their likely impact on test design or candidate performance. There were four key stages of development:

- feasibility study
- task design and trialling
- navigation design and trialling
- equivalence trialling.

It was agreed at an early stage that CB PET would retain the same exam format for the Writing (Reading/Writing) component. That is, the task types would be the same as in paper-based PET and candidate results would report on the same scale. This would allow schools to follow the same preparation course for both forms of the examination.

Feasibility study, task design and trialling

The aim of the feasibility study was to look at the suitability of the tasks for on-screen adaptation and to propose designs for trialling. Cambridge ESOL has produced computer-based tests in CD-ROM format since 1999, for example CB BULATS (Business Language Testing Service) and QPT (the Quick Placement Test, which is distributed and marketed by Oxford University Press), and development work had already been done on CB IELTS (launched in May 2005). Experience with developing such tests has enabled a body of knowledge and expertise to be established. One key difference between the majority of paper-based tests and on-screen display is 'aspect': most test papers are in portrait view (with candidates being able to view two pages at one time) whereas computer screens are in landscape.

An initial phase of the feasibility study was to identify those task types successfully used in previous Cambridge ESOL CB products and to undertake a risk assessment on any remaining task types in order to determine particular features of the processing of items that might raise problems for on-screen display and impact on the manner in which the candidate processes the task. The layout of previously used task-types was additionally reviewed in the hope that advances in technology would engender opportunities for improvement.

From a Writing perspective, the key CB PET issues appear to have been the impact of typing on candidate performance and the effect of typewritten script on examiner marking. A number of studies into this area have been carried out for CB IELTS and are reported in Chapter 5 above (Thighe et al

2001, and Green and Maycock 2004). Nevertheless, from the trials undertaken so far a preference for seeing questions one at a time has been expressed for Part 1, and most candidates have found typing as easy or easier than having to write by hand in Parts 2 and 3.

Navigation design and trialling

Following on from task template trialling and design modification, the navigation system was more fully developed: the primary aim being to allow candidates to progress through the PET test as they would in the more conventional format, selecting which questions to attempt first and re-visiting questions at any time throughout the test. Navigation trialling was tested on a mixed-nationality group of CEF A2/B1 level non-PET students from a UK language school in April 2004 (it was believed that if candidates with little or no knowledge of the PET test format were successful at navigating through the test, this should present few difficulties for real PET candidates). Findings from navigation trialling have been very encouraging: all candidates have been able to work their way through the test without instruction. Nevertheless, the Reading and Writing component contains a brief tutorial, available to candidates prior to starting the main test screen in line with British Standard BS:7988.

Equivalence trialling

Analysis of results from equivalence trials (where participating candidates scheduled to enter for the paper-based PET session soon after the trial also took a paper-based anchor test) found performance consistent in both forms of the test, replicating earlier studies in CB/PB equivalence (Jones 2000a, Green and Maycock 2004, Blackhurst 2005). Blackhurst (2005) concluded that 'The data gathered since 1999 has provided evidence that CB IELTS can be used interchangeably with PB IELTS, and that candidates, given adequate computer familiarity, will perform equally well on either version of the test.'

Candidate reaction to task design and navigation usability was garnered through questionnaire responses and post-test focus groups. An overwhelming proportion of candidates rated the test navigation easy to use, with 96% giving ratings of 3 or above on a scale of 1 to 5, where 5 indicates total agreement. A number of specific questions relating to candidates' reactions to reading and writing on computer were asked in order to gauge the general suitability of taking a Writing test on computer as opposed to on paper. In response to the question 'Did you find reading on computer easier than reading on paper?' 46% found it easier, whereas only 25% preferred reading on paper. This perhaps reflects an increasing familiarity with on-screen reading, at home, in school or at work. Typing written answers on computer was significantly more popular than writing by hand, with 67% showing a preference for typing and only 25% expressing a preference for handwriting. In general, a preference for taking CB PET was expressed by the majority of candidates: 63% preferred taking the Reading and Writing test on computer (as opposed to 20% preferring the paper-based version). These findings were corroborated by candidate comments gleaned from the focus groups. Whilst there was general satisfaction with the screen layout and navigation toolbars, a few candidates expressed a desire to be able to use a highlighting tool in the Reading section of the test, mirroring the function of underlining text on paper. The technology required to enable this function is currently being investigated for a future release of the software.

Early indications are that CB PET appears to be well suited to a sizeable proportion of the PET candidature and it is anticipated that it will become increasingly popular with centres looking for greater flexibility and faster turnaround times. However, it is appreciated that not all centres are equipped to deliver computer-based products and some candidates will still prefer to take the paper-based version, so CB PET has been developed as an additional service rather than a replacement for traditional PB PET sessions. CB PET was launched with a small number of European based centres in November 2005, prior to a wider worldwide rollout from March 2006.

Although the CB PET has been successfully received within the market-place, there is currently no backend process that allows examiners to mark the candidates' responses digitally, and responses have to be printed onto OMR (Optical Mark Reader) for paper-based marking. Cambridge ESOL would, therefore, like to prove that the online marking application developed by the ESM programme might enable CBT files to be marked on-screen.

Currently scoris – the web-based application which has been developed under the ESM programme to allow examiners to mark candidates' responses from their computer screen – only supports the marking of scanned paper scripts. ESOL would like to prove that it can also handle CBT files and, therefore, trials are underway to test how existing CBT systems will integrate with ESM systems, particularly scoris.

Trials will demonstrate that ESM technology can process CBT responses as well as scanned scripts. Examiners can mark the responses anywhere in the world provided they have the necessary training and the required IT equipment/internet connection.

The alternative (printing and paper-marking) is expensive, manually intensive and misses an opportunity to complete the entire testing and marking process in digital form.

APPENDIX H
Electronic Script Management in Cambridge ESOL: Issues and directions

Electronic Script Management (ESM) in Cambridge ESOL

The ESM Programme is a major cross-business stream strategic initiative within Cambridge Assessment. It has been described as the industrialisation of the examination process, impacting every activity from test production to awarding.

There are two major strands of work within the ESM umbrella:

ESM: The on-screen marking of candidate responses captured in electronic format, generally through the scanning of paper scripts (also known as Mark from Image or MFI), but potentially also through the electronic capture of a speaking interview. Mark from Object (MFO) is used in the context of marking from CBT responses. In addition ESM covers broader areas such as automated script tracking, and online co-ordination and standardisation.

ERM: Electronic Return of Marks (ERM) refers to marks being returned electronically for exams which cannot easily be marked on-screen such as Speaking tests (also known as Mark from Script or MFS).

The ESOL ESM Programme has adopted a phased implementation to manage the risks associated with such a large and complex project. This is being achieved through a series of trials, gradually ramping up the volume and complexity of implementation, and enabling Cambridge Assessment to develop software customised to the organisation's exact requirements.

Cambridge ESOL is already trialling ESM within the following key areas:

- CB PET Writing: the on-screen marking of CB PET Writing exams
- audio-digital investigation: research into the capture of Speaking tests as a digital object
- CB PET Speaking: the electronic return of marks for CB PET Speaking exams

- LIBS development: changes required to make question papers and mark schemes 'ESM-able'
- IELTS: exploration of IELTS-specific requirements for ESM.

The longer term implications of ESM developments for the wider ESOL community are still under evaluation.

Modelling facets of the assessment of writing within an ESM environment

It is becoming increasingly more important for Cambridge ESOL to be able to provide evidence of quality control in the form of assessment validity to the outside world. Whilst this is well advanced for objective tests of English, it is less so for the performance tests. In addition to the concern for reliability, a recent focus of language testing research has been the multiple features (or 'facets') of examiners and candidates engaged in tests that may systematically impact on test performance, but may not always be of relevance to the construct of communicative writing ability (see Milanovic and Saville 1996:1–12 for an overview of the facets involved in performance assessments). Bachman regards facets as 'an aspect of the measurement procedure which the test developer believes may affect test scores and hence needs to be investigated as part of test development' (2004a:146). As such they constitute potential sources of measurement error in test performance. Although these facets are already a consideration in the design and monitoring of Cambridge ESOL Writing tests, understanding of their impact remains limited and they are not systematically accounted for in reported test scores.

With the emergence of new technology an opportunity exists to radically alter the nature of future writing assessment. ESM, for example, potentially provides the rater performance data necessary to gather evidence in a timely manner, which is particularly important for reliability. ESM also has the potential to facilitate new marking models that will enable tighter control over current assessment quality and costs. ESM should not only provide for the capture and management of Writing test data, but should also open the facets of the test event to investigation, allowing for the adjustment of candidate scores if and as necessary. Conceptualising the assessment setting in terms of facets offers the possibility for estimation of the influence of examiner and task characteristics on ability estimates in the assessment setting. Moreover, such an approach can reveal interactions between different facets of the assessment situation which may have a systematic influence on scores. Ideally, the development of new approaches to scoring writing should allow Cambridge ESOL to investigate and address the behaviour of the individual examiner when confronted with particular candidate responses or particular writing tasks.

This section attempts to describe efforts to conceptualise the Cambridge ESOL Writing assessment setting as a workflow and in terms of the facets of the setting within an ESM environment.

Conceptualising writing assessment as a 'marking model workflow'

Writing assessment can be conceptualised as a 'marking model workflow'. A marking model workflow is a procedural approach for processing a candidate's response. At its very simplest, a candidate in response to an input task in the testing instrument provides a specified output and the output is the mark awarded to the candidate as an estimate of the ability which is being tested. Cronbach (1971:26) suggests that the test instrument can be thought of as 'a systematic procedure for observing a person's behaviour and describing it with the aid of a numerical scale or category system'. The test instrument either elicits a choice as output, as in *fixed response assessment*, or a more complex performance, as in *constructed response assessment*.

So, the input to a marking model is a candidate's work (e.g. a script) and the intended output is marks of known, consistent accuracy and precision that are independent of the marker who marked the script ('script' is the traditional ESOL word although the term being used for ESM is 'response set', covering CBT responses, audio recordings, etc.). Various marking and quality assurance processes take place between the input and output stages. This process constitutes a basic workflow which can be built into the organisation's standard procedures (and can be quality-assured).

In workflow terms, a *work item* is an instance of a workflow (e.g. the processing of a particular response such as a complete script, single question or part question) on which the actions of the workflow will be carried out. These actions or *work steps* are carried out/initiated by a user (a designated class of user such as Principal Examiner (PE); Team Leader (TL); Assistant Examiner (AE), etc.). A *role* defines a class of user that has access rights and other properties affecting how users in that class can interact with the workflow system. *Work introduction* can be thought of as the initial state for a work item in the workflow system. Responses are imported into the workflow system and located in a marking *work queue* (a place where a work item is stored awaiting a work step action to be carried out). *Workflow routing* is the logical linkage between two or more work steps such that the completion of one work step causes one or more other work steps to become enabled and the work items to be loaded into the work queue associated with the enabled work step(s) (see Figure 1H).

Figure 1H Marking model workflow

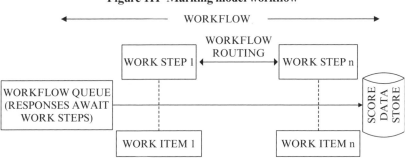

The potential for electronic data capture within a workflow in an ESM environment is of particular value in the following areas:

- workflow conceptualisation
- identification and manipulation of facets which constitute the data in the workflow
- subsequent movement and reconciliation of data within the workflow.

Test instrument elicitation: 'fixed format' tests from 'performance' tests

Slater (1980) alludes to distinctions between performance tests and non-performance tests (and the considerations that performance tests introduce). Commenting on Cronbach's definition above, Slater notes that:

> The big variable in this [Cronbach's] definition is how the term 'behaviour' is operationalised; doing so prescribes the characteristics of the stimulus eliciting the behaviour, the type of response called for, and the conditions under which the behaviour is displayed. Operationalising behaviour in these three respects is a heuristic technique for distinguishing between performance tests and other kinds of tests (1980:26).

Fixed format tests

Fixed response assessment scores are derived directly from the test instrument which tends to offer the candidate a number of options (such as multiple-choice items) of which only one is correct.

Possible responses from candidates are constrained and anticipated in the form of the instrument itself; the scoring task is simply to count responses of a particular type, which are easily and unambiguously indicated by a checked box, a circled number, or something similar (McNamara 1996:120–1).

Fixed format tests emphasise the **interaction between the candidate and the test instrument**. Responses gleaned from the candidate offer indirect verification (or not) of either the ability of the candidate or the value of the testing instrument (or both).

Performance tests

In assessment contexts, 'performance testing' is 'traditionally used to describe the approach in which a candidate produces a sample of spoken or written language that is observed and evaluated by an agreed judging process' (McNamara 1996). In this sense, performance assessments embrace processes (speaking assessment) and products (writing assessment). According to Fitzpatrick and Morrison (1971:238), a performance test is 'one in which some criterion situation is simulated to a much greater degree than is represented by the usual paper-and-pencil test'.

Figure 2H Fixed response and performance-based assessment: facets of assessment

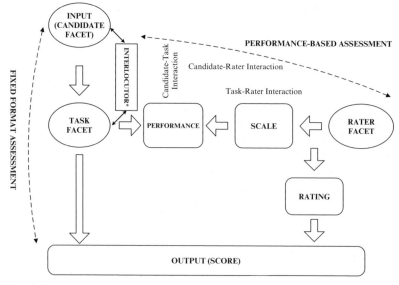

* *Speaking test only*
Source: based on McNamara 1996:86.

Performance-based assessment introduces new types of interaction between the rater and the rating scale (which mediates the scoring of the performance) and interaction between the rater and the candidate.

The marking model workflow: basic building blocks

Marking models can, for example, be built from basic types of marking: single; double; multiple; review; and gold standard. The diagrams below show the basic work and data flows (the types of marking can be integrated into full marking models).

Single-marking

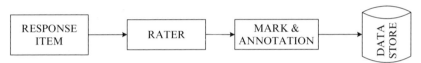

With single-marking, one rater records their marks and annotations, which are loaded into a data store for subsequent processing.

Double-marking

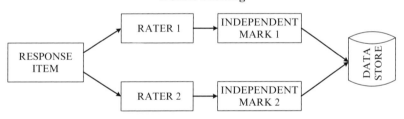

With double-marking, a response is independently marked by two raters, who both record their marks and any annotations. Both sets of marks and annotations are loaded into the data store for subsequent processing. A variant on the double-marking model is the multiple-marking model i.e. multiple observations (n) of the same sample of performance.

Multiple-marking

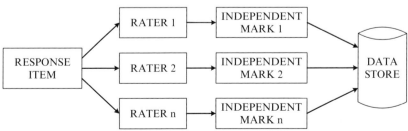

With review marking, a candidate's response and the original rater's marks and annotations are presented to the reviewer (TL, say), who enters their own marks and annotations for loading into the data store. Both sets of marks and annotations are stored for subsequent processing, though generally the reviewer's mark will take precedence.

Review marking

```
┌──────────┐        ┌──────────────┐
│          │───────▶│  CANDIDATE   │
│          │        │  RESPONSE    │
│  DATA    │        └──────────────┘              ┌──────────────┐
│  STORE   │                                      │  REVIEWER    │
│          │                                ─────▶│  RE-MARKS    │
│          │        ┌──────────────┐              │  RESPONSE    │
│          │───────▶│ FIRST RATER'S│              └──────────────┘
│          │        │   MARKS &    │                     │
└──────────┘        │ ANNOTATIONS  │                     ▼
     ▲              └──────────────┘              ┌──────────────┐
     │                                            │  REVIEWER'S  │
     └────────────────────────────────────────── │   MARKS &    │
         Reviewer's marks stored                  │ ANNOTATIONS  │
         together with first marks                └──────────────┘
```

With gold standard seeding, responses with pre-agreed but secret marks are introduced into a rater's work queue at certain intervals. A gold standard script is a clean copy of a script previously marked by a group of senior examiners. A PE would determine, in consensus with a small group of other PEs or senior TLs and in advance of marking, what the score should be on a sample number of scripts. These scripts would then be introduced on a periodic basis throughout the marking period for marking by AEs. The rater is unable to distinguish these gold standard responses from other responses and marks them as normal, their marks and annotations being loaded into the data store for subsequent comparison with the gold standard marks. In this way a rater's marks may be compared with a gold standard that is independent of any particular TL or supervisor.

Gold standard seeding

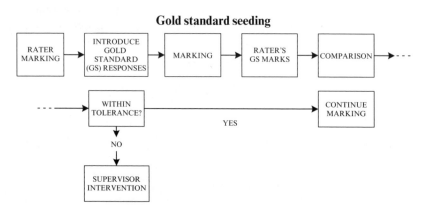

Conceptualising the writing assessment setting in terms of 'facets'

Writing tests are highly complex events involving multiple 'facets', some of which may be difficult to predict or control, which co-operate to produce a test score. Consideration of the various facets in writing assessment can reveal interactions between different facets of the assessment context which have a systematic influence on scores. The principal facets of the assessment context can be categorised into three groups: candidate (ability), task or item (difficulty) and rater (severity/leniency). Clearly, there are systematic facets of rater behaviour when confronted with particular candidates, particular tasks or particular test formats.

The modelling of the assessment characteristics – made possible by a faceted approach – has three primary functions:

1. A practical function – estimates of candidate ability may legislate for the features of both the rater and task thereby generating comparable candidate abilities which can be generalised across a universe of raters and tasks.

2. A planning and developmental function – for systems development, for example.

3. A research function – raising a host of research questions relating to facets of the rating assessment context. A clearly articulated research agenda would be required in order to investigate the significance for specific measurement variables that any proposed model may suggest are likely to be of some importance. Examples of research questions relating to the facet of scoring (say) might include:

   • In what ways do raters differ? Is there a gender effect? (facets of Rater Status; Rater Profile; and Rater Behaviour)

   • Is it possible to identify distinct rater types and certain patterns of rater behaviour? (facet of Rater Behaviour)

   • What amount of training/re-training is required? Can training improve raters' self-consistency? (facet of Rater Behaviour; facet of Rater Training)

   • How does assessment differ when marking electronically as opposed to paper-based marking (facet of Rater Profile; facet of Rater Behaviour).

Conceptualising writing assessment in terms of facets offers the potential for garnering complex data on the influence of rater and task characteristics on candidates' ability estimates in the assessment setting (McNamara 1996). For example, it is conceivable that certain raters variably respond to candidates of particular L1 backgrounds or that gender effects may exist – where the gender of rater and candidate may influence scores (facet of Rater

Behaviour or Rater Profile). It may be that the physical setting (which provides a context for the assessment) has an influence (facet of Rater Setting). In fact, any or all of the facets may exert a possible influence on the outcome of a test score. It is thus possible to collect information on the impact of any one of these facets (or any specific combination of them).

Each facet (or group of facets), assembled in a variety of ways, represents a potential source of data collection in the assessment context. If, for example, it is necessary to investigate finer-tuned aspects of the interaction of particular facets then the key facets must first be identified. These will constitute a focus for subsequent analyses. Facets of scoring validity, for example, can be identified and constructed for a particular assessment scenario, i.e. a particular kind of rating for a particular type of rater on a particular rating occasion (note that a rater, say, would no longer be conceived of as a 'person' but more in terms of a definition). Suitable mechanisms for data collection and storage can be built into the workflow systems and it would be necessary to ensure that adequate data is both collected and stored for retrieval. Decisions as to whether data is required in real time for grading purposes or whether it is needed for subsequent validation purposes will need to be taken.

A facet approach enables the researcher to deconstruct any assessment setting into relevant constituent facets in order to address specific research questions relating to facets of the rating assessment context. In this way, facets can be assembled/re-assembled in a variety of different ways offering a number of key benefits:

- score matching through tasks to best reflect both the knowledge and ability of candidates i.e. an effective scoring/procedural system
- knowledge and ability of candidates mediated through people (e.g. raters) and systems (e.g. scaling)
- introduction of stable and consistent scores
- ability to demonstrate an optimum marking model for score dependability
- greater control for assessment interactions (where there has been hitherto a lack of control)
- introduction of control mechanisms through data collection.

An argument can be made for conceptualising facets of the assessment setting in terms of the various constituent validity parts of Weir's Socio-Cognitive Validation Framework (2005b). The framework offers a perspective on the validity of examinations (developed in relation to Cambridge ESOL Main Suite Writing examinations throughout this volume). Of particular interest to the discussion here, are the *a priori* validation components of context and cognitive validity and the *a posteriori* component of scoring validity (which together constitute what is frequently referred to as construct validity). Cambridge ESOL follows this socio-cognitive approach in relation to the Main Suite examinations where attention is paid to both context validity and to cognitive validity in terms of the cognitive processing and resources that are activated by test tasks. The 'superordinate' facets of context and scoring validity and the test taker can thus be deconstructed into sub-facets:

Figure 3H Facets in testing and assessment

Facets of scoring validity

Facet of rating	Facet of rater profile	Facet of rater training	Facet of rater behaviour
• Automatic • Semi-automatic • Clerical • Semi-skilled subject expert • Expert	• Gender • Age • Background • Qualifications	• Recruitment • Screening • Induction • Training • Qualification • Monitoring • Grade review	• Severity • Fit statistics • Mean absolute difference from GS • Skew • Correlation • Grade (last session) • Duration

Facet of rater setting
- At Home
- On-site
- Individual
- Group

Facet of rater timing
- Time of day
- Session
- Period of year
- Period into marking episode

Facet of rater status
- Expert (AE/TL/PE)
- Experienced
- Inexperienced
- New/novice
- Subject expert
- Clerical

Facets of context validity

Task data facet
- Dichotomous
- Polytomous (without or ignoring judge mediation)
- Polytomous (taking judge mediation into account)

Output facet
- Transactional letter
- Essay
- Report
- Discursive composition
- Short story
- Article
- Proposal
- Word completion
- Open cloze
- Information transfer
- Sentence transformations
- Review

Channel facet
- Receptive
- Productive

Delivery facet
- On-demand
- Fixed date
- Paper-and-pencil
- Computer-based

Response facet
- Paper-based answer booklet
- Paper-based question paper
- Screen
- Multiple choice
- True/false
- Short answer question
- Extended answer

Input facet
- Instructions
- Rubric
- Task information

Facets of the test taker

Candidate skills
• Knowledge
• Experience
• Ability
• Use of computers
• World knowledge
• Cultural background

Candidate profile
• Gender
• Age
• Nationality
• L1
• School type
• Years of study
• Exam preparation
• Exams taken
• Reason for taking exam

The search for a satisfactory conceptualisation of second language writing performance and for an adequate writing assessment model is a challenging one and it is clear that there is a need to broaden current discussions of the issues involved. It is hoped that the issues addressed here will make a positive contribution to the widening nature of the performance assessment debate within Cambridge Assessment. Whilst the complexity and type of proposed assessment model have yet to be determined by research it is important that the model should be simple so that it is easily understood, easily implemented in software, and is computationally efficient – especially given the very large amounts of data that could be collected in an ESM environment. It is also a requirement that the model is able to identify problem marking accurately and precisely, and that this can be improved by adding complexity. In this sense, an iterative process of research and development is advocated, that starts with a simple model and subsequently adds complexity until the business is satisfied with the balance it has achieved. Such a model will probably explicitly model candidate, task and rater facets. There would be a need for the model to collect rich, robust data that facilitates the investigation and (if necessary) ongoing operationalisation of any issue considered relevant to understanding the nature of the assessment and promoting fairness. The data will need to embrace:

- details of the assessment (e.g. task parameters; administration; linguistic demands)
- candidate characteristics (e.g. gender; age; nationality; L1; years of study; knowledge; experience)
- examiner characteristics (e.g. biodata, qualifications, experience)
- rating details (clerical or 'expert' (AE/TL/PE) examiners; at home or residential rating; examiner behaviour; aspects of scoring).

Much of what is needed can already be found in existing examiner databases, test banks, candidate information sheet data stores and elsewhere. These sources would need to be related to test performances to facilitate investigations. As the scoring model is refined, some of the data might come to inform the operational management and calculation of test scores. The system would need to be designed with this level of flexibility in mind.

Capitalising fully on ESM would require a research agenda designed to:

- explore the significance for measurement of facets that the model may suggest are of importance (e.g. the effect of the characteristics of the rater on test scores)

- focus on the nature of interactions of the facets of assessment (e.g. the candidate/rater – rater/task interaction) especially given the interactional nature of performance assessment

- ascertain what it is appropriate and realistic to both consider and assess in any given assessment context (position/stance adopted and a supporting rationale, feasibility and practicality of assessment proposals, etc.).

To meet the requirements of the Research and Validation Group at Cambridge ESOL, the outcomes of ESM would need to include a practical, practicable, feasible and manageable business system which builds on existing ESOL structures, but supports sufficient flexibility to accommodate the needs set out above and can also manage interactions between constantly changing systems (e.g. IM considerations, issues related to examiner payment and contracts).

Proposing a marking model: future directions?

The means for achieving tight control over quality without the brute force approach of 100% double-marking (deemed profligate, expensive and inefficient especially in relation to reliable markers) needs to be realised. An alternative approach might be to adopt statistical modelling.

Statistical modelling

It is thought that the viability and usefulness of statistical monitoring will increase over the marking period as more marks become available. Initially, only large rater effects will stand out. It is in these early stages that it is most important to detect and resolve serious problems with rater quality. Once it has been established that raters *can* apply the mark scheme within a permitted tolerance, the focus of marker quality monitoring shifts to ensuring they maintain this standard – this is where more precise targeting is required and becomes possible as marking proceeds and more marks become available.

The complexity and type of statistical model used is still to be determined – there is a range to choose from. Whatever model is chosen, it will probably explicitly model candidate, task and rater variables. This will enable a mark to be predicted for each candidate-task-rater interaction and compared with the actual mark – the mark actually awarded by a particular rater to a particular task response. The results of this comparison are the basis for prioritising marking for review: raters with large mean differences are likely to be severe or lenient, those with a large variance of differences are likely to be erratic, and these flaws are likely to have been manifested most strongly in those marks with the largest difference. If a component contains a mixture of clerical and examiner marked items, the low judgement clerical marker items (items marked against a very 'tight' marking key by raters with no prior expertise) will be particularly useful since they may be treated as an objective comparator against which the higher judgement marks may be compared.

As marking proceeds, more data per candidate will become available which, if incorporated into the model, will enable candidates at risk of getting the wrong result to be more effectively targeted. For example, marks from other components taken by the candidate could be incorporated. The sooner actual or putative grade boundaries are known, the sooner a candidate's proximity to a grade boundary may be incorporated into the risk assessment. Random apportionment and instant return and loading of marks – two of the major benefits of ESM – will enable the statistical information used in determining boundaries to be available sooner; statistics should be fairly stable once complete marks for around 2,000 (say) candidates are available, providing they were truly drawn at random.

Raikes and Shaw (2005) have explored alternative ways of targeting the double-marking on the raters most likely to be aberrant and the scripts most likely to have been wrongly marked. If reliance is placed on more than the gut instinct of TLs and PEs, a marking model that enables the identification of anomalous marks that may reflect the problem marking needs to be developed. To do this it is necessary to separate out the various characteristics that influence marks so that it is possible to home in on those attributable to the rater.

Raikes and Shaw (2005) advocate two basic models, *untargeted gold standard seeding* and *targeted review*.

Untargeted gold standard seeding is thought to be most appropriate for clerical markers, who mark short, low judgement items – this is because the overheads of preparing and marking the seeds is low, and there is only a relatively small number of acceptable answers for such items, which makes it practical to test the marker on the full range. Moreover, such items are generally low value (typically 1 mark), making the impact of occasional rater error both hard to detect statistically and of relatively minor consequence. Such arguments might also apply to some of the items marked by expert-markers, but as the degree of judgement required by raters increases so the overheads of adequate gold standard seeding escalate and the costs of inefficiency rise. In such circumstances the targeted review model might be appropriate.

Targeted review marking is most suitable for items requiring raters to make non-trivial judgements. Statistical modelling could be employed to target marked responses for review marking. Since statistical modelling requires a certain amount of data to be available, there may be an initial stage right at the start of marking where review marking is untargeted, particularly for long answer, high judgement items (such as compositions) which take a long time to mark; for such items the initial rater approval and ongoing quality control processes may in practice overlap, particularly for inexperienced raters. However, the hallmark of such a model is that most review marking is targeted in most cases. Review marking should be done by a panel of trusted and experienced raters approved for this purpose, so that review raters are not individually responsible for particular raters.

Specifying classification error for each grade boundary (candidates at risk)

ESM offers the huge advantage of rapid identification of certain candidates who fall on the wrong side of the pass/fail boundary within one standard error of the passing grade. Such candidate information could be sent to senior examiners electronically for further scrutiny.

Consider candidates at risk close to the pass/fail boundary. Such candidates would have their scripts re-marked by a second AE unfamiliar with the first AE's score. Pairs of scores between the first and second raters can be lined up in columns and a correlation coefficient calculated between the two. The resulting coefficient is an estimate of the inter-rater reliability of the judgements made in either set of ratings. Though there is bound to be some variation between an AE's mark and another AE's mark or between an AE's mark and the standard mark, there must be a high degree of consistency overall if the test is to be considered reliable by its users.

Once the reliability index for candidates at the pass/fail grade boundary has been computed then the SEM index for the pass-fail cut-off score can also be calculated. The reliability coefficient can be used to estimate how reliable the test is in percentage terms but a more concrete and useful way of looking at the consistency of a set of scores is the SEM. Conceptually, this statistic is used to determine a band around a candidate's score within which that candidate's score would probably fall if the test were administered to the candidate repeatedly. Based on the percentages within a normal distribution, the SEM can also be used to estimate the probability with which the tester can expect those scores to fall within the band.

The purpose of the SEM is to estimate a sort of average of the distribution of error deviations across all the candidates who attempted the test. On the basis of this estimate, a tester is able to determine with certain amounts of probability how far candidates' scores would vary by chance alone if the candidates were to take the test repeatedly. Using this information, it is possible to report with certainty that, for any candidate, error alone can cause the scores to vary within a band of plus or minus one SEM (say) 68% of the time or two SEMs 95% of the time.

Consider those candidates at the extreme of the proficiency continuum. The narrower the SEM is, the narrower the band of possible fluctuations will be, or the more consistent the ratings (greater reliability due to second rating).

Reliability could be reported in relation to the SEM in terms of distance from a grade boundary, e.g. 'Every candidate is within two SEMs of a decision boundary'.

Figure 4H Estimating and reporting Standard Error of Measurement (SEM)

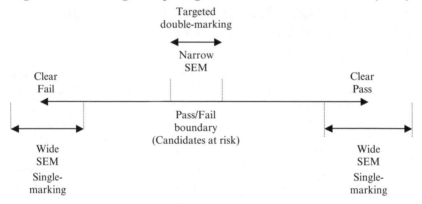

References

Adams, R (1981) *The reliability of marking of five June 1980 examinations*, mimeographed paper, Guildford: Associated Examining Board.

Akyel, A and Kamisli, S (1989) Word Processing in the EFL Classroom: Effects on writing strategies, attitudes, and products, in Pennington, M C (Ed.) *Writing in an Electronic Medium: Research with language learners*, Houston: Athelstan, 27–60.

Alderman, D L and Holland, P W (1981) *Item performance across native language groups on the Test of English as a Foreign Language*, TOEFL research report No.9, Princeton, New Jersey: Educational Testing Service.

Alderson, J C (1989) *Bands and scores*, paper presented at the IATEFL Language Testing Symposium Bournemouth, 17–19 November.

Alderson, J C (1991) Bands and scores, in Alderson, J C and North, B (Eds) *Language Testing in the 1990s*, London: Macmillan, 71–86.

Alderson, J C (2004) Washback in language testing: Research contexts and methods, in Cheng, L, Watanabe, Y and Curtis, A (Eds) London: Lawrence Erlbaum.

Alderson, J C (n.d.) Waystage and Threshold: Or does the emperor have any clothes? unpublished article.

Alderson, J C and Banerjee, J (1996) *How might Impact study instruments be validated?* A paper commissioned by UCLES as part of the IELTS Impact Study.

Alderson, J C, Clapham, C and Wall, D (1995) *Language test construction and evaluation*, Cambridge: Cambridge University Press.

Alderson, J C, Figueras, N, Kuijper, H, Nold, G, Takala, S and Tardieu, C (2004) *The development of specification for item development and classification within the Common European Framework of Reference for Languages: Learning, Teaching, Assessment (Reading and Listening)*, final Report of the Dutch CEF construct project.

Alderson, J C and Hamp-Lyons, L (1996) TOEFL preparation courses: a study of washback, *Language Testing* 13 (3), 280–97.

Alderson, J C and Urquhart, A H (Eds) (1984) *Reading in a Foreign Language*, London: Longman.

Alderson, J C and Urquhart, A H (1985) The effect of students' academic discipline on their performance on ESP reading tests, *Language Testing* 2 (2), 192–204.

Alderson, J C and Wall, D (1993) Does washback exist? *Applied Linguistics* 14 (2), 115–29.

Alderson, J C and Wall, D (1996) Special Issue: Washback, *Language Testing* 13 (3).

ALTE (1998) *Multilingual Glossary of Language Testing Terms*, Studies in Language Testing 6, Cambridge: UCLES/Cambridge University Press.

ALTE (1998a) *ALTE Handbook of European Language Examinations and Examination Systems*, Cambridge: UCLES.

References

American Educational Research Association, American Psychological Association, National Council on Measurement in Education (1999) *Standards for Educational and Psychological Testing*, Washington, DC.

Anastasi, A (1988) *Psychological Testing* (6th edition), New York: Macmillan.

Angoff, W H and Sharon, A T (1974) A comparison of scores earned on the Test of English as a Foreign Language by native American college students and foreign applicants to US colleges, *TESOL Quarterly* 5 (2), 129–36.

Aston, G and Burnard, L (1998) *The BNC Handbook: Exploring the British National Corpus with SARA*, Edinburgh: Edinburgh University Press.

Attali, Y and Burstein, J (2005) *Automated Essay Scoring with E-rater v 2.0*, ETS Research Report RR–04–45, November 2005, Educational Testing Service.

Bachman, L F (1990) *Fundamental Considerations in Language Testing*, Oxford: Oxford University Press.

Bachman, L F (2004) *Building and supporting a case for test utilization*, paper presented at the 26th Annual Language Testing Research Colloquium, March 2004, Temecula, California, USA.

Bachman, L F (2004a) *Statistical Analyses for Language Assessment*, Cambridge: Cambridge University Press.

Bachman, L, Davidson, F, Ryan, K and Inn-Chull Choi (1995) *An Investigation into the Comparability of Two Tests of English as a Foreign Language*, Cambridge: Cambridge University Press.

Bachman, L F and Palmer, A S (1996) *Language Testing in Practice*, Oxford: Oxford University Press.

Bailey, K M (1999) *Washback in Language Testing*, TOEFL Monograph Series 15, Princeton, NJ: Educational Testing Service.

Ball, F (2002) Developing wordlists for BEC, *Research Notes* 8, 10–13.

Banerjee, J V (1996) *The Design of the Classroom Observation Instruments*, Cambridge: UCLES internal report.

Banerjee, J V (2003) *Interpreting and using proficiency test scores*, unpublished PhD thesis, University of Lancaster.

Bangert-Drowns, R L (1993) The word processor as an instructional tool: A meta-analysis of word processing in writing instruction, *Review of Educational Research*, 63 (1), 69–93.

Barker, F (2004) Using Corpora in Language Testing: Research and validation of language tests, *Modern English Teacher* 13 (2), 63–67.

Barker, F and Betts, C (2004) Question uptake in the Certificate in Advanced English Writing Paper, *Research Notes* 16.

Belcher, D, and Hirvela, A (Eds) (2001) *Linking literacies: Perspectives on L2 reading-writing connections*, Ann Arbor: University of Michigan Press.

Benesch, S (1987) *Word processing in English as a second language: A case study of three non-native college students*, paper presented at the conference on College and Composition, Atlanta, GA (ERIC Document No. ED 281383).

Bennett, R E (2002) Inexorable and Inevitable: The Continuing Story of Technology and Assessment, *The Journal of Technology, Learning, and Assessment* 1 (1), 2–22.

Bereiter, C and Scardamalia, M (1987) *The Psychology of Written Composition*, Hillside, NJ: Lawrence Erlbaum Associates.

Berry, V (1994) Current assessment issues and practices in Hong Kong: A preview, in Nunan, D, Berry, R and Berry,V (Eds) *Bringing about change in language education: Proceedings of the International Language Education Conference 1994*, Hong Kong: University of Hong Kong, 31–34.

Berry, V (1997) *Gender and personality as factors of interlocutor variability in oral performance tests*, paper presented at the 19ᵗʰ Language Testing Research Colloquium, Orlando, Florida, USA.

Berry, V (2004) *A study of the interaction between individual personality differences and oral performance test facets*, unpublished PhD Thesis, Kings College, The University of London.

Betancourt, F and Phinney, M (1988) Sources of writing block in bilingual writers, *Written Communication* 5 (9), 461–78.

Biber, D (1991) *Variation across Speech and Writing*, Cambridge: Cambridge University Press.

Black, E L (1962) The marking of GCE scripts, *British Journal of Educational Studies* 11 (1), 61–71.

Blackhurst, A (2005) Listening, Reading and Writing on computer-based and paper-based versions of IELTS, *Research Notes* 21, 14–17.

Blanchard, J D and Reedy, R (1970) *The relationship of a test of English as a second language to measures of achievement and self-concept in a sample of American-Indian students*. Research and Evaluation Report Series No. 58. Washington, DC: Bureau of Indian Affairs, US Department of Interior.

Bonkowski, F (1996) *Instruments for the Assessment of Teaching Materials*, unpublished MA assignment, Lancaster University.

Boyd, E (2005) *Persuasion in CAE Part 1 Tasks: Overview Report*, Cambridge: Cambridge ESOL internal report.

Breland, H M and Jones, R J (1984) Perceptions of Writing Skills, *Written Communication* 1 (1), 101–119.

Bridgeman, B and Carlson, S (1983) *Survey of Academic Writing Tasks Required of Graduate and Undergraduate Foreign Students*, TOEFL Research Reports 15, Princeton, NJ: Educational Testing Service.

Bridges, G and Shaw, S D (2004) IELTS Writing: revising assessment criteria and scales (Phase 4), *Research Notes* 18, 8–12.

Briggs, D (1970) The influence of handwriting on assessment, *Educational Research* 13 (1), 50–5.

Brindley, G (1998) Describing Language Development? Rating Scales and SLA, in Bachman, L F and Cohen, A D (Eds) *Interfaces between Second Language Acquisition and Language Testing Research*, Cambridge: Cambridge University Press, 112–140.

British National Corpus: www.natcorp.ox.ac.uk

British Standards (2002) Code of Practice for the Use of Information Technology for the Delivery of Assessments, BS:7988:2002.

Brock, M N and Pennington, M C (1999) A comparative study of text analysis and peer tutoring as input to writing on computer in an ESL context, in Pennington, M C (Ed.) *Writing in an electronic medium: research with language learners*, Houston: Athelstan, (61–94).

Brossell, A and Ash, B H (1984) An experiment with the wording of essay topics, *College Composition and Communication* 35 (4), 423–25.

Brown, A (1995) The Effect of Rater Variables in the Development of an Occupation-specific Language Performance Test, *Language Testing* 12 (1), 1–15.

Brown, A (2003) *Legibility and the Ratings of Second Language Writing: An investigation of the rating of handwritten and word-processed IELTS Task Two essays*, IELTS Research Reports, Vol. 4, 131–51.

Brown, A (2004) *Legibility and the rating of second-language writing*, in Milanovic, M and Weir, C (Eds) *European Language Testing in a Global*

References

Context: Proceedings of the ALTE Barcelona Conference July 2001, Studies in Language Testing 18, Cambridge: UCLES/Cambridge University Press, 117–125.

Brown, A and Iwashita, N (1998) *The role of language background in the validation of a computer-adaptive test*, in Kunnan, A J (Ed) *Validation in Language Assessment: Selected papers from the 17th Language Testing Research Colloquium*, Mahweh, NJ: Lawrence Erlbaum Associates, 195–208.

Brown, J S, McDonald, J L, Brown, T L, and Carr, T H (1988) Adapting to processing demands of discourse production: The case of handwriting, *Journal of Experimental Psychology: Human Perception & Performance* 14, 45–59.

Buck, G (1988) Testing Listening comprehension in Japanese university entrance examinations, *JALT journal* 10 (1), 15–42.

Bull, R and Stevens, J (1979) The effects of attractiveness of writer and penmanship on essay grades, *Journal of Occupational Psychology* 52, 53–59.

Burrows, C (1998) *Searching for Washback: An investigation of the impact on teachers of the implementation into the Adult Migrant English Program of the assessment of the Certificates in Spoken and Written English*, unpublished PhD thesis, Macquarie University.

Burstein, J, Kukich, K, Wolff, S, Chi, Lu, Chodorow, M, Braden-Harder, L and Harris, M D (1998a) Automated scoring using a hybrid feature identification technique, Proceedings of the Annual Meeting of the Association of Computational Linguistics August 1998, Montreal.

Burstein, J, Kukich, K, Wolff, S, Chi, Lu, Chodorow, M, Braden-Harder, L and Harris, M D (1998b) Computer analysis of essays, in *NCME Symposium on Automated Scoring*, Montreal, Canada.

Burstein, J, Leacock, C and Swartz, R (2001) *Automated evaluation of essays and short answers*, paper presented at the 5th International Computer Assisted Assessment Conference, Loughborough University, 2001.

Butler, F A, Weigle, S C, Kahn, A B and Santo, E Y (1996) *Test development plan with specifications for placement instruments anchored to the model standards*, Los Angeles: University of California, Los Angeles, Centre for the study of Evaluation.

Callear, D, Jerrams-Smith, J, and Soh, V (2001) CAA of short non-MCQ answers, in *Proceedings of the 5th International CAA conference*, Loughborough. Retrieved from www.lboro.ac.uk/service/ltd/flicaa/conf2001/pdfs/k3.pdf

Cambridge Learner Corpus: www.cambridge.org/elt/corpus/learner_corpus.htm

Canale, M (1981) Communication: How to evaluate it? *Bulletin of the Canadian Association of Applied Linguistics* 3 (2), 77–94.

Canale, M (1983) From communicative competence to communicative language pedagogy, in Richards, J and Schmidt, R (Eds) *Language and communication*, London and New York: Longman, 2–27.

Canale, M and Swain, M (1980) Theoretical Bases of Communicative Approaches to Second Language Teaching and Testing, *Applied Linguistics* 1 (1), 1–47.

Carlson, J G, Bridgeman, B, Camp, R and Waanders, J (1985) *Relationship of admission test scores to writing performance of native and nonnative speakers of English*, TOEFL Report No. 19, Princeton, NJ: Educational Testing Service.

Carrell, P, Devine, J and Eskey, D E (Eds) (1988) *Interactive approaches to second language reading*, Cambridge: Cambridge University Press.

Carroll, B (1980) *Testing communicative performance*, Oxford: Pergamon.

Carson, J G (2000) Reading and writing for academic purposes, in Pally, M (Ed.) *Sustained content teaching in academic ESL/EFL*, 19–34.

Carter, R and McCarthy, M (2002) What constitutes a basic spoken vocabulary? *Research Notes* 13, 5–7.

Chadwick, S and Bruce, N (1989) The revision process in academic writing: From pen and paper to word processor, *Hong Kong Papers in Linguistics and Language Teaching* 12, 1–27.

Chapelle, C and Douglas, D (1993) Foundations and directions for a new decade of language testing, in Douglas, D and Chapelle, C (Eds) *A New Decade of Language Testing Research*, Arlington, VA: TESOL publications, 1–22.

Chapelle, C A, Enright, M K and Jamieson, J (2004) *Issues in developing a TOEFL validity argument*, draft paper presented at the Language Testing Research Colloquium, Temecula, California, March 2004.

Charney, D A (1984) The validity of using holistic scoring to evaluate writing: A critical overview, *Research in the Testing of English* 18 (1), 65–81.

Chase, C I (1986) Essay test scoring: Interaction of relevant variables, *Journal of Educational Measurement* 23 (1), 33–42.

Chen, Z and Henning, G (1985) Linguistic and cultural bias in language proficiency tests. *Language Testing* 2 (2), 155–63.

Cheng, L (1997) *The washback effect of public examination change on classroom teaching: An impact study of the 1996 Hong Kong Certificate of Education in English on the classroom teaching of English in Hong Kong secondary schools*, unpublished PhD thesis, University of Hong Kong.

Cheng, L (2005) *Changing Language Teaching Through Language Testing: A washback study*, Studies in Language Testing 21, Cambridge: UCLES/Cambridge University Press.

Cheng, L and Watanabe, Y (Eds) (2004) *Context and Method in Washback Research: The influence of language testing on teaching and learning*, Mahwah, NJ: Lawrence Erlbaum Associates.

Chou, F, Kirkland, J S and Smith, L R (1982) Variables in College Composition (Eric Document Reproduction Service No. 224017).

Clapham, C (1996) *The development of IELTS: A study in the effect of background knowledge on reading comprehension*, Studies in Language Testing 4, Cambridge: UCLES/Cambridge University Press.

Cochran-Smith, M (1991) Word processing and writing in elementary classrooms: A critical review of related literature, *Review of Educational Research* 61 (1), 107–55.

Cohen, A (1994) *Assessing Language Ability in the Classroom* (2nd Edition), Boston, MA: Heinle and Heinle.

Cooper, C R (1977) Holistic evaluation of writing, in Cooper, C R and Odell, L (Eds.) *Evaluating Writing: Describing, Measuring, Judging*, Urbana, IL: The National Council of Teachers of English, 3–31.

Cooper, R L (1986) An elaborated language testing model, *Language Learning*, Special Issue (3), 57–72.

Council of Europe (2001) *Common European Framework of Reference for Languages: Learning, teaching, assessment*, Cambridge: Cambridge University Press.

Coxhead, A (2000) A new academic word list, *TESOL Quarterly* 34 (2), 213–38.

Criper, C and Davies, A (1988) *ELTS validation project report*, ELTS Research Report 1(i), Hertford, UK: The British Council/UCLES.

Cronbach, L J (1971) Test Validation, in Thorndyke, R L (Ed.) *Educational Measurement* (2nd edition), American Council on Education: Washington, DC, 223–507.

Crystal, D (1996) *A Dictionary of Linguistics and Phonetics* (3rd Edition), Oxford: Blackwell.

Cumming, A (1998) *An investigation into raters' decision making, and development of a preliminary analytic framework, for scoring TOEFL essays and TOEFL 2000 prototype writing tasks*, Princeton, NJ: Educational Testing Service.

Dalton, D and Hannafin, M (1987) The effects of word processing on written composition, *Journal of Educational Research* 50 (6), 223–28.

Daiute, C (1985) *Writing and computers*, Reading, MA: Addison-Wesley.

Davies, A (1990) *Principles of Language Testing*, Oxford: Blackwell.

Davies, A (forthcoming) Assessing Academic English: Testing English proficiency 1950–2005 – the IELTS solution, *Studies in Language Testing* 23, Cambridge: Cambridge University Press/UCLES.

Davies, A, Brown, A, Elder, C, Hill, K, Lumley, T and McNamara, T (1999) *Dictionary of Language Testing*, Studies in Language Testing 7, Cambridge: Cambridge University Press/UCLES.

de Jong, J H A L and Stoyanova, F (1994) *Theory building: sample size and data-model fit*, paper presented at the 16th annual Language Testing Research Colloquium, Washington DC, March 1994.

DeLoughry, T J (1995) Duke professor pushes concept of grading essays by computer, *Chronicle of Higher Education*, A24–25, 20/10/1995.

De Mauro, G (1992) *An investigation of the appropriateness of the TOEFL test as a matching variable to equate TWE topics*, TOEFL Research Report 37, Princeton, NJ: Educational Testing Service.

Diederich, P B (1974) *Measuring Growth in English*, Urbana, Il: The National Council of Teachers of English.

Diederich, P B, French, J W and Carlton, S T (1961) Factors in Judgements of Writing quality, *Research Bulletin* 61–15, Princeton, NJ: Educational Testing Service.

Douglas, D (2000) *Assessing language for specific purposes: theory and practice*, Cambridge: Cambridge University Press.

Douglas, D and Chapelle, C (Eds) (1993) *A New Decade of Language Testing Research: Selected Papers from the Annual Language Testing Research Colloquium, March 1990*, Alexandria, VA: TESOL.

Dudley-Evans, T (1988) A consideration of the meaning of the word 'discuss' in examination questions, in Robinson, P (Ed.) *Academic Writing: Process and product*, Oxford: Modern English Publications, in association with the British Council.

Duran, P, Malvern, D, Richards, B and Chipere, N (2004) Developmental trends in lexical diversity, *Applied Linguistics* 25 (2), 220–42.

Ede, L and Lunsford, A (1984) Audience addressed/audience invoked: The role of audience in composition theory and pedagogy, *College Composition and Communication* 35 (2), 155–71.

Edgeworth, F Y (1888) The statistics of examinations, *Journal of the Royal Statistical Society* 51, 599–635.

Edgeworth, F Y (1890) The element of chance in competitive examinations, *Journal of the Royal Statistical Society* 53, 460–75 and 644–63.

Educational Testing Service (2002) ETS Standards for quality and fairness. Princeton, NJ: ETS.

Eignor, D, Taylor, C, Kirsch, I and Jamieson, J (1998) *Development of a Scale for Assessing the Level of Computer Familiarity of TOEFL Examinees*, TOEFL Research Report 60, Princeton, NJ: Educational Testing Service.

Elder, C (1992) How do subject specialists construe Second Language Proficiency? *Melbourne Papers in Language Testing* 1 (1), 17–33.

Elder, C (1993) How do subject specialists construe classroom language proficiency? *Language Testing* 10 (3), 235–54.

Ellis, R and Yuan, F (2004) The Effects of Planning on Fluency, Complexity, and Accuracy in Second Language Narrative Writing, *Studies in Second Language Acquisition* 26 (1), 59–84.

Emig, J (1971) *The Composing Process of Twelfth Graders*, Urbana, Il: National Council of Teachers of English.

Esmaeili, H (2002) Integrated reading and writing tasks and ESL students' reading and writing performance in an English language test, *The Canadian Modern Language Review* 58 (4), 599–622.

Eysenck, M and Keane, M (2005) *Cognitive Psychology* (5th edition), Hove: Psychology Press.

Falvey, P and Shaw, S D (2005) IELTS Writing: revising assessment criteria and scales (Phase 5), *Research Notes* 23, 7–12.

Field, J (2004) *Psycholinguistics: the Key Concepts*, London: Routledge.

Field, J (2005) *Second language writing: a language problem or a writing problem?* Paper presented at IATEFL Research SIG 'Writing Revisited' conference, Cambridge, 25–27 February 2005.

Fitzpatrick, R and Morrison, E. J (1971) Performance and product evaluation, in Thorndyke, R L (Ed.) *Educational Measurement* (2nd edition), American Council on Education, Washington DC (237–70), reprinted in Finch, F L (Ed.) 1991 *Educational performance assessment*, Chicago: The Riverside Publishing Company (89–138).

Francis, J C (1977) *Impression and analytic marking methods*, unpublished paper, Aldershot: Associated Examining Board.

Francis, W N and Kucera, H (1979) *Manual of information to accompany a standard corpus of present-day edited American English*, for use with digital computers, Technical report, (revised edition), Providence, Rhode Island: Department of Linguistics, Brown University.

Freedman, S W (1979) Why do teachers give the grades they do? *College Composition* 30 (2), 365–87.

Freedman S W (1981) Influences on evaluators of expository essays: beyond the text, *Research in the Teaching of English* 15 (3), 245–55.

Fulcher, G (1987) Tests of oral performance: the need for data-based criteria, *English Language Teaching Journal* 41 (4), 287–91.

Fulcher, G (1996) Does thick description lead to smart tests? A data-based approach to rating scale construction, *Language Testing* 13 (2).

Fulcher, G (2003) *Testing Second Language Speaking*, Harlow: Pearson.

Furneaux, C and Rignall, M (2000) *The effect of standardisation-training on rater-judgements for the IELTS Writing Module*, British Council internal report.

Gere, A R (1980) Written composition: Toward a theory of evaluation, *College English* 42 (1), 44–48.

Goulden, R, Nation, P and Read, J (1990) How large can a receptive vocabulary be? *Applied Linguistics* 11 (4), 341–63.

Grabe, W and Kaplan, R B (1996) *Theory and Practice of Writing: An applied linguistic perspective*, London: Longman.

Grabe, W and Stoller F L (2002) *Teaching and Researching Reading*, Harlow: Pearson Education Ltd.

Granger, S (2004) Computer learner corpus research: current status and future prospects, in Connor, U and Upton, T A (Eds) *Applied Corpus Linguistics: A multidimensional perspective*, Amsterdam and Atlanta: Rodopi, 123–45.

Green, A (2003) *Test Impact and EAP: a comparative study in backwash between IELTS preparation and university pre-sessional courses*, unpublished PhD thesis, University of Surrey at Roehampton.

Green, A (2005) *Composing and scoring CB scripts: Analysis of CB-IELTS Trial A and B Writing data*, Cambridge: UCLES internal report.

Green, A and Maycock, L (2004) Computer-based IELTS and paper-based versions of IELTS, *Research Notes* 18, 3–6.

Grobe, C (1981) Syntactic maturity, mechanics and vocabulary as predictors of quality ratings, *Research in the Teaching of English* 15 (1), 75–86.

Gutteridge, M (2003) *Dyslexia and ESOL Candidates*, Cambridge: UCLES internal report.

Haas, C (1989) How the writing medium shapes the writing process: Effects of word processing on planning, *Research in the Teaching of English* 23 (2), 181–207.

Haas, C and Hayes, JR (1986) What did I just say? Reading problems in writing with the machine, *Research in the Teaching of English* 20, 22–35.

Hale, G, Taylor, C, Bridgeman, B, Carson, J, Kroll, B and Kantor, R (1996) *A Study of Writing Tasks Assigned in Academic Degree Programs*, Princeton, NJ: Educational Testing Service.

Hamp-Lyons, L (1986) *Testing second language writing in academic settings*, unpublished doctoral dissertation, University of Edinburgh.

Hamp-Lyons, L (1990) Second Language Writing: Assessment issues, in Kroll, B (Ed.) *Second Language Writing: Research Insights for the Classroom*, Cambridge: Cambridge University Press, 69–87.

Hamp-Lyons, L (1991) What is a 'Writing Test'? in Hamp-Lyons, L (Ed.) *Assessing Second Language Writing in Academic Contexts*, Norwood, NJ: Ablex Publishing Corporation, 241–76.

Hamp-Lyons, L (1991a) Reconstructing 'Academic Writing Proficiency', in Hamp-Lyons, L (Ed.) *Assessing Second Language Writing in Academic Contexts*, Norwood, NJ: Ablex Publishing Corporation, 127–53.

Hamp-Lyons, L (1995) *Summary Report on Writing Meta-Scale Project*, Cambridge: UCLES internal report.

Hamp-Lyons, L (1996) The challenge of second-language writing assessment, in White, E M, Lutz, W D and Kamusikiri, S (Eds) *Assessment of Writing: Politics, Policies, Practices*, New York: Modern Language Association of America, 226–40.

Hamp-Lyons, L (2000) Social, professional and individual responsibility in language testing, *System* 28 (4), 579–91.

Hamp-Lyons, L (2002) The scope of writing assessment, *Assessing Writing* 8 (1), 5–16.

Hamp-Lyons, L and Kroll, B (1997) *TOEFL 2000 – Writing: Composition, Community, and Assessment*, TOEFL Monograph 5, Princeton: Educational Testing Service.

Hamp-Lyons, L and Mathias, S (1994) Examining expert judgments of task difficulty on essay tests, *Journal of Second Language Writing* 3 (1), 49–68.

Hamp-Lyons, L and Prochnow, S (1991) Difficulties in Setting Writing Assessments, *Language Reporter* 6.

Hargreaves, P (2000) How Important Is Collocation in Testing the Learner's Language Proficiency? in Lewis, M (Ed.) *Teaching Collocation – further developments in the Lexical Approach*, Hove: Language Teaching Publications, 205–23.

Hasselgren, A (1997) Oral test subskill scores: what they tell us about raters and pupils, in Huhta, A, Kohonen, V, Kurki-Suonio, L and Luoma, S (Eds) *Current Developments and Alternatives in Language Assessment*, Jyväskylä: University of Jyväskylä and University of Tampere, 241–56.

Hawkey, R (2001) *IIS Student Questionnaire*, Cambridge: UCLES internal paper.

Hawkey, R (2004) *CPE Textbook: Washback Study*, Cambridge: UCLES internal paper.

Hawkey, R (2004a) An IELTS Impact Study: implementation and some early findings, *Research Notes* 15, 12–16.

Hawkey, R (2004b) *A Modular Approach to Testing English Language Skills: The development of the Certificates in English Language Skills (CELS) examinations*, Studies in Language Testing 16, Cambridge: UCLES/Cambridge University Press.

Hawkey, R (2006) *Impact Theory and Practice: Studies of the IELTS test and Progetto Lingue 2000*, Studies in Language Testing 24, Cambridge: UCLES/Cambridge University Press.

Hawkey, R and Barker, F (2004) Developing a Common Scale for the Assessment of Writing, *Assessing Writing* 9 (2), 122–59.

Hawkey, R and Shaw, S D (2005) The Common Scale for Writing Project: implications for the comparison of IELTS band scores and Main Suite exam levels, *Research Notes* 19, 19–24.

Hayes, J R (1996) A new framework for understanding cognition and affect in writing, in Levy, C M and Ransdell, S (Eds) *The Science of Writing*, Mahwah, NJ: Lawrence Erlbaum Associates, 1–28.

Hayes, J R and Flower, L S (1980) Identifying the organisation of writing processes, in Gregg, L W and Steinberg, E R (Eds) *Cognitive processes in writing*, Hillsdale, NJ: Lawrence Erlbaum Associates, 3–30.

Hayes, J R and Flower, L S (1986) Writing research and the writer, *American Psychologist* 41 (10), 1106–13.

Henning, G (1991) Issues in Evaluating and Maintaining an ESL Writing Assessment Program, in Hamp-Lyons, L (Ed.) *Assessing Second Language Writing in Academic Contexts*, Norwood, NJ: Ablex Publishing Corporation, 273–91.

Herrington, R (1996) *Test-taking strategies and second language proficiency: Is there a relationship?* unpublished MA dissertation, Lancaster University.

Hill, K (1998) The effect of test taker characteristics on reactions to and performances on an oral English proficiency test, in Kunnan, A *Validation in Language Assessment: Selected papers from the 17th Language Testing Research Colloquium*, Mahwah, NJ: Lawrence Erlbaum, 209–30.

Hindmarsh, R (1980) *Cambridge English Lexicon*, Cambridge: Cambridge University Press.

Hinkel, E (1994) Native and nonnative speakers' pragmatic interpretations of English texts, *TESOL Quarterly* 28 (2), 353–76.

Hoetker, J (1982) Essay examination topics and students' writing, *College Composition and Communication* 33 (4), 377–92.

Hoetker, J and Brossell, G (1989) The effects of systematic variations in essay topics on the writing performance of college freshmen, *College Composition and Communication* 40 (4), 414–21.

Horak, T (1996) *IELTS Impact Study Project*, unpublished MA assignment, Lancaster University.

Horowitz, D (1986) Essay examination prompts and the teaching of academic writing, *English for Specific Purposes* 5 (2), 107–20.

Horowitz, D (1991) ESL writing assessments: Contradictions and resolutions, in Hamp-Lyons, L (Ed.) *Assessing Second Language Writing in Academic Contexts*, Norwood, NJ: Ablex Publishing Corporation, 71–85.

Hughes, A (1989) *Testing for Language Teachers*, Cambridge: Cambridge University Press.

Hughes, A (2003) *Testing for Language Teachers* (2nd edition), Cambridge: Cambridge University Press.

Hughes, D C, Keeling, B and Tuck, B F (1983) Effects of achievement expectations and handwriting quality on scoring essays, *Journal of Educational Measurement* 20 (1), 65–70.

Huhta, A, Kohonen, V, Kurki-Suonio, L and Luoma, S (Eds) (1997) *Current Developments and Alternatives in Language Assessment*, Jyvaskla: University of Jyvaskla and University of Tampere Finland.

Hult, C (1986) *The computer and the inexperienced writer*, paper presented at the Annual Meeting of the Conference on College Composition and Communication, New Orleans.

Huot, B (1990) Reliability, Validity and Holistic Scoring: What we know and what we need to know, *College Composition and Communication* 41 (2), 201–13.

Huot, B (1993) The Literature of Direct Writing Assessment: Major Concerns and Prevailing Trends, *Review of Educational Research* 60 (2), 237–63.

Huot, B (1996) Toward a new theory of writing assessment, *College Composition and Communication* 47 (4), 549–66.

Hyland, K (2002) *Teaching and Researching Writing*, Applied Linguistics in Action Series, London: Longman.

Hymes, D (1972) On communicative competence, in Pride, J and Holmes, J (Eds) *Sociolinguistics*, Harmsworth and New York: Penguin, 269–93.

Jacobs, H L, Zinkgraf, D R, Wormuth, V F, Hartfiel, V F and Hughey, J B (1981) *Testing ESL Composition: A Practical Approach*, Rowley, MA: Newbury House.

Jakobson, R (1960) Linguistics and Poetics, in Seboek, T A (Ed.) *Style in Language*, New York: John Wiley, 350–77.

Jones, N (2000) Background to the validation of the ALTE Can Do Project and the revised Common European Framework, *Research Notes* 2, 11–13.

Jones, N (2000a) BULATS: A case study comparing computer based and paper-and-pencil tests, *Research Notes* 3, 10–13.

Jones, N (2001) The ALTE Can Do Project and the role of measurement in constructing a proficiency framework, *Research Notes* 5, 5–8.

Jones, N (2002) Relating the ALTE Framework to the Common European Framework of Reference, in Council of Europe (Eds) *Case Studies on theUse of the Common European Framework of Reference*, Cambridge: Cambridge University Press, 167–83.

Jones, N (2002a) *Examiner scaling for Writing: Minimum number for scaling*, Cambridge: UCLES internal report.

Jones, N and Hirtzel, M (2001) The ALTE 'Can Do' statements, Appendix D, in Council of Europe, *Common European Framework of Reference for Languages: Learning, teaching, assessment*, Cambridge: Cambridge University Press. (Also downloadable from www.coe.int/T/DG4/Linguistic/Source/Framework_EN.pdf)

Jones, N and Shaw S D (2003) *Writing Examiner Behaviour in Response to Team Leader Feedback: a scrutiny of Batch Monitoring Forms and associated data*, Cambridge: UCLES internal report.

Jones, S and Tetro, J (1987) Composing in a second language, in Matsuhashi, A (Ed.), *Writing in real time: Modelling production processes*, Norwood, NJ: Ablex Publishing Corporation, 34–57.

Kane, M T (1992) An argument-based approach to validity, *Psychological Bulletin* 112 (3), 527–35.

Keddle, J S (2004) The CEF and the secondary school syllabus, in Morrow, K (Ed.) *Insights from the Common European Framework*, Oxford: Oxford University Press, 43–54.

Kellogg, R T (1994) *The Psychology of Writing*, New York: Oxford University Press.

Kellogg, R T (1996) A model of working memory in writing, in Levy, C M and Ransdell, S (Eds) *The Science of Writing*, Mahwah, NJ: Lawrence Erlbaum, 57–72.

Kerchner, L B and Kistinger, B J (1984) Language processing/word processing: Written expression, computers, and learning disabled students, *Learning Disability Quarterly* 7 (4), 329–35.

Khalifa, H (2003) *Student Achievement Test Development Manual*, (SATD), Egypt: United States Agency for International Development.

Kirsch, I, Jamieson, J, Taylor, C, and Eignor, D (1998) *Computer familiarity among TOEFL examinees*, TOEFL Research Report 59, Princeton, NJ: Educational Testing Service.

Kobayashi, H and Rinnert, C (1996) Factors affecting composition evaluation in an EFL context: Cultural rhetorical pattern and readers' background, *Language Learning* 46 (3), 397–437.

Krapels, A R (1990) An overview of second language writing process research, in Kroll, B (Ed.) *Second language writing: Researching insights for the classroom*, New York: Cambridge University Press, 37–56.

Kroll, B (1990) What does time buy? ESL student performance on home versus class compositions, in Kroll, B (Ed.) *Second language writing: Research insights for the classroom*, New York: Cambridge University Press, 140–154.

Kunnan, A J (1990) DIF in native language and gender groups in an ESL Placement test, *TESOL Quarterly* 24 (4), 740–46.

Kunnan, A J (1994) Modelling relationships among some test-taker characteristics and performance on EFL tests: An approach to construct validation, *Language Testing* 11 (3), 225–52.

Kunnan, A J (1995) *Test taker characteristics and test performance: A structural modelling approach*, Studies in Language Testing 2, Cambridge: UCLES and Cambridge University Press.

Lam, F S and Pennington, M C (1995) The computer vs. the pen: A comparative study of word processing in a Hong Kong secondary classroom, *Computer Assisted Language Learning*, 8 (1), 75–92.

Land, R E and Whiteley, C (1989) Evaluating second language essays in regular composition classes: Towards a pluralistic U.S. rhetoric, in Johnson, D M and

Roen, D H (Eds) *Richness in writing: Empowering ESL students*, New York: Longman, 284–93.

Landauer, T K, Laham, D and Foltz, P (2003) Automatic Essay Assessment, *Assessment in Education* 10 (3), November 2003.

Larkey, L S (1998) Automatic essay grading using text categorization techniques, in *Proceedings of the Twenty First Annual International ACM SIGIR Conference on Research and Development in Information Retrieval, Melbourne, Australia*, New York: ACM Press, 90–5.

Laufer, B (1997). What's in a word that makes it hard or easy: some intralexical factors that affect the learning of words, in Schmitt, N and McCarthy, M (Eds) *Vocabulary: Description, acquisition, and pedagogy*, Cambridge: Cambridge University Press, 140–55.

Laufer, B (1998) The development of passive and active vocabulary in a second language: same or different? *Applied Linguistics* 19 (2), 255–71.

Laufer, B and Nation, P (1995) Vocabulary size and use: Lexical richness in L2 written production, *Applied Linguistics* 16 (3), 307–22.

Lebus, S (2005) Internal ESM communications meeting, Cambridge: Cambridge Assessment.

Leech, G, Rayson, P, and Wilson, A (2001) *Word Frequencies in Written and Spoken English: based on the British National Corpus*, London: Longman.

Levelt, W J M (1989) *Speaking: From intention to articulation*, Cambridge, MA: MIT Press.

Lewkowicz, J (1997) *Investigating authenticity in language testing*, unpublished PhD dissertation, University of Lancaster.

Li, J and Cumming, A (2001) Word processing and second language writing: A longitudinal case study, *International Journal of English Studies* 1 (2), 127–52.

Lieberman, A (2000) Networks as Learning Communities – Shaping the Future of Teacher Development, *Journal of Teacher Education* 51 (3), 221–27.

Little, D, Lazenby Simpson, B and O'Connor, F (2002) Meeting the English language needs of refugees in Ireland, in *Council of Europe 2002*, 53–67.

Lowe, P (1988) The unassimilated history, in Lowe, P and Stansfield, C W (Eds.) *Second language proficiency assessment: current issues*, Englewood Cliffs NJ: Prentice Hall Regents, 11–51.

Lumley, T (2000) *The process of the assessment of writing performance: the rater's perspective*, unpublished PhD dissertation, Department of Linguistics and Applied Linguistics, The University of Melbourne.

Lumley, T and McNamara, T F (1995) Rater characteristics and rater bias: implications for training, *Language Testing* 12 (1), 54–71.

Lumley, T and O'Sullivan, B (2000) *The effect of speaker and topic variables on task performance in a tape-mediated assessment of speaking*, paper presented at the 2nd Annual Asian Language Assessment Research Forum, The Hong Kong Polytechnic University, January 2000.

Lunz, M E and O'Neill, T R (1997) *A longitudinal study of judge leniency and consistency*, paper presented at the Annual Meeting of the American Educational Research Association, Chicago, Illinois.

Lunz, M E, Wright, B D and Linacre, J M (1990) Measuring the impact of judge severity on examination scores, *Applied Measurement in Education* 3 (4), 331–45.

Luoma, S (2004) *Assessing Speaking*, Cambridge: Cambridge University Press.

MacArthur, A C (1988) The impact of computers on the writing process, *Exceptional Children*, 54 (6), 536–42.

Madsen, H S (1982) Determining the debilitative impact of test anxiety, *Language Learning* 32 (1), 133–43.

Marcu, D (2000) *The Theory and Practice of Discourse Parsing and Summarization*, Cambridge, MA: MIT Press.

Markham, L R (1976) Influences of handwriting quality on teacher evaluation of written work, *American Educational Research Journal* 13 (4), 277–83.

Marsh, H W and Ireland, R (1987) The assessment of writing effectiveness: A multidimensional perspective, *Australian Journal of Psychology* 39, 353–67.

Marshall, H (2006) The Cambridge ESOL Item Banking System, *Research Notes* 23, 3–5.

Marshall, J C and Powers, J C (1969) Writing neatness, composition errors, and essay grades, *Journal of Educational Measurement* 6 (2), 97–101.

Massey, A and Foulkes, J (1994) Audit of the 1993 KS3 Science national test pilot and the concept of quasi-reconciliation, *Evaluation and Research in Education* 8 (3), 119–132.

Maughan, S (2001) *On-line Teacher Support: A Teachers' Perspective*, Cambridge: Cambridge International Examinations, UCLES internal report.

Maycock, L (2004) *An Investigation into the Effects of Computer Familiarity and Attitudes Towards CBIELTS on Candidate Performance*, Cambridge: UCLES internal report.

Maycock, L (2004a) *CBIELTS: A Report on the Findings of Trial A (Live Trial 2003/4)*, Cambridge: UCLES internal report.

Maycock, L (2004b) *CBIELTS: A Report on the Findings of Trial B (Live Trial 2003/4)*, Cambridge: UCLES internal report.

Maycock, L and Green A (2005) *A Study of Candidate Reactions to Taking PET on Computer: Analysis of February 2005 Equivalence Trialling Questionnaires*, Cambridge: UCLES internal report.

McDonald, A (2002) The impact of individual differences on the equivalence of computer-based and paper-and-pencil educational assessments, *Computers and Education* 39 (3), 299–312.

McGarrell, H M (1993) *Perceived and actual impact of computer use in second language writing classes*, paper presented at the Congress of the Association Internationale de Linguistique Appliquee (AILA), Frije University, Amsterdam, August 1993.

McGuire, D W (1995) *A comparison of scores on the Kansas writing assessment for word processed and hand-written papers of eleventh graders*, Dissertation Abstracts International, A: The Humanities and Social Sciences; 1996, 56, 9.

McNamara, T F (1996) *Measuring Second Language Performance*, London: Longman.

McNamara, T F (2000) *Language Testing*, Oxford: Oxford University Press.

Mehnert, U (1998) The effects of different lengths of time for planning on second language performance, *Studies in Second Language Acquisition* 20 (1), 83–108.

Melka, F (1997) Receptive vs. productive aspects of vocabulary, in Schmitt, N and McCarthy, M (Eds) *Vocabulary: Description, Acquisition and Pedagogy*, Cambridge: Cambridge University Press, 84–102.

Messick, S A (1989) Validity, in Linn, R L (Ed.) *Educational Measurement* (3rd edition), New York: Macmillan, 13–103.

Messick, S A (1994) The interplay of evidence and consequences in the validation of performance assessments, *Educational Researcher* 23 (2), 13–23.

Milanovic, M and Saville, N (1994) *An Investigation of Marking Strategies using*

Verbal Protocols, Cambridge: University of Cambridge Local Examination Syndicate.

Milanovic, M and Saville, N (1996) *Considering the impact of Cambridge EFL examinations*, Cambridge: UCLES internal report.

Milanovic, M, Saville, N, Pollitt, A and Cook, A (1996) Developing Rating Scales for CASE: Theoretical Concerns and Analyses, in Cumming, A and Berwick, R (Eds) *Validation in Language Testing*, Clevedon: Multilingual Matters Ltd, 15–38.

Milanovic, M, Saville, N and Shuhong, S (1996) A Study of the Decision-making Behaviour of Composition markers, in Milanovic, M and Saville, N (Eds) *Performance Testing, Cognition and Assessment: Selected Papers from the 15th Language Testing Research Colloquium and Arnhem*, Studies in Language Testing 3, Cambridge: UCLES/Cambridge University Press, 92–114.

Mislevy R J, Steinberg, L S and Almond, R G (2002) Design and analysis in task-based language assessment, *Language Testing* 19 (4) 477–96.

Mislevy R J, Steinberg, L S and Almond, R G (2003) On the structure of educational assessments, *Measurement: Interdisciplinary Research and Perspectives* 1 (1), 3–62.

Miller, T (2003) *Essay Assessment with Latent Semantic Analysis*, German Research Centre for Artificial Intelligence, downloaded from www.dfki.uni-kl.de/~miller/publications/miller03a.pdf on 9 February 2006.

Mitchell, J S (1998) Commentary: SATs don't get you in, *Education Week on the Web*: www.edweek.org/ew/current/3mitch.h17

Mitchell, T, Russell, T, Broomhead, P and Aldridge, N (2002) Towards robust computerised marking of free-text responses, in *Proceedings of 6th International Computer Aided Assessment Conference, Loughborough*, 233–49.

Moore, T and Morton, J (1999) Authenticity in the IELTS Academic Module Writing Test: A comparative study of Task 2 items and university assignments, in Tulloh, R (Ed.) *IELTS Research Reports* Vol. 2, Australia: IELTS Australia Pty Ltd, 64–106.

Morrow, K (1979) Communicative Language testing: revolution or evolution? in Brumfit, C and Johnson, K (Eds) *The communicative approach to language teaching*, Oxford: Oxford University Press, 143–57.

Morrow, K (Ed.) (2004) *Insights from the Common European Framework*, Oxford: Oxford University Press.

Nation, I S P (2001) *Learning vocabulary in another language*, Cambridge: Cambridge University Press.

Newstead, S and Dennis, I (1994) The reliability of exam marking in psychology: Examiners examined, *The Psychologist*, May, 216–19.

Nicholls, D (2003) The Cambridge Learner Corpus – error coding and analysis for lexicography and ELT, in Archer, D, Rayson, P, Wilson, A and McEnery, T (Eds) *Proceedings of the Corpus Linguistics 2003 Conference*, UCREL technical paper number 16, Lancaster University: UCREL.

North, B (2000) *The Development of a Common Framework Scale of Language Proficiency*, New York: Peter Lang.

North, B (2002) A CEF-based self assessment tool for university entrance, in *Common European Framework of Reference for Languages: Learning, Teaching, Assessment*, Council of Europe, 146–66.

North, B (2004) Relating assessments, examinations, and courses to the CEF, in Morrow, K *Insights from the Common European Framework*, Oxford: Oxford University Press, 77–90.

Nystrand, M (1989) A social interactive model of writing, *Written Communication* 6 (1), 66–85.

O'Dell, F (2005) *Structural resources in Main Suite examinations*, Cambridge: UCLES internal report.

O'Dell, F (2005a) *Functional resources in Main Suite examinations*, Cambridge: UCLES internal report.

Odell, L (1981) Defining and Assessing Competence in Writing, in Cooper, C R (Ed.) *The Nature and Measurement of Competency in English*, Urbana, IL: National Council of Teachers of English, 95–138.

Odell, L and Cooper, C (1980) Procedures for evaluating writing: assumptions and needed research, *College English* 42 (1), 35–43.

Oltman, P K, Stricker, L J and Barrows, T (1988) *Native Language, English Proficiency and the Structure of the Test of English as a Foreign Language*, TOEFL Research Reports 27, Princeton, NJ: Educational Testing Service.

O'Loughlin, K (1992) The Assessment of Writing by English and ESL Teachers, unpublished MA thesis, The University of Melbourne.

Orr, L and Nuttall, D (London: Schools Council), (1983) *Determining Standards in the Proposed Single System of Examining at 16+*, Comparability in Examinations Occasional Paper 2, London: Schools Council.

O'Sullivan, B (2000) *Towards a Model of Performance in Oral Language Testing*, unpublished PhD Dissertation, University of Reading.

O'Sullivan, B (2006) *Issues in Testing Business English: The revision of the Cambridge Business English Certificates*, Studies in Language Testing 17, Cambridge: UCLES/Cambridge University Press.

O'Sullivan, B and Green, A (forthcoming) Test-taker characteristics, in Taylor, L (Ed.) *Examining Second Language Speaking: Research and practice*, Studies in Language Testing, Cambridge: UCLES/Cambridge University Press.

O'Sullivan, B and Porter, D (1995) *The importance of audience age for learner-speakers and learner-writers from different cultural backgrounds*, paper presented at the RELC conference, Singapore.

O'Sullivan, B and Rignall, M (2002) *Effect on rater performance of systematic feedback during the rating procedure – the IELTS General Training Writing Module*, UCLES/The British Council/ IDP Australia: IELTS Research Report.

O'Sullivan, B, Weir, C, and Saville, N (2002), Using observation checklists to validate speaking-test tasks, *Language Testing* 19 (1), 33–56.

Page, E B (1966) The imminence of grading essays by computer, *Phi Delta Kappan* 47 238–43.

Page, E B (1994) Computer grading of student prose, using modern concepts and software, *Journal of Experimental Education* 62 (2), 127–42.

Palmer, D and Raikes, N (2000) *ESM Pilot Study: Research Specification*, ITAL/CIE: UCLES internal report.

Papajohn, D (1999) The effect of topic variation in performance testing: the case of the chemistry TEACH test for international teaching assistants, *Language Testing* 16 (1), 52–81.

Park, D (1988) The meanings of 'audience', *College English* 44 (3), 247–57.

Pearson, I (1988) Tests as levers for change, in Chamberlain, D and Baumgartner, R (Eds) *ESP in the Classroom: Practice and Evaluation*, ELT Documents 128, London: Modern English Publications.

Pennington, M C (1996) The power of the computer in language education, in Pennington, M C (Ed.) *The power of CALL*, Houston: Athelstan, 1–14.

Pennington, M C (1999) The missing link in computer-assisted writing, in Cameron, K (Ed) *CALL: Media, design, and applications* (271–92). Lisse: Swets and Zeitlinger.

Pennington, M C and Brock, M N (1992) Process and product approaches to computer-assisted composition, in Pennington, M C and Stevens, V (Eds) *Computers in Applied Linguistics: An international perspective*, Clevedon, UK: Multilingual Matters, 79–109.

Perkins, K (1983) On the use of composition scoring techniques, objective measures, and objective tests to evaluate ESL writing ability, *TESOL Quarterly* 17 (4), 651–71.

Phinney, M (1989) Computers, composition, and second language teaching, in Pennington, M C (Ed.) *Teaching languages with computers: The state of the art*, La Jolla, CA: Athelstan, 81–96.

Phinney, M and Khouri, S (1993) Computers, revision, and ESL writers: The role of experience, *Journal of Second Language Writing* 2 (3), 257–77.

Phoenix, J and Hannan, E (1984) Word processing in the grade 1 classroom, *Language Arts*, 61 (8), 804–12.

Pienemann, M (1998) *Language Processing in Second Language Acquisition: Processability theory*, Amsterdam: John Benjamins.

Polio, C and Glew, M (1996) ESL Writing assessment prompts: How students choose, *Journal of Second Language Writing* 5 (1), 35–49.

Pollitt, A and Murray, N L (1996) What raters really pay attention to, in Milanovic, M and Saville, N (Eds) *Performance Testing, Cognition and Assessment*, Studies in Language Testing 3, Cambridge: UCLES/Cambridge University Press.

Porter, R (1986) Writing and word processing in year one, *Australian Educational Computing* 1 (1), 18–23.

Powers, D E, Fowles, M E (1996) Effects of applying different time limits to a proposed GRE writing test, *Journal of Educational Measurement*, 33 (4) 433–52.

Powers, D E, Fowles, M E, Farnum, M and Ramsey, P (1994) Will they think less of my handwritten essay if others words process theirs? Effects on essay scores of intermingling handwritten and word-processed essays, *Journal of Educational Measurement* 31 (3), 220–33.

Purpura, J (1999) *Learner Strategy Use and Performance on Language Tests*, Cambridge: Cambridge University Press.

Purves, A (1992) Reflection on research and assessment in written composition, *Research in the Teaching of English* 26 (1), 108–22.

Quellmalz, E S, Capell, F J and Chou, C P (1982) Effects of discourse and response mode on the assessment of writing competence, *Journal of Educational Measurement* 19 (4), 242–58.

Raforth, B A and Rubin, D L (1984) The impact of content and mechanics on judgements of writing quality, *Written Communication* 1 (4), 446–58.

Raikes, N (2006) An Evaluation of the Cambridge Assessment – Oxford University automatic marking system: Does it work? *Research Matters* 2, 17–21.

Raikes, N and Shaw, S D (2005) *ESM Marking Models and Quality Control*, Cambridge Assessment internal report.

Read, J (1990) Providing Relevant Content in an EAP Writing Test, *English for Specific Purposes* 9 (2), 109–21.

Read, J M (2000) *Assessing vocabulary*, Cambridge: Cambridge University Press.

Reid, G (2003) *Dyslexia in Different Languages: Review of the Literature*, Edinburgh: University of Edinburgh.

Richards, J C, Platt, J and Platt, H (1992) *Dictionary of Language Teaching and Applied Linguistics*, Harlow: Longman.

Roach, J (1945) *Some Problems of Oral Examinations in Modern Languages: An Experimental Approach Based on the Cambridge Examinations in English for Foreign Students*, Cambridge: UCLES internal report.

Russell, M (1999) Testing Writing on Computers: A Follow-up Study Comparing Performance on Computer and on Paper, *Educational Policy Analysis Archives* 7, 20.

Russell, M and Haney, W (1997) Testing writing on computers: an experiment comparing student performance on tests conducted via computer and via paper-and-pencil, *Education Policy Analysis Archives*, 5/3 http://olam.ed.asu. edu/epaa

Ruth, L and Murphy, S (1984) Designing topics for writing assessment: Problems of meaning, *College Composition* 35 (4), 410–21.

Ruth, L and Murphy, S (1988) *Designing writing tasks for the assessment of writing*, Norwood, NJ: Ablex Publishing Corporation.

Ryan, K and Bachman, K L (1992) DIF on two tests of EFL proficiency, *Language Testing* 9 (1), 2–29.

Salton, G (1989) *Automatic Text Processing: The Transformation, Analysis, and Retrieval of Information by Computer*, Reading, MA: Addison-Wesley.

Santos, T (1988) Professors' Reactions to the Academic Writing of Nonnative-Speaking Students, *TESOL Quarterly* 22 (1), 69–90.

Saville, N (2001) Investigating the impact of international language examinations, *Research Notes* 2, 4–7.

Saville, N (2003) The process of test development and revision within UCLES EFL, in Weir, C and Milanovic, M (Eds) *Continuity and Innovation: Revising the Cambridge Proficiency in English Examination 1913–2002*, Studies in Language Testing 15, Cambridge: UCLES/Cambridge University Press, 57–120.

Saville, N (2004) *The ESOL Test Development and Validation Strategy*, Cambridge: UCLES internal discussion paper.

Saville, N, Capel, A and Hamp-Lyons, L (1995) *Common Scale for Writing: Interim Project Report*, Cambridge: UCLES internal report.

Saville, N and Hawkey, R (2004) The IELTS Impact Study: Investigating washback on teaching materials, in Cheng, L, Watanabe, Y and Curtis, A (Eds) *Washback in Language Testing: Research contexts and methods*, Mahweh, NJ: Lawrence Erlbaum, 73–96.

Scardamalia, M and Bereiter, C (1987): Knowledge telling and knowledge transforming in written composition, in Rosenberg, S (Ed.) *Advances in Applied Psycholinguistics, Volume 2: Reading, writing and language learning*, Cambridge: Cambridge University Press, 142–75.

Schmitt, N (2005) *Lexical Resources in Main Suite examinations*, Cambridge: UCLES internal report.

Schmitt, N, Schmitt, D, and Clapham, C (2001) Developing and exploring the behaviour of two new versions of the Vocabulary Levels Test, *Language Testing* 18 (1), 55–88.

Schwartz, A E (1998) Graded by machine, *Washington Post* 26 April, 107.

Shaw, S D (2001) *The Effect of Standardisation Training on Rater Judgement and Inter-Rater Reliability (Revised CPE Writing Paper 2)*, Cambridge: UCLES internal report.

Shaw, S D (2002) *IELTS Writing Assessment: Towards revised assessment criteria and Band Descriptors: A quantitative and qualitative analysis of IELTS Writing examiner feedback*, Cambridge: UCLES internal report.

Shaw, S D (2002a) IELTS Writing: Revising assessment criteria and scales (Phase 1), *Research Notes* 9, 16–18.

Shaw, S D (2002b) IELTS Writing: Revising assessment criteria and scales (Phase 2), *Research Notes* 10, 10–13.

Shaw, S D (2002c) The effect of standardisation training on rater judgement and inter-rater reliability for the revised CPE writing paper 2, *Research Notes* 8, 13–17.

Shaw, S D (2003) *IELTS Writing Assessment Revision Project (Phase 3): Validating the Revised Rating Scale – A quantitative analysis*, Cambridge: UCLES internal report.

Shaw, S D (2003a) IELTS Writing: Revising assessment criteria and scales (Phase 3), *Research Notes* 16, 3–7.

Shaw, S D (2003b) Legibility and the rating of second language writing: The effect on examiners when assessing handwritten and word processed scripts, *Research Notes* 11, 7–10.

Shaw, S D (2003c) Electronic Script Management: Towards on-screen assessment of scanned paper scripts, *Research Notes* 12, 4–8.

Shaw, S D (2003d) *Writing Assessment Models: Writing Component Marking Procedures for Main Suite and Specialised Examinations (including Clerical Marking) August 2003*, Cambridge: UCLES internal manual.

Shaw, S D (2004) IELTS Writing: revising assessment criteria and scales (concluding Phase 2), *Research Notes* 15, 9–11.

Shaw, S D (2004a) *Approach to scaling under ESM: High Priority ESM Issue 3*, Cambridge: UCLES internal report.

Shaw, S D (2005) *IELTS Writing Assessment Revision Working Group: Summary of progress (June 2001–October 2005)*, Cambridge: UCLES internal report.

Shaw, S D (2005a) *Examining CAE Writing Examiner Behaviour (Phase 2): A Multi-faceted Rasch Measurement approach*, Cambridge: UCLES internal report.

Shaw, S D (2005b) *The impact of word processed text on rater behaviour: A review of the literature*, Cambridge: UCLES internal report.

Shaw, S D (2005c) *Item versus whole script marking in an ESM environment: A Cambridge ESOL perspective*, Cambridge: UCLES internal report.

Shaw, S D and Falvey, P (forthcoming) *The IELTS Writing Assessment Revision Project: Towards a revised rating scale*, Cambridge ESOL Web-Based Research Report 1.

Shaw, S D and Geranpayeh, A (2005) *Examining CAE Writing Examiner Behaviour: A Multi-faceted Rasch Measurement approach*, Cambridge: UCLES internal report.

Shaw, S D, Levy, S and Fenn, S (2001) *Electronic Script Management: Report on an exercise held 20, 21, 22 April 2001*, Cambridge: UCLES internal report.

Sherif, M (1935) A study of some social factors in perception, *Archives of Psychology* 27, 187.

Shohamy, E (1990) Discourse analysis in language testing, *Annual Review of Applied Linguistics* 11, 115–31.

Shohamy, E (2001) *The Power of Tests: A critical perspective on the uses of language tests*, Harlow: Pearson Education.

Silva, T (1993) Toward an understanding of the distinct nature of L2 writing: The ESL research and its implications, *TESOL Quarterly* 27 (4), 657–77.

Sitko, M C and Crealock, C M (1986) *A longitudinal study of the efficacy of computer technology for improving the writing skills of mildly handicapped adolescents*, paper presented at the Invitational Research symposium on Special Education Technology, Washington, DC.

Skehan, P and Foster, P (1997) The influence of planning and post-task activities on accuracy and complexity in task-based learning, *Language Teaching Research* 1 (3), 185–211.

Skehan, P and Foster, P (1999) The influence of task structure and processing conditions on narrative retellings, *Language Learning* 49 (1), 93–120.

Skehan, P and Foster, P (2001) Cognition and tasks, in Robinson, P (Ed.) *Cognition and second language instruction*, Cambridge: Cambridge University Press, 183–205.

Slater, S J (1980) Introduction to performance testing, in Spirer, J E (Ed.) *Performance Testing: issues facing vocational education*, National Centre for Research in Vocational Education, Columbus OH, 3–17.

Sleator, D K and Temperley, D (1991) *Parsing English with a link grammar*, Technical Report, October CMU–CS–91–196, School of Computer Science, Carnegie Mellon University, Pittsburgh, PA.

Sloan, C and McGinnis, I (1978) The effect of handwriting on teachers' grading of high school essays, *Journal of the Association for the Study of Perception* 17 (2), 15–21.

Smith, J (2004) IELTS Impact: a study on the accessibility of IELTS GT Modules to 16–17 year old candidates, *Research Notes* 18, 6–8.

Smith, W L, Hull, G A, Land, R E, Moore, M T, Ball, C, Dunham, D E, Hickey, L S and Ruzich, C W (1985) Some effects of varying the structure of the topic on college students' writing, *Written Communication* 2, 73–89.

Stahl, J A and Lunz, M E (1991) *Judge performance reports: Media and message*, paper presented at the annual meeting of the American Educational Research Association, San Francisco, CA.

Standards for Educational and Psychological Testing (1999) Washington, DC: American Psychological Association.

Stewart, M and Grobe, C (1979) Syntactic maturity, mechanics of writing and teachers' quality ratings, *Research in the Teaching of English* 13, 207–215, UCLES, 1976, *School Examinations and their Function* 3, Cambridge: UCLES.

Stiggins, R J and Bridgeford, N J (1983) An analysis of published tests of writing proficiency, *Educational Measurement: Issues and Practices* 2 (1), 6–19, 26.

Stock, P L and Robinson, J L (1987) Taking on testing, *English Education* 19 (2), 93–121.

Sudweeks, R R, Reeve, S and Bradshaw, W S (2005) A comparison of generalizability theory and many-facet Rasch measurement in an analysis of college sophomore writing, *Assessing Writing* 9 (3), 239–61.

Sukkarieh, J Z, Pulman, S P and Raikes, N (2005) Automatic marking of short, free text responses, *Research Matters* 1, Cambridge Assessment, 19–22, downloadable from www.cambridgeassessment.org.uk/research/

Susser, B (1993) ESL/EFL process writing with computers, *CAELL Journal*, 4 (2), 16–22.

Swan, M (1997) The influence of the mother tongue on second language vocabulary acquisition and use, in Schmitt, N and McCarthy, M (Eds)

Vocabulary: Description, Acquisition, and Pedagogy, Cambridge: Cambridge University Press, 156–80.

Swinton, S S and Powers, D E (1980) *Factor Analysis of the Test of English as a Foreign Language for Several Language Groups*, TOEFL Research Reports 6, Princeton, NJ: Educational Testing Service.

Taylor, C, Jamieson, J, Eignor, D and Kirsch, I (1998) *The relationships between computer familiarity and performance on computer-based TOEFL test tasks*, TOEFL Research Reports 61, Princeton, NJ: Educational Testing Service.

Taylor, L (1999) *Constituency matters: responsibilities and relationships in our testing community*, paper delivered to the Language Testing Forum, University of Edinburgh, 19–21 November 1999.

Taylor, L (2000) *Constituency Matters*, paper presented at the 1999 Language Testing Forum, Edinburgh; also appears as Stakeholders in Language Testing, *Research Notes* 2, 2–3.

Taylor, L (2003) The Cambridge approach to speaking assessment, *Research Notes* 13, 2–4.

Taylor, L (2004) *Special Arrangements: Summary report from the Special Circumstances Working Group relating to the provision of 'separate marking' as part of our current Cambridge ESOL provision for L2 candidates with dyslexia*, Cambridge: UCLES internal report.

Taylor, L (2004a) Issues of test comparability, *Research Notes* 15, 2–5.

Taylor, L (2004b) IELTS, Cambridge ESOL examinations and the Common European Framework, *Research Notes* 18, 2–3.

Taylor, L (2006) The changing landscape of English: implications for language assessment, *ELT Journal* 60 (1), 51–60.

Taylor, L (Ed.) (forthcoming) *Examining Second Language Speaking: Research and practice*, Studies in Language Testing, Cambridge: UCLES/Cambridge University Press.

Taylor, L and Barker, F (forthcoming) Using corpora in language assessment, in Shohamy, E (Ed.) *Encyclopedia of Language and Education* 7.

Taylor, L and Falvey, P (Eds) (2007) *IELTS Collected Papers: Research in speaking and writing assessment*, Studies in Language Testing 19, Cambridge: Cambridge University Press/UCLES.

Tedick, D J and Mathison, M A (1995) Holistic scoring in ESL Writing Assessment: What does an Analysis of Rhetorical Features Reveal? in Belcher, D and Braine, G (Eds) *Academic Writing in a Second Language: Essays on Research and Pedagogy*, Norwood, NJ: Ablex Publishing Corporation, 205–230.

Thighe, D, Jones, N and Geranpayeh, A (2001) *IELTS PB and CB Equivalence: A comparison of equated versions of the Reading and Listening components of PB IELTS in relation to CB IELTS*, Cambridge: UCLES internal report.

Tierney, R J and Shanahan, T (1991). Research on the reading-writing relationship: Interactions, transactions, and outcomes, in Barr, R, Kamil, M L, Mosenthal, P and Pearson, P D (Eds.) *Handbook of reading research*, New York: Longman, Vol. 2, 246–80.

Tittle, C K (1990) Test bias, in Walberg, H J and Haertel, G D (Eds) *The International Encyclopedia of Educational Evaluation*, Oxford: Pergamon, 128–33.

Toulmin, S E (1958) *The uses of argument*, Cambridge: Cambridge University Press.

University of Cambridge ESOL Examinations (1990) *KET Waystage Specification List*, Cambridge: UCLES.

University of Cambridge ESOL Examinations (1990a), *PET Threshold Level*, Cambridge: UCLES.

University of Cambridge ESOL Examinations (2001) Specifications and Sample Papers for updated examination, in *CAE Handbook*, Cambridge: UCLES.

University of Cambridge ESOL Examinations (2003) *CAE Examination Report*, Cambridge: UCLES.

University of Cambridge ESOL Examinations (2003a) *CPE Examination Report*, Cambridge: UCLES.

University of Cambridge ESOL Examinations (2003b) Specifications and Sample Papers for updated examination, in *CPE Handbook*, Cambridge: UCLES.

University of Cambridge ESOL Examinations (2003c) *FCE Examination Report*, Cambridge: UCLES.

University of Cambridge ESOL Examinations (2003d) *FCE, CAE and CPE: Information common to all papers*, Cambridge: UCLES.

University of Cambridge ESOL Examinations (2004) *BEC Handbook*, Cambridge: UCLES.

University of Cambridge ESOL Examinations (2004a) *Bulletin For Centres*, Issue 31, November 2004, Cambridge: UCLES.

University of Cambridge ESOL Examinations (2004b) *FCE/CAE/CPE Instructions to Local Secretaries, Supervisors and Invigilators for Examination Administration*, Cambridge: UCLES.

University of Cambridge ESOL Examinations (2004c) *KET/PET Instructions to Local Secretaries, Supervisors and Invigilators for Examination Administration*, Cambridge: UCLES.

University of Cambridge ESOL Examinations (2004d) *KET Examination Report*, Cambridge: UCLES.

University of Cambridge ESOL Examinations (2004e) Specifications and Sample Papers for updated examination from March 2004, in *KET Handbook*, Cambridge: UCLES.

University of Cambridge ESOL Examinations (2004f) *KET Item Writer Guidelines: Information common to all papers*, Cambridge: UCLES.

University of Cambridge ESOL Examinations (2004g) *PET Examination Report*, Cambridge: UCLES.

University of Cambridge ESOL Examinations (2004h) Specifications and Sample Papers for updated examination from March 2004, in *PET Handbook*, Cambridge: UCLES.

University of Cambridge ESOL Examinations (2004i), *PET Item Writer Guidelines: Information common to all papers*, Cambridge: UCLES.

University of Cambridge ESOL Examinations (2005) *BEC Handbook for teachers*, Cambridge: UCLES.

University of Cambridge ESOL Examinations (2005a) *CAE Handbook for teachers*, Cambridge: UCLES.

University of Cambridge ESOL Examinations (2005b) *CELS Handbook for teachers*, Cambridge: UCLES.

University of Cambridge ESOL Examinations (2005c) *CPE Handbook for teachers*, Cambridge: UCLES.

University of Cambridge ESOL Examinations (2005d) *FCE Handbook for teachers*, Cambridge: UCLES.

University of Cambridge ESOL Examinations (2005e) *IELTS Handbook for teachers*, Cambridge: UCLES.

University of Cambridge ESOL Examinations (2005f), *Instructions to Local*

References

*Secretaries, Supervisors and Invigilators for Examination Administration
(ILSSIEA)*, Cambridge: UCLES.
University of Cambridge ESOL Examinations (2005g) *KET Handbook for
teachers*, Cambridge: UCLES.
University of Cambridge ESOL Examinations (2005h) *PET Handbook for
teachers*, Cambridge: UCLES.
University of Cambridge ESOL Examinations (2005i) *Handbook for Centres*,
Cambridge: UCLES.
University of Cambridge ESOL Examinations (2006) *KET Vocabulary List*,
downloadable from www.CambridgeESOL.org/teach/ket
University of Cambridge ESOL Examinations (2006a) *PET Vocabulary List*,
downloadable from www.CambridgeESOL.org/teach/pet
University of Cambridge ESOL Examinations *(forthcoming)* Specifications and
Sample Papers for updated examination, in *FCE Handbook*, Cambridge:
UCLES.
Upshur, J A and Turner, C E (1995) Constructing rating scales for second
language tests, *ELT Journal* 49 (1), 3–12.
Urquhart, A H and Weir, C J (1998) *Reading in a Second Language: Process,
Product & Practice*, London: Longman.
Vahapassi, A (1982) On the specification of the domain of school writing, in
Purves, A C and Takala, S (Eds.) *An international perspective on the evaluation
of written composition*, Oxford: Pergamon, 265–89.
Van Ek, J A and Trim, J L M (1991) *Threshold 1990: Council of Europe*,
Cambridge: Cambridge University Press.
Van Ek, J A and Trim, J L M (1991a) *Waystage 1990: Council of Europe*,
Cambridge: Cambridge University Press.
Van Ek, J A and Trim, J L M (2001) *Vantage: Council of Europe*, Cambridge:
Cambridge University Press.
Vann, R J, Lorenz, F O and Meyer, D M (1991) Error Gravity: Faculty
Response to Errors in the Written Discourse of Nonnative Speakers of
English, in Hamp-Lyons, L (Ed.) *Assessing Second Language Writing in
Academic Contexts*, Norwood, NJ: Ablex Publishing Corporation, 181–95.
Vaughan, C (1991) Holistic Assessment: What goes on in the rater's mind? in
Hamp-Lyons, L (Ed.) *Assessing Second Language Writing in Academic
Contexts*, Norwood, NJ: Ablex Publishing Corporation, 111–25.
Wall, D (1997) Test Impact and Washback, in *Language Testing and Evaluation*,
Volume 7 of *Kluwer Encyclopedia of Language Education*, 291–302.
Wall, D (2005) *The Impact of a High-Stakes Examination on Classroom Teaching:
A Case Study Using Insights from Testing and Innovation Theory*, Studies in
Language Testing 22, Cambridge: Cambridge University Press/UCLES.
Wall, D and Alderson, J C (1993) Examining washback: the Sri Lankan impact
study, *Language Testing* 10 (1), 41–69.
Weigle, S (1994) Effects of Training on Raters of ESL Compositions, *Language
Testing* 11 (2), 197–223.
Weigle, S C (1998) Using FACETS to model rater training effects, *Language
Testing* 15 (2), 263–87.
Weigle, S (1999) Investigating Rater/Prompt Interactions in Writing Assessment:
Quantitative and Qualitative Approaches, *Assessing Writing* 6 (2), 145–78.
Weigle, S C (2002) *Assessing Writing*, Cambridge University Press: Cambridge.
Weigle, S C (2004) Integrating reading and writing in a competency test for non-
native speakers of English, *Assessing Writing* 9, 27–55.

336

Weigle, S C, Lamison, B and Peters, K (2000) *Topic selection on a standardized writing assessment*, paper presented at Southeast Regional TESOL, Miami, FL, October 2000.

Weir, C J (1983) *Identifying the language problems of overseas students in tertiary education in the United Kingdom*, unpublished doctoral dissertation, University of London.

Weir, C J (1988) Construct validity, in Hughes, A, Porter, D and Weir, C (Eds) *ELT Validation Project: Proceeding of a Conference Held to Consider the ELTS Validation Project Report*, Cambridge: The British Council and the University of Cambridge Local Examination Syndicate.

Weir, C J (1990) *Communicative Language Testing*, Englewood Cliffs, NJ: Prentice Hall.

Weir, C J (1993) *Understanding and Developing Language Tests*, New York: Prentice Hall.

Weir, C J (2003) A survey of the history of the Certificate of Proficiency in English (CPE) in the twentieth century, in Weir, C J and Milanovic, M *Continuity and Innovation: The History of the CPE 1913–2002*, Studies in Language Testing 15, Cambridge: Cambridge University Press/UCLES, 1–56.

Weir, C J (2005a) Limitations of the Council of Europe's Framework of Reference (CEFR) in developing comparable examinations and tests, *Language Testing* 22 (3), 281–300.

Weir, C J (2005b) *Language Testing and Validation: An Evidence-Based Approach*, Basingstoke: Palgrave Macmillan.

Weir, C J and Milanovic, M (Eds) (2003) *Continuity and Innovation: The History of the CPE 1913–2002*, Studies in Language Testing 15, Cambridge: Cambridge University Press/UCLES.

Weir, C J and Milanovic, M (Eds.) (2004) *European Language Testing in a Global Context. Proceedings of the ALTE Barcelona Conference July 2001*, Studies in Language Testing 18, Cambridge: Cambridge University Press/UCLES.

Weir, C J, O'Sullivan, B, Yan, J and Bax, S (2005) *Establishing Equivalence in EAP Writing Assessment: Effects of Computerization on Candidates' Cognitive Processing and Test Scores*, unpublished IELTS report.

Weir, C J and Wu, J (2006) Establishing Test Form and Individual Task Comparability – A Case Study of a Semi-direct Speaking Test, accepted for publication, *Language Testing* 23 (2), 167–97.

White, E M (1995) An apologia for the timed impromptu essay test, *College Composition and Communication* 46 (1), 30–45.

Whitehead, R (2003) Issues in the assessment of pen-and-paper and computer-based IELTS writing tasks, unpublished IELTS Research Report.

Wigglesworth, G (1993) Exploring bias analysis as a tool for improving rater consistency in assessing oral interaction, *Language Testing* 10 (3), 305–35.

Wigglesworth, G (1997) An investigation of planning time and proficiency level on oral test discourse, *Language Testing* 14 (1), 85–106.

Williamson, M M and Pence, P (1989) Word processing and student writers, in Britton, B Glynn, S M (Eds) *Computer writing environments: Theory, research, and design*, Hillsdale, NJ: Lawrence Erlbaum, 93–127.

Wilson, S C (1982) A comparison of the academic performance of high school graduates and GED certificate holders at Tulsa Junior College, unpublished doctoral dissertation, Oklahoma State University.

Winetroube, S (1997) The design of the teachers' attitude questionnaire, Cambridge: UCLES internal report.

References

Wolf, A (1995) *Competence-based assessment*, Bristol: Open University Press.
Wolfe, E W, Bolton, S, Feltovich, B and
Bangert, A W (1996) A study of word processing experience and its effects on student essay writing, *Journal of Educational Computing Research* 14 (3), 269–83.
Wood, R (1991) *Assessment and Testing: a survey of research*, Cambridge: Cambridge University Press.
Wresch, W (1993) The imminence of grading essays by computer – 25 years later, *Computers and Composition* 10 (2), 46–58.
Xiu Xudong (forthcoming) *An investigation of the construct validity of the tests used for assessing the academic writing ability in English of non-native speakers at tertiary level in China*, PhD in progress, Roehampton University.
Yang, H and Weir, C J (1998) *Validation Study of the College English Test*, Shanghai: Shanghai Foreign Language Education Press.
Yue, W (1997) *An investigation of textbook materials designed to prepare students for the IELTS test: a study of washback*, unpublished MA dissertation, Lancaster University.
Zipf, G K (2006) Bibliography on Zipf's Law, downloadable from www.nslij-genetics.org/wli/zipf/2006.html

Subject Index

Author Index